George Herbert's
Pastoral

George Herbert's Pastoral

New Essays on the Poet and Priest of Bemerton

Edited by
Christopher Hodgkins

DELAWARE

Newark: University of Delaware Press

Associated University Presses
2010 Eastpark Boulevard
Cranbury, NJ 08512

The paper used in this publication meets the requirements of the American National Standard for Permanence of Paper for Printed Library Materials Z39.48-1984.

Library of Congress Cataloging-in-Publication Data

George Herbert's pastoral : new essays on the poet and priest of Bemerton / edited by Christopher Hodgkins.
    p. cm.
    Includes index.
    ISBN 978-0-87413-022-5 (alk. paper)
    1. Herbert, George, 1593–1633—Criticism and interpretation.   2. Herbert, George, 1593–1633—Settings.   3. Pastoral poetry, English—History and criticism.   4. Country life in literature.   5. Theology in literature.   I. Hodgkins, Christopher, 1958–
    PR3508.G49   2010
    821'.3—dc22   2009015023

For Mary and Alice

Ladies, look here; this is the thankfull glasse,
That mends the lookers eyes. . . .
—"The H. Scriptures" (I)

Contents

Acknowledgments   9

Introduction: Reforming Pastoral: Herbert and the Singing
Shepherds   15
CHRISTOPHER HODGKINS

Part I. Pastoral Poetry and Pastoral Practice

Pastoral Conversions   35
DONALD FRIEDMAN

"Brittle Crazy Glass": George Herbert, Vocation, and the
Theology of Presence   52
GENE EDWARD VEITH

Herbert's Holy Practice   72
KENNETH GRAHAM

"Hallow'd Fire"; or, When Is a Poet Not a Priest?   91
HELEN WILCOX

Part II: Historical Personalities and Places

William Herbert's Gardener: Adrian Gilbert   113
CRISTINA MALCOLMSON

At the Porch to the Temple: Herbert's Progress to Bemerton   134
CLAYTON D. LEIN

The Country Parson's Flock: George Herbert's Wiltshire
Parish   158
JOHN CHANDLER

George Herbert and the Widow Bagges: Poverty, Charity,
and the Law   173
CHAUNCEY WOOD

"To Do a Piece of Right": Edmund Duncon and the
Publication of George Herbert   181
    ANTHONY MARTIN

Part III: Biblical and Liturgical Connections

George Herbert and the Liturgical Experience of Scripture   197
    PAUL DYCK

Herbert and Early Stuart Psalm Culture: Beyond
Translation and Meditation   211
    KATE NARVESON

Part IV: Pastor, Garden, and Pasture

Herbert's Pastor as Herbalist   235
    CURTIS WHITAKER

Part V: Beyond Bemerton

Under Salisbury Spire with the Fictional George Herbert   255
    SIDNEY GOTTLIEB

"Something Understood": From Poetry to Theology in the
Writings of George Herbert   273
    DAVID JASPER

Notes on Contributors   288

General Index   292

Index to Herbert's Writings   310

Acknowledgments

THIS BOOK IS MORE THAN USUALLY TIED TO A PARTICULAR PLACE—THE four miles extending westward from the Salisbury Cathedral Close through Bemerton to Wilton House—and it is to people of that place that I owe special thanks. In January 2006 I received a forwarded letter from Canon Judy Rees of Lower Bemerton (within sight of St. Andrew's parish church), asking whether anyone at the University of North Carolina at Greensboro still maintains Amy Charles's interest in George Herbert. In replying, I confirmed that not only did I still write and teach regularly on Herbert, but that UNCG houses one of the finest collections of rare Herbert editions in North America, including every first edition of Herbert's works and nearly every other edition since. Then in concluding I suggested that the time might be ripe for some sort of transatlantic event in Wiltshire devoted to Herbert and his work there as poet and pastor; and I asked if any of her friends in Bemerton, Salisbury, or Wilton might be interested in such an idea. Little did I imagine how many friends Judy Rees has or how interested they would be.

Soon Rees put me in touch with Rev. Tim Macquiban, principal of Sarum College—a theological school and retreat center literally in the shadow of Salisbury's cathedral spire—and by May 2006, we had laid plans for not just one but two Herbert conferences: one, "George Herbert's Pastoral," at Sarum College in October 2007, exploring the relations between Herbert's poetry and his pastoral life in early Stuart Wiltshire, and the other, "George Herbert's Travels," at UNCG in October 2008, devoted to Herbert's international print and cultural legacies in the four centuries since. The present collection represents the firstfruits of this collaboration, developed from the keynote addresses and selected papers presented at the Salisbury conference, which brought together about one hundred Herbertians from Great Britain, the United States, Canada, France, Iran, Australia, New Zealand, and Japan. And appropriately, an earlier version of John Chandler's essay, "The Country Parson's Flock: George Herbert's Wiltshire Parish," appeared in Salisbury's local history journal, *Sarum Chronicle*.

9

10   ACKNOWLEDGMENTS

In addition to these crucial Wiltshire partners, others helped to inspire this Herbert gathering. I owe the spark of the idea to my colleagues on the Renaissance Society of America's Cambridge 2005 panels, "George Herbert, Cambridge Scholar"—particularly Anne-Marie Miller Blaise, Elizabeth Clarke, Paul Dyck, Sidney Gottlieb, Helen Wilcox, and the panel organizer, Chauncey Wood— who over dinner in a Trumpington Street restaurant wondered aloud whether we might meet a few years hence at some other place important to Herbert's life and career. So the seed was sown, the letter from Judy Rees watered, and Salisbury gave the growth.

Seldom if ever did a conference so fully combine business with pleasure: Sarum College—itself an architectural gem housed in a building designed by Christopher Wren—boasts an attentive staff led by the indefatigable Linda Cooper and provides an atmosphere of simple comfort, friendly intimacy, aesthetic beauty, and easy access to all of the places important in Herbert's brief pastoral career. We enjoyed an embarrassment of riches: not only three outstanding plenary speakers and fourteen paper panels, but also a concert by the Farrant Singers, a dramatic reading by Sonia Woolley, a banquet with remarks by Bishop David Stancliffe, a session in St. Andrew's Church itself led by local people, a walk through Herbert's rectory garden, and a private tour of the inner rooms at Wilton House. Particular thanks are due to the novelist and poet Vikram Seth, who now owns Herbert's old Bemerton rectory, and to his friend, the composer Alec Roth, who hosted our visit to the grounds in Mr. Seth's absence; and to Ros Liddington, whose guided tour through Wilton's Double Cube Room and inner chambers and across the Palladian Bridge capped the conference unforgettably.

As abundant as the help of our Wiltshire friends has been, North Carolina and Delaware have played their parts, too. First and foremost in Greensboro have been the alumnae of the class of 1952, whose generosity helped to support my conference travel and made possible our group's special Wilton House tour. Also indispensable in planning and developing the Salisbury conference was the director of UNCG Special Collections, William Finley, who made a genial traveling companion to London and Salisbury; and my lead research assistant, Will Duffy, whose handling of every conceivable logistical and textual detail has been invariably thorough, foresighted, and good-humored. At the University of Delaware Press, I wish to thank Donald C. Mell, director and chair of the Board of Editors, for encouraging the development of this collection; Karen G. Druliner, managing editor, for shepherding it through the process of review; and the press's anonymous external and internal readers, for their helpful corrections and heartening affirmations. At the Associated University Presses, I am grateful to managing editor Christine A. Retz, and especially to the sharp eye of copyeditor Wyatt Benner. And the contributor Clayton D. Lein wishes to thank Ms. Jane Darwin for permission to quote from her Oxford University BL thesis on John Earle.

Above all I want to thank my family—my wife Hope, daughter Alice, and son George—who doubled the pleasures of Salisbury by joining me there; and my daughter Mary, who accompanied me to Cambridge in 2005, and to whom I still owe a return trip. I promise to take you all back! In the meantime, here is this book . . .

George Herbert's
Pastoral

Introduction: Reforming Pastoral: Herbert and the Singing Shepherds

Christopher Hodgkins

Pastoral is an ancient, urbane mode celebrating an imagined, ideal rural life—in other words, it has always been ripe for irony, or, to put it more harshly, prone to aesthetic hypocrisy. As Donald Friedman notes in his essay "Pastoral Conversions," below, "[P]astoral has from its beginning announced itself as a way of talking about matters under a guise, an approach to its genuine concerns that proceeds by dressing them in images and locutions drawn from a markedly different, imagined world."[1] As pastoral is virtually birthed in irony, its origins and course have won it much dispraise; as Edmund Gosse wrote long ago, perhaps echoing Keats, "[P]astoral is cold, unnatural, artificial, and the humblest reviewer is free to cast a stone at its dishonored grave."[2] But if we want to know why this sometimes dishonored mode has lasted well over two millennia, and why supposedly jaded urban and courtly poets have been and still are genuinely moved to invoke the pastoral, we need only look at Salisbury, at George Herbert's nearby village of Bemerton, and at the surrounding country.

A walk on a fine fall day around Salisbury's Cathedral Close, or through the water meadows and pastures of Wiltshire, with the distant bleating of their sheep and the fragrance of their new-mown hay, might well put even a hardened urbanite in a pastoral frame of mind. In the mood for this mode, we may envy, or at least admire, all sorts of country pastors: both the pastoralists who, at their own more leisurely pace, have for ages tended the flocks that produce some of the finest wool in the world; and the country parsons who for centuries have sought to guide, protect, and nurture their human flocks in these quiet rural places.

So the approximately one hundred poets, critics, historians, and sympathetic civilians who met in Salisbury for the "George Herbert's Pastoral" conference in October 2007 came to reflect extensively on the relations between the particularly pastoral locale of

15

Herbert's last years (1630–33) and the themes, images, and tenor of his writing. The conference's main site was Sarum College, situated in the Cathedral Close, two miles from Herbert's Bemerton church of St. Andrew, and four miles from Wilton House, home to his Pembroke cousins. How did the specific country place, time, and people shape the life and work of this especially lyrical country priest? What, in turn, can we learn from that life and work about his time and place? The fourteen new essays in this collection, drawn from more than fifty papers presented at the conference, address Herbert's pastoral poetry and practice, his actual relations with specific local personalities and places, some fresh connections to the inward biblical and liturgical spaces of his work, his links to the outward spaces of garden and pasture, and some fictional and theological reverberations beyond Herbert's rural life in Bemerton.

Though the Wiltshire historian John Chandler warns us in his essay below against thinking of Bemerton, even in Herbert's day, as a rural retreat, it is nevertheless powerfully tempting to romanticize such rural places—to be drawn into the organically embedded life of the nearby fields and pastures and to hope, perhaps under the influence of Theocritus, Virgil, Sidney, and Spenser, that there we may become more reflective, better people, perhaps more like Herbert himself. However, anyone opening Herbert's *Temple* in search of much bucolic tranquility is likely to be disappointed. This model country parson was apparently more of Edmund Gosse's mind; he would seem to want nothing of pastoral romance. It would not of course be the first time that a disillusioned local snorted at a swooning tourist; and Herbert in his turn has plenty of unsentimental things to say about rural life. For instance, early in "The Church-porch," which opens *The Temple*, Herbert exhorts his lazy countrymen using the full preacherly vocative:

> O England! Full of sinne, but most of sloth,
> Spit out thy flegme, and fill thy brest with glorie:
> Thy gentry bleats, as if thy native cloth
> Transfused a sheepishness into thy story:
>   Not that they all are so; but that the most
>   Are gone to grass, and in the pasture lost.

(lines 91–96)[3]

Far from praising the virtue-breeding delightfulness of Arcadian labor, or even celebrating the restorative beauty of meadow and stream, here Herbert associates pastoralism with the least glamorous of all the deadly sins—the sin of sloth—and presents the pasture as a place of bleating complaint, idle consumption, and aimless wandering, a condition caught like anthrax from the sheep themselves. It appears that rural life has made the gentry as dull and gross as common clods.

In fact, Herbert's call to an act of national expectoration suggests the snorting, hacking, and spitting of very real shepherds on a raw day—uncouth swains, no doubt, but hardly warbling their Doric lay. Overall, these deflating lines from "The Church-porch" have more in common with Raphael Hythloday's humorous antipastoral diatribe in book 1 of More's *Utopia*—where the sheep are merely unproductive eaters and the shepherds are fools[4]—than with the pastoral philosophers and poets of Spenser's *Shephearde's Calendar* or Sidney's *Arcadia*.

Yet even a casual reader of *The Temple* may recall another line about shepherds, a line from the initially antipastoral poem "Jordan" (I), and it involves neither sloth nor spitting: "Shepherds are honest people; let them sing . . ." (57, line 11). No doubt the two stanzas preceding this line often have been read as anti-Spenserian and anti-Arcadian—they clearly look askance at the romantic affectations of "enchanted groves," "sudden arbours," and deliberately archaic "coarse-spunne lines," and they seek to shine some harsh daylight behind the veils of allegory (56, lines 6–9). Nevertheless, in the final stanza of this apparently antipastoral lyric, Herbert evokes both Spenser's and Sidney's pastoral bards, praising the honesty of shepherds and proclaiming their freedom not merely to speak but to sing. Though the poem's speaker may, as Donald Friedman suggests, dismiss the singing shepherds by asserting the plain psalmic poetry of his final *"My God, My King,"* this praise of honest shepherds still leaves room for pastoral music—as does Herbert's most extensive pastoral work, his ministry manual *The Countrey Parson*. In fact, a closer look back at the antipastoral outburst in "The Church-porch" reveals that even here the explicit targets are not literal shepherds or country parsons per se, but instead the idle and sheepish country gentry. And there are enough moments in *The Temple* expressing awe at spring days and at dew and rain and flowers and larks to show that Herbert could indeed be moved to unbidden joy by a pastoral setting.

How then can we understand Herbert's apparently double impulses—on the one hand, to mock pastoral traditions while, on the other, to praise pastoral persons and places? The essays in this collection seek some concord from this discord in the details of multiple contexts: aesthetic, theological, historical, and local. In the process they discover Herbert finding a middle way. If we know

Herbert we know how typical it is of him to carry loyalties that are potentially complementary yet at times seemingly contradictory. These include his loyalties to poetic beauty and to truthful simplicity, to liturgical dignity and to extemporaneous devotion, to the demotion of erotic desire and to its redemption, to outer and inner spiritual architecture, and to the celebration and the correction of old country customs.

So we should not be too surprised to find Herbert tracing a via media between antipastoral satire and pastoral romance. As we have seen, the poem cannot reasonably be read as flatly antipastoral, in the sense of attacking the pastor as a shepherd or as a poet or as a parson. What Herbert seeks instead is a reformed pastoral—a poetic style that treats country life without courtly or urban fantasy and folly, yet recognizes its enduring attractions and so turns it to the purposes of the spiritual shepherd.

Also, any attempt to distinguish Herbert's honest shepherds from their Sidneian and Spenserian predecessors must note that these two earlier exemplars of the English Renaissance romance themselves expressed reservations about romantic frivolity and poetic excess. Sidney half-seriously mocks the monstrous fantasy of his own *Arcadia* in the dedication to his sister, Mary Sidney Herbert, the Countess of Pembroke and the wife of Herbert's cousin. In fact, it is worth noting that Sidney composed much of the *Arcadia* at Wilton House, only four miles from Salisbury.[5] And Spenser much more seriously condemns poetic excess by destroying the sensuous pastoral bower of Acrasia at the climax of Sir Guyon's quest for Temperance in *The Faerie Queene*, book 2.[6] So in problematizing the pastoral, Herbert was in the company of the mode's chief Renaissance proponents and practitioners.

Still, it speaks volumes that when Herbert chose to compose an extended pastoral work with a rural setting, this lyric master not only descended to the cooler element of prose, but descended further to the least fanciful and most practical pastoral of all: a how-to manual for country parsons, sometimes called by its longer title, *A Priest to the Temple; or, The Countrey Parson,* composed at Bemerton but not published until 1652, nineteen years after his death.[7] The distance of Herbert's pastoral from the classical poetic precedents is most obvious in his virtual dismissal of erotic desire from this clerical shepherd's life. We need not belabor how assiduously unromantic, indeed antiromantic, is "the parson's state of life" as described in chapter 9 of *The Countrey Parson:* no sporting *here* with Amaryllis in the shade, let alone in the sun, and perhaps not even in a marriage bed, if he can help it. In one of the most nearly medieval statements by this profoundly reformational soul, Herbert considers "that virginity is a higher state than matrimony," so that his parson "is rather unmarryed, then married" (236–37). But, as if remembering St. Paul's famous concession about marrying rather than burning (1 Cor. 7:9), Herbert immediately qualifies and effectively reverses himself, saying that "as the temper of his body may be, or . . . of his parish may be, where he may have occasion to converse with women, . . . he is rather married then unmarried" (237). Yet his choice of this necessary wife is made "rather by his eare then by his eye; his judgement not his affection [find] out a fit wife for him." The parson is no household tyrant: "[H]e gives her respect . . . and half at least of the government of the house" (238); but if Herbert knows the ways of sensual pleasure, as he asserts for instance in his poem "The Pearl" (88–89, lines 21–30), one might not guess it here.

Yet if this shepherd's rural state of life is not defined by gathering flowers and herbs for any shepherdess, it is nevertheless profoundly informed by the flowers and herbs themselves. A little like Andrew Marvell's happily solitary Adam in "The Garden," Herbert's parson would be inclined to bypass the sweetheart and embrace the bouquet.[8] His true passion is for the flora, both in book knowledge from his herbal catalogue and in direct knowing of the plants and their particular virtues. In chapter 23, entitled "The Parson's Completenesse," nothing completes or fulfills him more than what he calls his "recreation" and "diversion" with herbs and simples in the garden and countryside. The simple pleasure of these pursuits is both augmented and magnified by the powerful sense of divine presence that the workaday green world stirs in him: "[O]ur Saviour made plants and seeds to teach the people," Herbert says, so that "labouring people . . . might have everywhere monuments of his doctrine, remembring in gardens, his mustard-seed, and lillyes, in the field his seed-corn, and tares" (261).

Herbert warms further to this theme of "Nature serving Grace" in chapter 30, "The Parson's Consideration of Providence" (270–72). As in his similarly titled lyric poem "Providence" (116–21), here in this chapter he reads the creation with the practiced eye of a metaphysical exegete: a farmer's crop has not truly profited him, he says, until God enables him not only to harvest and sell the crop, but to interpret it correctly—that is, to turn "all outward blessings to inward advantages. . . . Better were his corne burnt than not spiritually improved" (271–72). Although, as we have seen in "Jordan" (I) Herbert satirizes the pastoral allegories where the reader "divines, / Catching the sense at two removes" (57, lines 11–12), here in this prose piece he treats the act of reading divine sense in an actual rural landscape as not only allowable to but expected of the ordinary Christian.

It is of course worth noting that the main mode of rural life that Herbert's country parson oversees is agricultural rather than literally pastoral, as if somehow the more righteous brother Abel, the spiritual shepherd, is appointed to watch over the potentially more dull and carnal Cains on the farm. Certainly Herbert resorts fairly often to images of a shepherd's far-reaching oversight, finding his country parson "at spare times from action, standing on a hill, and considering his Flock" (264). What the pastor sees from this height, and what he does with the knowledge, is the subject of one of *The Countrey Parson*'s most intriguing and lengthy chapters, chapter 32, "The Parson's Surveys" (274–78). Significantly, this chapter calls to mind the political pastoral mode of Spenser's *Shepheardes Calendar,* where supposedly simple rural shepherds rather surprisingly hold forth on matters of theological and political import. Similarly, in this chapter of *The Countrey Parson,* the ordinary rural clergyman reading the manual may be surprised to discover advice for everyone from justices of the peace and noblemen's sons to members of Parliament and colonial adventurers.

I have written elsewhere about this chapter as advancing a broader Protestant humanist social vision concerned not only with religious matters narrowly defined, but also with legislative action, industrial development, class tensions, courtly corruption, national security, and international relations.[9] And Cristina Malcolmson's recent literary life of Herbert makes abundantly clear how committed he was to the cause of worldwide Protestantism.[10] Although Herbert recommends reading "the Lives of the Primitive Monks, Hermits, and Virgins" (237), there is nothing quietist or retreatist about his country parson. Much as Sidney or Spenser put philosophy or policy in the mouths of simple rural swains, Herbert gives his rural parson the sanctifying but decidedly earthly mission of reforming the commonwealth one parish at a time. In effect, he tells his rural pastor to act locally while thinking nationally (and even globally). Significantly, it is these diligent "surveys" by the parson that would send the idle nobility and gentry back to work and thus cure the national disease of sheepish sloth that we noted earlier, and that Herbert warns against so sternly in "The Church-porch."

So Herbert, like the many creators of more poetic pastorals, used his prose pastoral to promote social progress. Yet Herbert is nevertheless quite careful to preserve and celebrate some ancient country customs, as in chapter 35. Though there is something potentially precious about a chapter entitled "The Parson's Condescending," Herbert presents this condescension as a matter of love. "The Country Parson is a Lover of old Customes, if they be good, and harmlesse; and the rather, because Country people are much addicted to them, so that to favour them therein is to win their hearts, and to oppose them therin is to deject them" (283). In particular, he praises the ancient practice of procession—that is, of walking the old boundaries while reciting the Litany and singing the Psalms—and here he sounds a good deal like the prototypical pastoral poet, the urbanite who is charmed by the found poetry of native rites and folkways. For Herbert, procession becomes a kind of three-dimensional prayer with, as he says, "4 manifest advantages. First, a blessing of God for the fruits of the field; Secondly, justice in the Preservation of bounds; Thirdly, Charity in loving walking, and neighborly accompanying of one another, with reconciling of differences . . .; Fourthly, Mercy in releeving the poor by a liberall distribution and largesse . . ." (284). Here is the pastoral in every positive sense: there are pastures and kind country folk, justice and mercy, divine blessing and human forgiveness, charity and the chanting of songs that bring, for the time being, a measure of peace in the valley.

Yet there is a reminder of the astringent antipastoral here, too—there is no peace without the police, in the person of the parson himself. Enforcing the ties that bind, "he exacts of all to be present at the perambulation, and those that withdraw, and sever themselves from it, he mislikes, and reproves as uncharitable, and unneighbourly; and if they will not reforme, presents them." Herbert's reformed pastoral is after all about the reformation of others too, through coercive church discipline if necessary. This language of "exacting" and spiritual enforcement falls harshly on the modern ear. Yet even in "presenting" the stubbornly "uncharitable" parishioner to the authorities, the parson's goal is after all the creation of loving presence: he must be "exacting" in his enforcement because, Herbert believes, "absence breeds strangeness, but presence love," and because "Love is his business, and aime." For Herbert pastoral authority, even in punishment, is not an end in itself, but rather a means to reconciliation and peace. "[S]ometimes, where he knows there hath been or is a little difference, hee takes one of the parties, and goes with him to the other, and all dine or sup together" (284). As at the end of "Love" (III), they all do sit and eat. Or so the pastor hopes.

Our recognition of Herbert's apparently double impulse toward the pastoral—to mock literary pastoral conventions while praising various pastoral persons and places—brings us back to the mixed conventions of the pastoral tradition itself, and to Herbert's conversion of these conventions for divine service. The first group of essays in this collection, under the heading "Pastoral Poetry and Pastoral Practice," directly considers the relations between literary pastoral and literal pastoral. As already noted above, Donald Friedman's opening essay, "Pastoral Conversions," recognizes that the habitual doubleness of the pastoral mode was well understood in Herbert's time, and that the inherent ambiguity of its perspective on rural life would not have been news to his first readers. Friedman sees this double aspect of pastoral poetics as central to Herbert's conception of his role as poet and priest. The question, then, is the larger purpose or purposes that doubleness is made to serve in the poems of *The Temple*. Friedman concludes that Herbert, like Marvell after him, was always conscious of his consciousness—in other words, aware of his complicity as poet in his own presentations or representations. Yet, Friedman adds, as Herbert grew in his priestly vocation, his Marvellian irony was tempered by a Miltonic concern with finding, defining, and creating his role and powers as a poet—the kind of poet who can fulfill the ancient duties of the prophet.

Next in this group, Gene Edward Veith's essay, "'Brittle Crazy Glass': George Herbert, Vocation, and the Theology of Presence," reasserts Lutheran contexts for Herbert and pastoral. Veith explores the tension that he perceives in Herbert's work between the early Reformation's stress on divine presence and the later Protestant reemphasis on confirming one's "vocation" through works and moral effort, with their potential legalism. Veith argues that in some of Herbert's poetry, but especially in *The Countrey Parson*, Herbert struggles to define the nature of God's calling upon his life. Generally, Veith claims, the pastoral manual expresses the latter understandings of vocation, sounding like most of his later Protestant contemporaries in his perfectionism, moralism, and earnest desire to serve God—goals that he finds tormenting in his inability to achieve them. In Herbert's poetry, though, the vocational conflicts that Herbert explores often are resolved with an epiphany of Christ's presence, the insight from the early Reformation that his calling—both as a priest and as a poet—is, in Luther's terms, a mask of God, who is truly and unconditionally present and active in human vocation. In Veith's view, it is in poetry that Herbert feels most in God's presence.

In "Herbert's Holy Practice," Kenneth Graham views the same

issue—the relation between Herbert's poetry and pastoral practice—through the lens not of Lutheran but of early Stuart English theology. He turns particularly to Herbert's exact contemporary and near Wiltshire neighbor, Robert Dyer, a clergyman whose book *The Christians Theorico-Practicon; or, His whole Duty, consisting of Knowledge and Practise* was published in 1633 specifically to be sold in a Salisbury bookshop. Graham compares Dyer's book to *The Temple*, revisiting poems such as "A Wreath," "The Windows," and especially "Discipline" to explore how, for Herbert, the very grace that unconditionally saves the believer also shows itself in good works if it was true grace to begin with. Thus, Graham would reconcile the inward devotion of Herbert's poetry with the outward pastoral practice of *The Countey Parson* in Herbert's own words from "The Windows":

> Doctrine and life, colours and light, in one
>   When they combine and mingle, bring
> A strong regard and aw: but speech along
>   Doth vanish like a flaring thing,
>   And in the eare, not conscience ring.

Like a sermon without the application, like words without works, like doctrine without life and discipline, "Knowledge, that sleeps, doth die," writes Jonson.[11] But, says Graham, Herbert suggests that knowledge that goes forth to direct practice not only survives, but multiplies.

The kinds of words that work best for the pastoral Herbert are poetic words, argues Helen Wilcox, concluding this section on pastoral poetry and practice with her essay, based on her conference keynote address, " 'Hallow'd Fire'; or, When Is a Poet Not a Priest?" Wilcox's answer to her title's question is: in Herbert's case, never. She argues that the functions of poet and priest are inseparably bound together in Herbert's writing, so that, in vocation and in practice, the priest is always the poet, and vice versa. His poems' representation of priesthood mirrors the aesthetic principles of *The Temple*, while the poetic texts themselves fulfill the duties of a priest in preaching and praying, word and sacrament. Herbert is a priest aesthetically as well as spiritually, whose "hallow'd fire" implies purity and sacrifice in both language and devotion. In "Jordan" (I), Herbert rejects the flowery rhetoric of traditional (secular) pastoral verse in favor of plainness in praise of God: in this way, beauty and truth will go hand in hand, and delight will indeed be turned into a sacrifice.

The next group of essays turns from this focus on literary and literal pastoralism to Herbert's actual relations with specific and local historical personalities and places. Cristina Malcolmson's essay, based on her keynote address to the Salisbury conference, takes up the case of nearby Wilton House and William Herbert's gardener: Adrian Gilbert. Malcolmson has written extensively about George Herbert's country parson as a figure deeply interested in and involved with public life.[12] Here she argues that Gilbert's landscape designs for the Earl of Pembroke at Wilton ensured that the garden would be experienced by those who visited it, including George Herbert, not as a mere rural retreat, but as a religious and scientific challenge. More specifically, Gilbert's presence at Wilton represented not only the memory of his half brother Sir Walter Raleigh, but also the glories and failures of Elizabethan overseas exploration, including its association with science and magic. Gilbert, with his expansive person and personality and his far-flung experience of travel, was a living link to Raleigh's great schemes for a Protestant empire, as well as to sophisticated courtly interest in the interconnections between gardening, chemistry, mathematics, navigation, and alchemy. In fact, these interconnections were visible in Gilbert's garden designs at Wilton—making a walk among the shrubberies a potential act of discovery.

From Malcolmson's argument that even in Wiltshire Herbert might still connect with the wider world, we turn next to Clayton D. Lein's consideration of how and why Herbert came to Wiltshire at all. His essay "At the Porch to the Temple: Herbert's Progress to Bemerton" supports Izaak Walton in certain aspects of his account about Herbert's pilgrimage from Westminster in 1624 to Bemerton in 1630. Acknowledging the lack of much firm documentary evidence, Lein attempts to explain this six years' gap, suggesting that Herbert is at moments in this period virtually incoherent in his motivations. Admitting that we cannot answer many questions concerning Herbert's "years in the wilderness," Lein nevertheless puts parameters on certain speculations. Herbert's long pilgrimage to Bemerton began with his retreat to his friend in Kent. From that point, Lein argues, there was either an acute crisis in patronage *or* Herbert did not truly decide to enter the priesthood until very late in this period. Even then, he received the barest nod of patronage, as his contemporaries were quick to perceive. Lein concludes that Herbert's choice, however sound for his soul, undeniably involved serious self-effacement.

Whatever Herbert's irresolution and winding ways in reaching Bemerton, there is no doubt that, once he arrived, he threw himself into his new pastoral life with quiet but famous intensity. It has been said on some authority that the good shepherd knows his sheep, and the Wiltshire historian John Chandler's important new research enables us to know Herbert's congregation in some surprisingly specific ways. In "The Country Parson's Flock: George Herbert's Wiltshire Parish," Chandler takes us into a roll call that survives of all adult males who were living in the parish in 1641/2, less than a decade after Herbert's death. Using this roster as a guide to specific persons and personalities, Chandler takes us into local records, introducing us, for instance, to the striving farmers Richard and John Thring, and their dowered sister Susan; to the rather improvident widow Elflet Young; and to Margaret Elliott Forman, the elderly sister-in-law to the notorious astrologer, magician, and medical quack (and Shakespearean companion), Dr. Simon Forman. These were the people whom Herbert visited, encouraged, cajoled, and sometimes sought to reconcile—and strove to "kindle" with his Sunday sermons. Chandler also attends helpfully to the land and landscape itself—its composition, its characteristic crops, its cycles of plenty and want—and to the sometimes tumultuous politics of early Stuart Salisbury. Here we see the local soil—both literally and metaphorically—in which both *The Temple* and *The Countrey Parson* grew to completeness.

The next essay in this group, Chauncey Wood's "George Herbert and the Widow Bagges: Poverty, Charity, and the Law," addresses through the lens of the Poor Law the tensions and apparent ambivalence in Herbert's writings about poverty, and about ministry to the poor. Noting that the Poor Law Statute of 1601 attempted for the first time to deal nationally with the problem of the "deserving poor," Wood closely reads Herbert's carefully nuanced response to the law in *The Countrey Parson,* chapter 12—"The Parson's Charity." Like John Chandler, Wood looks to local examples contemporary with Herbert, such as the lame-handed Widow Bagges of Salisbury, to draw out Herbert's praise—and subtle dispraise—of the Poor Law in practice. Wood argues that in creating his model country parson, Herbert takes issue with both local and national laws for the treatment of the poor, and tacitly censures both for ignoring the spiritual dimension of poverty. A shilling a week may make the lame-handed Widow Bagges comfortable, but in Herbert's view it will not make her good; her appearance on the Poor Bench serves others—the local burghers who desire their charity to be known and praised—but not the poor themselves. Instead, Herbert seeks to complete that "excellent statute" in the service of a "double aime"—to address both material and spiritual poverty, not only through law, but through grace.

This section on historical personalities and places ends, appropriately, with an essay about the largely neglected man who was instrumental in the posthumous preservation and transmission of Herbert's manuscripts on their indirect and sometimes difficult way to publication. In "'To Do a Piece of Right': Edmund Duncon and the Publication of George Herbert," Anthony Martin builds on Barnabas Oley's brief 1671 mention of Duncon's crucial role as a literary agent. Martin notes not only that Duncon delivered the manuscript of *The Countrey Parson* to Oley, thus enabling its publication as part of Herbert's 1652 *Remains;* Martin also clarifies Duncon's critical work in delivering the manuscript of *The Temple* to Nicholas Ferrar. Martin shows why this was a slightly testy transaction: Herbert's legal executor, Arthur Woodnoth, had plans to publish the book with the London bookseller Philemon Stephens, while Ferrar had already arranged its publication by Thomas Buck and Roger Daniel at the University Press in Cambridge. Thus, the very form, and perhaps the existence, of *The Temple* in print is due to Duncon. Furthermore, Martin notes that because Duncon was one of the few clerical associates of Herbert and Ferrar who lived long enough to witness both the Interregnum and the Restoration, study of his life can teach us more about Herbert's milieu as priest and poet in the 1630s, and also hypothetically about how Herbert himself might have fared had he lived so long.

Following these sections on the pastoral uses of poetry and on historical personalities and places, the two essays in the next section take up the related topic of 'biblical and liturgical connections.' In Herbert's historical moment, and especially in his writings, pastoral ministry was inseparable from biblical forms and formation, and in Herbert's English Church, biblical formation was inseparable from liturgy—which was itself founded on biblical forms. It is the interdependence of the biblical and the liturgical in Herbert's poetry that is the subject of Paul Dyck's essay, "George Herbert and the Liturgical Experience of Scripture." While acknowledging the Book of Common Prayer as a common site of political and even military conflict in the Tudor-Stuart era, Dyck argues primarily for Prayer Book liturgy as a way of reading scripture. Therefore he seeks to demonstrate that Herbert's poetry operates within a biblical discursive space that has been significantly formed by Prayer Book worship, and that the most immediately important aspect of this worship for *The Temple* is that it positions readers, and more particularly the reading church, as themselves being read by the living Word. Liturgy's spiritual significance, says Dyck, depends not so much on its internalization in the worshipper, but rather on its arrangement of scripture, which makes possible both outward prayer and inward communion. This way of reading liturgically does not negate the contests around the Prayer Book, nor does it equate Herbert's poetry with Prayer Book liturgy; but it does make clear that Prayer Book liturgy is not *an alternative to* being Word-centered, but, like the poetry of *The Temple,* is rather *a way of* being Word-centered.

If Prayer Book liturgy is essentially an arrangement of scripture, then the scriptures most likely to be so arranged are the Psalms—themselves, of course, the work of ancient Hebrew liturgists. In her essay "Herbert and Early Stuart Psalm Culture: Beyond Translation and Meditation," Kate Narveson clearly reconnects Herbert's literary and liturgical concerns with his sense of evangelical pastoral duty. Noting that most devotional writers in Herbert's day imitated not psalmic *form* but rather psalmic *devotional content,* Narveson argues that by examining points of similarity and difference between Herbert's lyrics and devotional writing rooted in the book of Psalms, we can gain a better sense of just how unprecedented was his choice to write poetry in the form of psalmic lyrics. By getting beyond mere psalm translation and the looseness of prose meditation, says Narveson, Herbert took early Stuart devotional literature in a fresh, and a more inward, direction. Although, as Paul Dyck suggests, Herbert's lyrics can be read liturgically and some could have been used, like the Psalms, by an individual or congregation to express devotion, Narveson concludes that overall "The Church" is closer to the evangelical treatise than to a new Psalter for public worship.

As we already have observed, Herbert's commitment to spiritual nurture, expressed so fully in his "pastoral" poetry and prose, extended beyond the walls of his parish church throughout his entire parish community in concrete ways that confound the usual distinctions between sacred and secular. The one essay in the next section, "Pastor, Garden, and Pasture," presses the writ of pastoral care even further, not only beyond the church's gates, but also beyond the human congregation and out among the local flora and fauna.

"Herbert's Pastor as Herbalist," by Curtis Whitaker, takes as its point of departure point "The Parson's Completeness," Herbert's chapter 23 in *The Countrey Parson* about the parson's omnicompetence—not only in the Gospels, but in the law, in anatomy, in diet, and most extensively, in herbal medicine. Whitaker observes that this blurring of professional boundaries tells us much about the relationship of religion and science in the sixteenth and seventeenth centuries. It was perfectly acceptable for a botanist to include biblical information in a scientific work such as an herbal and not unusual for a clergyman to dabble in the scientific study of plants. The essay first puts Herbert's apparently odd herbal recommendation in the context of early modern medicine—and science more generally—and then considers roses as a kind of medicinal test case, since they appear consistently in the herbals of the period, and appear as well as in Herbert's poetry. Noting the rose's beauty and sweetness, as well as its chemically purgative properties and its penitential associations, Whitaker concludes by reading Herbert's poem "The Rose" as an herbalist's emblem of restraint: restraint from indulgent pleasure, and restraint from arguing your opponent into submission. "The Rose" becomes all the more powerful in making its case through the gentleness with which it conveys its message.

Following this foray into the garden and the fields, the collection concludes with a section, "Beyond Bemerton," that reflects further outward from the book's decidedly local focus, first on fictional portrayals of Herbert that suggest something of his place in the popular imagination, and finally on the enduring theological implications of his poetry. As to the fictional Herbert, Sidney Gottlieb suggests that the fictionalizing began, if not with the many personae of *The Temple* itself, at least with Herbert's earliest biographers; and in "Under Salisbury Spire with the Fictional George Herbert," Gottlieb treats a largely unnoticed but fascinating contributor to this process, the late-Victorian novelist Emma Marshall. Two of her novels, *Under Salisbury Spire* (1889) and *A Haunt of Ancient Peace* (1896), include Herbert as a central character, and the way he figures in them gives us an intriguing view of Herbert's image in late nineteenth-century England, and reminds us of the extent to which a poet's reputation and persona can be mediated by the discourse of fiction.

As her first title suggests, Mrs. Marshall's novels are still locally specific to Herbert's Salisbury in the 1620s and 1630s, and taken together they amount to an implicit—and plausible—historical argument: that had there been more George Herberts to moderate Puritan and courtly passions while maintaining the liturgical "beauty of holiness," there might not have been an English Civil War. Blending the historical Herbert, Jane Danvers, and Arthur Woodnoth with the fictional Anthony and Magdelene Wydville, Carlo Valdessaro, and, yes, the Puritan Sir Marmaduke Peel, Mrs.

Marshall imagines Herbert not only as a pastoral mediator for a via media, but also as a pastoral lover of sorts, courting and winning Jane Danvers in the (rather unlikely) guise of rural romantic hero. Herbert's role as a warm but chaste lover and advisor to young lovers plays out in microcosm the impending national drama, as the Wydvilles' daughter Dorothea (apologies to George Eliot) resists the Malvolio-like advances of the Puritan Marmaduke in favor of the virtuous and courtly (and romantically Latin) Carlo. Mrs. Marshall's efforts at making Herbert a complex and dynamic character, says Gottlieb, support her strategic use of Herbert as a figure who embodies a model of spirituality, charity, love, and conflict resolution with historical as well as contemporary relevance.

Herbert's spiritual and pastoral model is central to the collection's concluding essay by the conference keynote speaker David Jasper, "'Something Understood': From Poetry to Theology in the Writings of George Herbert." Helen Wilcox argues that for Herbert the writing of true poetry is always a pastoral and priestly act, and many contributors to this book make quite reasonable claims that specific religious doctrines provide rich and proper contexts for experiencing Herbert's poetry; but Jasper wants to distinguish carefully between the poetic and the theological, particularly when theology verges into dogma. Jasper notes that Herbert's "Prayer" (I) abruptly ends, after a vivid montage of glorious and musical phrases, in deliberate and quiet indefinition, and he argues that Herbert's silent acceptance is truly his "something understood"—that is, his recognition of the limits of language, his acknowledgment of the essential unspokenness of true prayer. Herbert's verse, says Jasper, provokes the reader on competing, simultaneous levels, always profoundly aware of its limitations while yet opening up a polyphony of meanings that can be heard and felt only in the challenging grandeur of their harmony and their dissonance. Thus, Jasper would resist the reduction of Herbert's poetry to any particular kind of religious language, or to any set of doctrines. Jasper concludes instead that the brilliant and sometimes violent variety of Herbert's images and metaphors is finally consumed in a still, insistent voice—the voice of "something understood," with its final negation of all language and its demands, and yet their complete fulfillment in the silence of God's total presence.

Jasper's paradoxical point about both the negation and the silent fulfillment of language brings a fitting end to this collection—because the pastoral language that Herbert both mocks and uses in "Jordan" (I) is after all only a specific type of all language that is both emptied and finally understood in "Prayer" (I). I would agree with Jasper that no poet ever attended more carefully to the negative limits of language than did Herbert, and that this awareness of limits is the source of our ultimate fulfillment in reading his work—both as poetry and as prayer. For Herbert's powerful negation of language's glittering images leads to his even more powerful affirmation that prayer, and prayerful poetry, is indeed "something understood." That is, prayer in Herbert's view has an omniscient divine Understander, who does not need the splendid shards of metaphor to puzzle out a meaning, but who sees whole and true and clear. In this sense, for Herbert, prayer is the *only* utterance truly "understood," truly free from the beautiful and bewildering contingencies of language, and from the sad inevitabilities of misunderstanding.

I began by invoking the ancient pastoral dream—the fancy of Theocritus, Virgil, Sidney, and Spenser—that by drawing close to the simple shepherd's life, we may cease our striving for a time and become more reflective, better people. We have seen how Herbert mocked and parodied the pastoral—how he tried to free it of its "quaint metaphors" and "false hair," and how he laughed its follies to scorn. Yet we have seen that near the end of *The Countrey Parson* Herbert turns with a surprising sympathy to celebrate, with unsentimental clarity and practical charity, a deeply pastoral scene. The language is the plainest and simplest, but if beauty is the form of harmony made visible, then these words are beautiful indeed.

So it would seem that Herbert's reformed pastoral and his country parson have a touch of the poet about them after all. We might think that his plain honest shepherds would want only to *preach;* but Herbert also wants them to *sing.* For Herbert, the problem with pastoral poetry, as indeed with all poetic language, was not that it imagines too much pleasure, but that it imagines too little—Herbert had immortal longings in him, and his desire was not content with any merely mortal joy.

NOTES

1. See page 37, below.

2. *The Complete Works in Verse and Prose of Edmund Spenser,* ed. Alexander B. Grosart (London: Spenser Society, 1882), ix.

3. *The Works of George Herbert,* ed. F. E. Hutchinson (Oxford: Clarendon Press, 1964), 10. All further references to *The Temple* will be to this edition, and will be given parenthetically in the text.

4. Thomas More, *Utopia,* trans. Paul Turner (Harmondsworth, England: Penguin, 1965), 46–49.

5. *The Countess of Pembroke's Arcadia, Written by Sir Philip Sidney Knight. Now since the First [1590] Edition augmented and ended* (London: William Ponsonbie, 1593), 3r–3v. Sidney writes that his sister witnessed the composition of much of the book at Wilton, "being done in loose sheetes of paper, most of it in your presence. . . ."

6. Edmund Spenser, *The Faerie Queene*, ed. Thomas P. Roche, Jr. (New Haven, CT: Yale University Press, 1981).

7. Herbert, *Works*, (ed. Hutchinson), 10. All further references to *The Countrey Parson* will be to this edition, and will be given parenthetically in the text.

8. Andrew Marvell, *The Complete English Poems*, ed. Elizabeth Story Donno (New York: St. Martin's, 1974), 100–102.

9. Christopher Hodgkins, *Authority, Church, and Society in George Herbert: Return to the Middle Way* (Columbia: University of Missouri Press, 1993), 189–90.

10. Cristina Malcolmson, *George Herbert: A Literary Life* (New York: Palgrave Macmillan, 2004), 37.

11. Ben Jonson, "An Ode. To Himself," in *Complete Poems*, (Harmondsworth: Penguin, 1988). line 3.

12. Cristina Malcolmson, *Heart-Work: George Herbert and the Protestant Ethic* (Stanford, CA: Stanford University Press, 1999); Malcolmson, *George Herbert*.

I
Pastoral Poetry and Pastoral Practice

Pastoral Conversions
Donald Friedman

S̲URELY GEORGE HERBERT, OF ALL PEOPLE, WITH HIS LIMITLESS AND VIS-
ceral sensitivity to words, their meanings, their polyphonic historical and social resonances, and their emblematic force, was aware
of the ambivalences, literary and theological, inherent in the word
"pastoral." Therefore I will begin by noting an oddity. The major
critics and scholars who have written about the history of pastoral
have, pretty uniformly, defined the literary mode as one that bases
itself in representative fictions about shepherds in rural settings.[1]
And yet in all of Herbert's poems he mentions shepherds in only
four; of those one refers specifically to Christ,[2] another is a version
of Psalm 23 (and therefore requires the mention),[3] and a third,
"Christmas,"[4] has a similar biblical determinant. Only in "Jordan"
(I)[5] do actual (so to speak) pastoral shepherds appear, and they do
so only to be dismissed cordially as singers of the kinds of songs the
poet himself does not wish to sing.[6] In fact, although the singers of
pastoral songs—song is an indispensable feature of the literary type
Herbert is considering—are allowed as "honest people," there is no
mistaking the dissatisfaction, bordering on contempt, signaled by
the terms Herbert uses to characterize their poetry. It is full of "enchanted groves" and "purling streams," and its "sudden arbours"
cast an obscurantist shade on "coarse-spun lines." The last phrase
reveals Herbert as what we would call, I think, a literary critic, and
suggests that his rejection of pastoral (along with other poetic
modes identified in the poem by allusion and the inventive deploy-
ment of cliché, such as Petrarchan love poems, allegorical works of
all sorts, and perhaps even Donnean conceits) is grounded not
alone in its fundamental falsity but also in its inevitable, deteriorat-
ing effect on the fineness of diction that Herbert seeks in his own
verse.

The animadversions of "Jordan" (I) establish a connection between an ideal of the proper language of poetry—and not simply
devotional poetry—and the modes it employs to represent its subjects. That is, they question whether beauty and "good structure"

can be found in verse only if it resorts to the embellishments of imaginative reconstructions of reality—fictions—or artificially enhanced versions of that reality ("false hair"). Herbert explains how these acts of supererogatory substitution come about in "Jordan" (II), where he also discovers their source in his unacknowledged literary ambitions. He asks Plato's question about the relationship between the crafted representation and the created object it is meant to serve by that craft. An invocation of the contrast—or conflict—between a "true chair" and a "painted chair" leads to a more pointed examination of the purposes of contemporary poetic styles; thus, he hints that the meretricious charms of "enchanted groves" and the surprise of "sudden arbours" are little more than veils to hide inept versifying. Similarly, the passion of true love should not need to be "refreshed" by the aesthetics of landscape. Climactically, Herbert, with feigned naïveté, asks why any reader should be taxed by deliberate obscurity; implicit in his protest is the suggestion that not only is there no justification for "veiling" the truth, but that the very attempt to put difficulty in the way of the seeker after truth is tantamount to a confession that truth is not the object of the poem. "Jordan" (I) clinches its argument by asserting the near identity, in verse, of simplicity and directness of diction and "the truth" that should be the only aim, and the proper measure, of both poem and poet. He then offers proof of that identity by writing "My God, My King," a statement that in itself creates an identity, then identifying that statement as saying itself "plainly," and finally by demonstrating that he has not suffered "losse of rime," because clearly the word "King" completes the rhyme scheme of the stanza.

Nevertheless, that stanza begins by dismissing "shepherds," sending them off to sing whatever they will, so long as Herbert can write the kind of verse he aspires to. It would seem to be the case, then, that when we wish to consider Herbert's relation to pastoral poetry as it has been regarded and classified historically, we must attend to some clear and distinct ideas. One worth thinking, about, I suggest, is that if we accept the notion that the literary form we commonly call "pastoral" begins in the Western tradition with the *Idylls* of Theocritus, we must also recognize that those poems, while they dwell on the speech and behavior, as well as the natural settings, of rustic personae, are written by, and from the viewpoint of, sophisticated urbanites; and, furthermore, that the presumptive audience for such poems understands the parallax effect that is both the intent and the consequence of the distance between what is represented and the representer. In essence, pastoral in its original form is ironic; by that I mean that it responds to the meaning and the etymology of Greek *eironeia*, a verbal compound made of the word for speech itself and the word for dissembling. In other words, pastoral has from its beginning announced itself as a way of talking about matters under a guise, an approach to its genuine concerns that proceeds by dressing them in images and locutions drawn from a markedly different, imagined world.

As any number of books and essays testify, this is one of the Greek inventions that were imitated, expanded, and in some cases radically altered by Roman civilization. For us, the most important figure in this process is, of course, Virgil, in whose hands the evolution of pastoral poetry encompassed politics, history, social criticism, and the nature of poetic art, to mention only a few aspects of this increasingly comprehensive mode. But throughout its own history, and notably during its reflorescence during the Renaissance, pastoral maintained its fundamentally ironic, or Janus-like, stance toward the truths it attempted to comment on. At times this trait is attributed to authorial intent, as in "E.K.'s" remark that Spenser masqueraded as Colin Clout because "he chose rather to unfold great matter of argument covertly, then professing it,"[7] or when Puttenham grants us a glimpse into the paranoid society of Francis Walsingham's regime by revising the received history of the eclogue, arguing that it was devised "not of purpose to counterfait or represent the rusticall manner of loves and communication, but under the vaile of homely persons and in rude speeches to insinuate and glaunce at greater matters, and such as perchance had not bene safe to have been disclosed in any other sort."[8]

Whether determined by self-censorship, modesty, or diffidence on the part of the poet, the habitual doubleness of the representative mode of pastoral was well understood in Herbert's time; and the inherent ambiguity of its perspective on rural life had always been acknowledged. It is that aspect of the poetics of pastoral that seems to me to be central to Herbert's conception of his role as poet and priest. The question, then, is the larger purpose or purposes that doubleness is made to serve in the poems of *The Temple*. One further point of clarification may be pertinent: some of the most prominent critics who have written about pastoral—in particular Paul Alpers in his magisterial book, *What Is Pastoral?*—have argued that a view of the mode (Alpers, and others, prefer that term to "genre" or similarly generic designations)[9] that identifies its primary trope as irony is basically mistaken.[10] They reject the well-worn characterization of pastoral as an exercise in nostalgia, dominated by visions and theories of a lost golden age. Most recently,

Nancy Lindheim, in a book on the life of Virgilian pastoral in Western literature, has seconded Alpers in the contention that pastoral
is in essence a way of representing timeless human problems of
moral choice and the individual's place in the world.[11] I believe
these positions are also consonant with some held by Cristina Malcolmson, in her examinations of Herbert's involvements (I had almost said "entanglements") in contemporary political and social
structures.[12]

I would like to make it clear that I do not find such arguments in
contradiction to what I have been saying about pastoral's fundamental manner of representing its subjects. But on occasion, they
tend to fuse with speculation about the autobiographical component of *Temple* poems, and thereby enter the foggy terrain of "sincerity." Many, if not most, commentators on "The Church" feel the
need to decide to what extent the poems in that part of *The Temple*,
especially those that do not appear in the Williams manuscript, and
so presumably date to the period of the Bemerton priesthood, are
cast in the voice of Herbert himself, rather than of a presumptive
speaker. Thus, they tend to minimize or ignore the recurrence in
that volume of Herbert's presenting himself in the guise or role of
persons clearly different from what we and he know him to be. Of
course, that mannerism—or witty device—is quite often a way to
mock, knowingly, his own knowingness, and therefore enacts a serious moral criticism. If we credit Walton's account of what Edmund Duncon told him of Herbert's dying wishes,[13] perhaps we
should attend more closely to the precise wording of the advice and
request sent to Nicholas Ferrar with the "little book": he is told he
will find "a picture of the many spiritual Conflicts that have past
betwixt God and my Soul" in the course of Herbert's spiritual journey. "A picture"—and we know with what care Herbert chose his
words—is a representation, an artful, artificial, consciously crafted
version of an experience. The word, and the concept, indicates the
artist's consciousness of the gap between that experience—or
thought, or proposition, or memory—and his rendition of it in the
material of words and the medium of verse. Here, again, I would
say, is evidence not only of Herbert's deliberate exploitation of an
intrinsic feature of the rhetoric of pastoral, but of its indispensable
function in that rhetoric.

Let me make what may be a necessary comparison between the
literary, or secondary, pastoral and the kind of pastoral we encounter in the famous similes in the *Iliad,* those moments when Homer
turns our attention from a scene of gory devastation to a vision of
tranquil fields and peaceful domestic activity. There can be little

doubt that the singer/poet means us to be struck by the contrast, and we might legitimately speculate that he is making a point about the pains and costs of war, however glorious. The poet is transparent in his presence, as is his device; the voice is clearly his own, and his intent is unmistakable. But whereas the pastoral mode originated in the impulse, as Empson once defined it, to "put the complex in the simple"[14] by dressing sophisticated questions in rustic costume, that process of conversion confronted Herbert with challenges infinitely more complex and daunting. Perhaps the first task that lay before him was to trace the connections between the numinous and the natural in the world he was given and had chosen. But ultimately he needed to find the proper dress in which to clothe his living recollections of those conflicts and to make of them "something understood."

I hope that I have cleared enough ground to allow me to plant my own preferred sapling of pastoral theory, which grows from the conviction that Herbert's version of pastoral, while it makes little enough of the contents of the box where the many conventions of pastoral "compacted lie"[15]—precious few shepherds, and no purling streams at all—is deeply aware of and dependent on the mode's genius for looking at the object of its interest through an initially distorting, but ultimately illuminating, mirror or glass. What gives Herbert's poetry its coruscating clarity is his unfailing—and courageous—honesty about the necessity of this sleight of hand, his dissatisfaction, approaching despair, at having to yield to that necessity, and his struggle to find sufficient evidence that even that necessity is not the work only of his will, but of some purpose that embraces and motivates his own, and in some measure justifies it. I mean to suggest that the cognitive distance between the presented rurality of the typical pastoral poem, say, and the evaluative consciousness responsible for that presentation is reflective of and ineluctably involved with the fundamental poetic act—the rendering of experience as felt and grasped at in a medium not entirely of one's own creation and not entirely under one's control.

To add to the difficulties facing him as he assumed the burdens of priesthood and the curacy of a small rural parish, Herbert's version of pastoral had to engage not only its archetypal play with the discrepancies between the objects of its contemplation and the consciousness of the contemplator, but also the almost ineffable incongruities discovered by an attempt to address, attract, complain to, catch, argue, and even compete with the creator of the creation that supplies both the material and the language that the pastoralist must use. That is to say, he had to address his God, but had first to forge the language adequate to that address, guided by the word handed down to him in scripture, while remaining true to his own knowledge of the world he lived in and through.

The world of *The Temple*—and I think it is true of all the manifestations of that word "temple" that Herbert might have had in mind—is filled with things of the world we know; it is a world of extraordinary particularity, concreteness, and familiarity, of chairs and boxes, coins and clocks and stones, grapes and lutes, even swords and crowns, and most of all, flowers. They are represented to us, with rare exceptions, in clear but rather abstract outlines, a mode that allows for what I will call a kind of ideational parallax, in which the mention of a homely object summons a view, or a recognition, or a memory, of that object *sub specie aeternitatis*. It is a way of representing the penetration of the diurnal by the timeless, or, we might say, of revealing the interpenetration of the literary language of pastoral and the divine language from which it descends to do its work on the earth. To co-opt one of Herbert's most revealing images, familiar domestic *things* appear in *The Temple* as if seen in or through a glass.[16] What is at issue is the purity or clarity of that medium, the extent to which it distorts or colors the object of vision, and whether it is capable of revealing, by transmitting, the full reality of the thing looked at or looked for. Herbert puts the matter quite succinctly in "The Elixir," where, as if explaining to God what he asks to be taught, he says,

> A man that looks on glasse,
> On it may stay his eye;
> Or if he pleaseth, through it passe,
> And then the heav'n espie.

(lines 8–11)

The poet is here rehearsing Augustine's well-known distinction between the "use" and the "enjoyment" of creation,[17] wherein he articulates the differences, practical, psychological, and moral, between "using" the things of this world as means to achieve other desires or goods, and "enjoying" them—that is, recognizing and accepting them for their intrinsic value, their true significance in their unique and transcendent identities.[18] The Augustinian position, and the philosophical-theological tradition that flows from it, has many versions; Milton's, for example, notably in book 9 of *Paradise Lost,* casts it in terms of the crucial imperative to recognize the hand of the creator in his creation; the formula works its way through history, to the Declaration of Independence, with its invocation of "the law of nature and of nature's God" and onward still.

Some years ago, Elizabeth Cook entitled her work on "late Renaissance poetry" *Seeing Through Words*,[19] and I can think of no better phrase to suggest what Herbert tries to accomplish by shaping his vocabulary to the true pastoral he has imagined, one that will be able to discover the divine meaning implicit in the things of this world. I would point out, too, that the play on words that distinguishes Professor Cook's title chimes very well with Herbert's penchant for playfully serious puns, puns that suggest harmonies between the human and the divine. His resort to puns and wordplay is related to his search for a language that can convey those harmonies; the kind of word that functions on two or more planes is his familiar device for making his poem an expression of such relationships. In this sense, Herbert proposes to teach us that we may find realities by looking confidently *through,* or beyond, the words and signs by which we find our way usually. From this perspective, our words and other means of representation, while they are our principal avenues of inquiry, communication, and understanding, have also inevitably the potentiality to confuse or obscure or misrepresent what they purport to reveal. But Cook's pun also suggests that, in our state of limited perception, words, insofar as they are the creation and the manifestation of the Word who was "in the beginning," may provide our best access to true meaning— if, as Herbert says, "we could spell." His sense, or his intuition, of the ways in which meaning is embedded in our everyday words, almost in spite of the use we make of them in our everyday pursuits, is close to a fundamental insight about the medium of poetry itself; but it is also clearly applicable to his thoughts about the pastoral mode in particular, and thus to his argument in "Jordan" (I) against the literary pastoral as he knew it. To put the matter perhaps too bluntly, while he holds that those other poets who call themselves "shepherds" are "honest people," and may sing of nightingales and spring as freely as may be, he parts company with them because they find it necessary or appropriate to refine their verses with fictions and equivalent deliberately misleading disguises, which he figures as elaborate wigs. He goes on to yoke them with allegorists of all stripes, rejecting them all either for their feckless attempts to make their poems more attractive by adding glitter and surprise, or for their presumptuousness in confusing difficulty with subtlety. Both characteristics of style show contempt for the reader's powers of judgment and for the integrity of the ostensible subject of the poem. We might note that, aside from the work of

Sidney, his admired distant relation, and that of the pastoralists of
the great Elizabethan miscellanies, the pastoral poets Herbert
would have known most immediately were probably the mob of allegorical Spenserians who published so liberally during his youth
and early manhood. Perusal, let alone close study, of Browne and
the Fletchers, or Wither, or even Drayton, will help to explain Herbert's position with respect to the responsibilities and even the
powers of pastoral; for, after all, he of all people was conscious of
the intrinsic ambivalence of the word itself and of the literary mode
it generated. From its classical beginnings it had allegorized the
roles of shepherd and poet, and throughout Christian history it had
enriched and complicated those concepts with that of the priesthood and of its ultimate progenitor, Jesus. No wonder Herbert committed himself so categorically and so passionately to "truth," in
"Jordan" (I). That poem sounds with the same passion that infused
the sonnet he sent to his mother in his seventeenth year, in which
he deplores the cooling of "that ancient heat" toward the divine, a
sonnet that seems, rather eerily, to predict the later, adult poem in
its structure, made almost entirely of rhetorical, but sharply
pointed, questions.[20] It should be no surprise to find that while the
youthful aspirant to devotional verse sounds primarily indignant,
the mature poet speaks as a literary critic and as a "verser" confi-
dent in the correspondence between his language and his intent.

I hoped by giving the title "Pastoral Conversions" to this essay to
point to the correspondences between the spiritual processes that
Herbert is concerned with in *The Temple,* the literary conventions
characteristic of pastoral poetry, and the basic action of transformation that underpins the poetic act itself; except that in the case
of Herbert's poetry I would convert Empson's dictum and describe
it as the act of taking the simple out of the complex, an act of revelation, or freeing reality from the shadow of its representation. At
least, that is what Herbert often seeks, wishes for, or fails at, or de-
spairs at not being able to achieve. Poetry, priesthood, language itself—all depend on changing one thing into another, converting a
word, or a thought, or a soul from what it has been held to be to
what it is in its essence. I am sure that Herbert knew full well, and
delighted in the knowledge, that the root meanings of "convert"
come from the Latin for "together" and to "turn"; but more to the
point, that the compound embraces the ideas not only of changing
one thing into another, but also of directing a thing to its proper
place, and also of turning a thing right around, or upside down: in
short, of causing change, whether by force, or force of argument,
or the sheer poetic power of truth.[21]

Few words of movement occur more frequently in *The Temple* than "stay" and "change." They seem to be in contention with each other as ideas that dominate Herbert's thinking, just as they speak of the tensions within the religious life, caught in the rhythms of time and transience, looking toward the place of sameness and timelessness promised by the Word, that garden where flowers will no longer "glide."[22] Indeed, the mere conception of a flower that glides draws deeply upon Herbert's contemplation of his enterprise, the search for a language adequate to his experience and to his ambitions. (By the way, the word "glide" appears only this once in all of Herbert's verse.) One perspective on that search might focus on specific adaptations of those pastoral motifs he found acceptable. Early on in "The Church," in fact in "The Thanksgiving,"[23] that utterance of frustration that follows the immense pathos of "The Sacrifice," Herbert wonders whether the response he seeks can possibly be met by converting Christ's sufferings into a pastoral celebration of the "triumph" of the Cross; shall he sing of flowers and posies and bowers? But this will not do as imitation, and it is an *imitatio Christi* that he imagines as the appropriate thanksgiving; of course it is, but not in the way he has conceived. A good deal of the vocabulary of the poem is colored as retaliatory or even vengeful, so that the offered gestures of self-denial are revealed, progressively and subtly, as acts of self-aggrandizement. Herbert even invokes the Augustinian complex mentioned earlier, when he promises,

> Then I will use the works of thy creation,
> As if I us'd them but for fashion.
>
> (lines 35–36)

Thus he misses the point, and *mis*uses the—so to speak—letters that have been provided for the further creation of the words that will express the meaning of "thy creation."

The same figure appears, although in a somewhat different context, in "Employment" (I), where he acknowledges that

> The measure of our joys is in this place,
> The stuffe with thee.
>
> (lines 11–12)[24]

The poem, which is largely concerned with his almost obsessive concern with being made use of, speaks in the persona of a part of nature that feels itself barred from the normal processes of nature;

in the end, the minimal employment he pleads for is to be admitted as a member of a consort; as a solitary creature, he asks to be allowed to sing in harmony with the rest of creation. The recurrent plea is to be shown how to establish the way from the world of experience to the realm of ideas, or meaning, or reality—the terms shade into one another in the tradition in which Herbert places himself.

It is worth noting, too, that this range of ideas is manifested in other of Herbert's genres; in the moral epigrams of *Lucus*,[25] for example, while many are devoted to satiric thrusts at the pope and Catholicism in general, and some indicate support for King James's pacific foreign policy and for Protestant positions on both domestic and European matters, epigram 24, *In Angelos,* discourses on the superiority of their "*Intellectus adultus*"[26] to ours, which perforce must depend on images of the concrete in order to understand ourselves. The angels, by contrast, because all knowledge is directly open to them, know themselves as if they were "*ipsi sibi mola & farina*" [to themselves both grain and mill]."[27] Epigram 31, *In Solarium*,[28] describes the sundial as a "machine" that connects heaven and earth, and interprets its function as analogous to the earth's need for sunlight and the need of man's body for the mind, the light without which it would exist in a terrified state of darkness.

The same figure appears later in Herbert's life, in *Memoriae Matris Sacrum*,[29] where, in epigram 14, a visitor to Lady Danvers's grave is told that the mind finds its true resting place in a star, because light seeks light as its natural domain. His mother's beauty, thus, is not subject to change or mortality; rather, during her life it existed as light that glowed through her mortal body, but now it flashes through heaven as if through a glass. The Neoplatonic metaphors are, of course, widely familiar in the literature of the period; I mean merely to point to their presence in Herbert's English, Latin, and Greek poems as signs of his continuing meditation on the relation of the divine and the human.

Although the way that leads to the promised land of biographical interpretation tends to follow a less reliable palmer than Guyon's in *The Faerie Queene,* I think it is clear that the poems in the latter part of "The Church" have been arranged so as to suggest changes in the poet's presentation of self as the dilemmas he faces change as well. "Providence"[30] is fairly conventional in its organization on a psalmic model; but it is there that Herbert announces his new title, "Secretary of Praise," as he surveys the stuff of creation. Not only does he conduct his survey with a distinct note of confidence in his knowledge and capability, but he boasts that in this poem he has gone beyond his previous offerings to the power that orders things of this world. As "secretary" of creation, he takes upon himself the responsibility of offering the praise owed by all living (and inanimate) members of the chain of being that make up the world he surveys. He discovers divinely purposed order in the abundance of creation, in its wondrous plenitude, and perhaps even more admirably in the principle of balance that provides sand to "Check the proud sea, ev'n when it swells and gathers" and antidotes to poisons (lines 47–48, 87). Even though he attributes to God the power to praise, the pen he has put in his hand, and the ability of the hand itself to write, Herbert declares quite straightforwardly that "Man is the worlds high Priest" (line 13).

I would venture a comparison to one of Milton's expositions of the "great chain being" in *Paradise Lost,* not the angel Raphael's account of the process and order of creation, but rather Adam's conduct of his and Eve's morning prayer, in book 5, where, in effect, the first "Man" acts as the "high Priest" of the newly created world. What is noteworthy is that rather than speaking *for* the languageless flora and fauna, Adam calls them to the act of praise and instructs them in its rhetoric. Their proper "speech" is constituted by their essences, which in turn consist in filling their places in the order of beings. The best example I can think of to illustrate the understanding of the natural world that Milton gives voice to through Adam is the passage demonstrating the true meaning of the laws of meteorology:

> Ye mist and exhalations that now rise
> From hill or steaming lake, dusky or grey,
> Till the sun paint your fleecy skirts with gold,
> In honour to the world's great author rise,
> Whether to deck with clouds the uncoloured sky,
> Or wet the thirsty earth with falling showers,
> Rising or falling still advance his praise.
>
> (lines 185–91)[31]

In short, each member of the "chain" justifies its position by serving those above and those below appropriately; different levels of the hierarchy require different kinds of service. Herbert's vision of the "supply" of providence focuses rather on the intrinsic organization that preserves stability by counterbalancing opposing forces, desires, and proclivities. One might say that he finds (or hopes to find) in the order of nature the "neatness" that he discovers with such delight in "Man" (line 42).[32]

All of this moves toward the position from which he turns to the four last things and the conquests of "Love" (III) that close "The Church." But there is a sequence that precedes it that I would suggest is illustrative of Herbert's conversion of pastoral to his newly defined objectives. While he continues to understand and accept his responsibilities for interpreting the world around him (and within him) in a medium that may distort as radically as it can reveal, his commitment to unadorned and perspicuous language has become more particular. The "fineness" he cherishes in "A True Hymn" is understood less as the product of conscious literary choice and more clearly as the issue of a submission of will to the source of true expression. Thus, in "Grief"[33] he speaks as a microcosm whose sorrows are too "rough" for verse, which he repels as "too fine a thing," fit rather for "some lovers lute." His suffering, rather, "excludes both measure, tune, and time," although his protest is somewhat muted by the fact that it is cast in regular iambic quatrains and a couplet. Nor does his ironic humor desert him even in this depth of despond; he tells "verses" to "keep your measures for some lovers lute, / Whose grief allows him musick and a ryme" (lines 17–18), reverting to the categorizations of "Jordan" (I).

"The Crosse"[34] marks a descent still further into despair, the fear of being abandoned, of being denied the benefice of song, despite having summoned "all [his] wealth and familie" (line 5), as well as talent and desire to praise. His "power to serve" has been given and then taken, leaving him "ev'n in Paradise to be a weed" (line 30), thus conjuring Herbert's recurrent fear and loathing of being rendered useless. Crushed by "contrarieties," his heart "cut" by God's "crosse actions" (lines 31–32) he is led finally to surrender: *Thy will be done*"(line 36). This latest of his "many spiritual Conflicts" resolves itself in "The Flower,"[35] which, tellingly, follows the act of submission. God's "crosse actions" come to be seen as points and stages in a process not necessarily understood, but purposefully undergone. Moreover, the analogy on which the poem is built—that between the poet and the flower, whose fortunes, in good and bad weather, seem to be related—is revealed as a misreading. Human beings are subject to, and experience, change in ways crucially different from other denizens of the creation; thus, they are "flowers that glide," an image that, imperfectly interpreted, would border on the incoherent or ludicrous. But the achievement of this great poem is to arrive at the realization that, despite the unmaking of its metaphoric foundation, there exists a garden where human beings may flourish as flowers, but of their own species.

Suffice it to say that from this point the way of "The Church" leads almost uninterruptedly upward; indeed, in "The Sonne,"[36] the second poem to follow "The Flower," Herbert rediscovers the language he has been seeking, and it turns out to be his native English; the reason is, of course, that it has always had the wit to use one word for the sun of heaven and the Son of God.[37] And of course, that is the kind of pun that has always been at home in the pastoral mode, where shepherd, poet, and priest have fused into a single figure—and in doing so have shown how creation speaks the language of the creator, as we would realize, if only we could spell. I would submit that the pun and the pastoral are responses to, or evidences of, an impulse to assert identities beneath apparent dissimilarities. Another example from Milton may illustrate the point: in book 5 of *Paradise Lost* the "affable angel" Raphael, while explaining to Adam how things came to be and how they are related one to another, cites the growth cycle of a flower:

> So from the root
> Springs lighter the green stalk, from thence the leaves
> More airy, last the bright consummate flower
> Spirits odorous breathes: flowers and their fruit
> Man's nourishment, by gradual scale sublimed
> To vital spirits aspire, to animal,
> To intellectual, give both life and sense,
> Fancy and understanding, whence the soul
> Reason receives. And reason is her being.
>
> (lines 479–87)

The description conflates the idea of service we noted in Adam's prayer (the subordination of lesser to higher goods), the facts of biology, and the family connection of trees and flowers to human beings, whose "roots" support the flowering of their natures in the faculty of reason.[38] Such an attempt runs parallel with the period's interest in retrieving the "original" language supposedly spoken by Adam, which in essence was a wish to bridge the gap between the word and the thing, a gap that could easily be compared (as it was) to the distance between the Word and his creation, and that our own age has translated as the distance between sign and signified. The consciousness of that distance is, I suggest, the ground of all metaphor, and thus the seedbed of poetry itself.[39] Pastoral, of all the inherited genres, is the one most obviously involved in that eternal search.

As noted above, Herbert resorts to puns and wordplay because he is working at a language that can convey the relationships between the world of daily reality and the world of transcendent reality that gives it meaning. The kind of word that functions on two or more planes is his familiar device for making his poem an expression of that relationship and a way for us to glimpse the filiations that he wants us to recognize.

Pastoral, as we have seen, is always saying something by pretending to be talking about something else. Herbert is closer to Marvell than to Milton in his view of pastoral, in that Marvell was always conscious of his consciousness—in other words, aware of his complicity as poet in the presentation or representation he was engaged in. That awareness added a complication to the basic structure of deploying pastoral symbols and conventions in the service of other kinds of ideas and perspectives—mainly the political, but also what I would call the epistemological.[40] For Milton the situation was, in a way, simpler, but not altogether different. He, of course, chose to "see" from a pastoral viewpoint often and consistently throughout his career; but his resort to pastoral was often underpinned or undermined or shadowed by his awareness of its inherent potential for misrepresentation. The best example of his thinking about the use of pastoral disguise—the appearance of a shepherd, to characterize both Comus and Lawes in *A Masque presented at Ludlow Castle,* 1634 ("Comus")—has as one of its main concerns the ability of the individual to perceive the difference between falsehood and reality. The fact that Milton chooses the disguise of shepherd raises questions not only about perception per se but also more pointedly about the role that traditional identifications, like that of priest and shepherd (and by implication, poet), play in social institutions. Milton's choice also resonates with his treatment of pastoral in "Lycidas," where the conventions of the form are summoned to illuminate a moment of personal crisis, and are found, one by one, to be inadequate to the task. Of course, this being a poem by Milton, his problem is resolved by his discovery, or creation, of a new form of pastoral—one that openly reverts to the motifs of Christian symbolism. Marvell, by contrast, remains skeptical of any ultimate solution to the dilemma created by the relation between his mind and the world it contemplates; Milton is more openly concerned with finding, defining, and eventually creating his role and powers as a poet—and the kind of poet who can fulfill the ancient duties of the prophet, and perhaps even those of an unanointed priest. Clearly, Herbert is alive to the puzzles that were central to Marvell's kind of pastoral; but he moved closer to Milton's understanding of the possibilities of pastoral, as his thinking as a poet became infused by his explorations of the meaning of his priestly vocation.

Notes

1. A paradigmatic account is that of Frank Kermode, in *English Pastoral Poetry* (London: George G. Harrap and Co., 1952), in the introduction, but particularly p. 16.

2. "Antiphon" (II), where "the God of love" is referred to as "The great shepherd of the fold." All quotations of Herbert are from *The Works of George Herbert,* ed. F. E. Hutchinson (Oxford: Clarendon Press, 1959). "Antiphon" (II) is on p. 92.

3. "The 23d Psalme," in Herbert, *Works* (ed. Hutchinson), 172–73.

4. "Christmas," in Herbert, *Works* (ed. Hutchinson), 80–88.

5. Herbert, *Works* (ed. Hutchinson), 56–57.

6. In *Musae Responsoriae* (unpublished, but most probably written about the time Herbert was elected public orator at Cambridge, ca. 1620), countering Andrew Melville's attack on the Anglican establishment, epigram 39, *Ad Seren. Regem,* addresses King James as the shepherd who guides his sheep safely between the threatening waves of Puritanism and Catholicism. Not surprisingly, both the country parson and Christ are called "shepherd" in *The Priest to the Temple* (see e.g., Herbert, *Works* [ed. Hutchinson], 230, 234).

7. So "E.K." explains in the "Epistle" that introduces *The Shepheardes Calender;* see *Spenser's Minor Poems,* ed. E. De Selincourt (Oxford: Clarendon Press, 1950), 7.

8. Puttenham, *The Arte of English Poesie,* chap. 18, in *Elizabethan Critical Essays,* ed. G. G. Smith (London: Oxford University Press, 1904), 2:40.

9. The reasons for the distinction are presented in "Mode and Genre," chap. 2 of Paul Alpers, *What Is Pastoral?* (Chicago: University of Chicago Press, 1996), 44–78.

10. Although he says that pastoral "makes explicit a certain disproportion between its fictions . . . and the meanings they bear or imply" (*What Is Pastoral?* 16), Alpers, drawing on Kenneth Burke's theoretical concept, argues that the identifying mark of the pastoral mode, its "representative anecdote," has to do with "herdsmen and their lives, rather than landscape or idealized nature" (22). Alpers also provides a useful précis of modern theories of pastoral on page 11, n. 4.

11. In *The Virgilian Pastoral Tradition* (Pittsburgh: Duquesne University Press, 2005), Nancy Lindheim argues that "pastoral is not a poetry of place but of ethos," because "it strips away the encumbrances of . . . societies to explore what is more basic to our fully human needs" (4). She also follows Alpers in rejecting the critical linking of pastoral with nostalgia and ideas of a golden age; rather, she suggests that pastoral makes the reader consider what one is and what one values, so that its emphasis "becomes ethical stability in one's present world rather than yearning for one's past" (6). In both critics, the "doubleness of perspective" I have sketched above is rejected, but for slightly different reasons: Alpers, in "*Lycidas* and Modern Criticism," *ELH* 49 (1982) contends that to understand the speaker of *Lycidas* as something like a dramatic character is to indulge in an ironic view, which would allow us—inappropriately, in his view—"to understand things better

and see them more fully than he does" (477). This argument minimizes the meanings generated by the course of the poem, which itself reflects the successive attempts of a mind to achieve control of its reactions to and questionings of apparently meaningless events. Moreover, it fails to deal adequately with the effect of the ottava rima passage that concludes the poem, where the speaker (whether he is taken to be Milton or not) tells us that we have been listening to the "Doric lay" of an "uncouth swain," and thus differentiates his voice from the swain's, or at least allows for a degree of (ironic?) distance between the two voices and personages. Lindheim (*Virgilian Pastoral Tradition,* 121) seconds Alpers's analysis of the poem's structure, and thinks that "*Lycidas*" simply proceeds "sequentially, as longer poems normally do." More sternly, she asserts that an ironic perspective is found in the poem primarily because of "the critic's unwillingness to see pastoral as a serious form of literature."

12. These are presented comprehensively in Cristina Malcolmson, *Heart-Work: George Herbert and the Protestant Ethic* (Stanford, CA: Stanford University Press, 1999), and more concisely in Malcolmson, *George Herbert: A Literary Life* (New York: Palgrave Macmillan, 2004).

13. Izaak Walton, "The Life of Mr. George Herbert," in *Izaak Walton's "Lives"* (New York: Thomas Nelson and Sons, n.d.), 281.

14. William Empson, *Some Versions of Pastoral* (New York: New Directions, 1960); the phrase appears in the chapter entitled "Proletarian Literature" (23).

15. "Vertue," line 10 in Herbert, *Works* (ed. Hutchinson), 87–88.

16. The most familiar, and apposite, example is, of course, "The Windows"; but see also "The Sacrifice"; "The H. Scriptures" (I); "Justice (II)"; and "The Elixir." Interestingly, the figure occurs as well in "The Church-porch" and "The Church Militant," suggesting that the range of the metaphor attracted Herbert early on as well as later in his career (Herbert, *Works* [ed. Hutchinson], 67, 119, 58, 141, 184, 14, 196).

17. Augustine, *The City of God,* chap. 25, "Of the Division of Philosophy into Three Parts." Augustine treats the subject also in book 1 of *On Christian Doctrine.* Heather Asals has a wide-ranging discussion of Herbert's Augustinianism in chap. 3 of *Equivocal Predication: George Herbert's Way to God* (Toronto: University of Toronto Press, 1981).

18. Earlier, in *The Confessions,* chap. 26, Augustine had outlined a cognate distinction, between "the gift" and "the fruit," which had more clearly to do with the intent of the giver and the understanding of the receiver ("fruit" is the result of the cognizance of the deeper meaning of the "gift," which is primarily of immediate utility), but which shares with the passage in *The City of God* an emphasis on the connections that underlie the surface discontinuities between the mundane and the spiritual.

19. Elizabeth Cook, *Seeing Through Words* (New Haven, CT: Yale University Press, 1986).

20. The first of two sonnets printed in Walton's *Lives* (Herbert, *Works* [ed. Hutchinson], 206).

21. *OED,* 2nd ed., vb. 1–11.

22. "The Flower," line 44, in Herbert *Works* (ed. Hutchinson), 167.

23. Herbert, *Works* (ed. Hutchinson), 35–36.

24. Ibid., 57.

25. Ibid., 410–21.

26. Translated as "perfected mind," in *The Latin Poetry of George Herbert,* ed. M. McCloskey and P. R. Murphy (Columbus: Ohio University Press, 1965), 101.

27. Ibid., 103.

28. Ibid., 109.

29. Herbert, *Works,* (ed. Hutchinson), 422–31.

30. Ibid., 116–21.

31. John Milton, *Paradise Lost*, ed. A. Fowler, 2nd ed. (New York: Longman, 1998), 293. All citations to Milton are to this edition.

32. Herbert, *Works* (ed. Hutchinson), 90–91.

33. Ibid., 164.

34. Ibid., 164–65.

35. Ibid., 165–67.

36. Ibid., 167–68.

37. See Mary Ellen Rickey, *Utmost Art: Complexity in the Verse of George Herbert* (Lexington: University Press of Kentucky, 1966), 59–60.

38. Cf. Herbert's wistful version of the idea in "Affliction" (I) in Herbert, *Works* (ed. Hutchinson), 46–48, where he can only "sigh and wish [he] were a tree," for then he would "grow / To fruit or shade," and thus "should be just." As always, the crux of the matter for Herbert is being used properly. Marvell has a playful version of the trope in "Upon Appleton House," remarking that if he were to stand upside down, one would see he "was but an inverted tree" (line 568).

39. Bridging that distance is one way of thinking about the Incarnation.

40. Epistemological concerns are most obvious in "The Garden," but are also surprisingly prominent in the "Mower" poems. Few pastoral figures are as conscious of their mental disturbance and dislocation as Damon, or of the breach that consciousness has caused with the natural scene they inhabit and that defines them.

"Brittle Crazy Glass":
George Herbert, Vocation, and
the Theology of Presence
Gene Edward Veith

GEORGE HERBERT, IN MANY WAYS, EMBODIES WHAT CHARLES PORTER-field Krauth called the "conservative Reformation"; that is, the Reformation understanding of grace, faith, and the Bible expressed in terms of the historical liturgy and a high view of the sacraments. But in Herbert's day, the conservative Reformation—which Krauth identifies with Lutherans and with early Anglicans[1] but which could also apply to the early Calvin—was already giving way in England to the more radical Reformation of the separatists.

The conservative Reformation emphasized God's work in the act of salvation, as mediated in Christ's "real presence" in the Lord's Supper and the Holy Spirit's effectual presence in baptism and in the Word of God. The more radical Reformation drew away from this Protestant sacramentalism[2] into a more rationalistic approach to God and to the Christian life. This was accompanied, to one degree or another, by a reemphasis on human works, whether, with the Arminians, as acts of will that contribute to one's salvation or, with later Calvinists and Anglicans, as the cultivation of moral effort understood as the sign of salvation. This same shift away from an emphasis on God's presence and on God's work to an emphasis on human responsibility and human work is also evident in the development of one of the most important contributions of the Reformation, the doctrine of vocation.

Herbert in many ways was caught between the old Reformation and the new. Herbert scholarship has often interpreted his sacramentalism and his liturgical worship in terms of Roman Catholicism, or at least of nineteenth-century Anglo-Catholicism. Other scholars have noted Herbert's evangelical emphasis on justification by faith alone, his Calvinist understanding of grace, and his Protestant dependence on scripture. These two equally evident dimensions of Herbert's poetry, however, are by no means contradictory, as much recent scholarship has shown.[3] Rather, taken together, they define the sixteenth-century Church of England. In the early seventeenth century, however, this middle way was attacked from all sides. Some insisted that worship according to the Book of Common Prayer required too much ceremony, while others insisted that it required not nearly enough ceremony. The Church of England's initial Reformation position that salvation is by grace through faith, as mediated by the Word and the sacraments, was challenged by the Arminianism that characterized not only the Laudians but also many separatists.

These conflicts were also evident in the doctrines of vocation, or "calling," which was the Reformation's practical theology of the Christian life. Luther's doctrine of the real presence of Christ characterized not only his theology of the sacraments but also his theology of vocation. Just as Luther and Calvin both emphasized God's work in accomplishing salvation and bringing people to faith, so Luther emphasized God's work in and through human vocation. Just as later Protestants would put more of the burden of salvation back on human beings, so they often treated vocation as a burden, as a set of duties, obligations, and requirements necessary to please God.

Herbert struggled greatly to find his vocation. Cristina Malcolmson has argued that Herbert did not enter the pastoral ministry until after his aristocratic ambitions for public service were thwarted when his family patrons fell out of favor at court and the Arminians rose in both religious and political influence.[4] When he did enter the ministry, however, Herbert threw himself into his divine calling, exploring that vocation in his book *The Country Parson*. Robert Shaw and Diana Benet, among other scholars, also have shown that Herbert understood his identity as a poet to be a divine vocation.[5]

In his poetry, some of which predates the three years he spent in the pastoral ministry before his death, Herbert writes about his difficulties in recognizing and in living out God's calling upon his life. Often he does so in terms of the later understandings of vocation, sounding like many of his Protestant contemporaries in his perfectionism, moralism, and earnest desire to serve God, goals that he finds tormenting because of his inability to achieve them. The vocational conflicts he explores in his poetry, though, are often resolved with an epiphany of Christ's presence, the insight from the conservative Reformation that his calling—both as a priest and as a poet—is, in Luther's terms, a mask of God, who is truly present and active in human vocation.

TWO DOCTRINES OF VOCATION

Izaak Walton presented Herbert's taking of divine orders as a pious renunciation of the world.[6] Herbert's life, however, as part of an important and politically active family, was complicated, as were his ambitions.[7] Complicating the issue still further is that, for a Reformation-minded Christian, it was not necessarily true that church work was a more pious alternative than service in the world. As John Maxfield observes, contrary to ancient and medieval spirituality, "Luther and his earliest followers—many of the clergy coming like him from monastic orders—regarded the way of obedience not as a journeying from the world into the cloister, but from the cloister into the world."[8]

Maxfield goes on to describe the distinctive features of what he calls "evangelical" identity as opposed to that of medieval Catholicism:

> Evangelical holiness was defined in terms that included all Christians and not just clerics and monks. Its place was not the cloister, nor was it limited to the sphere of churchly life. Rather it comprehended, in addition to *ecclesia* [the church], vocations in the realms of *politia* [the state] and *oeconomia* [the household, comprising both the family and the workplace] as well, as Christians lived out their vocations in each of these realms by faith. In these three "holy works and orders of God," and particularly in the *tentatio* [the trials, temptations, and conflicts] experienced by Christians living in these holy orders, God works his divine righteousness in the lives of his people.[9]

Thus, the very struggles over vocation and the troubles that each vocation entails—whether in the church, the state, or the family— were accepted as a facet of evangelical piety.

Luther's doctrine of vocation was, arguably, one of his most important contributions to Christian spirituality.[10] It was rather different, however, from that of Calvin and, especially, Calvin's later followers.

Luther thought of vocation primarily in terms of God's action: God gives us our daily bread, as we pray in the Lord's Prayer, through the vocation of the farmer. He creates new human beings through the vocation of mothers and fathers. God protects us through magistrates. Christ baptizes, distributes his Body and

Blood, and proclaims his Word by means of pastors. God milks the cows, said Luther, through the hands of the milkmaid. Luther called vocation *larva dei,* the mask of God.

Each Christian, therefore, is a mask of God when acting in his or her various callings. The Christian's callings are multiple, occurring in the three estates established by God for the earthly life: the family, the church, and the state. Christians also may have a calling in the workplace, which Luther classified under the family estate as the way the household (*oeconomia*) supported itself.

A major distinguishing characteristic of Luther is his "theology of presence." Luther's insistence on the Real Presence of Christ in the bread and wine of Holy Communion is the best-known example, but he also believed that God is really present in vocation. In the sacramental controversies, Zwingli argued that since Christ ascended bodily into heaven, he is no longer present on earth. This effectively removed him not only from the Sacrament but also from vocation.

For Luther and his followers in the conservative Reformation—including Calvin, with his strong sense of God's providential governance—vocation is a manifestation of how God works in governing the secular world. Both Luther and Calvin consistently emphasize God's action rather than human action, in vocation just as in salvation. In time, however, this emphasis would become turned around. With the rise of Arminianism, salvation began to be seen once again—as it had been under medieval Catholicism—as having to do with the human will and human works. Calvinists in particular condemned this view as legalism, but many of the newer Protestant theologies were legalistic. Similarly, vocation began to be understood legalistically, as a matter of law, of what God demands of the Christian, rather than what God performs through the Christian.

Later Protestant divines tend to talk about vocation in terms of serving God, but Luther resisted this language. Our relationship to God, he said, does not depend upon our works, including the works of our vocations, but only on the work of Christ on the Cross on our behalf. God does not need our good works, said Luther, but our neighbor does. Luther developed a radically neighbor-centered ethic, redirecting morality's orientation from the service of God—which Luther associated with Catholicism's "salvation by works"—to the service of one's neighbor in the world.[11]

Thus, the purpose of every calling is not so much to love and serve God but to love and serve one's neighbors—that is, the specific human beings that God brings into a person's life in the course of every vocation. In the vocation of marriage, for example, the neighbor who is to be loved and served is one's spouse. Those with the vocation of parenthood are to love and serve their children. In the workplace, one's neighbors to love and serve are the customers, the employer, and the fellow workers. In the church, a person's neighbors are the fellow members; in the state, the fellow citizens. Furthermore, according to Christ's account of the sheep and the goats—in which he says, "Inasmuch as ye have done it unto the least of these my brethren, ye have done it to me" (Matt. 25:40)—he turns out to be really present in the neighbor as well. Thus, for Luther, a person does serve Christ after all in vocation, but he does so by serving the neighbor.

Malcolmson, in her book *Heart-Work,* after quoting numerous of Herbert's contemporaries on the subject, shows that the doctrine of vocation displaced spirituality away from even private meditation into the workplace, in effect, displacing monastic asceticism into the secular arena. This surely overstates the point, since personal meditations remained popular throughout the seventeenth century. But Einar Billing has shown how Luther's theology of vocation did displace the monastic virtues into the secular sphere: chastity became fidelity within marriage; poverty became the struggle to make a living; obedience became submission to earthly authorities.[12] Originally, the doctrine of vocation was perceived as a liberation from the cloister. But it might be taken as an extension of the cloister. This is the way Malcolmson takes it, quoting Max Weber: "Now every Christian had to be a monk all of his life."[13]

Weber reduced the doctrine of vocation to a Protestant work ethic, which it never was for Luther, though it arguably had become so by Herbert's time. Certainly Herbert was sometimes caught up in this secular monasticism. He strives for perfection and is tormented when he fails. He is obsessed with the necessity to serve God. There are few neighbors in his poetry. Herbert writes remarkably little, if anything, about his wife, his parishioners, or his social circle. Herbert's poetry is inhabited, for the most part, by himself and God alone. And yet, Herbert ultimately finds God hidden in vocation and serves a neighbor after all.

THE COUNTRY PARSON

Herbert's *The Country Parson* is a treatise on vocation. Though its subject, in the words of the subtitle, is the "character" and the "rule of holy life" of the rural pastor, it also explicitly discusses the doctrine of vocation as it relates to the parson's parishioners. Throughout *The Country Parson,* both as Herbert discusses his own calling and that of the people to whom he gives pastoral care, the tension between the different understandings of vocation is evident.

In the chapter "The Parson Surveys," Herbert gives a good overview of the doctrine according to the Reformation consensus. "Even in Paradise man had a calling,"[14] he says, alluding to the Reformers' arguments against the Roman Catholic doctrine of vocation, in which only churchly offices—with their vows of poverty, celibacy, and obedience that set priests, monks, and nuns apart from the worldly estates—are to be thought of as divine callings. This view considers marriage to be less spiritual than celibacy, which is a counsel of "perfection." Similarly, the necessity of physical labor was often seen in terms of the curse of original sin. But the Reformers pointed out that marriage—including sexuality— was instituted before the Fall and so partakes of perfection. Adam and Eve were also told to tend the Garden, a command given before the Fall, so that not work but only the pain and the frustrations of work (the sweat of the brow; bringing forth thorns) are signs of the curse. But physical labor itself, which alleviates poverty, is to be valued as a true calling from God, a divine vocation.

Furthermore, says Herbert, "every gift or ability is a talent to be accounted for, and to be improved to our Master's advantage" (Tobin, 248). What a particular human being is able to do is a "gift" from God. He creates each individual with particular abilities, personality, interests, and opportunities, all of which lead to God's various callings.

Herbert believes that one facet of the parish priest's calling is to make sure that all of those under his pastoral care find callings of their own. Herbert maintains that the major sin of the land is idleness—that is, not attending to vocation—and this carelessness, whether "having no calling" or "walking carelessly in our calling," leads to vices such as drunkenness, stealing, whoring, scoffing, reviling, and gambling (248). Thus, the country parson "represents to everybody the necessity of a vocation" (248).

Herbert goes on to comment on the various estates in which Christians are to find their callings. Of the family, he observes that "[m]en are either single or married. . . . His family is his best care, to labour Christian souls and raise them to their height, even to heaven" (249). He surveys the ways a gentleman may be called to serve the state: "No commonwealth in the world hath a braver institution than that of Justices of the Peace. . . . When there is a parliament, he is to endeavour by all means to be a knight or burgess there" (249-50).

Herbert, like the early Reformers, says relatively little about vocation in the modern sense—namely, the workplace—though with later Protestants that would become the primary emphasis and the source of the word "vocation" in the modern sense of "employment," as in "vocational training." The country parson in the agrarian economy of the place and time, which had far fewer employment options, is thinking mainly of the gentry throughout this discussion, the peasants and tradesmen having their callings more or less laid out for them. Herbert worries about the "younger brothers, those whom the parson finds loose, and not engaged into some profession by their parents, whose neglect in this point is intolerable and a shameful wrong both to the commonwealth and their own house" (250-51). The older brother will inherit the land, so the younger brothers need to find other callings. The parson recommends the study of civil law "because it is the key of commerce." Herbert also "commends mathematics as the only wonder-working knowledge," with its practical applications "fortification and navigation" (251). If all else fails, the young man with nothing to do can always go to America: "But if the young gallant think these courses dull and phlegmatic, where can he busy himself better than in those new plantations and discoveries, which are not only a noble, but also as they may be handled, a religious employment" (251).

Herbert's parson also counsels people who are already in their vocations, "those that he finds busy in the works of their calling" (223).

> He admonisheth them of two things: first, that they dive not too deep into worldly affairs, plunging themselves over head and ears into carking and caring, but that they so labour as neither to labour anxiously nor distrustfully nor profanely. Then they labour anxiously when they overdo it, to the loss of their quiet and health: then distrustfully when they doubt God's providence, thinking that their own labour is the cause of their thriving, as if it were in their own hands to thrive or not to thrive. Then they labour profanely when they set themselves to work like brute beasts, never raising their thoughts to God nor sanctifying their labour with daily prayer. . . . Secondly, he adviseth them so to labour for wealth and maintenance as that they make not that the end of their labour but that they may have wherewithal to serve God the better and to do good deeds (223).

The parson urges people in their vocations to avoid "carking" (that is, fretting) and being anxious. He wants them to realize that their work is not just in their hands, but is a function of God's providential working. He also wants them to be conscious of God in their work and to labor not for wealth but "to serve God the better" (the later Protestant emphasis), and also "to do good deeds" (the Lutheran emphasis). The parson's goal in his discourse is to encourage people in their callings, to lighten the sense of burden they may carry, "so they go on more cheerfully in their vocation" (223).

The focus of *The Country Parson,* of course, is on the vocation of the parish priest. Here Herbert indeed shows a pastoral heart, a genuine caring and sensitivity to the neighbors whom he is called to love and to serve. In catechizing his flock, he is concerned with "helping and cherishing the answerer" (231). He writes chapters entitled "The Parson Comforting" and "The Parson a Father." In his chapter "The Parson's Courtesy," he writes—with some understandable class consciousness for someone of his blood—of extending hospitality to the poor as well as to the rich. In "The Parson's Charity," he stresses almsgiving, giving money but also helping the unfortunate to alleviate their condition by encouraging them to "take more pains in their vocation" (220).

In that chapter too, Herbert alludes to what Luther called the "general estate," the social realm in which people from the various estates interact with each other. Luther's example was the parable of the Good Samaritan, in which God calls Christians to love and serve the neighbor whom he brings into their lives as they go about their ordinary routines, the neighbor lying bleeding by the side of the road. Luther called the general estate "the common order of Christian love."[15] Thus, Herbert says that the parson must attend not only to the people of his parish—that is, the people for whom he is responsible in his calling in the estate of the church—but to those in the neighborhood and "those at his door, whom God puts in his way and makes his neighbors" (Tobin, 220).

Herbert spends much of his book suggesting ways that parsons can counsel those who are tormented spiritually. He models what it means to "love and serve" his parishioners. Herbert's compassion for his parishioners is evident throughout the book. This climaxes in perhaps the most moving passage in *The Country Parson,* in which Herbert, for all of his noble blood, discerns the presence of Christ in the lowliest of his neighbors: "Nothing is little in God's service: if it once have the honour of that Name it grows great instantly. Wherefore neither disdaineth he to enter into the poorest cottage, though he even creep into it and though it smell never so loathsomely. For both God is there also and those for whom God died" (224). Here is the theology of presence: In that loathsome smelling hovel, "God is there."

The motif of condescension—the well-born parson stooping to enter the lowly cottage; the exalted God being present in the poor—is intensified with the statement that "God died" for the inhabitants of the foul-smelling cottage. That formulation, that in Christ's death "God died," is distinctly Lutheran. Indeed, that phrase occasioned a major controversy between Lutherans, who taught "the communication of attributes" between the divine and the human natures of Christ, and the Reformed, who insisted that the two natures are absolutely separate and only the human nature of Christ suffered death. [16] The authoritative Lutheran confession called *The Formula of Concord* quotes Luther, using the metaphor of someone being weighed on a scale: "If it is not true that God died for us, but only a man died, we are lost. But if God's death and God dead lie in the opposite scale, then his side goes down and we go upward like a light and empty pan. . . . God dead, God's passion, God's blood, God's death."[17]

This communication of attributes, as taught by Lutheran Christology, is the basis of its theology of presence. Because the Son of God shares in the Father's omnipresence, the body of Christ can be present in the bread and wine of Holy Communion. The Reformed, by contrast, insisted that since Christ ascended into heaven, his body cannot at the same time be present on the multiple altars of the church. (Calvinists, it must be emphasized, do believe that Christ is spiritually—rather than bodily—present in the Sacrament. Zwinglians believe the elements are merely symbolic.) The communication of attributes also allows Lutherans to speak of Christ's presence in vocation and, as Herbert stresses here, in the neighbor whom vocation serves.

Herbert believes in the theology of God's presence in his parishioners, and yet he speaks of his own vocation as a pastor in very different terms. The book begins, "A pastor is the Deputy of Christ for the reducing of man to the obedience of God" (Tobin, 201). Luther would agree about the pastor being Christ's "deputy," though he would emphasize that his calling is to proclaim the gospel of Christ's forgiveness, rather than coercing "obedience." But notice the implications that Herbert draws: "Out of this charter of the priesthood may be plainly gathered both the dignity thereof, and the duty: the dignity, in that a priest may do that which Christ did, and by his authority, and as his viceregent; the duty, in that a priest is to do that which Christ did, and after his manner, both for doctrine and life" (202). Here the pastor shares Christ's dignity and authority; moreover, he has the duty to do what Christ did and in the way that he did it. Strikingly missing, however, in this passage, is the active presence of Christ in the priest's vocation. Without that, the standards the priest sets for himself—"to do that which Christ did, and after his manner, both for doctrine and life"—are impossibly high.

Indeed, the life of the *country parson,* as Herbert describes it, is austere and ascetic. "The country parson is generally sad," he says, "because he knows nothing but the Cross of Christ" (241). He knows "he must be despised" (242). On fast days he ensures not only that he eats little but that the "quality" is "unpleasant" (218).

Though the Reformation doctrine of vocation had the effect of sanctifying the secular realm, Herbert feels the parson must strenuously avoid the taint of the world. This extends to the callings of his children. Herbert and his wife were childless, but he urges parsons to take special care in finding callings for their children. The eldest son should be encouraged to enter the ministry. The others should be kept away from callings that are overly worldly:

> He afterwards turns his care to fit all their dispositions with some calling, not sparing the eldest, but giving him the prerogative of his father's profession, which haply for his other children he is not able to do. Yet in binding them prentices (in case he think it fit to do so) he takes care not to put them into vain trades, and unbefitting the reverence of their father's calling, such as are taverns for men and lace-making for women; because those trades, for the most part, serve but the vices and vanities of the world, which he is to deny, and not augment (215).

This is the mind-set of secular monasticism, if the monks had children.

Meanwhile, Herbert piles more and more responsibilities onto the pastoral office. "The country parson desires to be all to his parish, and not only a pastor, but a lawyer also and a physician" (234). So he reads law books and medical treatises, settling his people's disputes like a justice of the peace and tending to their physical ailments. "The country parson is not only a father to his flock," Herbert writes, but carries "it about with him as fully as if he had begot his whole parish" (225). As if his own vocation were not arduous enough, this country parson feels constrained to take upon himself everyone else's vocations.

In traditional monasticism, the person with a divine vocation separated himself from the world with its necessary but spiritually inferior occupations; he took vows of celibacy and poverty, so as to be set apart from the demands of the family and the workplace.

Again, in the early Reformation, the family and the workplace, no less than the spiritual estate, were seen as divine vocations. In *The Country Parson,* Herbert situates the priest in the world, with all of its family and social responsibilities, but he brings his monastic asceticism with him.

HERBERT'S POEMS ON VOCATION

No wonder, in the privacy of his own poetry, Herbert chafes against his own high standards for himself. What the country parson counsels his parishioners not to do, he does himself. He plunges himself "over head and ears into carking and caring." He labors "anxiously," "distrustfully," and "profanely." He has a tendency to "overdo it, to the loss of [his] quiet and health." He doubts God's providence, "as if it were in [his] own hands to thrive or not to thrive" (223). Such struggles tend to constitute the conflict in Herbert's poems, especially the poems about his pastoral vocation. That conflict is generally resolved, though, in an epiphany of the theology of presence. As the parson/poet struggles and fails to measure up to his high calling, he finds that Christ himself is present in his vocation.

The later Protestant sense of vocation emphasized the necessity of "busy-ness." Herbert does too, sometimes. "Employment" (II) expresses the conventional late-Reformation view of vocation, as documented by Malcolmson, the secular monasticism that resulted in so many businessmen striving to prove their election. "In this doctrine," she observes, "the 'new man' emerged during business hours, perhaps even more than amidst private meditation."[18] Thus, Herbert, reflecting on "employment" in the second poem of that title, says, "Life is a business, not good cheer" (line 16). In this poem, as elsewhere, Herbert laments that he is not producing enough "fruit," referring to the Reformation teaching that good works are to be the fruit of faith:

> O that I were an Orange-tree,
>   That busy plant!
> Then should I ever laden be,
>   And never want
> Some fruit for him that dressed me.

(lines 21–25)

On the basis of such lines, Malcolmson concludes that "Herbert weaves a connection between labor and grace, piety and employment."[19]

In the companion poem on that topic, "Employment" (I), Herbert writes about the same frustration, associating being "busy" with the right service of God in vocation.

> All things are busy; only I
> Neither bring honey with the bees,
> Nor flow'rs to make that, nor the husbandry
> To water these.
>
> (lines 17–20)

Instead, the poet/parson feels he is languishing and is being "barren to thy praise," a praise that should be expressed in "busy" and productive labor. Notice these lines, which would be quite out of sync for the conservative Reformation:

> For as thou dost impart thy grace,
> The greater shall our glory be.
> The measure of our joys is in this place,
> The stuff with thee.
>
> (lines 9–12)

Here the goal of grace is "our glory," as opposed to the *soli deo gloria* of the early Reformation, including Calvin, who more than anyone insisted that God alone is to be glorified and not ourselves. More significantly, the distinction between what is "in this place" and what is "with thee" separates the man in his vocation down on earth (where he can measure his joys) from God (who has the essence of joy where he is). This recalls that later Protestant sense of separation and distance between Christ in his heaven and man in the world, as opposed to Luther's emphasis on Christ's presence in the world and in vocation.

In Herbert's "The Family," he is not writing about the Christian vocation of having a family, as one might expect. Rather, he internalizes everything in a way uncomplimentary to that vocation, using loud whining children as a metaphor for "this noise of thoughts within my heart" (line 1). In this poem, Herbert alludes to a theology of presence, but it is highly qualified ("perhaps") and transient:

> This is thy house, with these it doth abound:
> And where these are not found,
> Perhaps thou com'st sometimes, and for a day;
> But not to make a constant stay.
>
> (lines 21–24)

In a few poems, though, Herbert pushes the conflicts and the frustrations he feels in vocation further, until he finds a resolution in God's saving presence. The paradigmatic example, of course, is "The Collar." The parson here rebels against the sort of lofty standards that he urges in *The Country Parson*. Striking the board and crying, "No more" (line 1), he calls in his monastic death's-head and leaves his "cold dispute of what is fit and not" (line 20). He raves against the demands and poses of his pastoral office. But then, in the course of this extraordinarily honest artifice of meditation, his Lord breaks in, "calling" him, as the poem says, with the word of love, grace, and the Gospels: "Child" (line 35). With this "call," the emotions and the poetic form are resolved. What this poem dramatizes is a pastor encountering the Lord's real presence in his vocation.[20] The frustrations and restrictions—the sense in which the speaker feels his "calling" to be a "collar"—are reexperienced in the presence of the "Caller." The parson/poet realizes that the "Caller" is calling him "at every word," even his words of complaint about the responsibilities and demands of his office, so that the "one calling" animates his vocation.[21]

According to Luther's doctrine of vocation, God is "hidden" in vocation, which is a way of speaking of his presence, just as a child hiding in the room is present, though not seen. Luther stresses that the Christian in vocation is often in conflict with the presence of God. The temptations in vocation are wanting to be served rather than to serve, acting for the self rather than for the neighbor, ascribing saving merit to one's work rather than trusting in God's grace alone.[22] Just as Christians must struggle against legalism when it comes to their salvation, so they must struggle against legalism in their vocations. Vocation, too, must be seen as the action of God's grace. Conflicts between legalism and grace, both in salvation and in vocation, run throughout *The Temple*. Often, as in "The Collar," this is resolved with the discovery of the One who is hidden.

In "Aaron," another poem about the pastoral vocation, the priest compares himself unfavorably to the measure of what a priest should be, until his vocation is wholly filled, inhabited, and covered by the presence of Christ. The repeated rhyme words in each stanza, which establish the point-by-point comparison, are telling, especially the changes Herbert rings on the word "rest." The priest is to lead his people "unto life and rest" (line 4). Hell is a place "where is no rest" (line 9). Without Christ, "I could have no rest" (line 14). In Christ, to the "old man" of sin "I may rest" (line 19). Each of these references is to the "rest" of the Gospels, to the conservative Reformation notion that salvation entails *not* working, but rather abiding securely and peacefully in the grace of God.

The final stanza applies the concept to vocation: The parson/poet's ability to exercise the priesthood does not lie in his own merits, of which he has none, only "profaneness," "defects," and "darkness" (lines 6–7). Rather, he can be a priest not to the extent that he is "busy," as in the "Employment" poems, but because Christ "lives in me while I do rest" (line 24).

For Luther, one must *rest* in vocation, trusting in the hidden God to work in and through the calling, as the person who is called subjugates the sinful tendencies of the self through love and service to the neighbor. Significantly, "Aaron" ends with something relatively rare in the introversions of *The Temple*—namely, a turn away from the self, preoccupied with its interior relationship to God, to other people, to the neighbor: "Come people; Aaron's dressed" (line 25) and ready to serve them.

In "The Windows," Herbert works out with theological precision how the Lord is present in and works through the pastoral vocation and also why the human being who holds that office is likely to experience conflicts with that divine presence. The preacher is described as a window, a transparent or at least translucent medium through which the light of God's grace shines to illumine his people. But the preacher himself is "a brittle crazy glass" (line 2). What must happen for God's Word to shine through is for Christ to "anneal in glass thy story / Making thy life to shine within the holy preacher's" (lines 6–8). God's Word manifests itself through the preacher's sermon just as a story from the life of Christ manifests itself in a stained-glass window. The preacher himself is brittle, cracked glass, but he has been colored and inscribed with Christ. The preacher should accord himself with Christ who is in him, but this is not a moralistic attempt to imitate the virtues of Jesus. Rather, it is a matter of Christ's work—the poem has *Christ* doing the annealing, *Christ* making his life to shine within the preacher's—so that the theology of presence intersects with justification by faith.

As Richard Strier observes, speaking of "Aaron," "[T]he conditions for being a 'true priest' [are] basically identical with those for being a true Christian."[23] The doctrine of justification by faith led to the Reformation doctrine of the priesthood of all believers, which, in turn, was largely defined by the doctrine of vocation. The priesthood of all believers by no means meant, at least for the conservative Reformation, that pastors were not necessary or that everyone was to be a pastor. Rather, the priesthood of all believers

meant that one did not have to be a pastor to be a priest, that all
vocations—since they involve sacrifice, intermediation, and coming into the presence of God—are priesthoods.

Thus, in his poem that most explicitly treats vocation, "The
Elixir," Herbert uses the same imagery he used to describe the pastoral office in "The Windows" to describe a servant girl sweeping
the floor: "A man that looks on glass, / On it may stay his eye; / Or
if he pleaseth, through it pass, / And then the heav'n espy" (lines
9–12). Again, we have the figure of the translucent glass. Recalling
Luther's example of the milkmaid as a mask of God, Herbert says
that while our eyes might stop on the surface of the servant, if we
look deeper, we can see God shining through her. Just as God gives
"colours" to the brittle, crazy glass of the preacher in "The Windows" (line 11), he gives "his tincture" to the glass that is the servant girl. She partakes of God, who "doth touch and own" her (line
23), so that her "drudgery" is "divine" (line 18).

Herbert universalizes this insight into a theology of presence that
embraces "all things" and all labor:

> Teach me, my God and King,
> In all things thee to see,
> And what I do in anything,
> To do it as for thee.
>
> (lines 1–4)

The servant sweeping the floor for her master is doing it for God
because he is "in all things" and he is in her. This discovery Herbert applies also to himself, and he describes this particular doctrine of vocation as the philosopher's stone "that turneth all to
gold" (line 22), an alchemy that transfigures ordinary life with the
presence of God.

Helen Wilcox, in her edition of Herbert's poetry, cites this poem,
which exists in three versions, as an example of Herbert's skill in
revision.[24] The title was originally "Perfection," with the poem focusing on the speaker's desire to perfect his works. In the draft, the
first stanza originally focused on human works, what "I doe" to
please God:

> Lord teach me to referr
> All things I doe to thee
> That I not onely may not erre
> But also pleasing bee.
>
> (lines 1–4)

The final stanza uses the imagery of light as an external illumination that shows human actions "as they are."

> But these are high perfections:
> Happy are they that dare
> Lett in the light to all their actions
> And show them as they are.

(lines 21–24)

In the final revision, however, the pressure for personal perfection changes, as the speaker presents the action done in faith as partaking in God's perfection ("his perfection," line 8). As Herbert revises the poem, he revises his understanding of vocation, shifting away from a negative judgment of human actions to an apprehension that even the humblest of callings are illuminated with God's own presence.

THE SACRIFICE OF PRAISE

Priests offer up sacrifices. An important facet of the priesthood of all believers is the concept of sacrifice in vocation. While Roman Catholicism teaches that the priest offers up an unbloody sacrifice in the mass, the Reformers all taught that Christ on the Cross offered the one unrepeatable sacrifice for the sins of the world. John Pless, in his study of vocation and Lutheran liturgy, observes that "Luther relocated sacrifice. He removed it from the altar and repositioned it in the world."[25] That is, sacrifice takes place in vocation.

"The Christian brings his sacrifice as he renders the obedience, offers the service, and proves the love which his work and calling require of him," writes Vilmos Vatja, summarizing Luther. "The work of the Christian in his calling becomes a function of his priesthood, his bodily sacrifice. His work in the calling is a work of faith, the worship of the kingdom of the world."[26]

This displacement of priesthood with its sacrifices from the church into the world did result in the "secular monasticism" that Malcolmson writes about, though the effect for those with a conservative Reformation sense of vocation was to bring the presence of Christ into everyday life, thus sacralizing the secular realm. The later Protestants, in separating Christ from the world, arguably secularized the sacred realm. They did so while retaining an ascetic intensity about their work, understood, however, as the obligations

of God's commands, rather than as a manifestation of God's love
and its outworking in service to the neighbor.

So what are the sacrifices in vocation? The Reformers turned to
the New Testament, which speaks not only of Christ's sacrifice but
of other kinds of sacrifice that take place in each of the Christian's
multiple vocations. St. Paul said, "[P]resent your bodies a living
sacrifice" (Rom. 12:1). That was taken to refer to hard labor, self-
denial, and physical suffering. The New Testament also refers to
another kind of sacrifice, one that is unexpected, because unlike
other sacrifices it is inherently joyful: "Through him then let us
continually offer up a sacrifice of praise to God" (Heb. 13:5).

This work of the priesthood—offering up the sacrifice of the body
and the sacrifice of praise—was to take place in every vocation. As
Herbert writes in his poem "Providence," "Man is the world's high
Priest: he doth present / The sacrifice for all" (lines 13–14), which
consists of praising and lauding God (line 17).[27] In that poem, Herbert explores the concept of God's providence in terms of a theology
of presence: "Thou art in small things great, not small in any . . . .
For thou art infinite in one and all" (lines 41, 44).

In that poem, Herbert writes specifically about how God provi-
dentially works through vocation:

> O Sacred Providence, who from end to end
> Strongly and sweetly movest! Shall I write,
> And not of thee, through whom my fingers bend
> To hold my quill? shall they not do thee right?
>
> Of all the creatures both in sea and land
> Only to Man thou hast made known thy ways
> And put the pen alone into his hand,
> And made him Secretary of thy praise.
>
> (lines 1–8)

The description here is of Herbert himself as he writes the poem
that we are reading. He feels that Providence is moving through
him as he writes. The vocation that Herbert writes about here is
that of the poet. In the poet's act of writing a poem—this poem—
God is present. God calls and equips the poet—puts the pen alone
into his hand—so that he can be a "Secretary" writing out praise.

Herbert's imagery brings together the priesthood of all believers,
Herbert's own vocation as priest, and Herbert's vocation as a poet,
praising God for the universe, giving voice to all creation on its behalf:

Man is the world's high Priest: he doth present
The sacrifice for all; while they below
Unto the service mutter an assent,
Such as springs use that fall, and winds that blow.
He that to praise and laud thee doth refrain,
Doth not refrain unto himself alone,
But robs a thousand who would praise thee fain,
And doth commit a world of sin in one

. . . .
Wherefore, most sacred Spirit, I here present
For me and all my fellows praise to thee.

(lines 13–20, 25–26)

The man/poet/priest is offering up the sacrifice of praise for the whole universe, which mutters its assent like congregants repeating the responses in the liturgy. If human beings do not praise, the universe will be silent. "Man" in his vocation acts as a priest for all creation.

Throughout *The Temple*, Herbert refers to his vocation as a poet in terms of sacrifice, praise, and the presence of Christ. In "The Altar," which is a place of sacrifice, what Herbert offers up is praise: "Wherefore each part / Of my hard heart / Meets in this frame, / To praise thy name: / That if I chance to hold my peace, / These stones to praise thee may not cease" (lines 9–14). The lines serve as the dedication to the entire poetic sequence of "The Church," and establish the theme of the poet's vocation for the poems that follow.

As for Christ's presence in the poet's vocation, Tim McKenzie has shown how Herbert at many points "claims that Christ intervenes directly into the process of poetic composition."[28] This happens in "The Collar," as we have seen, and also in "The Cross" ("these thy contradictions / Are properly a cross felt by thy Son, / With but four words, my words, *Thy will be done*" [lines 34–36]), "A True Hymn" ("God writeth, *Loved*" [line 20]); and "The Banquet" ("take up my lines and life" [line 51]).

But where is the neighbor in Herbert's poetry? The understanding of vocation as expressed in the conservative Reformation, with its sacrifices of suffering and praise and its sense of God's active presence, is incomplete without the real presence of a neighbor, whom the vocation loves and serves. There are neighbors in *The Country Parson*, whom Herbert serves in his calling as priest. There are hints of neighbors in *The Temple*—the young man being counseled in "The Church-Porch," the "friend" in "Love Unknown"—but they are hardly present, even in the sense that Christ is present in these poems. But the poet's neighbor, the human being to whom the vocation of putting words on paper is directed, is the reader. The poet loves and serves the reader of the poems, who finds delight and edification in the poet's artifice, born as it is out of the poet's sacrifice.

Though all vocations have their distinct sacrifices, both in their sufferings and in their praises, and though in all vocations the presence of God is hidden, the poet has the calling, in love and service to the reader, to put such things into words.

NOTES

1. Charles Porterfield Krauth, *The Conservative Reformation and Its Theology* 1871; reprint, St. Louis: Concordia Publishing House, 2007), xli–xliii.

2. The major difference with Roman Catholic sacramentalism is that the early Protestants construed baptism and the Lord's Supper in terms of justification by faith: the tangible manifestation of Christ offering the free gift of salvation to those who believe. Roman Catholicism tends to treat the sacraments as offerings to God and as holy and meritorious human works, a conception the early Reformers rejected. Roman Catholicism, of course, employs a much more complex system of seven sacraments, while the early Protestants insisted that the only sacraments are those that bear the Gospel, namely, baptism and the Lord's Supper. The early Protestants also saw the Word of God in sacramental terms, particularly in the proclamation of the gospel of Christ's forgiveness in preaching and, for Lutherans, in the words of absolution. Krauth gives a full account of these differences and similarities throughout *The Conservative Reformation and Its Theology.*

3. See, for example, my book *Reformation Spirituality: The Religion of George Herbert* (Lewisburg, PA: Bucknell University Press, 1985); Christopher Hodgkins, *Authority, Church, and Society in George Herbert: Return to the Middle Way* (Columbia: University of Missouri Press, 1993); and Daniel W. Doerksen, *Conforming to the Word: Herbert, Donne, and the English Church before Laud* (Lewisburg, PA: Bucknell University Press, 1997).

4. See Cristina Malcolmson, *Heart-Work: George Herbert and the Protestant Ethic* (Stanford, CA: Stanford University Press, 1999); and Malcolmson, *George Herbert: A Literary Life* (New York: Palgrave Macmillan, 2004).

5. See Robert Shaw, *The Call of God: The Theme of Vocation in the Poetry of Donne and Herbert* (Cambridge, MA: Cowley Publications, 1981); Diana Benet, *Secretary of Praise: The Poetic Vocation of George Herbert* (Columbia: University of Missouri Press, 1984); and Tim McKenzie, *Vocation in the Poetry of the Priest-Poets George Herbert, Gerard Manley Hopkins, and R. S. Thomas* (Lewiston, NY: Edwin Mellen Press, 2003).

6. See Izaak Walton's *The Life of Mr. George Herbert.*

7. See Malcolmson, *Heart-Work;* and Malcolmson, *George Herbert.* See also Jeffrey Powers-Beck, *Writing the Flesh: The Herbert Family Dialogue* (Pittsburgh: Duquesne University Press, 1998).

8. John Maxfield, *Luther's Lectures on Genesis and the Formation of Evangelical Identity* (Kirksville, MO: Truman State University Press, 2008), 112.

9. Ibid., 135.

10. See Gustaf Wingren, *Luther on Vocation,* trans. Carl S. Rasmussen (Eugene, OR: Wipf and Stock, 2004); and Einar Billing, *Our Calling* (Philadelphia: Fortress, 1964). See also my own study of vocation in *God at Work: Your Christian Vocation in All of Life* (Downers Grove, IL: Crossway Books, 2002). The following description of Luther's teaching on the subject is taken from Wingren.

11. See, for example, Luther's treatise *The Freedom of the Christian.* See also Paul Althaus, *The Ethics of Martin Luther* (Philadelphia: Fortress Press, 1972).

12. Billing, *Our Calling,* 30.

13. Malcolmson, *Heart–Work,* 39. Weber himself was quoting Sebastian Franck. Malcolmson documents this seventeenth-century understanding of vocation.

14. George Herbert, *A Priest to the Temple, or, The Country Parson: His Character and Rule of Holy Life,* in *George Herbert: The Complete English Poems,* ed. John Tobin (New York: Penguin Books, 2004), 248. Page numbers to Tobin's edition of *The Country Parson* are henceforth cited in the text.

15. *Luther's Confession of March, 1528,* in *The Augsburg Confession: A Collection of Sources,* ed. M. Reu, in the public domain and posted online at http://show case.netins.net/web/bilarson/pc.html.

16. For the Calvinist position on this controversy, drawing on the writings of Calvin and on the official Reformed confessions of faith, see F. N. Lee, "Did God Die on Calvary?" posted at *The Works of the Rev. Prof. Dr. F. N. Lee,* http://www.dr-fnlee.org/index.html.

17. From *Concerning the Councils and the Church.* In "Formula of Concord, Solid Declaration," article 8, section 43. In *The Book of Concord: The Confessions of the Evangelical Lutheran Church,* trans. Theodore G. Tappert (Philadelphia: Fortress Press, 1959), 599.

18. Malcolmson, *Heart-Work,* 37.

19. Ibid., 8.

20. This is essentially what Shaw sees, who says that "Herbert's concept of vocation is fundamentally sacramental" and is "rendered acceptable by the transforming presence of God" (*Call of God,* 90). The Reformers would not use "sacramental" to refer to vocation, since the term denoted for them the saving action of the Gospels in baptism and the Holy Communion. Shaw, however, is using "sacramental" in the sense of the theology of presence.

21. See my book *Reformation Spirituality,* 108–9.

22. See Wingren, *Luther on Vocation,* 100.

23. Richard Strier, *Love Known: Theology and Experience in George Herbert's Poetry* (Chicago: University of Chicago Press, 1983), 127. See McKenzie, *Vocation,* 77, and his reading of this poem.

24. Helen Wilcox, ed., *The English Poems of George Herbert* (Cambridge: Cambridge University Press, 2007), 637–39. Quotations of the earliest draft of the poem are taken from this edition.

25. John T. Pless, "Taking the Divine Service into the Week: Liturgy and Vocation." Concordia Theological Seminary. http://www.ctsfw.edu/academics/faculty/pless/DS_Into_Week.html.

26. Vilmos Vatja, *Luther on Worship* (Philadelphia: Muhlenberg Press, 1958), 169.

27. See McKenzie, *Vocation,* 12; and Benet, *Secretary of Praise,* 175–76.

28. McKenzie, *Vocation,* 208. See also Diana Benet on Herbert's sense of poetry as a vocation (*Secretary of Praise,* 175–76).

Herbert's Holy Practice
Kenneth Graham

In 1633, A WILTSHIRE CLERGYMAN NAMED ROBERT DYER PUBLISHED *The Christians Theorico-Practicon: or, His whole Duty, consisting of Knowledge and Practise*.[1] Dyer's book comprises two sermons on John 13:17—"If ye know these things, Happy are ye if ye doe them"—a favorite text in discussions of Christian practice. The verse was said by Dyer to express "the perfect Idea of a Christians life" (Dyer, 5). The first sermon focuses on Christian knowledge, the second on Christian practice, but Dyer's concern throughout is with the relationship between the two. "In a word," he writes, employing a suggestively circular antimetabole, "*Scientia conscientiam dirigit, conscientia scientiam perficit:* Our knowledge must bee the directory of our conscience in it's [sic] practise, and our practise the perfection of our knowledge" (21). He goes on to stress "the absolute necessity of practice to Salvation" (56), while carefully noting that all good works are finally caused by grace. Published in London, *The Christians Theorico-Practicon* was, according to its title page, to be sold by Henry Hammond in his bookshop in Salisbury.

Of course, Dyer was not the only Wiltshire clergyman thinking about the relationship between Christian knowledge and practice at this time, or the only one to find his way into print in 1633. A poem such as "A Wreath" bears obvious comparison to Dyer, especially in its concluding quatrain:

> Give me simplicitie, that I may live,
> So live and like, that I may know, thy wayes,
> Know them and practise them: then shall I give
> For this poore wreath, give thee a crown of praise.[2]

Herbert's use of the rhetorical figure of *gradatio* and his repetition in reverse order of the rhymes of the opening quatrain emphasize his point about the circular or perhaps spiral shape of holy practice: life leads to knowledge, which in turn leads to more life (or "practise"). The poem's interest in the relationship between theory and practice has not gone unnoticed. William Nestrick, for example, states that the "familiar Renaissance imperative to join *gnosis* and *praxis* receives special force here," a point William Flesch develops with reference to modern philosophy: "[F]or both Herbert and Wittgenstein," he writes, "knowledge is an epiphenomenon of action."[3] Both Nestrick and Flesch approach the poem from the perspective of gift exchange, and criticism in general has understandably concentrated on Herbert's conception in the poem of his poetic gift. But the poem, like Dyer's sermons, clearly raises the question of what happens to practice in a religion where the essential fact is the gift of grace—of how knowing and doing interact when the knowledge in question is that of a gift that renders doing inessential.

Until the 1980s Herbert criticism tilted heavily toward the knowing side of this equation. Herbert's reputation was that of an impractical poet whose introspective lyrics exemplified what William Halewood called "the poetry of grace."[4] In 1985, Chana Bloch could complain that "Herbert's explicitly didactic poems are often scanted in anthologies and critical commentaries today, giving us a bowdlerized Herbert congenial to current tastes."[5] Since then much has changed. Without challenging the view of Herbert's Protestant theology established by Richard Strier in particular, important work by Claude Summers and Ted-Larry Pebworth, Sidney Gottlieb, Michael Schoenfeldt, Christopher Hodgkins, Daniel Doerksen, Cristina Malcolmson, and many others has painted a portrait of a poet who was deeply involved in the contemporary world.[6] Herbert's practical if idealistic pastoral guide, *The Country Parson,* has consequently received increased scrutiny, leading to the publication of Ronald Cooley's excellent book-length study.[7] Yet the idea, expressed most memorably by Debora Shuger, that there is a split in Herbert between the realm of grace and the realm of practical action persists.[8] For example, in *Moral Identity in Early Modern English Literature* Paul Cefalu criticizes Shuger's understanding of two kingdoms theology, but argues nevertheless that "Herbert maintains a distinction between the spheres of morality and grace, a distinction that . . . sets his theology apart from the mainstream English Protestant belief in the interfused nature of justification and sanctification."[9] Similarly, Gregory Kneidel observes that "critics have had a hard time reconciling the introspective spirituality of *The Temple* with the pastoral worldliness of *The Country Parson,*" yet his own insightful essay largely endorses the separation, suggesting only that we might view the individual "heartbreak" in *The Temple* as "a technique of passage for creating the kind of religious experience described in *The Country Parson*."[10]

The practical religious experience advocated in *The Country Parson,* however, is debated, valued, and illustrated in some of the lyrics in *The Temple.* Moreover, Herbert's representation of such experience in both works is by and large consistent with what we find in works like Dyer's. Writers on Christian practice typically distinguish three types of value that inhere in a holy life, one for each of three audiences. Dyer is typical: "[W]ee affirme the necessity and injoyne the performance of good works, both in respect of God, our selves, and others" (Dyer, 88). Herbert echoes this popular formula when he describes the honest man in "Constancie" as "To God, his neighbour, and himself most true" (line 3). The first of these three is the most straightforward. We should do good works, writes Christopher Sibthorp, "to shew our obedience, dutie, and thankefulnesse to God."[11] The second and third will be my concern here. What, for Herbert, is the value of holy practice to others and to the self? How does he understand the relationship between the knowledge of justification and the practice of sanctification?

DOCTRINE AND LIFE

Dyer writes in *The Christians Theorico-Practicon* that good works are necessary "[i]n respect of others, that wee may edifie them by our pious example, that wee may gaine unbeleevers from their infidelity, and lastly that we may avoide all scandal" (Dyer, 89). This emphasis on the power of example is conventional and consistent with Herbert's understanding of the value of a holy life to others.[12] This is illustrated by "The Windows," Herbert's most admired poem on the ministry, where Herbert asks how a minister can effectively communicate his knowledge of doctrine. The poem's opening question—"Lord, how can man preach thy eternall word?" (line 1)—is answered by the addition of "life" to doctrine:

> Doctrine and life, colours and light, in one
>   When they combine and mingle, bring
> A strong regard and aw: but speech alone
>   Doth vanish like a flaring thing,
>   And in the eare, not conscience ring.

(lines 11–15)

As many have noted, the phrase "doctrine and life" also appears in *The Country Parson,* where the first chapter ends by stating that "a Priest is to do that which Christ did, and after his manner, both for Doctrine and Life."[13] It has also been pointed out frequently that the phrase did not originate with Herbert; it was a commonplace, found in the New Testament, in the Prayer Book, in the 1604 Canons, and throughout Reformation culture.[14] For Herbert, as for this culture, "doctrine and life" bespoke an ideal connection that was valued for its rhetorical power. When life is added to doctrine, a sermon "more doth win" (Hutchinson, 9), or persuade, because, as Herbert explains in "The Parson arguing," a "strict religious life" and a "humble, and ingenuous search of truth" are "powerfull perswaders" when men "consider, that God cannot be wanting to them in Doctrine, to whom he is so gracious in Life" (263).

But what is the nature of the ideal connection that the phrase "doctrine and life" indicates? Cristina Malcolmson argues that it is a transparent connection between "an outward sign and an inward spiritual state"—that is, between the word preached ("doctrine") and an inner reality signified by "life."[15] For Malcolmson, the poem illustrates a new character of holiness in *The Temple,* a holiness defined not by the difference between internal holiness and external surface, but by this transparency. In "The Parson preaching," Herbert himself identifies such transparency as an element of the rhetorical character of holiness, which is gained in part "by dipping, and seasoning all our words and sentences in our hearts, before they come into our mouths, truly affecting, and cordially expressing all that we say; so that the auditors may plainly perceive that every word is hart-deep" (Hutchinson, 233). The word must match the heart, and, Malcolmson concludes, in "The Windows" it does.

In "The Windows," however, the word must match not the heart so much as the deed. The principal contrast is not between speech that is transparent or "hart-deep" and speech that lies on the surface, but between "speech alone," mere prattle without practice, and speech that matches the actions of a holy life.[16] The key word is not "within," which Malcolmson mistakenly sees as the centerpiece of Herbert's "illogical" (Malcolmson, 138) development of the metaphor (a stained-glass window is not transparent, after all),[17] but "storie," or history, the persuasive and mnemonic power of which Herbert notes in "The Parson preaching": "Sometimes he tells them stories, and sayings of others, according as his text invites him; for them also men heed, and remember better then exhortations" (Hutchinson, 233). The ideal preacher of "The Windows" goes this advice one better: instead of telling stories about

others, he illustrates the best of those stories with his own life. And
though the poem emphasizes God's agency in this successful imitation, it is still the actions of the preacher's personal history that
make credible the doctrinal story he tells. "A good life is a main
argument," wrote Ben Jonson.[18] This idea, like the phrase "doctrine and life," was a commonplace. For example, in *The Happiness of Practice* (1621), another sermon on John 13:17, Samuel
Ward observes that "words are but wind, and vanish into the winde,
leaving no print or impression, more then a Ship in the Sea, in
comparison of actions which men take markes and notice of."[19] By
observing that "speech alone / Doth vanish like a flaring thing,"
then, "The Windows" testifies in conventional terms to the way in
which an exemplary life produces a persuasive rhetorical ethos.[20] A
holy life increases credibility, not because it transparently reveals
essence, but because people trust those who practice what they
preach.

Because it emphasizes God's transformation of the preacher and
the persuasive power of the preacher's own holy life, "The Windows" has little to say about the minister's use of the preaching
arts. Yet, as Malcolmson notes (139), such artifice is a major part
of the picture Herbert paints in *The Country Parson*. The parson
does not rely simply upon the persuasive ethos his holy life gener-
ates. Instead, Herbert's idea of a practice beneficial to others requires that it be informed by rhetorical knowledge, particularly
knowledge of audience. Like any good rhetorician, the parson is an
expert at "particularizing," or adjusting "his speech now to the
younger sort, then to the elder, now to the poor, and now to the
rich" (Hutchinson, 233). When he reproves, "he distinguisheth,"
reproving a "plaine countryman . . . plainly," and those of "higher
quality," who are "quick, and sensible, and very tender of reproof,"
more delicately (248). Herbert frequently notes the parson's dis-
cretion, which is another word for prudence, a virtue closely associated with rhetoric.[21] Some readers have been uncomfortable with
this aspect of Herbert's parson, finding him tainted by courtliness
or Machiavellianism or worse.[22] But Kneidel demonstrates that *The
Country Parson* illustrates a "sophisticated pastoral rhetoric" that
was modeled in good measure on Paul's epistles.[23] For Herbert,
applying doctrine to the lives of others requires a prudent consideration of circumstances; holy practice is necessarily rhetorical.

The lyric in "The Church" that best illustrates the rhetorical nature of holy practice is "Constancie," which is also probably the
poem that most resembles Herbert's pastoral manual. "Constancie," Heather Asals writes, "is Herbert's 'Character' of the Preacher

whose life is one with rigorous rule."[24] As *The Country Parson* presents "a Mark to aim at" (Hutchinson, 224), so "Constancie" describes "the Mark-man" (line 34), whose honest life is a goal for
others to aim at. Indebted in part to the portrait of the righteous
man in Psalm 15, "Constancie" illustrates many of the virtues possessed by the "holy, just, prudent, temperate, bold, [and] grave"
country parson (Hutchinson, 227).[25] As Marion Singleton has
shown, the cardinal virtues are especially prominent.[26] To "giv[e]
all their due" (line 5) is a concise definition of justice. The ability
to withstand "great trials" (line 11), neither seeking nor shunning
them, illustrates fortitude. One who "never melts or thaws / At
close tentations" (lines 21–22) clearly possesses temperance. (We
will see in a moment the presence in the poem of prudence.) Thus,
while Kneidel is correct in general that self-control is "ridiculed in
The Temple,"[27] "Constancie" shows that this is not invariably so.

A possible misreading of "Constancie" arises from the Stoic associations of its title and the emphasis on honesty with which the
poem begins. The word "constancy" may suggest an unwillingness
to change one's behavior and hence a lack of responsiveness to the
world; "honesty" may suggest a person who answers only to a fixed
inner truth, which his constant behavior and plain words show
forth. The fourth stanza in particular encourages this reading:

> Whom none can work or wooe
> To use in any thing a trick or sleight;
> For above all things he abhorres deceit:
>   His words and works and fashion too
> All of a piece, and all are cleare and straight.

> (lines 16–20)

Focusing on these lines, Malcolmson comments that "[t]he honest
man abhors deceit not only because he doesn't lie, but because his
external behaviour is 'cleare' (line 20), transparently communicat-
ing the internal realm within" (144). She compares the lines to
"The Parson in Reference": "The Countrey Parson is sincere and
upright in all his relations. And first, he is just to his Countrey. . . .
To do otherwise, is deceit; and therefore not for him, who is hearty,
and true in all his wayes, as being the servant of him, in whom
there was no guile" (Hutchinson, 252–53). For Malcolmson, "Constancie" is the final, clinching example of transparent holiness in
The Temple.

However, transparency no more defines holiness in "Constancie" than it does in "The Windows." The point of the fourth stanza,

like the point of "The Windows," is not that words reveal an inner reality. On the contrary, the formula "words and works," like "doctrine and life," signifies the agreement of word and deed. As Thomas Saltern wrote in a 1630 sermon, it is unfortunate when "the doctrines and deeds, the words and works, the profession and practice of Christians" disagree. "Gods livery is a good life," which declares us God's servants "when words shall prove but winde."[28] In addition, honesty is a necessary virtue of which the parson makes strategic use: "[B]ecause Countrey people (as indeed all honest men) do much esteem their word, it being the Life of buying, and selling, and dealing in the world; therfore the Parson is very strict in keeping his word, though it be to his own hinderance, as knowing, that if he be not so, he wil quickly be discovered, and disregarded: neither will they beleeve him in the pulpit, whom they cannot trust in his Conversation" (Hutchinson, 228).

Just as honesty is another arrow in the parson's rhetorical quiver, so the honest man in "Constancie" observes and responds decorously to the demands of every occasion. "What place or person calls for," Herbert writes, "he doth pay" (line 15); and "when he is to treat / With sick folks, women, those whom passions sway," he "allows for that, and keeps his constant way" (lines 26–28). The allowances that must be made here are prudent adjustments to his behavior for these difficult audiences, for, whatever faults and failings others may have, the honest man must continue to "play" "his part" (line 30). Herbert means to place full weight upon the theatrical metaphor, which he would know as a commonplace of humanist prudence, the fourth and final cardinal virtue. Like the character More in book 1 of *Utopia*, Herbert's honest man does not think "all things meet for every place"; rather, he prefers a "philosophy more civil which knoweth . . . her own stage," and which, "thereafter ordering and behaving herself in the play she hath in hand, playeth her part accordingly with comeliness, uttering nothing out of due order and fashion."[29] "Constancie" does not describe Raphael Hythloday.

Wherein, then, lies "his constant way"? Not in a simple sameness of "words and works," but in a constant purpose. The ideal is that stated in *The Country Parson*: the parson has "throughly studied" patience and mortification not for their own sake but "that he may be an absolute Master and commander of himself, for all the purposes which God hath ordained him" (Hutchinson, 227). In "Constancie," these purposes are to "still and strongly good pursue" (line 2), to be true "[t]o God, his neighbour, and himself," and, by so doing, to be an example for others, "the Mark-man."

Doctrine and Discipline

According to Dyer, good works are necessary "[i]n respect to our Selves, that wee may discerne the truth and livelie-hood of our Faith; as also, that it may be exercised, nourished and corroborated thereby; that wee may ascertaine our selves of our Election, and remission of sinnes; that wee may avoide punishments both temporall and eternall, and obtaine those rewards of our obedience, both corporall and spirituall, which are annext to good works, by God's free and gracious promise" (Dyer, 88–89). The passage is typical of contemporary treatments of the benefits of Christian practice to the self in the way it balances the need for works and talk of rewards with a final emphasis on God's free grace. In this section I will explore Herbert's depiction of the value of works to the self in his treatment of religious discipline. A synonym for practice, discipline was defined by Milton as "the execution and applying of Doctrine home"; for Richard Hooker, the concern of church discipline, or, as he prefers to call it, "spirituall Jurisdiction," was "Doctrine referred unto action and practice."[30] The phrase "doctrine and life" closely resembles a second popular pairing, "doctrine and discipline." Herbert's *Country Parson* is above all a book about church discipline, and I will begin there; but I will concentrate on the representation of disciplinary practice in "The Church," where its presence is less obvious but where Herbert treats it with a balance similar to that of Dyer and other contemporaries. Like Dyer, I will argue, Herbert maintains that justification is by faith alone while still sometimes writing as if holy practice were directly beneficial to the person who performs it.

In the chapter of *The Country Parson* entitled "The Parsons Knowledg," Herbert cites John 7:17 (which Judy Kronenfeld and William Flesch rightly link to "A Wreath"): "if any do Gods will, he shall know of the Doctrine" (Hutchinson, 228).[31] Like John 13:17, which John 7:17 resembles, this is a favorite text of writers on Christian practice. "Theologie or Divinity is a practical science," writes one author, before citing it.[32] But while 13:17 places knowing before doing, 7:17 says that doing will lead to knowledge, a potential challenge to the Protestant insistence that works are the fruits of faith. For Augustine, to do God's will here "is the same thing as to believe." The passage concerns "faith that worketh by love," and such faith enables a better understanding of the Word: "[L]et this faith be in thee, and thou shalt understand concerning the doctrine."[33] For Protestants involved in doctrinal controversy, the passage had to be consistent with the priority of faith. Thomas

Cartwright, for instance, replied to the Catholic gloss of the Rheims translation—"The way to come to know the truth, is to live well"—by adding, "Hee that lives well, lives by faith in the son of God. . . ." For Cartwright, then, the text essentially means "if any has faith and so does what he knows of God's will, he will continue to learn more about that will," a meaning that for Cartwright is consistent with scriptural statements of God's bounty toward his own people: "And those that thus live well," he continues, "shall have further revelation of the will and doctrine of Christ, as here he himself speaketh: for to him that hath shall be given."[34] The negative corollary of this is stated by Ward in *The Happiness of Practice*: "[H]e that will obey, shall know my Father's will; and such as will not doe what they know to bee good, shall soone unknowe that which they know."[35] But it is the positive implications of the passage that drew most attention. John 7:17, the text Herbert cites to show that a holy life is the first means for understanding the best knowledge, led Protestants to think about the benefits of holy practice to the holy, and in particular raised the intriguing possibility that works may have a spiritual value that doctrinal statements of the priority of faith can obscure.

In "The Church," this possibility is considered in two of the poems most directly concerned with disciplinary practice. The first of these is "Lent." Lent was one of the most controversial parts of church discipline; with other occasions for fasting, it is the subject of about one-fifth of Calvin's influential chapter on discipline in the *Institutes*.[36] In the poem's sixth stanza, Herbert notes the biblical injunction to "Be holy ev'n as he," and exhorts his audience to do their imperfect best. The seventh stanza follows:

> Who goeth in the way which Christ hath gone,
> Is much more sure to meet with him, then one
>   That travelleth by-wayes:
> Perhaps my God, though he be farre before,
> May turn, and take me by the hand, and more
>   May strengthen my decayes.

(lines 37–42)

Herbert is characteristically cautious here. He establishes a temporal sequence, with human action preceding the reception of "more" strength from God, but he does not claim that there is a causal connection between the two: we do not know why the meeting is "more sure." And though "more sure" sounds like a good bet, "sure" turns out to mean "likely." God "May turn"—the word is significant, since Protestant theology denied men and women the power to "turn" toward God, or convert, of their own free will—"Perhaps."

Herbert's causal uncertainty links "Lent" to works on Christian practice such as Dyer's. Dyer writes that our own virtue cannot "formally" cause our salvation, "though perhaps dispositively it may, for as the golden mouth'd Father [Chrysostom] affirmes; that when wee endeavour the constant practise of morall virtue and diligently performe what wee can, God often in mercy supplyes what is wanting, and so brings us to the knowledge of his truth" (Dyer, 35). The key term here is "dispositively," which Dyer opposes to "formally" and qualifies with "perhaps." The *OED* defines the obsolete, Latinate word *dispositive* as having "the quality of disposing or inclining," and notes that, in its adverbial form, it is often opposed to "effectively" or "actually." Dyer may have picked the term up from Bishop Francis White's *Replie to Jesuit Fishers Answere* (1624), which he appears to have been reading. For White, the word "dispositive" helps to correct Fisher's erroneous views on merit and satisfaction; it is closely linked to a second term, "impetrant," which White cites in Augustine and translates as "obtaining by request."[37] (The *OED* provides examples of both words from White.) Dispositive and impetrant causes are for White alternatives to meritorious causes (White, 546). His argument rests on two related distinctions. The first is between "Merit of Condignitie" and "Merit of Impetration." The former, upheld by Fisher, is a fiction; the latter is real but limited. White explains: "[D]ivine grace doth not elevate virtuous actions by adding unto them a force of meriting, but onely by making them susceptible of a free and liberall reward, and by placing them in the state and order of causes impetrant, or dispositive conditions" (512). The second distinction clarifies the nature of the "free and liberall reward" promised by scripture. Reward does not imply merit, White stresses, since "there is a reward of mere bountie, as well as of desert" (545–46). For White, then, "disposition" is opposed to "desert" (514) and condign merit (517), and refers not to earning a reward but to the condition of one who by God's free grace has performed good works and thus has been put in position to receive an eternal reward, again of God's free grace. Since Dyer, too, distinguishes between the "reward of free grace and bounty" and that "of due debt or desert" (Dyer, 102), it is likely that he has a similar distinction in mind when he says that virtue may help us "dispositively" toward salvation.[38] "Perhaps" Herbert, too, believed that "the constant practise of morall virtue" that he calls for in "Lent" could serve as a "dispositive" cause of God's turning to us, rather than as a meritorious one.

Theologically this is tricky territory. "Dispositively" could carry the sense of "preparatory," suggesting the doctrine of preparation for grace, with which seventeenth-century Protestants increasingly struggled. The *OED* cites as an example William Sclater's *The Christians Strength* (1612): "Papists . . . allow to nature a power dispositive, and ability to prepare itself to regeneration." White himself is usually identified as an Arminian, though I am not sure that the relatively early *Replie to Fisher* supports this identification. As for Dyer, he leaves no doubt that he believes justification is by faith alone, but he can still consider the possibility that moral striving may lead to and even in a limited sense cause some divine benefits, even if it follows from and is caused by others. And the same is true of Herbert. Christopher Hodgkins's description of the seventh stanza of "Lent" as "Bunyanesque" is especially apt.[39] There can be no question of the Protestant orthodoxy of Bunyan's belief in the doctrine of justification by faith, yet his great allegory proclaims, in the words of its central character, that "[t]he Soul of Religion is the practick part," while conveying imaginatively, as Christopher Drummond has brilliantly argued, not only that Christian belief is the true way through the world, but that coming truly through the world is true belief.[40]

The characteristically Protestant balancing act that this involves—believing in the priority of faith while giving works their due, believing the will is impotent to effect salvation while simultaneously encouraging the will to join in the practice of Christian life fostered by grace—may be best expressed in another poem whose title links it to practice, "Discipline."[41] "Discipline" is as much about the inward state of the believer as it is about God's behavior, and the discipline it envisages is as much a property of the believer as it is of God's treatment of him. By expressing the claims of both the believer's will and God's will, Herbert presents the gentle discipline the poem's speaker seeks as both an undeserved, regenerative love and a well-deserved reward for the regenerate self's holy practice.

The poem begins with a forceful request to God to discipline and not to punish:

> Throw away thy rod,
> Throw away thy wrath:
>   O my God,
> Take the gentle path.

(lines 1–4)

The rhyme-enforced distinction between "wrath" and "the gentle path" recalls the distinction between God's customary treatments of the unregenerate and of the godly. Calvin, for example, distinguishes between the judgment of "vengeance" and that of "chastisement." God exercises the former "upon his enemies; so that he exercises his wrath against them, he confounds them, he scatters them, he brings them to nought." By the latter God reproves the sins of his people; it is not "punishment or vengeance, but correction and admonition."[42] Herbert makes the same distinction in the "Notes on Valdes," observing that "the godly are chastized but not punished."[43] The speaker, then, appears to ask for a treatment different from the harsh punishment inflicted on the ungodly.

Surprisingly, however, the next three stanzas offer no enlightenment about this treatment. Instead, they turn from God's behavior to the speaker's in order to build a carefully qualified case that he is a fit recipient of such treatment. Their starting place is the heart:

> For my hearts desire
> Unto thine is bent:
> > I aspire
> To a full consent.
>
> (lines 5–8)

The lines claim a partial identification of the speaker's will with God's, and proclaim his desire for a perfect agreement in the contractual language of "consent." The freedom this implies, however, is limited by the slight pun on "bent," which nicely captures the relation of the two wills becoming one, indicating that the speaker's desire is both curved, as if by an outside force, and determined, strongly tending or inclined of its own accord. Determination and determinism coexist. This version of the desire for union that Herbert expresses most insistently in "Clasping of hands" acknowledges need and dependency while still suggesting that the discipline the poem contemplates is already being enacted by the speaker, and should be rewarded.

The third and fourth stanzas add important support for the claim of the second. The third grounds desire in scripture:

> Not a word or look
> I affect to own,
> > But by book,
> And thy book alone.
>
> (lines 9–12)

Herbert deserves gentle treatment, he argues, not only because he desires to do God's will but because he has devoted himself to study of the scriptures, seeking knowledge to guide his practice. Again, however, Herbert qualifies the stanza's argument, this time by undercutting the language of property. Through another slight pun, the speaker owns (acknowledges) his insignificant ownership of his "own" knowledge and desires. They come only "by . . . thy book," so how much merit can he claim?

The fourth stanza continues to build the Pyrrhic argument for desert, adding contrition and progress to the speaker's qualifications:

> Though I fail, I weep:
> Though I halt in pace,
>   Yet I creep
> To the throne of grace.
>
> (lines 13–16)

The stanza conveys a humility consistent with penitence. To "creep" in particular suggests a physical prostration that may externalize the penitent's feeling of unworthiness, as it also does in "Longing": "Behold, thy dust doth stirre, / It moves, it creeps, it aims at thee" (lines 37–38). But here confession and humility offer necessary support for the argument that the speaker deserves "gentle" treatment. Given the nature and importance of repentance for Herbert, the claims made in the second and third stanzas could not be true were the speaker's contrition not real.[44] In the poem's argument, weeping and creeping, which are understood to be identical actions—their identity heightened by the rhyme—constitute reasons for throwing the rod away. Like the pun on "bent," the fourth stanza's parallel statements perfectly capture the poem's ambivalent position toward the value of practice. The speaker is not exactly asking to be treated according to desert, as the concessive clauses make clear: he fails and halts in pace. Yet he also cannot be said to be asking for a gift to which he has no claim, since he is doing what he can to reach his goal.

Herbert returns in the fifth stanza to the delayed consideration of the "gentle path," which proves to be the way of love:

> Then let wrath remove;
> Love will do the deed:
>   For with love
> Stonie hearts will bleed.

> Love is swift of foot;
> Love's a man of warre,
>   And can shoot,
> And can hit from farre.
>
> Who can scape his bow?
> That which wrought on thee,
>   Brought thee low,
> Needs must work on me.

(lines 17–28)

The poem changes abruptly here from a fairly plain style to a highly metaphoric style of wonder that Herbert uses to convey a sense of love's awe-inspiring power.[45] But because these stanzas define love mainly through the contrasts to the erotic and wrathful powers whose figurative traditions they borrow and transform, they tell us surprisingly little about the change love brings about. We learn that love's effect is internal, the softening of hard hearts, and, probably, that it involves a humbling or bringing low. But on the whole these stanzas stress the fact of love's power without telling us much about what specifically that power does.

The reason for this omission is that the first half of the poem has already told us what love does: it brings desire for union, an obedient will and reason, repentance, humility, and the confidence of acceptance. Why then, having spent three stanzas describing love's effects in him, does Herbert request that he be treated, as if for the first time, with love? One answer lies in the distinction between justification and sanctification that underlies the poem.[46] The speaker has already been justified by the imputed righteousness of Christ and so is able to begin to desire God's will; hence he does not need anything new. But he remains bound to sin and therefore continues to depend on God's grace to carry forward his sanctification. The third and final stanza on love clarifies the poem's position on this important theological point. Until then, the poem appears to argue that the speaker's love of God deserves love in return. But the reminder of the Incarnation reverses this priority, showing Herbert's understanding that God loved him first. In this way "Discipline" implies the priority of faith to works, and of doctrine to discipline, that so many of Herbert's poems insist upon. This does not mean, however, that Cefalu is right to argue that Herbert departs from the "mainstream English Protestant belief in the interfused nature of justification and sanctification."[47] Rather, the poem agrees with most of Herbert's contemporaries in suggesting that while justification is a work of faith alone, the process of sanctification is cooperative and repetitive, fusing grace and effort over time. Because of God's initial gift, the justified sinner is "sanctifi'd . . . to do good"("Trinitie Sunday," line 3), meaning he can give God something in return and so "earn" more, "dispositively," from God, which then permits more holy practice, more grace, and so on.

The symmetrical conclusion of "Discipline" provides a final illustration of how this circularity issues from the poem:

> Throw away thy rod;
> Though man frailties hath,
>   Thou art God:
> Throw away thy wrath.

(lines 29–32)

The stanza hinges on Herbert's most brilliant use of the short third line, the strikingly direct "Thou art God." By itself, the line states as simply as possible Herbert's acknowledgment of the nature of God in accordance with the first commandment. But the poem has set up two possible corollaries of this statement, each of which gives the stanza a different meaning. The first, following from the description of the God of love in the second half of the poem, is "Therefore you love me." If this corollary is emphasized, the final stanza's condensed argument reads: "Though man has frailties or sins which are deserving of harsh punishment, you are a God of love and therefore will not treat man according to his deserts." The second corollary of "Thou art God," following from the profession of faith and love in the first half of the poem, is "Therefore I love you." (So read, the line implies less the Mosaic first commandment than Christ's "great commandment": "Thou shalt love the Lord thy God with all thy heart, and with all thy soul, and with all thy mind." [Matt. 22:37].) If this corollary is stressed, the final stanza means: "Though man's sins taken by themselves deserve harsh punishment, the love to which I have testified is a convincing reason for you to treat me gently." The question, in short, is whether God should throw away his rod because he loves man or because man loves him. In doctrinal terms, the answer must be only the first; but as a sanctifying process discipline allows for the impurity of experience and practice reflected in the second. In Herbert's "Discipline" both answers are possible.

The conclusion of "Discipline" returns us to the circularity of "A Wreath," of Dyer's Latin slogan, and of our two texts from John's Gospel. Holy practice, they all suggest, is not only a consequence of a changed understanding or experience of God; it also changes our understanding and experience of God. And, as Herbert and his contemporaries agree, it changes others' understanding and experience of God, so long as the exemplary life that lends credence to doctrine plays its part prudently. Like a sermon without the application, like words without works, like doctrine without life and discipline, "[k]nowledge, that sleeps, doth die," writes Jonson.[48] But Herbert and others suggest that knowledge that goes forth to direct practice not only survives, but multiplies.

NOTES

1. Robert Dyer, *The Christians Theorico-Practicon: or, His whole Duty, consisting of Knowledge and Practise* (London, 1633). Further references will appear parenthetically in the text. The sermons had been delivered in Oxford; in 1633, Dyer was a lecturer at Devizes in Wiltshire.

2. *The Works of George Herbert*, ed. F. E. Hutchinson (Oxford: Clarendon Press, 1941), lines 9–12. Further references to the line numbers of Herbert's English poetry appear in the text.

3. William Nestrick, "The Giver and the Gift," *Ploughshares* 2 (1975): 197; William Flesch, *Generosity and the Limits of Authority: Shakespeare, Herbert, Milton* (Ithaca, NY: Cornell University Press, 1992), 43. On the theology of "A Wreath," see Judy Kronenfeld, "Imperfect Efforts Redeemed by Grace," *ELH* 48 (1981): 290–309.

4. William Halewood, *The Poetry of Grace: Reformation Themes and Structures in English Seventeenth-Century Poetry* (New Haven, CT: Yale University Press, 1970).

5. Chana Bloch, *Spelling the Word: George Herbert and the Bible* (Berkeley and Los Angeles: University of California Press, 1985), 170.

6. Richard Strier, *Love Known: Theology and Experience in George Herbert's Poetry* (Chicago: University of Chicago Press, 1983); Claude J. Summers and Ted-Larry Pebworth, "Herbert, Vaughan, and Public Concerns in Private Modes," *George Herbert Journal* 3, nos. 1–2 (1979–80): 1–21; Sidney Gottlieb, "The Social and Political Backgrounds of George Herbert's Poetry," in *The Muses Common-Weale: Poetry and Politics in the Seventeenth Century*, ed. Claude J. Summers and Ted-Larry Pebworth (Columbia: University of Missouri Press, 1988), 107–18; Michael C. Schoenfeldt, *Prayer and Power: George Herbert and Renaissance Courtship* (Chicago: University of Chicago Press, 1991); Christopher Hodgkins, *Authority, Church, and Society in George Herbert: Return to the Middle Way* (Columbia: University of Missouri Press, 1993); Daniel W. Doerksen, *Conforming to the Word: Herbert, Donne, and the English Church before Laud* (Lewisburg, PA: Bucknell University Press, 1997); Cristina Malcolmson, *Heart-Work: George Herbert and the Protestant Ethic* (Stanford, CA: Stanford University Press, 1999).

7. Ronald W. Cooley, *Full of All Knowledg: George Herbert's "Country Parson" and Early Modern Social Discourse* (Toronto: University of Toronto Press, 2004).

8. Debora Kuller Shuger, *Habits of Thought in the English Renaissance: Religion, Politics, and the Dominant Culture* (Berkeley and Los Angeles: University of California Press, 1990), chap. 3.

9. Paul Cefalu, *Moral Identity in Early Modern English Literature* (Cambridge: Cambridge University Press, 2004), 136.

10. Gregory Kneidel, "Herbert and Exactness," *English Literary Renaissance* 36 (2006): 290, 302.

11. Christopher Sibthorp, *A Friendly Advertisement to the Pretended Catholickes of Ireland* (Dublin, 1622), 152.

12. Scandal is a concern of Herbert's in "Lent" and in "The Parson arguing," but I will not consider it here.

13. George Herbert's *A Priest to the Temple or, The Country Parson,* in Hutchinson, *Works of George Herbert,* 225. Further references will appear in the text.

14. For example, see Robert B. Shaw, *The Call of God: The Theme of Vocation in the Poetry of Donne and Herbert* (Cambridge, MA: Cowley Publications, 1981), 92; and Doerksen, *Conforming to the Word,* 75. So far as I am aware, the presence of the phrase in the 1604 Canons has not been noted. See *Constitutions and Canons Ecclesiastical,* in Edward Cardwell, *Synodalia: A Collection of Articles of Religion, Canons, and Proceedings of Convocations in the Province of Canterbury,* 2 vols. (Oxford, 1842), 1:266, 290.

15. Malcolmson, *Heart-Work,* 138. Further references will appear in the text.

16. On plainness as a trope of belief rather than of transparency, see my *The Performance of Conviction: Plainness and Rhetoric in the Early English Renaissance* (Ithaca, NY: Cornell University Press, 1994).

17. Judy Z. Kronenfeld correctly observes that "[a]ny reading that emphasizes transmission or translucency as at issue in the poem ultimately faces the problem that colored windows, which presumably are less translucent than plain windows, are compared favourably, on the metaphorical level, to those plainer windows." See Kronenfeld, "Probing the Relation between Poetry and Ideology: Herbert's 'The Windows,'" *John Donne Journal* 2, no. 1 (1983): 57.

18. Ben Jonson, *Timber: or Discoveries,* in *The Complete Poems,* ed. George Parfitt (New Haven, CT: Yale University Press, 1982), line 115.

19. Samuel Ward, *The Happiness of Practice* (London, 1621), 22.

20. On Herbert's view of ethos, see Sheridan D. Blau, "George Herbert's Homiletic Theory," *George Herbert Journal* 1, no. 2 (1978): 24–25.

21. On rhetoric and prudence in the Renaissance, see especially Thomas O. Sloane, *Donne, Milton, and the End of Humanist Rhetoric* (Berkeley and Los Angeles: University of California Press, 1985); and Victoria Kahn, *Rhetoric, Prudence, and Skepticism* (Ithaca, NY: Cornell University Press, 1985).

22. For suspicious readings of *The Country Parson,* see especially Douglas Swartz, "Discourse and Direction: *A Priest to the Temple, or the Country Parson* and the Elaboration of Sovereign Rule," *Criticism* 36 (1994): 189–212; and Stanley Fish, "Void of Storie: The Struggle for Insincerity in Herbert's Prose and Poetry," in *Writing and Political Engagement in Seventeenth-Century England,* ed. Derek Hirst and Richard Strier (Cambridge: Cambridge University Press, 1999), 31–51. More balanced readings include Hodgkins, *Authority, Church, and Society,* chap. 4; and Cooley, *Full of All Knowledg.* Castiglione's courtier and Machiavelli's prince do resemble Herbert's parson in their awareness of the related demands of rhetoric and practical wisdom.

23. Kneidel, "Herbert and Exactness," 291. On Herbert and rhetoric, see also my "'Clear as Heav'n:' Herbert's Poetry and Rhetorical 'Divinitie,'" in "Early Modern God," ed. Michael O'Connor, special issue of *Renaissance and Reformation* 29, nos. 2–3 (2005): 183–201.

24. Heather Asals, *Equivocal Predication: George Herbert's Way to God* (To-

ronto: University of Toronto Press, 1981), 85. Malcolmson, *Heart-Work,* and Marion White Singleton, *God's Courtier* (Cambridge: Cambridge University Press, 1987), also note the poem's relation to the genre of charactery. Sidney Gottlieb mentions Joseph Hall's *Characters of Virtues and Vices* in relation to "Constancie" to suggest that both attempt to reconcile Stoicism and Christianity. See Gottlieb, "'Content' to 'Affliction (III)': Herbert's Anti-Court Sequence," *English Literary Renaissance* 23 (1993): 486.

25. On the poem's relation to Psalm 15, see Noel J. Kinnamon, "The Psalmic and Classical Contexts of Herbert's 'Constancie' and Vaughan's 'Righteousness,'" *George Herbert Journal* 8, no. 1 (1984): 29–42.

26. Singleton argues that in "Constancie" "The virtues are restored to their proper place in the exemplary Christian life by being 'raised to godliness'" (*God's Courtier,* 181).

27. Kneidel, "Herbert and Exactness," 294.

28. Thomas Saltern, *Dorcas: A True Patterne of a Goodly Life, and Good End* (London, 1631), 5.

29. Thomas More, *Utopia,* trans. Ralph Robynson, ed. David Harris Sacks (Boston: Bedford-St.Martin's, 1999), 121.

30. John Milton, *Of Reformation,* in *The Riverside Milton,* ed. Roy Flannagan (Boston: Houghton Mifflin, 1998), 877; Richard Hooker, *Of the Lawes of Ecclesiasticall Politie: The Sixth and Eighth Books* (London, 1648), B3v.

31. Kronenfeld, "Probing the Relation between Poetry and Ideology," 71; Flesch, *Generosity and the Limits of Authority,* 43–44.

32. Unsigned preface to Lancelot Andrewes, *The Pattern of Catechistical Doctrine at Large, or, A Learned and Pious Exposition of the Ten Commandments* (London, 1650), **1v–**2r.

33. St. Augustine, *Homilies on the Gospel of John,* trans. John Gibb and James Innes, in *A Select Library of the Nicene and Post-Nicene Fathers of the Christian Church,* ed. Philip Schaff, 1st ser., vol. 7 (1888; reprint, Grand Rapids, MI: Eerdmans, 1956), 185.

34. Thomas Cartwright, *A Confutation of the Rhemists Translation* (n.p., 1618), 229.

35. Ward, *Happiness of Practice,* 29. Bradin Cormack and Carla Mazzio begin *Book Use, Book Theory: 1500–1700* (Chicago: University of Chicago Library, 2005) by citing Geffrey Whitney's *Choice of Emblemes,* where the same fate threatens if the use required by proper reading practices is neglected: "Firste reade, then marke, then practise what is good, / For without use, we drinke but LETHE flood" (*Book Use, Book Theory,* 2).

36. John Calvin, *Institutes of the Christian Religion,* ed. John T. McNeill, trans. Ford Lewis Battles, Library of Christian Classics, vol. 21 (Philadelphia: Westminster Press, 1960), 4.12.14–21.

37. Francis White, *A Replie to Jesuit Fishers Answere* (London, 1624), 548. Further references appear in the text.

38. Dyer could have found the distinction between the reward of merit and the reward of grace elsewhere in anti-Catholic controversial writing. It appears, for example, in Sibthorp's *A Friendly Advertisement,* and, exactly contemporary with Dyer's and Herbert's texts, in George Downame's *A Treatise of Justification* (London, 1633). But the use in English of the unusual term "dispositively" increases the likelihood that Dyer was reading White.

39. Hodgkins, *Authority, Church, and Society,* 79.

40. John Bunyan, *The Pilgrim's Progress,* ed. N. H. Keeble (Oxford: Oxford

University Press, 1984), 65; C. Q. Drummond, "Believing and Coming in *The Pilgrim's Progress*," in *In Defence of Adam: Essays on Bunyan, Milton and Others,* ed. John Baxter and Gordon Harvey (Harleston, England: Edgeways Books, 2004), 1–58. Not surprisingly, Bunyan's character Faith, responding to Talkative, quotes John 13:17 (Bunyan, *Pilgrim's Progress,* 67).

41. I examine the relationship of Herbert's "Discipline" to contemporary debates about church discipline in "George Herbert and the 'Discipline' of History," *Journal of Medieval and Early Modern Studies* 31 (2001): 349–77.

42. Calvin, *Institutes of the Christian Religion* (ed. McNeill), 3.4.31.

43. George Herbert, "Briefe Notes on Valdesso's *Considerations*," in Hutchinson, *Works of George Herbert,* 311. Richard Strier discusses this distinction in "Changing the Object: Herbert and Excess," *George Herbert Journal* 2, no. 1 (1978), 24–37, and in "Herbert and Tears," *ELH* 46 (1979): 221–47.

44. See Strier, "Herbert and Tears."

45. Herbert's use of such a style in the poem supports James Biester's contention that Herbert, like other seventeenth-century religious poets, normally directs wonder away from the poet and toward God. Biester, *Lyric Wonder: Rhetoric and Wit in Renaissance English Poetry* (Ithaca, NY: Cornell University Press, 1997), 148.

46. On sanctification in Herbert, see especially Gene Edward Veith, Jr., *Reformation Spirituality: The Religion of George Herbert* (Lewisburg, PA: Bucknell University Press, 1985), chap. 6.

47. Cefalu, *Moral Identity,* 136.

48. Jonson, "An Ode. To Himself," in *Complete Poems,* line 3.

"Hallow'd Fire"; or, When Is a Poet Not a Priest?
Helen Wilcox

W HEN I WAS RESEARCHING THIS ESSAY ON THE INTERRELATEDNESS OF the roles of poet and priest in the work of George Herbert, I happened to visit a stately home near my home in North Wales. The family seat of the Marquess of Anglesey, Plas Newydd, is a fine eighteenth-century house overlooking the Menai Strait, and includes one rather unusual room in which the artist Rex Whistler painted a magnificent panorama during the 1930s. There are times when the influence of George Herbert seems to reach the most unexpected corners of one's experience, and that Sunday afternoon in Anglesey was one of them. Among the items on display in a small exhibition about the life of Rex Whistler was a model of a church made from a hatbox. It transpired that this was created by Whistler to be carried in the 1933 pageant at Wilton House to celebrate the tercentenary of Herbert's death and of the publication of *The Temple*. Whistler, as a visual artist, had chosen to represent Inigo Jones in the procession, and had therefore designed the miniature church in a classical mode—in fact, in the style of a temple.

In this unique combination of the hatbox with the architect's model, an everyday item with aesthetic achievement, and the church with the temple, we may see an emblem of Herbert's life and work. In his writing and life he brought together the homely and the skillful, the plain style and divine rhetoric, and the role of rector of a church and that of poet-psalmist of *The Temple*. What better evocation could there be of his double vocation as priest and poet than this strange hatbox-church that was also a temple?

POET AS PRIEST

Taking my cue from this happy coincidence at Plas Newydd, I wish to demonstrate—using evidence that is a little more substan-

91

tial than an old hatbox—that the functions of poet and priest are inseparably bound together in Herbert's writing. It is important to state from the outset that this is not a claim based solely on Herbert's biography; it is inspired by his lyrics on what it means to be both a priest and a devotional poet. The tradition of the poet as priest is, after all, a symbolic idea with ancient origins; poetry itself was born in a liturgical context, and firmly connected to oral and oracular methods of teaching, prophesying, and inspiring. As Virgil wrote in *Georgics* 2.675, in the translation by Dryden:

> Ye sacred Muses, with whose beauty fir'd,
> My Soul is ravish'd, and my Brain inspir'd:
> Whose Priest I am, whose holy Fillets wear;
> Wou'd you your Poet's first Petition hear?
> Give me the Ways of wandring Stars to know:
> The Depths of Heav'n above, and Earth below.[1]

Here Virgil, through Dryden, makes clear that the poet is a "Priest" of the sacred "Muses," a role that suggests spiritual and rational inspiration ("Soul" and "Brain" are both affected by this priesthood) as well as a vocation to serve (the special garments or "holy Fillets" display allegiance). The poet as priest also hopes to gain from this willingness to serve: the fruits of human obedience will be the knowledge of both "Heav'n above, and Earth below."

This was the sense in which the romantic poets, too, envisaged their bardic responsibility, being called to be "Nature's priest" and therefore to receive what Wordsworth referred to as "the vision splendid."[2] Yet their priestly custodianship was supremely of the imagination, as Keats makes clear in his "Ode to Psyche":

> Yes, I will be thy priest, and build a fane
>   In some untrodden region of my mind,
> Where branched thoughts, new grown with pleasant pain,
>   Instead of pines shall murmur in the wind.[3]

This priesthood goes beyond nature into the landscape of the mind, where "branched thoughts" will "murmur" a litany at a hidden shrine, a "fane" built faraway from the distractions of everyday existence. And although much modern poetry may shy away from these romantic claims of a priesthood of the imagination, there is certainly a residual sense of the spiritual burden of the poet who is a servant of a larger force—that is, of the power of words themselves. In his acceptance speech for the Nobel Prize for Literature, Seamus Heaney referred to poetry as the "ark of the covenant" between language and sensation, a metaphor that casts the poet in the role of Jewish priest preserving and protecting holy things.[4] In his earlier account in *The Redress of Poetry*—in which he responded to Herbert's verse among other sources of inspiration—Heaney also put forward a view of poetry as a redemptive force, countering and correcting the imbalances of worldly experience (as the term "redress" in the title implies) through both metaphysical insight and formal skill.[5]

The extensive tradition of the poet as priest, therefore, draws on classical, Celtic, Jewish, and Christian images to cast the writer in the role of one whose vocation brings responsibilities as well as insights. Knowledge is given to the priest, but must be shared; special gifts are received but must be honored. Priest-poets are called to be go-betweens, finding an equilibrium between spiritual and worldly perceptions; they are "charged" (like the "world" in Hopkins's sonnet) with the burden and honor of proclaiming the "grandeur of God"[6] or the "mystery of things."[7]

In the light of this tradition, it would be quite legitimate to suggest that Herbert, too, regarded his roles as poet and minister of God as a dual vocation, inextricably interwoven in his life and writing. But my purpose is to go further and examine in greater detail how the priestly calling is represented in *The Temple,* and then to consider the specific ways in which the role of a priest underlies, and even defines, his poetry.

PRIESTLY QUALITIES

First, what does Herbert the poet say about priesthood? *The Temple* contains three main poems that envisage and enact the role of a priest in the Judeo-Christian tradition. Let us begin with "Aaron," in which the speaker contrasts his own imperfections with a vision of ideal priesthood, "true Aarons":

> Holinesse on the head,
> Light and perfections on the breast,
> Harmonious bells below, raising the dead
> To leade them unto life and rest.
> Thus are true Aarons drest.
>
> Profanenesse in my head,
> Defects and darknesse in my breast,
> A noise of passions ringing me for dead
> Unto a place where is no rest.
> Poore priest thus am I drest.[8]

The poem's metaphors of dress are inspired by the elaborate description in Exodus of the robing of Aaron, the first high priest in the Old Testament; his garments are said to "consecrate him, that he may minister . . . in the priest's office."⁹ Herbert's opening line specifically recalls Aaron's miter, which had the words "Holiness to the Lord" engraved upon it in gold, while line 3, the "Harmonious bells below," refers to the hem of Aaron's robe, which was hung with "bells of gold."¹⁰ In the second stanza of the poem, however, in contrast to the biblical ideal evoked in the first, priestly holiness and harmony have been displaced by a profane and passionate earthliness: the "poore priest" is merely human. How can the "Defects and darknesse" of mortality possibly be overcome?

The subsequent stanzas suggest the answer by changing the poem's focus from the original priest of the Jewish covenant to the "great high priest"¹¹ of the New Testament, Christ himself:

> Onely another head
> I have, another heart and breast,
> Another musick, making live not dead,
> Without whom I could have no rest:
> In him I am well drest.
>
> Christ is my onely head,
> My alone onely heart and breast,
> My onely musick, striking me ev'n dead;
> That to the old man I may rest,
> And be in him new drest.

As the Jewish priestly tradition is seen to be fulfilled in the Messiah, so the individual priest is transformed and renewed—"new drest"—in the image of Christ. The old harmonies have become a new and redeeming "musick," Jesus himself, whose impact is so overwhelming that the priest is made "live not dead." This phrase enacts its promise even in grammatical terms: the word "live" functions here as both adjective and verb, investing the line with dynamic potential. Within the given pattern of the Jewish tradition and the limitations of human existence—fixed frameworks suggested by the repeated rhyme scheme shaping each stanza of the poem—the presence of Christ offers a genuine prospect of enlivened perfection. With Jesus within, then, is the poet-priest "drest" and ready to lead the people "unto life and rest":

> So holy in my head,
> Perfect and light in my deare breast,

> My doctrine tun'd by Christ, (who is not dead,
>   But lives in me while I do rest)
>   Come people; Aaron's drest.

The key quality of a priest highlighted by this poem is the capacity to be Christlike. The holiness, light and harmony of Aaron all find their fulfilment through the indwelling Christ; his presence becomes the very head, heart, breast, and "onely musick" of those called to the ministry.[12] The tasks implied here are liturgical—the priest dresses for holy office, and the "people" are invited to attend—but they are based upon the fact that Christ has gone before the priest, setting the example of sacrifice and salvation. In the first chapter of *A Priest to the Temple,* Herbert writes of the "Dignity" and the "Duty" of priesthood, both of which are defined by their Christlike nature: the "Dignity" lies in the fact that a priest is given the authority to "do that which Christ did," and the "Duty" is indeed to do so.[13] As we shall explore more fully in the subsequent section of this essay, these aspects of priesthood are strongly suggested in Herbert's lyrics, particularly in the frequent links made between "that which Christ did" and the experience of the speaker. The closeness of Christ as Master, example, friend, host, companion, and "my onely light"[14] is a hallmark of *The Temple,* and quite often Herbert's personae end up doing "that which Christ did" almost without intending it. In "Redemption," the rabble of "theeves and murderers" to which the speaker is eventually drawn turns out to be the crowd at the foot of the Cross, while the narrator of "Christmas" stops casually at "the next inne," only to discover that Christ was already there "expecting" him.[15] As poet as well as priest, and in sorrow as well as joy, Herbert perceives that his savior goes before (or "prevents") him in every experience.[16] The example of Christ is the "onely musick" of his lyrical poetry as well as his vision of priesthood.

While "Aaron" is concerned with the fundamentally Christlike quality of a spiritually "well drest" priest, Herbert's poem "The Windows" emphasizes a second priestly characteristic, and that is vulnerability:

> Lord, how can man preach thy eternall word?
>   He is a brittle crazie glasse:
> Yet in thy temple thou dost him afford
>   This glorious and transcendent place,
>   To be a window, through thy grace.
>
> But when thou dost anneal in glasse thy storie,
>   Making thy life to shine within

The holy Preachers; then the light and glorie
            More rev'rend grows, & more doth win:
            Which else shows watrish, bleak, & thin.

Doctrine and life, colours and light, in one
            When they combine and mingle, bring
A strong regard and aw: but speech alone
            Doth vanish like a flaring thing,
            And in the eare, not conscience ring.[17]

Unlike "Aaron," in the course of which the dark places of human weakness are filled with the light of Christ, leading to the final triumphant cry, "Come people: Aaron's drest," the prevailing impression of the priest in "The Windows" is of human frailty. Despite the shining and colorful presence of Christ's "storie," the preacher here is merely a "brittle crazie glasse"—one of Herbert's most expressive phrases for the dangerously flawed nature of humankind. In the second and third stanzas we are reminded of this feebleness: without Christ, the preacher is plain glass through which light "shows watrish, bleak, & thin," and the priest whose words are not supported by action is just a "flaring thing," a flash in the pan that will "vanish" as quickly as it came. Yet, despite—or even because of—this vulnerability, the priest is afforded a "glorious and transcendent place" in the Christian temple: the window that lets in the "light and glorie" of the redemption.

The frailty of the priest, therefore, though always potentially problematic, is absolutely crucial to the nature and success of priestly vocation. In keeping with the principle of the Incarnation, it is essential that priests share in the vulnerability of humanness. As St. Paul asserts: "For every high priest taken from among men is ordained for men in things pertaining to God, that he may offer both gifts and sacrifices for sins: Who can have compassion on the ignorant, and on them that are out of the way; for that he himself is also compassed with infirmity."[18]

That final Pauline phrase, "compassed with infirmity," vividly encapsulates priests' necessary weakness; they are, in Herbert's terms, "brittle," and can act on behalf of the people precisely because they are defined by and enfolded within the realms of human "infirmity." As Herbert notes in *A Priest to the Temple,* the parson discharges his duties in accordance with what is possible for a "poore, and fraile man."[19] The speaker in "Even-song" confesses a similar limitation: "I ranne; but all I brought, was fome."[20] Here, indeed, is the negative impact of "speech alone," as Herbert puts it in "The Windows." Even the "colours" of rhetoric, hinted at in the metaphor of stained glass, can be instances of language that is empty of meaning; to quote "Even-song" again, those words can prove to be "bubbles, balls of winde" when spoken without inspiration.[21] Yet the priest is called to preach, in spite of these dangers— not to hide human weakness but to be beneficially transparent. This priestly glass must not strike the eye "darkly" but offer a clear vista through which redemption can be glimpsed.[22] As Herbert suggests in "The Elixer,"

> A man that looks on glasse,
> On it may stay his eye;
> Or if he pleaseth, through it passe,
> And then the heav'n espie.[23]

A priest, then, who is truly vulnerable—brittle and seen-through, like glass—can be a means of spiritual inspiration; heaven may be glimpsed when "Doctrine and life, colours and light, . . . combine," as "The Windows" states. Here Herbert echoes the prayer for the clergy included in the order for Holy Communion, which asks that, by the workings of heavenly grace, "all bishops, pastors, and curates . . . may both by their *life and doctrine* set forth thy true and lively Word."[24] In this prayer, and in "The Windows," the key word is "grace." The priest's vulnerability is transformed into effective ministry, and the "brittle crazie glasse" is enabled to "be a window, through thy grace."

This sense of vulnerability as a crucial quality of priesthood—the priest being, as St. Paul puts it, "compassed with infirmity"—also has consequences for Herbert's vision of the poet's effectiveness. In an interesting overlapping of priesthood and poetry, "The Windows" contains one of the few references to the "temple" in Herbert's entire collection of the same name.[25] In the first stanza of the poem, by means of God's "grace," a frail human being is allowed a place "in thy temple," a phrase that has a double reference, both to the role of the priest in the church and the function of the poet in *The Temple.* Just as "Doctrine and life" must work hand in hand for the priest to be able to "preach thy eternall word," so the poet's words and beliefs must be in tune with one another if a poem is to be genuinely effective. As Herbert declares in "A true Hymne," "The finenesse which a hymne or psalme affords, / Is, when the soul unto the lines accords."[26] The parallel between the frail preacher and the poet whose "verse may be somewhat scant" extends to the similarity of the solution to these shared weaknesses;

in both cases, mortal vulnerability is not overcome through human effort but by divine intervention. In "The Windows," it is Christ who colors the preacher's plain glass with his "storie," and as a result more listeners are won to the faith. In "A true Hymne," if the poet's heart is appropriately "moved," the poem's simple words can become "the best in art," since "God doth supplie the want." Priest and poet are equally frail and dependent on the inspiration of God; in each function, Christ has gone before them, fulfilling the roles of high priest and the poet who is himself the "Word."[27]

After the Christlike nature of the priestly role as emphasized in "Aaron" and the human vulnerability of the priest as stressed in "The Windows," a third key quality is found—and celebrated—in "The Priesthood." The poem begins with a profound sense of awe at the combination of the two aspects that we have noted in the previous two poems. The priest is "but earth and clay," yet is called upon to carry out Christlike tasks:

> Blest Order, which in power dost so excell,
> That with th' one hand thou liftest to the sky,
> And with the other throwest down to hell
> In thy just censures; fain would I draw nigh,
> Fain put thee on, exchanging my lay-sword
>   For that of th' holy word.
>
> But thou art fire, sacred and hallow'd fire;
> And I but earth and clay: should I presume
> To wear thy habit, the severe attire
> My slender compositions might consume.
> I am both foul and brittle; much unfit
>   To deal in holy Writ.[28]

The speaker here, contemplating the possibility of being ordained as a priest, is struck by the awesome nature of the vocation and, echoing the "brittle crazie glasse" of "The Windows," considers himself "foul and brittle" and thereby in danger of being consumed by the "hallow'd fire" of priesthood. Fire in Herbert's poems can be either rash and brief, or thrilling and life-changing. In "The Windows," the unsuccessful preacher's sermon is like "a flaring thing" and soon dwindles to nothing, whereas the "fire-work" of "The Starre," for example, can with positive effect "burn to dust" both folly and lust.[29] "The Priesthood" favors the purging and hallowing impact of fire, as in the oven that turns mere "clay" into a useful or beautiful pot.[30] By this means the poem goes on to resolve the clash between the frail or "slender" speaker and the overwhelming responsibilities of a priest of Christ. The third critical feature of priesthood, therefore, is that the priest is neither wholly Christlike nor simply human, but rather an earthen "vessel" in which heavenly matters are conveyed to earthly contexts.

The fifth and sixth stanzas explain this metaphor:

> But th' holy men of God such vessels are,
> As serve him up, who all the world commands:
> When God vouchsafeth to become our fare,
> Their hands conuey him, who conveys their hands.
> Oh what pure things, most pure must those things be,
>> Who bring my God to me!
>
> Wherefore I dare not, I, put forth my hand
> To hold the Ark, although it seem to shake
> Through th' old sinnes and new doctrines of our land.
> Onely, since God doth often vessels make
> Of lowly matter for high uses meet,
>> I throw me at his feet.

The flawed "lowly matter" of human nature, which is (as stanza 2 reminded us) but "earth and clay," is honored in the priesthood with the task of conveying God to the world. As Donne wrote in "To Mr Tilman . . . ," "Maries prerogative was to beare Christ, so / 'Tis preachers to convey him, for they doe / As Angels out of clouds, from Pulpits speake."[31] Herbert's poem makes clear that this bringing of Christ to others can occur not only through the reading and interpretation of "holy Writ" (stanza 2) in the pulpit, but also in the distribution of the eucharistic elements, "our fare" in bread and wine (stanza 5), and in the absolutions and "censures" administered by the priest (as described in stanza 1).[32] The priest is a "vessel"—a term used three times in "The Priesthood"—in which divine presence is briefly contained and through which it is transferred to those who need it. Like the apostles, whom Herbert depicts as "pipes of gold" in "Whitsunday,"[33] priests form a channel along which grace flows.

Once again, the parallels between this crucial quality of priesthood and the function of an author are clear to see. The poet of *The Temple,* whose "fingers bend / To hold [his] quill" through God's creative influence,[34] is a vessel for the divine Word: his task is to copy out the sweetness *"readie penn'd"* in God's love.[35] Many of the poems in *The Temple* find their resolution in the words of the Bible, for which Herbert's lyric forms act as frames or containing forms—vessels, thus. This can be seen in the well-known instance of "Jordan" (I), for example, which centers on and ends with the simple biblical phrase, "*My God, My King,*"[36] and most clearly in the simultaneous containment and exposition of the diagonal text in "Coloss. 3.3," "*My Life Is Hid, In Him, That Is My Treasure.*"[37] These poems are able, as the fifth stanza of "The Priesthood" expresses it, to "bring my God to me" (or in this case to the reader) in the form of biblical word and an almost sacramental embodiment in the visual and verbal matter of the text. Like the priestly servants of God as they are represented in the final stanza of "The Priesthood," the poet is the raw material or "some mean stuffe" whereon God can "show his skill."

As this discussion suggests, I should like to argue that the roles and responsibilities of priesthood indicated in these poems underlie Herbert's aesthetic principles in *The Temple*. Each of the three key qualities of a priest—the vocation to be like Christ, the awareness of being vulnerable, and the capacity to be a vessel for God's saving force—is, as we have briefly seen, matched in a fundamental aspect of the poems and their functions. The paradoxical natures of both the priesthood and the poetic calling are summed up in the metaphor from "The Priesthood" that I have chosen as the title of this essay—"hallow'd fire"—which suggests honor and danger, divinity and destruction, spirit and matter, all simultaneously. The priest is, as we have seen, a holy and liturgical figure and yet a site of conflict and passion; an individual who has the power to judge and yet is fundamentally frail; a go-between who conveys Christ to the world, yet is in constant need of grace. These conflicting aspects define the vocation of the devotional poet, too. In "The Flower," for example, Herbert's poet-persona shares this mixture of obligation and inadequacy, joyful honor and painful anguish. The speaker has experienced the hardship of "grief" and "tempests," but has also known the restoration of life in a spiritual springtime: "Who would have thought my shrivel'd heart / Could have recover'd greennesse?"[38] The poem is a celebration of the "wonders" of the God who shows both "power" and "love," particularly to those who recognize their own vulnerability. The sweetness of the "returns" of and to this God must be conveyed to the world in poetry, which, like the priest in Herbert's vision, functions as a vessel for God's own message: as "The Flower" asserts, "Thy word is all, if we could spell." Spiritual health is signified in this poem by writing, which—like the "glorious and transcendent" role of the priest in "The Windows"—is a fulfillment of the vocation to tell and retell the story of the resurrection:

> And now in age I bud again,
> After so many deaths I live and write;
>   I once more smell the dew and rain,
> And relish versing:[39]

As these splendid words imply, the call to "versing" involves an obligation that is perceived at times as onerous but is ultimately life-affirming. The same may be said of the vocation to the priesthood as expressed in the three poems that we have examined. If there is ever any tension within or between the two roles of poet and priest, it lies in the constant sense of the human inability to respond fully to the demands of the vocation, whether in words or in priestly ministry. However, as we have already seen, recognition of that inadequacy is, ironically, one of the most important qualities of both a true hymn and a true priest.

The Practice of Poetry

In the preceding section of this essay, we have been considering what Herbert the poet had to *say about* priesthood, and suggesting ways in which the priestly vocation is reflected in and through the aesthetics of *The Temple*. At this point I wish to turn the question around, now asking in what ways the poems *themselves enact* the functions of a priest. As implied in the title of this section, which echoes Lewis Bayly's best-selling devotional manual of 1612, *The Practise of Piety*, my aim is to examine Herbert's poetic practice and to outline its parallels with the pious work expected of an ordained priest in the Church of England in the early seventeenth century.[40]

Looking at the overall structure of Herbert's volume, it becomes clear that the poems in their entirety carry out the main tasks of a priest.[41] *The Temple* begins by drawing its congregation into the entrance porch, over the threshold, and into a holy place. First, "The Church–porch" urges readers to "Hearken unto a Verser" whose poetic preaching will be more effective than a prose sermon: "A verse may finde him, who a sermon flies, / And turn delight into a sacrifice."[42] Then "Superliminare" invites them, suitably taught by the "precepts" of "The Church-porch," to leave the profane world behind in order to "approach, and taste / The churches mysticall repast."[43] "The Altar," the opening poem of the next section, "The Church," begins to participate in the church's unceasing acts of praise, and builds a poetic altar upon which the sacrifice of

Christ is laid—fulfilled in the subsequent poem, "The Sacrifice."
These opening poems thus form a sequence of priestly acts:
preaching to the fallen, welcoming the penitent, praying with them,
and celebrating the redemptive death of Jesus as reenacted in the
Communion rite. "The Church" is eucharistic from beginning to
end, and after urging readers, like a congregation, to "Come ye
hither all," this main section of *The Temple* closes, significantly,
with "Love" (III) and a final acceptance of the invitation to the
heavenly banquet: "So I did sit and eat."[44] The volume closes with
"The Church Militant," in which the priest sends out the congregation to live and work as "Christ's Church militant here in earth,"
as the Book of Common Prayer describes the active Christian presence in the world.[45] Thus, *The Temple* does not conclude in heaven
but in the rough-and-tumble of church history and the battle
against sin—not a comfortable place for Herbert's volume to end,
but certainly evoking the everyday arena in which a priest must
work just as much as within the church building. As Herbert notes
in *A Priest to the Temple,* the parson's work with those around him
in his parish forms a major part of his vocation and is "in effect a
Sermon."[46]

While the larger patterns of *The Temple* encompass the range of
priestly functions in word and sacrament, and include poetic versions of both the contemplative and the active ministry, the variety
of lyric modes within "The Church" reflects the spectrum of
priestly methods and tactics adopted by Herbert the poet. For example, Herbert's storytelling poems such as "Redemption," "Love
unknown," and "Peace" use narrative tones that are based on parables, folktales and proverbs; as he advises in *A Priest to the Temple,*
the congregation will have no difficulty in remembering "stories
and sayings,"[47] and Jesus himself chose to speak in parables since
by the use of "familiar things" doctrine can be made to "slip the
more easily into the hearts."[48] Indeed, the influence of the Bible
underlies virtually every lyric of *The Temple,* whether the speaker
is teaching, praying, or complaining.[49] As we have already seen in
the previous section, numerous poems expound the specific scriptural passages that are either referred to in their titles, used as refrains, or embedded in their vocabulary.[50] This, too, is a poetic
version of a priestly task—in fact, a combination of two important
roles of the priest: the liturgical reading of lessons from the Bible,
and the interpretative and meditative preaching on a scriptural
text.

As Stanley Fish has pointed out,[51] yet another function of a
priest—teaching the people by means of the question-and-answer

mode of the catechism—inspires the conversational tone of Herbert's verse. The interaction of catechist and pupil lies behind phrases such as "what wouldst thou know?" and "do you understand?" that occur in the course of his poems,[52] and the interaction generally informs the dialogic structure of many of the lyrics in "The Church." As titles such as "A Dialogue-Antheme" and "Antiphon" indicate, the use of contrasting voices is also a liturgical phenomenon, reminding us that a further priestly attribute of Herbert's poems is their constant interaction with the Book of Common Prayer[53] and, consequently, their implicitly communal function. The lyrics express intimate spiritual experience yet, like the Psalms, simultaneously convey a sense of shared ritual.[54] It is no coincidence that Herbert's first definition of "prayer" (in his poem of the same title) is "the Churches banquet,"[55] implying the primary role of public prayer as the communal feast of God's people. Since so many of the lyrics of *The Temple* begin or end as prayers, the collection as a whole, like a priest, leads its readers into prayerful conversation with God.

Herbert's devotional poems, then, enact a range of functions expected of a priest, by means of both the poetic architecture of *The Temple* as a sequence, and the lyric forms and modes sharing the chief characteristics of the ministry such as preaching, expounding scripture, catechizing, and praying. Not only are the poems concerned with the church as a subject, from porch to altar and from floor to monuments,[56] but, as we have seen, they also mirror in their rhetoric and purpose the church's tasks as performed by the priest. This is particularly true in the case of the sacramental qualities of the poems. Three lyrics in *The Temple* feature the name of a sacrament in their title, and several others focus directly or indirectly on Holy Communion,[57] but many more of Herbert's poems work in the same way as sacraments—that is, they take earthly elements such as water, bread, and wine and transform them, and those they touch, with heavenly power. This is the basic principle of Herbert's rhetoric of the plain style, in which homely simplicity is potentially holy, for "True beautie dwells on high: ours is a flame / But borrow'd thence to light us thither."[58] One of Herbert's apparently simple—or even simplistic—poems, "Jesu," clearly demonstrates the way in which his poetic art parallels the function of a priest celebrating the Eucharist:

> JESU is in my heart, his sacred name
> Is deeply carved there: but th'other week
> A great affliction broke the little frame,

> Ev'n all to pieces: which I went to seek:
> And first I found the corner, where was *J,*
> After, where *E S,* and next where *U* was graved.
> When I had got these parcels, instantly
> I sat me down to spell them, and perceived
> That to my broken heart he was *I ease you,*
> And to my whole is *J E S U.*[59]

If we are able to see beyond the superficial naïveté of this narrative, its symbolic effect becomes that of the Eucharist, in which bread is taken, broken, and shared as the body of Christ. In the poem's verbal Eucharist, the word "Jesu" (who is himself the Word) is read, broken, "parcel'd out" and found to be doubly efficacious.[60]

Herbert's poetry, therefore, works as a priest would work. To borrow the phrase used by Herbert's contemporary Joseph Fuller when describing ministers, the poems can even be "[d]ispensers of the mysteries of God."[61] In the same statement, however, Fuller reminded his readers that ministers are merely "earthen vessels, men loaden with infirmities, like the rest of their Brethren," and it is important to note that Herbert's poetry is immensely conscious of "infirmities."[62] There is a refreshing humility to *The Temple,* stemming from the many speakers in the lyrics who are misguided and troubled; the priestly quality of these poems lies as much in the flawed humanity that they represent and forgive as it does in the preaching offered from its poetic pulpit. Like the work of the more recent Welsh poet-priest R. S. Thomas, Herbert's poems teach by example; their lyric selves are uneasy, even resentful, and the congregations they address are their own unruly passions or "peevish heart."[63] In "Silence," Thomas writes of his relationship with God as "answering / his deafness with dumbness," and his tongue lolls like the "clapper of a disused / bell"[64]—lines that recall Herbert's poem "Deniall" with its painful sense of God's "silent eares" apparently oblivious to the "tongue" of mere "dust." In the penultimate stanza, Herbert's speaker virtually gives up in despair:

> Therefore my soul lay out of sight,
> Untun'd, unstrung:
> My feeble spirit, unable to look right,
> Like a nipt blossome, hung
> Discontented.[65]

In contrast to many of Thomas's poems, however, lyrics in *The Temple* such as "Deniall" and "The Collar" suggest that there *is* healing for those who feel that God gives them "no hearing," and absolution for the rebellious heart that cries "No more. / I will abroad."[66] These priestly poems offer comfort and reassurance in their example of honesty in weakness as well as the redeeming strength of their endings; they function in a manner similar to the repeated "comfortable words" spoken by the priest in the service of Holy Communion in the Book of Common Prayer.[67]

Above all, the very nature of poetry itself in *The Temple* may be seen as priestlike, since in Herbert's view it brings the reader into the presence of God. In "The Quidditie," we are informed that "a verse is not a crown, / No point of honour, or gay suit, / No hawk, or banquet, or renown, / Nor a good sword, nor yet a lute."[68] In contrast to these negative statements, Herbert concludes the short poem by offering a simple positive definition: addressing God, he declares that a verse is "that which while I use / I am with thee, and *Most take all*."[69] This startling final phrase, echoing the language of gambling, hints at the power of poetry to cross from earth to heaven "As from one room t'another,"[70] and wittily suggests the eternal winnings to be gained through the sacred ministerings of poetry.

PRIEST AS POET

We began this essay with the artist Rex Whistler in the procession at Wilton in 1933 with his hatbox model of a church, symbolizing the seventeenth-century priest who built a written temple out of the materials of ordinary life and language. As I hope to have shown, Herbert's extraordinary achievement is a combination of the vocation of a priest and the art of an orator.[71] The answer to the question posed in my title—"When is a poet not a priest?"—is, therefore: in Herbert's case, never. In vocation and in practice, the priest is always the poet, and vice versa. The poems' representation of priesthood mirrors the aesthetic principles of *The Temple,* while the poetic texts themselves fulfill the duties of a priest in preaching and praying, word and sacrament. Herbert is a priest aesthetically as well as spiritually, and his "hallow'd fire" implies purity and sacrifice in both language and devotion. In "Jordan" (I), Herbert rejects the flowery rhetoric of traditional (secular) pastoral verse in favor of a glorious plainness in praise of God: in this way, beauty and truth will go hand in hand, and delight will indeed be turned into the sacrifice called for by genuine devotion.[72]

In the chapter of *A Priest to the Temple* entitling "The Parson's Church," Herbert describes how the country parson should look after his church building, keeping it clean and in good repair, and decorating it appropriately for "great festivalls."[73] The principle that guides this priestly care of the church is, not surprisingly, biblical: the parson is "following the Apostles two great and admirable Rules," a reference to St. Paul's advice in 1 Corinthians 14. The first rule is, *"Let all things be done decently, and in order:* The second, *Let all things be done to edification."*[74] We may see in this a final, succinct summary of Herbert's sense of his double vocation as priest and poet. His work strives to delight with the beauty of its plainness and to teach with the truth of its perceptions; both of these principles apply, whether the medium is the rhetoric of poetry or the liturgy of the church.

NOTES

1. *The Works of John Dryden, vol. 5, The Works of Virgil in English (1697)*, ed. William Frost and Vinton A. Dearing (Berkeley and Los Angeles: University of California Press, 1987), 2.673–78, p. 203.

2. William Wordsworth, "Ode. Intimations of Immortality," line 72, in *Poetical Works,* ed. Thomas Hutchinson, rev. E. De Selincourt (London: Oxford University Press, 1966), 460.

3. John Keats, "Ode to Psyche," lines 50–53, *Poetical Works,* ed. H. W. Garrod (London: Oxford University Press, 1972), 212.

4. Seamus Heaney, *Opened Ground* (London: Faber and Faber, 1998), 450. Compare the reference to the "Ark" in Herbert's poem "The Priesthood."

5. Seamus Heaney, *The Redress of Poetry* (Oxford: Clarendon Press, 1990); see also Heaney, *Opened Ground,* 467.

6. Gerard Manley Hopkins, *God's Grandeur,* ed. W. H. Gardner and N. H. Mackenzie (London: Oxford University Press, 1970), 66. For a comparative study of Herbert and Hopkins as priests and poets, see Mary Theresa Kyne, *Country Parsons, Country Poets: George Herbert and Gerard Manley Hopkins as Spiritual Autobiographers* (Greensburg, PA: Eadmer Press, 1992).

7. Shakespeare, *King Lear* 5.3.16, when Lear speaks to Cordelia of taking on the role of "God's spies"(line 17), in *The Riverside Shakespeare,* ed. G. Blakemore Evans (Boston: Houghton Mifflin, 1974), 1291. Compare the expression used by Wordsworth in "Tintern Abbey" for the power of the poet who becomes "a living soul": "We see into the *life of things,"* (lines 46, 40, in *Poetical Works,* ed. Thomas Hutchinson, rev. E. de Selincourt (London: Oxford University Press, 1966), 164, my italics.

8. *The English Poems of George Herbert,* ed. Helen Wilcox (Cambridge: Cambridge University Press, 2007), 601, stanzas 1 and 2. All further references to Herbert's poems are given by page number in this edition.

9. Exod. 28:3. All biblical quotations are taken from *The Bible: Authorised King James Version,* ed. Robert Carroll and Stephen Prickett (Oxford: Oxford University Press, 1997).

10. Exod. 28:36, 33.

11. Heb. 4:14.

12. "Head" also implies Christ's position as head of the church; see Eph. 5:23.

13. Herbert, *A Priest to the Temple*, in *Works,* ed. F. E. Hutchinson (Oxford: Clarendon Press, 1941), 225.

14. See "The Odour," "The Thanksgiving," "Unkindnesse," "Love" (III), and "Mattens"; the quotation is from "The Flower," in Herbert, *English Poems,* 568.

15. "Redemption," in Herbert, *English Poems,* 132; "Christmas," in Herbert, *English Poems,* 292.

16. In "The Thanksgiving," the speaker wishes to grieve for the Savior in his passion, but Christ "in all grief preventest me" (Herbert, *English Poems,* 113); compare "Easter," in which Christ is "up by break of day" ahead of the speaker (140), and "Redemption," "Deniall," and "The Collar," in which God anticipates the speakers' needs before they can express them.

17. Herbert, *English Poems,* 246–47.

18. Heb. 5:1–2.

19. Herbert, *Priest,* 236.

20. Herbert, *English Poems,* 231.

21. Ibid.

22. 1 Cor. 13:12: "For now we see through a glass, darkly; but then face to face."

23. Herbert, *English Poems,* 641.

24. John E. Booty, ed. *The Book of Common Prayer 1559: The Elizabethan Prayer Book* (Charlottesville: University Press of Virginia, for the Folger Shakespeare Library, 1976), 254, my italics.

25. It is quite possible that the title was in fact added by Nicholas Ferrar, who oversaw the publication of Herbert's Poems; see Herbert, *English Poems,* 39–40.

26. Herbert, *English Poems,* 576.

27. John 1:14, "And the Word was made flesh."

28. Herbert, *English Poems,* 551.

29. Ibid., 268.

30. Compare "The Church-porch," lines 429–30: "Do not grudge / To pick out treasures from an earthen pot." See Diana Benet's discussion of this image of priesthood in *Secretary of Praise: The Poetic Vocation of George Herbert* (Columbia: University of Missouri Press, 1984), 182.

31. John Donne, "To Mr *Tilman* after he had taken orders," lines 41–43, in Donne, *Complete English Poems,* ed. C. A. Patrides (London: Dent, 1985), 471.

32. Compare line 44 of "To Mr *Tilman*": "And blesse the poore beneath, the lame, the weake."

33. Herbert, *English Poems,* 214.

34. "Providence," lines 3–4, in ibid., 416.

35. "Jordan" (II), in Herbert, *English Poems,* 367.

36. Herbert, *English Poems,* 200.

37. Ibid., 305.

38. Ibid., 567–8.

39. "The Flower," in ibid., 568.

40. It will be already evident that the priesthood discussed in this essay is the ordained ministry, rather than the New Testament doctrine of the priesthood of all believers (1 Pet. 2:9).

41. For a full account of these duties as outlined in *A Priest to the Temple,* see Christopher Hodgkins, *Authority, Church, and Society in George Herbert: Return to the Middle Way* (Columbia: University of Missouri Press, 1993), 103–26.

42. Herbert, *English Poems,* 50.

43. Ibid., 85.

44. "The Invitation," in ibid., 624; "Love" (III), in Herbert, *English Poems,* 661.

45. Booty, *Book of Common Prayer,* 253.

46. Herbert, *Works,* 245.

47. Ibid., 233; compare also the use of "sayings" in Herbert's poem "Charms and Knots."

48. Herbert, *Works,* 261.

49. For a full consideration of this aspect of Herbert's poems, see Chana Bloch, *Spelling the Word: George Herbert and the Bible* (Berkeley and Los Angeles: University of California Press, 1985).

50. See above, 99, for the discussion of "conveying" God or his words to the congregation, in relation to "The Priesthood." In addition to the poems highlighted there—"Jordan" (I) and "Coloss. 3.3"—see also "Ephes. 4.30," "The Pearl," "The 23 Psalme," "The Odour," "Church-musick," "Antiphon" (I), and "Easter."

51. Stanley Fish, *The Living Temple: George Herbert and Catechizing* (Berkeley and Los Angeles: University of California Press, 1978).

52. "The Discharge," in Herbert, *English Poems,* 502, "Love unknown," 454.

53. This is made clear, for example, by poem titles such as "Christmas," "Easter," "Whitsunday," and "Even-song." See also R. M. van Wengen-Shute, *George Herbert and the Liturgy of the Church of England* (Oegstgeest, Netherland: de Kampenaer, 1981).

54. See the broader discussion of this phenomenon in Ramie Targoff, *Common Prayer: The Language of Public Devotion in Early Modern England* (Chicago: University of Chicago Press, 2001).

55. "Prayer" (I), in Herbert, *English Poems,* 178.

56. "The Church-porch," "The Altar," "The Church-floore," "Church monuments."

57. "The H. Communion," "H. Baptisme" (I) and (II); for example, "The Agonie," "The Invitation," "The Banquet," "Love" (III).

58. "The Forerunners," lines 28–29, in Herbert, *English Poems,* 612.

59. Herbert, *English Poems,* 401.

60. The phrase "parcel'd out," which echoes the "parcels" of letters in "Jesu" line 7, is found in "Love" (I) and "Dooms-day" (Herbert, *English Poems,* 189, 651, respectively). For further discussion of the "Sacramental Voice" in Herbert's lyrics, see Heather Asals, *Equivocal Predication: George Herbert's Way to God* (Toronto: University of Toronto Press, 1981), 38–56.

61. Joseph Fuller, *Joseph's Party-Coloured Coat* (1640), 171.

62. Ibid. In these phrases, Fuller brings together two of the most important qualities of the priesthood identified in the earlier part of this essay: the necessary vulnerability of the priest (as illustrated by "The Windows") and the priest's role as one who conveys God to humankind (seen preeminently in Herbert's poem "The Priesthood").

63. "Sion," in Herbert, *English Poems,* 382.

64. R. S. Thomas, *Collected Later Poems, 1988–2000* (Tarset, England: Bloodaxe, 2004), 287.

65. Herbert, *English Poems,* 289.

66. "Deniall," in ibid., 288; "The Collar," in Herbert, *English Poems,* 526.

67. Booty, *Book of Common Prayer,* 260: the priest invites the congregation to listen to sayings from the Bible, with the words "Hear what comfortable words our Savior Christ saith, to all that truly turn to him."

68. Herbert, *English Poems,* 253.

69. Ibid., 254.

70. "The H. Communion," line 36, in ibid., 183.

71. Before becoming a priest, Herbert was public orator of Cambridge University. For a discussion of the relationship between his evident rhetorical expertise and his desire for poetic simplicity, see my "Herbert's 'Enchanting Language': The Poetry of a Cambridge Orator," *George Herbert Journal* 27 (2003/4): 53–66.

72. In "Jordan" (I), Herbert asks, "Is there in truth no beautie?" (*English Poems,* 200). Herbert's promise in "The Church-porch" that poetry will "turn delight into a sacrifice" (l. 6, p. 50) echoes Philip Sidney's claim, based on Horace, that poetry should "teach and delight." Sidney, *An Apology for Poetry,* ed. Geoffrey Shepherd (Manchester: Manchester University Press, 1973), 49.

73. Herbert, *Works,* 246.

74. Ibid.; the biblical quotations are from 1 Cor. 14:40, 14:26.

II
Historical Personalities and Places

William Herbert's Gardener: Adrian Gilbert
Cristina Malcolmson

I HOPE TO MAKE TWO POINTS ABOUT WILLIAM HERBERT'S GARDENER IN this essay. First, his biography suggests strongly that neither gardening nor the country could represent a world separated from politics for the Pembroke circle, including William's fourth cousin George Herbert. Adrian Gilbert lived at Wilton House from around 1610 to 1628 and designed William Herbert's garden there; Gilbert was also Sir Walter Raleigh's half brother. Therefore, William Herbert, the third Earl of Pembroke, was steadfast in his loyalty to a family directly associated with the Protestant cause, despite the strong distaste that King James had for the memory of Raleigh, whom the King executed in 1618. Second, Adrian Gilbert represented not only the memory of Raleigh, but also the glories and failures of Elizabethan overseas exploration, including its association with science and magic. Gilbert's presence at Wilton required remembrance of Raleigh and his great schemes for a Protestant empire, as well as the interconnections between gardening, chemistry, mathematics, navigation, and alchemy. In fact, these interconnections were visible in the garden that Gilbert laid out for the Herberts, and this ensured that the garden would be experienced by those who visited it, like George Herbert, not as a pastoral retreat, but as a religious and scientific challenge.

Although George Herbert became a country parson and chaplain to Wilton House in 1630, two years after Gilbert's death, the poet lived in Wiltshire from 1628 and presumably visited Wilton House before that as a near relative. George would have found it indispensable to know the cast of characters at Wilton, given the strong possibility that George sought and obtained the patronage of the third Earl of Pembroke for the position of public orator at Cambridge in 1620, the seat in Parliament in 1624, and the post of rector of Bemerton St. Andrew and Fuggleston St. Peter in 1630. It is interesting to try to imagine a conversation between the well-mannered George Herbert and the acerbic Adrian Gilbert on their patron's estate. John Aubrey calls Gilbert "a Man of excellent naturall

113

Parts; but very Sarcastick, and the greatest Buffoon in the Nation; [he] cared not what he said to man or woman of what quality soever." The *OED* defines a buffoon as a comic actor, like a jester or fool, or a joker who "practises indecent raillery," a bit like Shakespeare's Falstaff. Gilbert is also described in a court case as "corpulent." One critic has even suggested that Gilbert was the original for Falstaff. Imagine George Herbert and Falstaff meeting in the garden. No doubt both George Herbert and Adrian Gilbert would have been quite witty, but perhaps with different purposes in mind.[1]

My plan here is to examine Gilbert's biography and the significance of his presence at Wilton, to consider the relationship between gardening, science, and overseas exploration during the period, and to analyze some of George Herbert's poems to evaluate how he responded to the vision of a Protestant empire espoused by Raleigh and his half brothers, the Gilberts.

We know that Adrian Gilbert lived and worked at Wilton House through John Aubrey's account of Mary Sidney Herbert in his *Brief Lives* and through his manuscript "Memoires of Naturall Remarques in the County of Wilts." John Taylor, the Water Poet, praises Gilbert and the garden he constructed for William Herbert in *A new discouery by sea,* published in 1623. There is no entry for Adrian Gilbert in the *Oxford Dictionary of National Biography,* but the article on his brother Humphrey gives Adrian's life span as 1541 to 1628. During those eighty-seven years, Gilbert lived through both the Elizabethan and Jacobean periods. Indeed, by far the most material on Gilbert is found in the literature of early English overseas exploration.[2]

Queen Elizabeth granted to Sir Humphrey Gilbert and his brother Adrian Gilbert letters patent to search for a northwest passage from Europe to Asia in the 1570s and 1580s. Sir Humphrey and Raleigh were also granted patents to establish colonies in North America, "to discover, finde, search out, and view such remote, heathen and barbarous lands, countreys and territories not actually possessed by any Christian prince or people." Sir Humphrey had been knighted after a brutal but successful campaign in Ireland in the 1560s, and he and Raleigh sailed to North America in 1578, funded in part by Adrian Gilbert. Sir Humphrey became a martyr for the cause of "western planting" when he drowned in 1583 after claiming Newfoundland for the Queen. His brother Adrian as well as Raleigh became the new leaders in the movement. Raleigh sent out ships in 1584 that claimed Roanoke Island in what is now North Carolina for Queen Elizabeth, and he attempted to settle a colony there in 1585 and 1587. Adrian Gilbert

received letters patent in February 1584 for "the search and discouery of the Northwest Passage to *China*," and he funded the famous navigator John Davis on his three voyages between 1585 and
1587. Davis was no more successful than Sir Humphrey or Martin
Frobisher before him in finding a northwest passage; I suppose
there was no global warming in 1585, and Davis found instead the
Arctic ice that none of these investors expected.[3]

Adrian and his brother Humphrey were older than their half
brother Sir Walter Raleigh by about fourteen years, and Raleigh
learned the business of western exploration from them. Raleigh, of
course, became far better known, particularly for his writing and
his position as the favorite of Queen Elizabeth. King James did not
share Queen Elizabeth's appreciation for Raleigh, and imprisoned
him in the Tower for treason from 1603 to 1616. Raleigh argued for
and won his release in order to mount an expedition to Guiana to
search for El Dorado, the city of gold, with promises that he would
not attack the Spanish. People in 1616 thought he was either de-
luded or had plans to undermine the influence over King James
held by the Spanish ambassador, Gondomar. Raleigh's expedition
was a disaster; his men did attack the Spanish; no gold was discovered; and he was executed on October 29, 1618.[4]

Adrian Gilbert experienced all of this, first, in the 1580s as one
of the leading participants in the plans for an English empire overseas; second, after his fortunes declined in the 1590s, as an overseer or steward on Raleigh's estate; and third, at some point after
Raleigh was imprisoned in the Tower, at which time Gilbert was a
chemist, housekeeper, and gardener at Wilton House.

During his lifetime, Adrian Gilbert moved up and down the ladder of status and wealth. His father was a wealthy landowner, and
Adrian attended the Middle Temple. He is referred to as Master
Adrian Gilbert in the letters patent, and as an "esquire" in the list
of investors for Sir Humphrey's voyages. He certainly had considerable wealth at one time, given his investment in so many expeditions. In 1587, he held a lease on a lucrative silver-rich lead mine
in Devon, and, for the next two years, he and Sir Bevis Bulmer received 10,000 pounds profit each, but this declined to 1,000
pounds by 1590. Gilbert seems to have become dependent on Raleigh by 1593; he served as overseer on Raleigh's estate at Sherborne, and built a new lodge and set of elaborate gardens there. In
1603, Raleigh urged his wife from the Tower to look after his half
brother: "I recommend unto you my poor brother A[DRIAN] GIL-
BERT. The lease of Sandridge is his, and none of mine. Let him
have it, for God's sake. He knows what is due to me upon it." Later,

in a court case in 1612, Gilbert complained about how badly Raleigh had provided for him, and sued over the money Gilbert had "spent at Sherborne, about Sir Walter Raleigh's business, in making and planting of his walks and gardens, and about other [of] his affairs, by the space of seven years, or thereabouts." But Raleigh had been in the Tower for nine years, and had no money to pay out. Aubrey notes that Gilbert had a pension, which may have been granted by Queen Elizabeth, given King James's aversion to his half brother Raleigh. However, if this pension existed, it was probably not enough to live on. Perhaps by 1612 Gilbert had moved to Wilton. This would be quite a falling off for a leader in the "western planting" movement.[5]

Gilbert may have protested this remarkable shift in fortune by refusing to respect the rules of status and to care about "what he said to man or woman of what quality soever," as Aubrey put it. Certainly his role as gardener, which we will see included a great deal of manual labor, exploded any expectations about the leisure and clean hands of the gentleman.

According to Aubrey, Gilbert was primarily known as a chemist in the seventeenth century, and he originally came to Wilton to assist Mary Sidney Herbert in her laboratory. Christopher Thacker has suggested that Gilbert's garden might actually have been made for Mary Sidney Herbert, rather than her son William.[6] Aubrey writes in *Brief Lives:* "In her time, Wilton House was like a College, there were so many learned and ingeniose persons. She was the greatest Patronesse of witt and learning of any Lady in her time. She was a great Chymist, and spent yearly a great deale in that study. She kept for her Laborator in the house Adrian Gilbert (vulgarly called Dr. Gilbert) halfe-brother to Sir Walter Raleigh, who was a great Chymist in those dayes . . ."[7]

Aubrey adds in his memoirs on Wiltshire, "[Gilbert] was Housekeeper at Wilton . . . it is not forgot that he did many admirable cures with his Chymicall Medicines. But those Secrets are lost, or died with him."[8] However one of his secrets was published in *The Queens closet opened* (1659), a recipe called "Dr. Adrian Gilberts most Sovereign Cordial Water," which includes forty-two different plants and fruits, used in the healing of several diseases.[9] This recipe suggests the close connection at the time between chemistry, gardening, and medicine.

Gilbert must have been at Wilton for some time before 1614, when Mary Sidney Herbert left Wilton for the continent. She returned in 1616, but settled in her new home, Houghton House in Bedfordshire.[10] John Taylor reports that Gilbert was still at Wilton in 1623, and, although "an ancient gentleman," was still "toyling and tilling."[11] (And this at the age of eighty-two!) William Herbert, the master of Wilton after 1601, was probably happy to keep Gilbert at Wilton after Herbert's mother left in 1614, given Herbert's strong commitment to the family of Sir Walter Raleigh. In 1616, Herbert argued in favor of Raleigh's voyage to Guiana, and in 1618, against his execution. It is important to note that Gilbert lived at Wilton House throughout Raleigh's trial and execution. William Herbert also presented Walter Raleigh's third son, Carew Raleigh, at court in 1621. However, King James saw too much of a resemblance to his father, and Carew set off for a year on the continent. In 1624, both houses of Parliament passed a bill to restore Carew to his father's estates, but James refused to sign it. Certainly the King's refusal to accept Raleigh's son at court would have brought back to mind Raleigh's resistance to the Spanish and plans for an English empire. After his death, Raleigh became a Protestant hero, through works like *Sir Walter Rawleighs Ghost, or, Englands Forewarner,* written in 1626 by Thomas Scott. In 1628, Raleigh's *Dialogue betweene a Counsellor of State and a Justice of the Peace,* originally written in 1614 to convince King James to recall Parliament, was renamed *The Prerogative of Parliaments* and reprinted three times, perhaps in conjunction with the Petition of Right submitted to Charles I. William Herbert supported Raleigh's legacy by investing in overseas exploration and colonization, particularly in Bermuda, East India, Guiana, and Virginia, and, in 1612, in the pursuit of the discovery of the northwest passage, Adrian Gilbert's dream in 1584.[12] William Herbert and his gardener would have had a lot to discuss.

The link between Adrian Gilbert's early career in the western planting movement and his later career as a gardener for Raleigh and at Wilton can be found through the figure of John Dee, the famous English polymath who lived from 1527 to 1609. Dee was both a scientist and a magician. Dee supported overseas exploration through maps, his knowledge of navigation and the civil law pertinent to acquiring territory, justifications for British imperialism written to Queen Elizabeth, and his conversations with angels. One attendant at some of these angelic conversations recorded in Dee's "Spiritual Diaries" in 1583 was Adrian Gilbert. All major works on Dee mention Gilbert in this capacity.[13] Why was Gilbert visiting Dee? Did he share Dee's desire to be a Renaissance magus?

Explorers and investors in voyages frequently visited Dee, and not necessarily because of any interest in magic. Since the 1550s, Dee had been championing the cause of what he was the first to

call "the British Empire," and he continued to provide justifications for English imperialism into the 1590s. He trained explorers
in the use of navigation, maps, globes, and compasses. Sir Humphrey Gilbert visited Dee in 1577 to gain support for his project to
discover a northwest passage. The Frobisher expeditions to Canada
to discover a northwest passage in 1576 to 1578 had moved Dee to
develop maps and methods of navigation for exploring lands and
conveying metals by sea. Frobisher had brought back a large quan-
tity of ore with the promise of great wealth; this promise later
proved false, but Dee maintained his belief in the northwest passage as well as the possibility of finding rich metals in Canada. Dee
gave a map to Humphrey Gilbert in 1582 that made a northwest
passage look quite viable, and the map he gave to Queen Elizabeth
in 1580 probably did the same.[14]

Dee's patrons and pupils included many from the Sidney and
Herbert circles. The first Earl of Pembroke, William Herbert, had
taken Dee into his service in 1552, and consulted with him on the
enlargement of his estate through mines and metallurgy. Dee provided the first earl and his sons with information on mineralogy,
law, and cartography. One of these sons eventually became the second Earl of Pembroke, the husband of Mary Sidney Herbert. The
first earl and his countess were also investors in Frobisher's expeditions. Dee had one of the most remarkable libraries in England at
the time, and provided instruction on mathematics, navigation,
and geography. Dee became the tutor to Robert Dudley, the Earl of
Leicester, and Sir Philip Sidney studied with Dee as well. In the
biography of Sidney commissioned by Mary Sidney Herbert for the
instruction of her son William Herbert, Thomas Moffett, himself a
physician to the second Earl of Pembroke and Mary Sidney Herbert, records that Sidney learned chemistry from Dee, but had no
interest in astrology. Sir Francis Walsingham, a representative of
Elizabeth's court and Sidney's father-in-law, met with Dee, Adrian
Gilbert, and John Davis in 1583 to discuss the expeditions to discover a northwest passage. Both Sidney and Dee planned to invest
in Sir Humphrey Gilbert's voyage to North America in 1583, and
both Dee and Sidney were to receive vast amounts of land to use
for colonization. Sidney intended to sail on the expedition, but at
the last minute Queen Elizabeth forbade it.[15]

When Sir Humphrey visited Dee in November 1577, and when
he and his brother Adrian visited again in January 1583, they may
have been seeking only technical help on their upcoming voyages.[16]
A controversy has developed among Dee scholars about the relationship between his science and his magic. Frances Yates and

Peter French claim that the two should be seen as fully conjoined at this early period. William Sherman and others have argued that Dee's concern about the British Empire as well as his abilities in the practical sciences like navigation and geography were quite distinct from any interest in magic.[17] Sherman's argument should keep us from concluding that the Gilbert brothers were calling on Dee's powers as a magician to help them succeed in their colonial projects. They were probably seeking out Dee's help on practical matters—for instance, on charting a course for their voyages, as well as getting approval from the Queen. However, Adrian's attendance at Dee's seances suggests that Gilbert might have had other interests as well.

The magic that Dee embraced was based on the power of the stars and of numbers. The stars and the planets were believed to have magical powers, and the magician manipulated things on earth through these powers. Dee also believed that God created through numbers, and to grasp the significance of such numbers was to gain control over God's creation.[18] This control was wielded not in opposition to God, but through divine inspiration. Frances Yates argues that, for Dee, such subjects as navigation, surveying, fortification, proportion in architecture, and moving water from one place to another were not entirely separate from the power of the magus, but rather lower forms of the same thing: the ability to control matter for one's own purposes.[19]

It seems likely that Adrian Gilbert not only consulted with John Dee about overseas exploration, but also studied in Dee's famous library. The first recorded meeting between Adrian Gilbert and Dee was in 1579. Indeed, Robert Baldwin in an article published in 2006 concludes that Gilbert was one of Dee's pupils.[20] From Dee, Gilbert could have learned about geometry, mining, architecture, and navigation. According to David Quinn, both Adrian Gilbert and John Davis were closely associated with Dee "in his chemical, astrological, and spiritual experiments."[21] Dee believed in the existence of the philosopher's stone, and his lessons in chemistry may have included alchemy. It is interesting to note how many people in the Pembroke circle had an interest in chemistry: Philip Sidney, Mary Sidney Herbert, and her son Philip Herbert, the fourth Earl of Pembroke.[22] Aubrey tells us that Raleigh was also "a great chymist," and his quarters in the Tower included a laboratory and a garden.[23] There was apparently a committed alchemist in the area important to Mary Sidney Herbert; according to Aubrey, it was "one Boston, a good Chymist, a Salisbury man borne, who did undoe himselfe by studying the Philosopher-stone, and she [Mary

Sidney Herbert] would have kept him [or provided for him], but he would have all the golde to himselfe, and so dyde, I thinke, in a Gaole."[24] It is not at all clear that the sciences practiced at Wilton were entirely divorced from Dee's alchemy.

However, there is no doubt that Adrian Gilbert would have obtained technical knowledge through studying with Dee in his famous library. Gilbert and John Davis probably learned from Dee how to chart out Davis's three voyages to discover a northwest passage. Davis became the finest navigator of the time, and developed the ancient astrolabe into the backstaff or English double quadrant, which allowed navigators to measure the height of the sun more accurately.[25] (Apparently, Davis also stole several maps and books from Dee while he was out of the country, and Dee never could recover all of them when he returned.)[26] Gilbert also acquired from Dee a knowledge of mining, and used it to strike it rich at least for a few years between 1587 and 1589 in the silver-rich lead mine near Coombe Martin in Devon, known as Fayes Mine.[27] Indeed, Baldwin tells us that the first lease acquired on the mine was obtained by John Dee in March 1583, and that Gilbert seized the mine after Dee left for the continent in September 1584. At Dee's return to England in 1589, Gilbert was persuaded to give his teacher a considerable amount of the money he had earned from the mine, and this allowed Dee to settle his debts. It is not clear whether Gilbert had an attack of conscience or was threatened with legal action.[28]

In addition to training in navigation and mining, Gilbert may have learned from Dee the science of proportion and understanding of architecture he used to build a new lodge for Raleigh at Sherborne. Frances Yates demonstrates that, in Dee's *Mathematical Praeface to the Elements of Geometry of Euclid* published in 1570, Dee highlights "the geometrical and mathematical basis of [the] classical theory of architectural proportion," and coordinates as well the architecture of Vitruvius with the occult philosophy of Cornelius Agrippa.[29] This knowledge of proportion, as well as the practical art of moving water from one place to another, may have helped Gilbert to develop the elaborate gardens he laid out at Sherborne and at Wilton.

Gilbert's garden at Wilton displays the variety of skills available through Dee's teaching and library. Some of Gilbert's designs verge on magical symbols. The garden at Wilton that exists now was laid out in the eighteenth and nineteenth centuries, and was influenced by Capability Brown. It is far more naturalistic than early modern gardens, and highlighted by a beautiful Palladian bridge. The gardens of the seventeenth century were much more formal and emblematic. John Taylor, the Water Poet, provided in 1623 a description of Adrian Gilbert's garden as well as of Adrian Gilbert himself:

> But amongst the rest, the paines and industrie of an ancient Gentleman Mr. *Adrian Gilbert,* must not be forgotten, for there hath he (much to my Lords cost and his owne paines) vsed such a deale of intricate Setting, Grafting, Planting, inocculating, Rayling, hedging, plashing, turning, winding, and returning circular, Trianguler, Quadranguler, Orbiculer, Ouall, and euery way curiously and chargeably conceited: There hath he made Walkes, hedges, and Arbours, of all manner of most delicate fruit Trees, planting and placing them in such admirable Artlike fashions, resembling both diuine and morrall remembrances, as three Arbours standing in a Triangle, hauing each a recourse to a greater Arbour in the midst, resembleth three in one, and one in three: and he hath there planted certaine Walkes and Arbours all with Fruit trees, so pleasing and rauishing to the sense, that he calls it *Paradise,* in which he plaies the part of a true *Adamist,* continually toyling and tilling. Moreouer, he hath made his Walkes most rarely round and spacious, one Walke without another, (as the rindes of an Onion are greatest without, and lesse towards the Center) and withall, the hedges betwixt each Walke are so thickly set, that one cannot see thorow from the one walke, who walkes in the other: that in conclusion, the worke seemes endlesse, and I thinke that in *England* it is not to be fellowed, or will in hast be followed.[30]

In his book, *The Renaissance Garden in England,* Sir Roy Strong categorizes Gilbert's work as "geometric and symbolic." This may show the influence of Dee's *Praeface to the Elements of Geometry of Euclid.* Strong points out that Gilbert uses the triangle in his garden as an emblem for the Trinity in the placement of fruit trees, and that the circle is used in the placement of hedges, one circle within another. Strong concludes that the garden represents "a personal iconographical programme based on symbolic geometry."[31] The religious implications in Gilbert's garden are clear, particularly in the references to the Trinity and to Eden. But the garden also has scientific and perhaps magical significance, not only in the geometric figures, but also in the image of the cosmos. Gilbert's circular walk is similar to that at Twickenham Park, developed for Lucy, Countess of Bedford, and the garden at Chastleton House. The representations of those gardens in Strong's book demonstrate that putting circles within circles suggests the pre-Copernican universe.[32] Such images were frequently used in Renaissance hermeticism. Perhaps Gilbert learned this through Dee's work *Monas Hieroglyphica,* which has been described as "a mystical alchemical text, dedicated to the penetration of divine mysteries though an occult explanation of geometric figures."[33] One such figure was Dee's hieroglyph on the title page of his work. French defines this hieroglyph as "a unified construction of significant astro-alchemical symbols that embodied the underlying unity or *monas* of the universe." The hieroglyph includes a point in the middle of a circle, corresponding to the earth and the cosmos.[34] Like Gilbert's garden of concentric circles, Dee's hieroglyph represents the Ptolemaic universe.

Whether or not Gilbert's garden had magical significance, it certainly took a great deal of labor to create. Taylor emphasizes this in his account. Though an "ancient gentleman," Gilbert goes to great "pains" and uses a great deal of "industry" to develop the garden, whose planning and structuring seems to continue as Taylor writes, since, in his garden paradise, Gilbert is still "toyling and tilling." Aubrey's comments on the garden emphasize labor as well: "[Gilbert] made that delicate Orchard, where the stately Garden now is. [Aubrey refers to "the stately Garden" put in by Isaac de Caus in the 1630s for Philip Herbert, the fourth earl.] He took up choice Apple-trees, and Pear-trees &c. out of the ground, and fetched them eight or ten miles off or more: and planted them with respect to their first position sc. as to North & South: about the later end of October: they did all grow very well; and many of them did beare fruit the second yeare."[35] October is a bit late for establishing the roots of trees, but Gilbert's care to reproduce the original position of the trees ensures fruit even in the second year. Taylor reports that Gilbert is also well versed in the knowledge of "Grafting, Planting, inocculating, Rayling, hedging, plashing, turning, winding." "Plashing" is a method of making a hedge with trees by "cutting stems partly through, bending them down, and interlacing them with growing branches and twigs, so as to form a close low fence which will grow in height" (*OED*).[36] (Apparently, there are plashed or pleached trees in a garden now at Wilton built by the seventeenth earl to honor his father: the trees enclose a garden with herbaceous plants around a central fountain.)[37] In his garden, Gilbert spares no expense in creating the circular hedges, probably using fruit trees, since Taylor writes that "[t]here hath he made Walkes, hedges, and Arbours, of all manner of most delicate fruit Trees," and Aubrey calls the garden "that delicate Orchard."[38] If so, these trees are so thick that someone in one circle cannot see through to someone in the next circle. The roundness of the walks particularly strikes Taylor, who adds the footnote, "A round worke is endlesse, having no end."[39] Roundness in shape suggests endlessness in time. Although the representation of the Garden of Eden implies an eventual fall, the circular walk suggests the endlessness of eternity, and the restoration of the effects of the Fall. Taylor hints at this in a poem he writes on Gilbert: "As *Nature* rudely doth supply our wants, / *Art* is deformed *Natures* reformation."[40]

If Gilbert was an alchemist as well as a chemist, then he may have been guided by alchemical ideals in his construction of the garden. According to Deborah Harkness, John Dee believed that alchemy could purify the corruptions of fallen nature, and restore nature to health. Dee's belief in "the healing, perfecting, and restorative powers of alchemy was not unique." The philosopher's stone was thought to perfect other substances, and Paracelsus believed alchemy was the foundation of medicine.[41] Thus, the perfection of the endless circular walk restores the imperfections of fallen nature. It also provides a model for Gilbert's other work, that of physician; as Aubrey had said, "[H]e did many admirable cures with his Chymicall Medicines."[42] It is useful to note that one ingredient in "Dr Adrian Gilbert's most sovereign cordial water" was a unicorn's horn.[43] This suggests that Gilbert as gardener, architect, and physician considered science and the supernatural to be allies rather than in opposition to each other.

Whether or not Gilbert was an alchemist, entering his garden would not have been a retreat, but rather a challenge, simultaneously biblical and scientific, to imagine perfection in the world and the cosmos. As Curtis Whitaker notes in his essay "The Pastor as Herbalist," religion and science were not mutually exclusive at the time, and Gilbert interweaves images of the Trinity and Eden with models of the pre-Copernican universe.[44] Given Gilbert's position within the history of the "western planting" movement and his half brother Raleigh's legacy, such imaginings would most likely have included the vision of a Protestant reform in England as well as in the rest of the world.

What was George Herbert's response to the vision of a Protestant empire espoused by Raleigh, the Gilberts, and the Sidney-Herbert circle? In his poetry, George Herbert includes several direct and indirect satires of alchemy. Because of the possibility of an interest in alchemy at Wilton, these satires seem even more pointed. They may in fact indicate a general censure of all of the grandiose schemes of the "western planting" movement, and the Sidney-Herbert family that invested in them. It is remarkable how frequently the plans of Raleigh and the Gilbert brothers resulted in spectacular failure—for instance, in the search for a northwest passage, in the search for the precious metal that the Gilbert's expeditions never found in Canada, in the original colonies established by Raleigh on Roanoke Island, and in his search for the city of gold in Guiana. George Herbert may rebuke all of this vast expense of time, energy, and money in one of his Outlandish Proverbs, "No alchymy to saving."[45]

However, there is evidence that George Herbert supported not only overseas exploration, but also the program of study developed by John Dee that made these expeditions possible. In "The Parson's Surveys" from *The Country Parson,* Herbert gives advice to younger sons in a passage that suggests his knowledge of Dee: "[H]e first commends the study of Civil Law as a brave and wise knowledg, the Professours whereof were much imployed by Queen *Elizabeth,* because it is the key of Commerce, and discovers the Rules of forraine Nations. Secondly, he commends the Mathematicks, as the only wonder-working knowledg, and therefore requiring the best spirits. After the severall knowledg of these, he adviseth to insist and dwell chiefly on the two noble branches thereof, of Fortification and Navigation. . . ."[46]

Herbert's comment on professors of law employed by Queen Elizabeth could refer to John Dee. Through his knowledge of civil law, John Dee developed a justification for exploring and taking possession of foreign lands in his work *The Limits of the British Empire.* In this work, he refuted the papal bull of 1493 that granted all lands still unexplored by Europeans to either Spain or Portugal.[47] After Dee gave Queen Elizabeth his treatise in May 1578, Sir Humphrey Gilbert was granted a patent in the next month to explore North America and claim it for the Queen.[48] Herbert's description of civil law as "the key of commerce" may seem far more benign in its reference than the confiscation of foreign territory. Yet Dee's knowledge of "the rules of foreign nations"—for instance, of the papal bull of 1493—allowed Dee to provide alternate legal justification for English colonization of foreign lands. It is also significant that, in Herbert's passage, he moves immediately from discussing civil law to praising mathematics as "the only wonder-working knowledge" fundamental to "fortification and navigation." Fortification and navigation were two of the most important practical applications of mathematics considered by Dee in his *Praeface* to Euclid.[49] Surely "wonder-working" is remarkable praise from Herbert, and matches exactly the power that Dee attributed to his subject. In fact, later in the passage, Herbert refers to colonization, overseas exploration, and artifices and manufactures, all subjects considered by Dee in his *Praeface.* In her analysis of Dee's mathematics, E. G. R. Taylor stresses the importance of his program of study for young men without inheritance: "The impact of his *Preface* to the English Euclid . . . upon young men of the middle class, sons of tradesmen and craftsmen, was very great, setting out as it did the ways in which geometry could advance technique and foster inventions."[50] George Herbert simply applies this principle to younger brothers of the upper classes.

Herbert also refers to mathematics in his speech as public orator of Cambridge to Prince Charles in October 1623. Charles had just returned to England from his voyage to Spain to meet his possible bride, the Spanish infanta. Herbert is chiding those who complained about the voyage as frivolous. He reminds them that youthful romantic adventures can foreshadow a promising future.

> Who knows whether also the load of love skillfully fastened and tied, and carried easily through so many miles, may indicate a mind capable of greater things? There flourish with us [that is, at Cambridge] all the arts, amongst which also are the mathematics; and though these are occupied in describing figures, than which nothing may seem more futile and useless to an inexperienced person, yet when they have been transferred to practical business, they construct wonderful engines for the defence of the State; so the same mind which lately has been occupied in the form and features of a face, when circumstances demand will defend a kingdom.[51]

Herbert praises the "practical business" of fortifications and gunnery as "wonderful engines" (in the Latin original, "machinas . . . mirabiles"). "Mirabiles" is defined as "wonderful, marvellous, extraordinary, amazing, admirable, strange, singular," and is quite similar to the phrase "wonder-working," used by Herbert in *The Country Parson* seven years later.[52] Although his representation of gunnery, particularly cannons, is quite negative elsewhere, here it turns what seems "futile and useless"—mathematical figures—into a fundamental resource for national survival.

It is true that, elsewhere in his writing, Herbert expresses a tough opposition to Dee's program. Not only is alchemy rebuked, but also mining and gunnery. The demonization of the cannon in "Triumphus Mortis" in *Lucus* is well known, as is his attack on mining in the poem "Avarice." Herbert sums up his view of mining in the poem "Providence," which praises God for his creation of the world, and the lessons it teaches:

> Thou hast hid metals: man may take them thence;
> But at his perill: when he digs the place,

He makes a grave; as if the thing had sense,
And threat'ned man, that he should fill the space.

(lines 81–84)

Mines are graves to Herbert, and that is the end of it. Not only Adrian Gilbert, but George's patron, William Herbert, invested in mining, particularly through his lease of the ironworks in the Forest of Dean in 1612 and 1627–28.[53]

George Herbert is equally dismissive of the study of alchemy. I will briefly summarize this issue, because many have discussed it, but it is valuable to consider Herbert's specific reaction to the study of chemistry and alchemy within the Sidney-Herbert family.

As many have pointed out, the poem "Elixir" began as a poem entitled "Perfection" and ended through revision with a much stronger emphasis on the analogy of alchemy in the poem.[54] The elixir is the philosopher's stone that perfects other substances. In the poem, the substance being perfected is the speaker's soul, and the tincture used is the dedication, "for thy sake," a purification of motive that refines God's servant and all his actions. Although the emphasis on alchemy increases in the revised version, both versions of the poem indirectly satirize alchemy by providing a much more humble and heartfelt transformation of the soul than the spiritualization of the alchemist outlined in alchemical treatises, particularly Dee's. Both poems also point out the fundamental flaw inherent in the pursuit of perfection in alchemy or Gilbert's garden, especially in a Calvinist universe. This point is made very explicitly in the last stanza of the original version:

But these are high perfections:
Happy are they that dare
Lett in the Light to all their actions
And show them as they are.

So Herbert admonishes the seekers of gold in his extended family circle, including Adrian Gilbert and Sir Walter Raleigh.

Herbert also directly criticizes the discipline of chemistry in his poem "Vanitie" (I). Moffett described Sidney's study of chemistry as a heroic endeavor: "[H]e pressed into the inner-most penetralia of causes; and by that token, led by God, with Dee as teacher . . . he learned chemistry, that starry science, rival to nature." "Penetralia" can mean "inner sanctum" or the "mysteries" themselves.[55] Moffett has some anxiety about the issue, since he puts God firmly in the lead rather than the teacher Dee. In fact Moffett exclaims in the preceding passage that Sidney loathed astrology because of his commitment to "true religion," and Moffett himself explicitly condemns astrology, "which," he attests, "only chance and vanity have made an art."[56] Herbert suggests that the search for the secrets of chemistry is itself "vain," and not a method of finding God's law:

> The subtil Chymick can devest
> And strip the creature naked, till he finde
> The callow principles within their nest:
> There he imparts to them his minde,
> Admitted to their bed-chamber, before
> They appeare trim and drest
> To ordinarie suitours at the doore.
>
> (lines 15–21)

Hutchinson helps us with an explanation of this stanza: "The chemist in his laboratory is, as it were, *admitted to* the *bedchamber* of the object of his inquiry, and he can there unclothe it (*devest*) and *strip* it of the feathers which disguise it (cf. *callow,* featherless), so as to discover its interior *principles;* he can give his mind to their study (1. 18) with better opportunity than those can who only see them emerge from *the doore* fully drest."[57] In Herbert's stanza, the principles are "callow," raw or bald, not "starry," or heroically discovered, as in Moffett's account of Sidney. It is worthwhile to note that, according to the *OED,* "chymick" could mean both "chemist" and "alchemist."[58] Perhaps something else happens in this bedchamber rather than simply the chemist giving his mind to the study of the creatures; rather, he transforms them before presenting them to the "ordinary suitors at the door," perhaps "common customers." The image itself transmutes from birds in the nest to young women vulnerable to the intruder's "minde." Herbert suggests through the image of illicit penetration into the bedroom that the chemist or alchemist is a kind of pander or pimp. When Herbert recommends a guide for medicine in "The Parson's Completeness"—namely, Fernel's *Universa medicina*—he is advocating the work of a physician who explicitly turned away from Paracelsian alchemy by "dispelling some of the period's reliance on astrology and magic in matters of health."[59]

There is no doubt that Herbert often coordinates and questions most of the aspects of the program of study practiced and advocated by John Dee. "The Pearl" names law (perhaps civil), astrology, chemistry, "old discoveries, and the new found seas" all in one stanza as the "ways of learning" inadequate to the pursuit of salvation.[60] However, the poem "Providence" is interestingly ambivalent on the subject. It condemns mining and the pursuit of exotic goods as forms of greed, and yet finds that navigation is indeed helpful:

> The sea, which seems to stop the traveller,
> Is by a ship the speedier passage made.
> The windes, who think they rule the mariner,
> Are rul'd by him, and taught to serve his trade
> . . . .
> All countreys have enough to serve their need:
> If they seek fine things, thou dost make them run
> For their offence; and then dost turn their speed
> To be commerce and trade from sun to sun.
>
> (lines 89–92, 105–8)

Human beings abuse "the ways of learning"; God's providence turns them all to good. The universe in the poem "Providence" is in many ways static, since each part of it is filled: "all the guests sit close, and nothing wants" (line 134); therefore, "All countries have enough to serve their need." Given this plentitude, the pursuit of "fine things" is an "offence." Nevertheless, "commerce and trade" seem to be legitimate outcomes of a problematic desire: perhaps one country can legitimately need the resources of another. The lines between 92 and 105 consider a number of "goods," but these waver between God's blessings and commodities exchanged in trade. It may be that Herbert would have preferred a world in which the English stayed away from other countries, given their ability to ravage them. This ambivalence about navigation is expressed in a stanza on "the Indian nut" or coconut:

> Sometimes thou dost divide thy gifts to man,
> Sometimes unite. The Indian nut alone
> Is clothing, meat and trencher, drink and can,
> Boat, cable, sail and needle, all in one.
>
> (lines 125–28)

Since God gives "enough" to each country, Herbert would prefer that each group of people could "sit close," and nothing want, since this would protect them from the vanity of overseas exploration. However, he cannot resist the promise of the "old discoveries and the new found seas." This stanza takes its cue from a travel narrative written by Edward Terry, "A Relation of a Voyage to the Easterne India," found in Samuel Purchas's *Purchas His Pilgrimes*. Therefore the passage refers to India, not to the Americas:

The Coquer-nuts (of which this Iland [near Goa] hath abundance) of all the Trees in the Forrest (in my opinion) may have preeminence, for merely with it, without the least helpe from any other, a man may build, and furnish a ship to Sea; for the heart of this Tree will make Plankes, Timbers, and Masts, a Gumme that growes thereon, will serve to calke our ship. The Rind of the same Tree will make Cordage and Sailes, and the large Nut thereof being full of kernel, and pleasant liquor, will for a need serve for those that saile in this shippe for meate and drinke, and the store of these Nutes for Merchandize.[61]

In this passage, Terry refers to the coconut tree as providing meat and drink as well as material for boat, cable, and sail. I am not sure where Herbert got the idea that the coconut could also provide clothing and a needle. In any case, Herbert's stanza is ambiguous about who "man" is in the line, "Sometimes thou dost divide thy gifts to man, / Sometimes unite." Is he praising the East Indians who stay home and enjoy the blessings that God provides? Or is he advocating the "commerce and trade" of the English, who acquire a "store of these Nutes for Merchandize" in their visit to the island? At least to some extent, Herbert regarded overseas exploration, as well as trade, commerce, navigation, and fortification, as an act of Providence.

I find this stanza on "the Indian nut" amazing, because it proves that Herbert read travel narratives. Indeed, he probably read the most famous collection of travel narratives at the time, *Purchas His Pilgrimes*. It would have been difficult for Herbert to avoid the widespread fascination with such works, given his extended family's remarkably long engagement in the "western planting" movement.

Adrian Gilbert's biography helps us to understand the history of George Herbert's extended family, because it reveals the central role that John Dee and Sir Walter Raleigh played in that history. From 1552 when the first Earl of Pembroke took John Dee into his service, through Mary Sidney Herbert's engagement in chemistry and Gilbert's construction of his garden, to her son William's investment in colonization and his brother Philip's interest in chemistry, Dee's linking of magic, science, and empire inspired the Sidney-Herbert circle. William Herbert's commitment to Raleigh's family, including his half brother Adrian Gilbert, kept alive the dream of a northwest passage and British colonies in the Americas. George Herbert rejected the claim to perfection inherent to Dee's alchemy, but found the technologies used by Raleigh and Gilbert to be "wonder-working." He criticized the gold-seeking in colonizers

but praised colonization as a noble and potentially "religious imployment." In 1632, when Herbert wrote *The Country Parson,* we
find him in no pastoral retreat from the stresses of Parliament or
the court, but industriously advocating Dee's program of study. We
can speculate that he had learned something about Dee's program
and Raleigh's use of it through visiting Adrian Gilbert and his
garden.[62]

NOTES

I am very grateful to the participants at the conference "George Herbert's Pastoral" for their questions and comments on this essay.

1. On Herbert's patronage, see Cristina Malcolmson, *Heart-Work: George
Herbert and the Protestant Ethic* (Stanford, CA: Stanford University Press, 1999),
15–25. Clayton Lein argues in the following essay, below, that Philip rather than
William Herbert named George to the post at Bemerton. David Novarr agrees in
"Review: *A Life of George Herbert* by Amy Charles," *George Herbert Journal* 1, no.
2 (1978): 56, 62. However, either patron ties George strongly to Wilton House.
Aubrey describes Gilbert in *Aubrey's Brief Lives,* ed. Oliver Lawson Dick (London:
Secker and Warburg, 1958), 139. For the definition of buffoon, see the *Oxford
English Dictionary* (hereafter cited as *OED*) #2 and 4. *Gentleman's Magazine*
considers the court case in which Gilbert was described as corpulent (January
1854, 20). William Amos suggests that Gilbert was the model for Falstaff in *The
Originals: The A–Z of Fiction's Real-Life Characters* (Boston: Little, Brown,
1985), 175.

2. Aubrey, *Aubrey's Brief Lives,* p. 139. Aubrey's "Memoires of Naturall Remarques in the County of Wilts," Royal Society Library, Aubrey MS.92, 248. Some
of the same material appears in *"The Natural History of Wiltshire" of John Aubrey,* ed. John Britton (London: Wiltshire Topographical Society, 1847), 90. John
Taylor considers Gilbert in *A new discouery by sea, with a vvherry from London
to Salisbury; or, A voyage to the West, the worst, or the best That e're was express*
(London: Edward Allde, 1623), C2v–C3. For Adrian and Sir Humphrey, see the
entry on Sir Humphrey Gilbert in *Oxford Dictionary of National Biography,* hereafter cited as *ODNB.*

3. On the letters patent and the various expeditions, see David Quinn, ed. *The
Voyages and Colonising Enterprises of Sir Humphrey Gilbert,* 2 vols., Hakluyt Society, 2nd ser., (London: Hakluyt Society, 1940), esp. 1:35–100, 188–94, and
2:485–89; and Richard Hakluyt, *The principal nauigations, voyages, traffiques
and discoueries of the English nation* (London, 1599–1600), vol. 2, pt. 2, pp. 143–
61. See also entries for John Davis, Sir Humphrey Gilbert, and Sir Walter Raleigh
in the *ODNB.*

4. *ODNB,* entry for Raleigh. See also Stephen J. Greenblatt, *Sir Walter Raleigh: The Renaissance Man and His Roles* (New Haven, CT: Yale University Press,
1973). Queen Elizabeth had put Raleigh in the Tower in 1592 for marrying Elizabeth Throckmorton, one of the Queen's ladies-in-waiting (thanks to Christopher
Hodgkins for pointing this out to me).

5. For Adrian's father, see *ODNB* on Sir Humphrey Gilbert. For the letters patent, see Quinn, *Voyages.* Lesley Whitelaw cites 1562 as the date Adrian entered

the Middle Temple in "The Virginia Company," *Middle Templar,* no. 37 (2005): 2 http://www.middletemple.org.uk/Downloads/VirginiaCo.pdf. On mining, see the entry for Sir Bevis Bulmer in *ODNB.* On the lodge, see *ODNB* on Raleigh. Edward Edwards prints Raleigh's letter in *The Life of Sir Walter Raleigh,* 2 vols. (London: Macmillan and Co., 1868), 2:386. Cecil Monro records Adrian's suit against Raleigh in *Acta Cancellaria, or Selections from the Courts of Chancery* (London: William Benning and Co., 1847), 176–87; see also Rachel Lloyd, *Dorset Elizabethans: At Home and Abroad* (London: John Murray, 1967), 286. On Adrian's pension, see Aubrey MS.92, 248; and Britton, *"Natural History of Wiltshire" of John Aubrey,* 90.

6. Christopher Thacker, "A Note on Wilton and Adrian Gilbert," *Wiltshire Gardens Trust Journal,* no. 24 ([DATE?]): 13–15.

7. Aubrey, *Aubrey's Brief Lives,* 139. See also Margaret Hannay, "'How I These Studies Prize': The Countess of Pembroke and Elizabethan Science," in *Women, Science and Medicine, 1500–1700,* ed. Lynette Hunter and Sarah Hutton (Phoenix Mill, England: Sutton Publishing, 1997), 108–21.

8. Aubrey MS.92, 248.

9. M.W., *The Queens closet opened incomparable secrets in physick, chyrurgery, preserving, and candying &c. which were presented unto the queen by the most experienced persons of the times, many whereof were had in esteem when she pleased to descend to private recreations* (London: Nath. Brooke, 1659), 11–12.

10. Hannay, "How I These Studies Prize," 114.

11. John Taylor, *New discovery by sea,* C2v.

12. *ODNB,* entries on Raleigh and William Herbert.

13. To name just a few, Peter French, *John Dee: The World of an Elizabethan Magus* (London: Routledge and Kegan Paul), 1972, 62, 172, 179–80; and Deborah E. Harkness, *John Dee's Conversations with Angels: Cabala, Alchemy, and the End of Nature* (Cambridge: Cambridge University Press, 1999), 52.

14. On Dee and "the British Empire," see John Dee, *The Limits of the British Empire,* ed. Ken MacMillan with Jennifer Abeles (Westport, Ct: Praeger, 2004), 1–29. esp. 2, 11. See also William Sherman, *John Dee: The Politics of Reading and Writing in the English Renaissance* (Amherst: University of Massachusetts Press, 1995); and Christopher Hodgkins, *Reforming Empire: Protestant Colonialism and Conscience in British Literature* (Columbia: University of Missouri Press, 2002), 11–32. On Frobisher, see Robert Baldwin, "John Dee's Interest in the Application of Nautical Science, Mathematics, and Law to English Naval Affairs," in *John Dee: Interdisciplinary Studies in English Renaissance Thought,* ed. Stephen Clucas (Dordrecht, The Netherlands: Springer, 2006), 97, 103.

15. On Dee's library, see Frances Yates, *The Theatre of the World* (Chicago: University of Chicago Press, 1969), 1–44; and Sherman, *John Dee,* 29–52. On the Sidney-Herbert circle, see French, *John Dee,* 126–59; Baldwin, "John Dee's Interest," 97, 109–11.

16. Quinn, *Voyages,* 1:96–8, 170; 2:484.

17. Yates, *Theatre of the World,* 1–19; French, *John Dee,* 4–19; Sherman, *John Dee,* 12–26.

18. French, *John Dee,* 106.

19. Yates, *Theatre of the World,* 8, 22.

20. Baldwin, "John Dee's Interest," 105.

21. Quinn, *Voyages,* 1:96.

22. Aubrey, *Aubrey's Brief Lives,* 139; see also Hannay, "'How I These Studies Prize,'" 109.

23. Aubrey, *Aubrey's Brief Lives*, 254; *ODNB*, entry on Raleigh.

24. Aubrey, *Aubrey's Brief Lives*, 139; Britton, *"Natural History of Wiltshire" of John Aubrey*, 90.

25. *ODNB*, entry on John Davis.

26. Baldwin, "John Dee's Interest," 99, 118, 120.

27. Ibid., 111.

28. Ibid., 107, 111.

29. Yates, *Theatre of the World*, 20–41, and esp. 33.

30. Taylor, *new discouery by sea*, C2v.

31. Roy Strong, *The Renaissance Garden in England* (London: Thames and Hudson, 1979), 123.

32. Ibid., 120–22.

33. Allen G. Debus, "Mathematics and Nature in the Chemical Texts of the Renaissance," *Ambix* 20, no. 1 (February 1968): 11.

34. French, *John Dee*, 78.

35. Aubrey MS.92, 248.

36. *OED*, "plash," v.1.

37. "In the late 20th century the 17th Earl had a garden created in Wyatt's entrance forecourt, in memory of his father, the 16th Earl. This garden enclosed by pleached trees, with herbaceous plants around a central fountain, has done much to improve and soften the severity of the forecourt," http://en.wikipedia.org/wiki/Wilton_House.

38. Taylor, *New discouery by sea*, C2v; Aubrey MS.92, 248.

39. Taylor, *New discouery by sea*, C3.

40. Ibid.

41. Harkness, *John Dee's Conversations with Angels*, 196–201, esp. 96.

42. Aubrey MS.92, 248.

43. Hannay, "'How I These Studies Prize,'" 112.

44. See 235 in this collection.

45. George Herbert, *Outlandish Proverbs*, #114, in *The Works of George Herbert*, ed. F. E. Hutchinson (Oxford: Clarendon Press, 1941), 324. All subsequent quotations from Herbert's poetry in the text will be from this edition. See also "Astrology is true, but astrologers cannot find it," #641, 342. Thanks to Christopher Hodgkins for this reference.

46. Hutchinson, *Works of George Herbert*, 277–78.

47. Dee, *Limits of the British Empire*, 13–19.

48. Ibid., 18.

49. Yates, *Theatre of the World*, 22.

50. E. G. R. Taylor, *The Mathematical Practitioners of Tudor and Stuart England* (Cambridge: Cambridge University Press, 1968), 170.

51. Translated from the Latin by Richard Wilton in *The Complete Works in Verse and Prose of George Herbert*, ed. Rev. Alexander Grosart (London: Robson's and Sons, 1874), 3:414.

52. http://www.perseus.tufts.edu/cgi-bin/morphindex?lookup=mirabiles&.submit=Analyze+Form&lang=la&formentry=1.

53. Malcolmson, *Heart-Work*, 196.

54. Discussions of Herbert's use of alchemy in "The Elixir" include Hutchinson, *Works of George Herbert*, 541; C. A. Patrides in *The English Poems of George Herbert*, ed. C. A. Patrides (London: Dent, 1974), 207–8; Helen Vendler, *The Poetry of George Herbert* (Cambridge, MA: Harvard University Press, 1975), 269–73; and Clarence H. Miller, "Christ as the Philosopher's Stone in George Herbert's 'The Elixir,'" *Notes and Queries* 45, no. 1 (1998): 39–41.

55. *OED,* "penetralia."

56. Moffett, *Nobilis,* 75.

57. Hutchinson, *Works of George Herbert,* 505–6.

58. *OED,* "chemic," a. and n.

59. Hutchinson, *Works of George Herbert,* 261; http://www.faqs.org/health/bios/21/Jean-François-Fernel.html

60. See Christopher Hodgkins, " 'Yet I love thee': The 'Wayes of Learning' and 'Groveling Wit' in Herbert's 'The Pearl,' " *George Herbert Journal* 27 (2004/6): 24–31, particularly his discussion of the poem in terms of "an Augustinian Christianity which, particularly in its Calvinistic forms, has always had a lovers' quarrel with learning" (23).

61. Samuel Purchas, *Purchas His Pilgrimes,* Glasgow: James MacLehose and Sons, 1905–1907. pt. 2, chap. 6, 1466.

62. "But if the young Gallant think these Courses dull, and phlegmatick, where can he busie himself better, then in those new Plantations, and discoveryes, which are not only a noble, but also, as they may be handled, a religious imployment?" (Hutchinson, *Works of George Herbert,* 278). See Christopher Hodgkins's analysis of Herbert's mixed attitude toward empire: he was in the "tradition of Protestant imperial 'trusteeship' "—that is, he "was not flatly opposed to empire yet sought . . . to ameliorate its worst evils" (Hodgkins, *Reforming Empire,* 138; see also 153). However, I do not agree that Herbert's recommendation of employment cited above was a "concession" within Herbert's largely negative view on empire (see Hodgkins, *Reforming Empire,* 153 and note 21). For more on Herbert's engagement in the public world throughout his life, see Malcolmson, *Heart-Work,* chaps. 1 and 2; and Malcolmson, *George Herbert: A Literary Life* (Basingstoke, England: Palgrave Macmillan, 2004), ix–xiii, and especially 151 n. 5.

At the Porch to the Temple: Herbert's Progress to Bemerton

Clayton D. Lein

I WISH TO SUPPORT IZAAK WALTON IN CERTAIN ASPECTS OF HIS ACCOUNT of Herbert's pilgrimage from Westminster in 1624 to Bemerton in 1630. Almost anything can be (and has been) said about Herbert's path to the ministry in 1630, because we possess so little firm documentary evidence to work with. Nonetheless, a number of key points in Walton's narrative, I think, remain valid, and some previously unexplored circumstantial evidence can be brought to bear upon various claims that complicate our often too simple assessment of Herbert's actions. I personally believe that Herbert is at moments in this period virtually incoherent in his motivations. My larger perspective is that we should be careful not to dismiss Walton out of hand and should pay attention to Walton's hesitations, for he displays notable caution on certain points, more so than many later critics. Walton's caution on Herbert's move to the priesthood is particularly striking. Amy Charles's contrasting efforts to portray Herbert as persistently pursuing a sacred career, for example, is patently unconvincing.[1] Like others, I find this interpretation entirely inadequate to account for the huge gap between Herbert's move to the diaconate and his ordination and acceptance of the cure of Bemerton.

Walton possessed a sufficient number of well-informed sources to know that Herbert stalled in this period.[2] As Jeffrey Powers-Beck contends, there was almost certainly no single cause for the delay: illness almost certainly played a part; family responsibilities intervened (the care of his sister's children); so did literary responsibilities (work on volumes paying tribute to Bacon and to his mother); and, last but far from least, particularly if we follow Walton's and Christopher Hodgkins's positions, Herbert hesitated owing to serious doubts about his calling.[3] We can certainly be sympathetic to Herbert on all of these matters; nevertheless, in another mood, we may find it quite possible to regard some of these matters as willful

134

evasion—the seizing of occasions on Herbert's part to avoid making fundamental decisions. However we proceed, issues of motive and, as Walton insisted, patronage remain paramount, and we can recover some intriguing features about the contexts of Herbert's presumed patronage.

That Herbert's parliamentary career, quickly followed by the death of King James, provoked the essential crisis seems on the mark, yet assessing the relative importance of each is delicate. Walton ignored Herbert's parliamentary career, just as he ignored Herbert's involvement with figures deeply concerned with the Virginia Company and firmly opposed to the King. To emphasize such activities would have seriously threatened the royalist orientation of his biography, his crafted portrayal of church and state working in harmony in a nostalgically reimagined prerevolutionary past.[4] Nonetheless, the death of King James was almost certainly a decisive blow to Herbert's aspirations, for he had used his considerable skills to court James, at Cambridge and at Newmarket, and even in the aftermath of the tempestuous Parliament of 1624, he probably had a greater chance to advance with James than with Charles and Buckingham, whom he had possibly offended.[5]

Walton is almost certainly right, moreover, in describing Herbert's reaction to the crisis—the retreat from the court and Parliament. Walton's account, of course, insists on God's guiding hand:

> God, in whom there is an unseen Chain of Causes, did in a short time put an end to the lives of two of his most obliging and most powerful friends, *Lodowick* Duke of *Richmond,* and *James* Marquess of *Hamilton;* and not long after him, King *James* died also, and with them, all Mr. *Herbert's* Court-hopes: So that he presently betook himself to a Retreat from *London,* to a Friend in *Kent,* where he liv'd very privately, and was such a lover of solitariness, as was judg'd to impair his health, more then his Study had done.[6]

Walton alone records this final fact, and he is unlikely to be mistaken. Walton married, not long after this time, into a very well-connected Kentish family. His friendship with Sir Henry Wotton, a proud Kentishman, likewise began about this time; and before the end of this decade we find him engaged on behalf of Sir Edward Dering, another notable Kentish figure and parliamentarian, in the latter's attempts to secure the hand of a fabulously wealthy London widow.[7] Walton unquestionably recovered this fact from his extensive Kentish sources, sources he had used earlier on behalf of his lives of Sir Henry and Richard Hooker. Herbert's retreat, moreover, was the first of a series of removals throughout the following half a dozen years—removals to Kent, Chelsea, Woodford, Dauntsey, Lavington, and finally Baynton House.[8]

Those retreats are, among other things, the signs of personal crisis and the crisis of patronage, and we need to examine the larger patterns carefully. Cristina Malcolmson, in particular, has done invaluable work on those larger patterns in the 1620s, stressing that the members of Herbert's extended family were his "most important patrons."[9] But that familial condition, in fact, is more complicated than Malcolmson indicates. Walton's insistence on the collapse of Herbert's patronage at court about 1624–25 seems generally sound, although, in the absence of specific documentary evidence, there is considerable room for debate on the particulars and on the figures involved.[10] The well-known transformation of court patronage under King Charles and Laud commencing about 1625 has led to the common assumption that Herbert's lack of promotion was largely owing to the unacceptable character of his ideas and to his political allegiances.[11] That this was at least partly responsible for Herbert's situation seems to me virtually impossible to deny. Far more difficult to explain, however, is the noticeable lack of patronage on Herbert's behalf on the part of the very figures we might expect to advance him.

As Malcolmson insists, the members of Herbert's family were indeed his "most important patrons," but their responses to Herbert's clerical career are, to say the least, confusing. I begin with the earls of Pembroke. If we start at 1624, the earls of Pembroke made six presentations in Wiltshire through 1630, the last two (one of which is to Bemerton) quite possibly made by Philip Herbert, William's brother and successor. For whatever reason, Herbert was not high enough on William Herbert's list in either 1628 or 1629 to warrant ecclesiastical patronage. Instead, the earl presented Thomas Chafin, MA, to two separate Wiltshire livings at that time.[12] In February 1630 his presentation went to John Lee, BD.[13] Nor did Herbert receive the lucrative appointment in the gift of the earl to the Hospital of St. Nicholas in Salisbury. That appointment later in 1630 went to Matthew Nicholas, the son of the previous incumbent, at the concession of the earl.[14] Only with the ambiguous presentation to Bemerton late in the winter of 1630 did Herbert seem sufficiently important to one of the earls.

Nor was Herbert much in the eye of the King. Charles appointed others to livings in Wiltshire in 1625 and 1626, and evinced little interest in Herbert in 1629, when Matthew Nicolas, mentioned above, was preelected, "at the king's presentation," to the next canon residentiary's place at Salisbury Cathedral.[15] Equally revelatory, early in 1630, upon the translation of Herbert's predecessor, Walter Curle, to the bishopric of Bath and Wells, Charles presented Richard Steward, DCL, the future provost of Eton, to the cure of Mildenhall, one of Curle's two Wiltshire livings, Bemerton being the other, and Mildenhall was the more prestigious one. The bishop presented Steward to the vicarage of Aldbourne in the same period.[16] And even though the King had already appointed Steward to a prebend in Worcester Cathedral in July 1629, in mid-March 1630 Steward received further advancement (from the King as well as the bishop) to the prebend of Alton Borealis in Salisbury Cathedral.[17] Steward thus received three Wiltshire appointments in quick succession in early 1630.

Steward's case is particularly pertinent because in some important respects his career parallels Herbert's. Like Herbert, he was educated at Westminster School. From there Steward matriculated at Magdalen Hall, Oxford, from which he received his BA in 1612; elected fellow of All Souls in 1613, he advanced there to earn his MA, BCL, and finally his DCL in July 1624, previously having served as proctor.[18] In 1626, Steward resigned his fellowship to accept the living of Harrietsham, Kent, from his college, beginning his clerical career. Steward thus began his church career at roughly the same time as Herbert himself. Like Herbert, too, Steward held a prebend's place in another diocese. Steward's career, moreover, reveals what the fast track in ecclesiastical promotion looked like at this time. From a prebendary in Worcester Cathedral in 1629 he advanced to a prebend's place at Sarum the following year, to the positions of royal chaplain in 1633, dean of Chichester in 1634, clerk of the closet in 1636, and then prebend, by the King's gift, in Westminster Abbey in 1638, just to narrate his appointments in this brief period.[19]

The immediate point is that during the winter of 1629–30, the period in which the presentation to Bemerton must also have been considered, if not awarded, Charles was demonstrably not keen on advancing Herbert further in the upper ranks of the ecclesiastical establishment. In February 1630, Charles presented Edmund Mason, DD, to the deanery of Salisbury; and the following April, the very month in which Herbert received or accepted Bemerton, the King presented Roger Bates, DD, to the prebend of Lyme and Halstock there, a position customarily in the patronage of the Earl of Pembroke.[20] Then, little more than a year later, King Charles awarded the prebend of Beminster Secunda to Thomas Lushington, BD.[21] Herbert was clearly not on track for fast advancement, at either the local or national level. Steward's case demonstrates that possession of a prebend's place in another cathedral did not hinder advancement from the King at Salisbury. Furthermore, if we apply the argument characteristically advanced in the case of Herbert's presentation to Bemerton—that the King would be unlikely to make the appointment to Lyme and Halstock without consulting the earl—we again do not find Herbert at the top of any patron's agenda.[22]

Similar patterns emerge when we scour the records searching for other reasonable sources of patronage. Herbert's prominent friend Bishop Lancelot Andrewes made three Wiltshire presentations in this period: two in 1625, and one in 1626.[23] Bishop John Williams, Herbert's earliest ecclesiastical patron, doubtless in part through the influence of John Hacket, Herbert's childhood friend and a man much in Williams's presence and good graces, presented another man to one of his Wiltshire livings in February 1630.[24] Yet another candidate, Henry Danvers, the Earl of Danby, the elder brother of Herbert's stepfather, Sir John Danvers, made two presentations in 1627 and 1628, both to Edward Bridges, the curate of Dauntsey.[25] Nor was Herbert singled out for favor by John Davenant, the bishop of Salisbury, though, as several have argued, he was undoubtedly known to Herbert from their times at Cambridge.[26] Davenant independently awarded twelve prebends between 1626 and June 1632, not one to Herbert. Nor did he favor him with one of the cathedral "dignities." When the archdeaconry of Berkshire became vacant in 1631, he presented Edward Davenant, DD, to the office.[27] Neither the King nor the bishop was inclined to promote Herbert within the ranks of the cathedral.

One may quite reasonably quibble with Walton, then, about the nature and range of Herbert's patrons, but the evidence concerning patronage in Wiltshire convincingly documents that patronage was indeed slow in coming Herbert's way and that Herbert did not seem to rate highly in the eyes of any of his most likely patrons, *including* those within his own family and friendship networks. Neither ecclesiastical *nor* secular patrons set him on a swift track for advancement. The contrast with Donne, who upon taking orders was quickly offered fourteen benefices, is striking.[28] The conclusion seems inevitable: Either Herbert did indeed have marked difficulty finding patronage, as Walton contended, or, equally possible, Herbert was not actively seeking patronage until late, perhaps extremely late, in this puzzling period.

It thus seems to me that Walton assessed the general situation of Herbert's life in this period correctly. The 1620s were a volcanic period in Herbert's life. The year 1624 was a critical year, one that created huge problems for him regarding career and patronage. And, we must recognize that Herbert hedged his bets. Taking deacon's orders did cut off a parliamentary career, as Charles insists, but she errs badly when she insists that a clerical career was Herbert's only future.[29] Michael Schoenfeldt has pointed out that "[m]any men, in the ordinary course, entered the diaconate without any intention of becoming priests."[30] To such comments, we can add that we know from the letters of Donne's friend, George Garrard, among others, that such a move made Herbert eligible to head a number of charitable and educational institutions, institutions ranging from Charterhouse in Clerkenwell to Eton College and Winchester College.[31] Herbert may have regarded such possibilities favorably in this tumultuous period, and such a position may have suited Herbert well in light of his collegiate experience. Sir Francis Bacon's own bid for the provostship of Eton College in 1624 may have recommended such a future to his young friend, and each of these institutions gained a new leader in the period from 1624 to 1637.[32]

Yet issues of patronage and sense of purpose remain, beginning with Herbert's flight from Cambridge. Amy Charles, ever on the alert to diminish Herbert's secular interests, adroitly tries to gloss over this circumstance by presenting Herbert as a man reluctantly fulfilling family obligations to a powerful kinsman, William Herbert, the Earl of Pembroke.[33] This allows her to avoid forthrightly confronting the circumstance that that change of course also allowed Herbert to continue to postpone taking orders, as demanded by the statutes governing his college.[34] This hesitation had, moreover, telling consequences. As the example of Richard Steward demonstrates, it meant that Herbert simultaneously made himself unavailable for ecclesiastical patronage at the disposal of the college itself, patronage he utterly cut himself off from when he resigned his various posts in January 1628.[35]

No matter which set of facts one considers, Herbert seems paralyzed, perhaps stymied on occasion, but in general genuinely lost throughout much of this period. He will suddenly act boldly in one direction, only to retreat or change course shortly thereafter.[36] But he is not eager to enter the priesthood; nor does he seem to be actively courting patronage. Herbert's repeated retirements throughout this crucial period are a case in point. Such retreats, by removing himself from the circles of the great and the chief sites of political commingling, were most unlikely to help in the quest for patronage.[37]

The identity of Herbert's final patron, moreover, is genuinely vexed. Recent critics insist that Herbert was presented to the benefice of Bemerton by William Herbert, the third Earl of Pembroke.[38] We need to note, however, that this insistence flies in the face of the equally firm and *contemporary* testimony not only of Izaak Walton, but also of John Aubrey, a point universally swept under the table.[39] Aubrey, in fact, goes even farther than Walton and informs us that Herbert also served as Philip Herbert's chaplain.[40] We are thus tossed between competing authorities, but it is possible, I believe, to contextualize the issue. The larger point is that we need to pay attention not only to where Walton and Aubrey differ, but to where they agree. Aubrey, in this case, does not reveal his sources for his specific remarks, but we *can* recover much about Walton's own, and they are revealing.

Chief among Walton's informants in this particular context was George Morley, the bishop of Winchester when Walton penned Herbert's life. Walton, as is well known, was Morley's steward at the time of the Restoration, and he dedicated the *Lives* of 1670, which included the *Life of Herbert,* to Morley, claiming that Morley had a legitimate claim on all of the lives collected.[41] Crucial here is the knowledge that Morley was the godson of Anne Clifford, the Countess of Dorset and, shortly after Herbert's presentation to Bemerton, the Countess of Montgomery and Pembroke as well, following her marriage to Philip Herbert in June 1630.[42] Morley was particularly close to the countess in the early 1630s, when she was actively engaged in attempts to promote his own career, and it was undoubtedly through Morley that Walton obtained Herbert's letter to the countess, which he published in 1675.[43] Morley may well have arranged for Walton to speak directly with the countess; he undoubtedly consulted her on Walton's behalf.

Equally pertinent, one of Morley's oldest and "dearest" friends was John Earle, dean of Westminster in the early years of the Restoration and, at the time of his death, bishop of Salisbury. Earle lived with Philip Herbert, serving as his household chaplain throughout most of the 1630s, and in 1639 Philip presented him to the living of Bishopston in Wiltshire.[44] We also know from the biography that Walton spoke directly about Herbert to Humphrey Henchman, prebend and precentor at Salisbury Cathedral during Herbert's period at Bemerton, who participated in Herbert's ordination as priest. Walton quite likely spoke with Arthur Woodnoth as well, whom he directly associates with the presentation to Bemerton.[45] Walton was likewise the good friend of the church historian Thomas Fuller, who knew the Herbert family well, having served as chaplain to Sir John Danvers and his family in the 1650s.

He also served as prebend at Salisbury Cathedral in the early 1630s.[46]

Needless to say, this is a stellar collection of informants, and it is inconceivable to me, given this range of well-connected sources, that Aubrey and Walton are wrong about Philip Herbert playing a direct role in Herbert's presentation to Bemerton.[47] We should note, too, Walton's careful references to the two earls in his narrative. King James, Walton informs us, attracted to Herbert through his performances as university orator, summoned Herbert to Royston, "where after a Discourse with him, His Majesty declar'd to his Kinsman, the Earl of *Pembroke,* 'That he found the Orators learning and wisdom, much above his age or wit.'" The anecdote concerns William Herbert and is quite possible, since as lord chamberlain of the royal household then, William was in constant attendance upon the King.[48] Walton subsequently informs us that Magdalen Herbert herself "undertook to sollicit *William* Earl of *Pembroke* to become another" subscriber to Herbert's project to restore the church at Leighton Bromswold, toward which he then donated £50.[49] These precede Walton's description of the King's presentation of Bemerton: "but *Philip,* then Earl of *Pembroke* (for *William* was lately dead) requested the King to bestow it upon his kinsman *George Herbert.*"[50] These are careful designations, clearly distinguishing the contributions of the two earls, the kind of designations likely from members of the households.

The situation is, in fact, more complicated than commonly presented. William Herbert, the third earl, is now characteristically presented as the governing force behind many activities and successes of George's family.[51] William and Philip so often coordinated their activities, moreover, especially their political activities, that they seem as one; but there are subtle distinctions. Critics err technically when they claim that in 1624 George owed his seat in Parliament to the third earl.[52] In the largest sense this may be true; but technically Herbert owed his seat to Philip Herbert, the Earl of Montgomery, because Montgomery was a pocket borough in the control of the Herberts of Montgomery. We know, moreover, that Philip exerted himself strenuously through letters to influence elections in the early seventeenth century.[53] Hence, while there are good reasons to regard Edward and Henry Herbert as the clients, principally, of the third earl, this political distinction and the testimony of Aubrey and Walton suggest that George may have principally been the client of William's brother.[54]

This leads us to complications concerning the earls of Pembroke. Although Herbert finally found patronage from one of the earls, that eventuality may not have seemed particularly close in 1624. If, as several critics have hinted, the experience of the 1624 Parliament was such as to severely disillusion Herbert, to the extent, perhaps, of making such a career repulsive, he may well have alienated the third earl, his family's most powerful patron.[55] As Diana Benet has argued, in Parliament Herbert learned the price of political allegiance in a turbulent period. William Herbert had become firmly identified with the interests of the "Protestant faction," and he was engaged in a bitter struggle with Buckingham for influence. Herbert, as a client, had little chance of being his own man. Buckingham demanded subservient "vassals," and the earl seems to have been of the same mold.[56] He obviously needed every supporter he could muster. The defection of a kinsman in such circumstances may well have been resented, and Herbert's demonstrable lack of promotional support from that earl in the period from 1624 to 1630 may possibly be a sign of William's displeasure at Herbert's political withdrawal.

The other leading possibility is the very one Walton advanced: Herbert strongly resisted the movement toward ordination because of fierce personal doubts about his fitness for such a career. It may well have been such doubts that formed the basis of many conversations with Donne in the middle years of this decade. Herbert unquestionably knew of Donne's own tortuous path to the ministry, and may have found in Donne a mentor well versed in the labyrinthine and tortuous ways of the soul, a mentor with whom he could share his dilemmas.[57] Herbert received no appointment during this period, by this scenario, because he was far from resolved on taking orders and hence made no concerted effort to obtain patronage from the most likely patrons. Bishop Williams had been willing to lead Herbert to the porch of the temple, but he clearly did not feel compelled to provide further assistance, assistance such as he readily offered Herbert's friend John Hacket. At the very least, we should recognize the likely presence of some evasion and indecisiveness on Herbert's part to account for Williams's withdrawal. Christopher Hodgkins's proposal, noted above, that Herbert was waiting for a sign of God's favor is particularly enticing in these conditions.

But despite his hesitations, there may well have some movements behind the scenes that supported Herbert's choice. Biographers of Herbert commonly note Donne's intimacy with the family and his possible influence upon Herbert, but they have not considered an unexpected development in Donne's life precisely in this critical period. On July 6, 1626, Donne was chosen one of the governors of Charterhouse (or "Sutton's Hospital"), and he was a dedicated and energetic governor until the very end of his life.[58] The group that chose Donne included Archbishop Abbot; Thomas Coventry, lord keeper of the privy seal; George Mountain, bishop of London, Donne's friend; Sir Henry Martin, dean of Arches; and, significantly, William Herbert, the third Earl of Pembroke.[59] About eight months following his election, they were joined by Philip Herbert, then Earl of Montgomery, and Donne served with both men steadily until his death in early 1631.[60] Donne's friendship with both men, however, was more extensive than this suggests, for he also served with both men in the royal household. William Herbert had served as lord chamberlain since 1615. In 1626, Charles appointed William lord steward of the household, and allowed Philip Herbert to succeed to his brother's former place as lord chamberlain.[61] This service as lord chamberlain is particularly important, for the lord chamberlain had utter control of the rota of Lenten preachers. Donne's constant appearance on these lists is thus a major sign of his good standing in the eyes of both brothers.[62]

Donne's intimacy with Magdalen Herbert, Sir John Danvers, and George Herbert himself makes it likely that he was aware of Herbert's final movements toward the priesthood. He, along with Anne Clifford, thus may well be a figure who suggested to William and Philip that they should support their kinsman in his decision to enter the priesthood.[63] Whether Philip made the presentation in accordance with his brother's wishes or independently, overriding his brother's hesitations, remains unknown, but that Philip is the figure technically responsible at the very least for the presentation is made virtually certain not only by Walton's informed testimony, but by Aubrey's account, for Aubrey distinctly calls Philip "Lord Chamberlayn" and indicates that he found a record of the presentation in his name "[i]n the records of the Tower."[64]

There remain the actual conditions of Herbert's acceptance of a benefice, a decision that noticeably startled and puzzled his contemporaries. Barnabas Oley, recounting Herbert's academic honors and the wayward path of his career, confides, "*[P]robably he might, I have heard (as other Orators) have had a Secretary of States place.*"[65] The critical dimension of the movement of Herbert to Bemerton *is* its obscurity and ambiguous remuneration. Barnabas Oley was honest enough, despite his deep admiration for Herbert, to foreground the matter: "*And for our Authour* (The sweet singer of the Temple) *though he was one of the most prudent and accomplish'd men of his time, I have heard sober men censure him as a man that did not manage his brave parts to his best advantage and preferment, but lost himself* in an humble way; *That was the phrase, I well remember it.*"[66]

Critics of Herbert often moderate, mitigate, at times even ignore, the lowly condition of Bemerton as a clerical appointment; but the fact remains that it was not regarded as an appropriate living for one of Herbert's heritage, training, and talents. Oley addressed the issue because he knew it was a matter of acute interest.[67] John Gauden confronted similar problems when assessing the life of Richard Hooker. Confessing that Hooker "was some time in hewing and polishing," he found it necessary in all honesty to admit that Hooker's career "seemed not to have been to any great *conspicuity* or *expectance,* while he continued in the *Colledge,* if we may take an *estimate* of the opinion had of him by the first *offer of preferment,* or rather imployment, made to him, yea and accepted by him, as to those small obscure livings; one of which was first given him by the Colledge, and *leaving* that, another was conferred on him by some private Patron, each of them being though *competent* entertainments, even for Mr. *Hookers plainness and simplicity of living,* at least they were better then some Fellowships of that Colledge." Gauden's further commentary on Hooker is especially informative. Showcasing Hooker's goodness, he contends, "Nor did the good man [Hooker] disdain either the one or the other (when he left the first:) And this not out of covetousness or *ambition,* alas there was no such bait or temptation in either."[68]

This is the larger context for Walton's adroit handling of the presentation to the living. Walton has Philip Herbert urge the King to "bestow it upon his kinsman *George Herbert;* and the King said, *Most willingly to Mr.* Herbert, *if it be worth his acceptance.*"[69] As gently and imaginatively as possible, Walton conveys that the King himself doubted the "worthiness" of the offer for a man of Herbert's lineage and qualifications, but let the decision remain in Herbert's hands. We can manufacture excuses and explanations, but the fact remains that Herbert's contemporaries were far from impressed with his decision. And Gauden's precise perspective is worth further elaboration: as Ronald Cooley has pointed out, the clerical order was becoming more professional in Herbert's time and perforce more competitive. Gauden's comments inform us as to how a clerical career would be evaluated: an estimation of the likely future of a cleric could be obtained by examining the first offer of preferment made to him, or, a slight modification, the first "entertainment" accepted by him. The collective contemporary reaction is also consistent: Herbert's contemporaries either evinced marked reservations about the suitability of Herbert's choice, or strongly disapproved of it. John Aubrey certainly knew the region about Salisbury well. His tart description of Bemerton—"a pittifull little chappell of ease to Foughelston"—reveals a parallel contemporary lay opinion.[70]

Oley and Gauden, moreover, knew whereof they talked. Oley was Herbert's contemporary at Cambridge, where he likewise reached prominence within his college and within the university. A probationer fellow at Clare College in 1623, a senior fellow in 1627, and later yet, proctor, his first living, to which (like Steward and Earle) he was appointed by his college, was the comfortable living of Great Gransden, Huntingdonshire, which he held until his death. Gauden enjoyed nowhere near so prominent a career at Oxford, but his patron, Sir Francis Russell, presented him (as his first appointment) to the lucrative living of Chippenham. Gauden was chaplain at the time, moreover, to Sir Robert Rich, the Earl of Warwick, who within a year was instrumental in securing his appointment to the deanery of Bocking in Essex.[71] To men such as these, Herbert's acceptance of Bemerton could only have seemed strange and eccentric.

Amy Charles makes the best possible case for the appropriateness of Bemerton. Ignoring Aubrey and disputing the common description of Bemerton as "a poor country parish," she countered that it "was a good living, nearly double the value of the neighboring Wilton." She is wrong, as we have seen, and this is, moreover, a very narrow perspective.[72] She suppresses as much as possible the careerist perspective of Herbert's clerical contemporaries, substituting a partial—and, I stress, economic—perspective. The career of Herbert's Westminster and Trinity College friend, John Hacket, is more informative. Like Herbert a fellow and tutor at Trinity College, Hacket came to the notice of Lord Keeper Williams, who made him his chaplain in 1621; within a year Hacket was instituted to two livings. By 1623, he had become chaplain to King James, during which year Williams also promoted him to the lucrative prebend of Aylesbury in Lincoln Cathedral. The following year he was presented to the rich London living of St. Andrew's Holborn and also to that of Cheam in Surrey.[73] No matter which way we turn, we discover contemporaries who were equal to Herbert in training and status receiving more lucrative appointments. Donne, we recall, to provide further perspective, was offered fourteen rural benefices, all of which he refused. The London appointment he accepted, that at Lincoln's Inn, was considerably more prestigious than was Bemerton. Nick Page's ironic comment on Bemerton— "Charles may even have taken a wry pleasure in presenting such a tiny and unprepossessing living to the man who had once criticised his war plans"—has a wider extension.[74] What Herbert's contemporaries pondered was the fact that at the outset Herbert *accepted* positions involving ruined churches and decayed living quarters.

We should exercise decided caution, too, in assessing Herbert's psychology in accepting Bemerton. Few of us are free of conflicting aspirations; but to presume that Herbert accepted Bemerton with the *express* intent of climbing the ecclesiastical ladder is stretching the facts rather far. Nothing in Herbert's situation could have assured him of inevitable, or high, advancement. Within the immediate context of his own appointment, for example, Herbert must have known that his patron, Philip Herbert, had not enjoyed much success at promoting his candidates for ecclesiastical advancement, presumably because of opposition from William Laud.[75] Nor did Bemerton by itself provide any guarantee for advancement.

Bemerton enjoyed the services of a number of distinguished clerics in the sixteenth and seventeenth centuries, but the living did not itself provide the key to advancement. Of the fifteen clerics serving as rectors of Bemerton during the sixteenth and seventeenth centuries, only six enjoyed significant positions beyond Bemerton.[76] The majority did not advance. There are important exceptions on either side of Herbert's tenure: Nicholas Shaxton, William Bettes, Robert Hooper, Walter Curle, Thomas Lawrence, and Joseph Kelsey. Shaxton, Curle, and Lawrence I shall consider later. Of the remaining three, William Bettes, associated with the Earl of Pembroke, held a subdeacon prebend in the cathedral prior to obtaining the living of Bemerton, and held both until his death in 1535.[77] Robert Hooper, who received the living from the Earl of Pembroke in 1560, was elected master of Balliol College, Oxford, in 1563, and remained content with those positions until his death in 1571.[78] Joseph Kelsey, like Bettes, had already secured a prebend in Salisbury Cathedral before obtaining the living of Bemerton from a later Earl of Pembroke in 1681.[79] He had also obtained a presentation from the King for the right to a residentiary's place in 1680, but was not able to enjoy the presentation until 1695, when he became archdeacon of Salisbury and prebend of Grantham Australis.[80]

The lives of the three figures who did advance further in the church are more complicated. The career of Nicholas Shaxton does indeed establish that a rector of Bemerton could rise to a bishopric, but as we shall find with the other two figures considered here, his credentials were considerably different from Herbert's. A Cambridge man, Shaxton received his advanced degrees from Gonville Hall, including a bachelor's degree (1521), and later, a doctor of theology degree (1531). More important, he early became one of Anne Boleyn's "protégés," and in 1534 became a court preacher through the influence of Thomas Cranmer, by which time he had become Queen Anne's almoner.[81] He already held the living of Mattishall, Norfolk (as well as his Fellowship at Gonville Hall), when in 1533 he was presented to Bemerton and appointed treasurer of Salisbury Cathedral.[82] Appointments quickly followed to a canonry in St. Stephen's Chapel and finally, early in 1535, to the bishopric of Salisbury, both through the influence of the Queen.[83]

The other figure who rose to a bishopric was Herbert's predecessor, Walter Curle. Comparisons between Curle and Herbert, however, are worrisome, for their careers have little in common. Curle had been marked out for advancement in the church for some time. A fellow of Peterhouse, Cambridge, where he received his degree of doctor of divinity in 1612, Curle received two Wiltshire livings from the Earl of Pembroke in 1611, relinquishing his fellowship upon obtaining the subdeacon prebend of Lyme and Halstock from the King in 1615.[84] All of these livings were within the customary patronage of the Earl of Pembroke, so Curle was clearly a major client of William Herbert's patronage, to use Cristina Malcolmson's terms.[85] In 1619, William extended his patronage by presenting Curle to the comfortable living of Mildenhall (where he lived), to which, the following year, was added the living of Fugglestone with Bemerton, at the concession of the earl.[86] Curle likewise became a royal chaplain within this period, quite possibly as early as 1616, when he first appears in the list of Lenten preachers.[87] In 1622, King James presented him to the deanery of Lichfield Cathedral, which he held with the livings of both Mildenhall and Fugglestone with Bemerton.[88] In 1628 he was elected prolocutor of the lower house of Convocation, and in July that same year King Charles made him bishop of Rochester, promoting him little more than a year later to the bishopric of Bath and Wells.[89]

This leaves Thomas Lawrence, Herbert's successor. Lawrence matriculated from Balliol College in 1615, migrating to All Souls in 1618, where he became the colleague of Gilbert Sheldon and Brian Duppa, the latter one of the figures most active in the election of Laud to the chancellorship of the university in 1630.[90] In January 1629, a few weeks before he received his BD degree, he was appointed treasurer of Lichfield Cathedral, to which the prebend of Sawley was attached, a dignity he kept until his death.[91] At some point in the 1620s he became household chaplain to Philip Herbert, who managed through his post as lord chancellor to have him appointed as a royal chaplain.[92] Then in March 1633, Herbert, now Earl of Pembroke and Montgomery, granted Lawrence the living of Bemerton; four months later Lawrence received his DD.[93] Other appointments followed. In November 1637, Lawrence was elected master of Balliol College, and in 1638 the King appointed him Lady Margaret Professor of Divinity at the University of Oxford.[94]

What should strike us at once, as with the case of Richard Steward earlier, is the markedly greater degree of patronage received by each of these latter men compared to that garnered by Herbert himself. All of them, moreover, were firmly fixed at court as court preachers and royal chaplains, positions Herbert's contemporaries, Curle and Lawrence, held *before* obtaining the living of Bemerton.[95] (Curle and Lawrence were likewise close associates of Laud, a position Herbert is unlikely to have sought.)[96] In addition, Shaxton, Curle, and Lawrence *all* had secured positions as cathedral dignitaries, Shaxton and Lawrence as treasurers, Curle as a dean. Finally, all three men, the only rectors of Bemerton to advance far in the ecclesiastical establishment, held the highest degrees in divinity.

What kind of advancement, then, *if* he truly harbored hopes of great advancement, could Herbert reasonably have maintained? Here the careers of Shaxton, Curle, and Lawrence are instructive. First, Herbert would have needed to find occasions to preach at court and then to become a royal chaplain, which increasingly meant currying the favor of William Laud.[97] Herbert would also necessarily have had to obtain a higher degree in divinity. Residentiary canons, deans, and royal chaplains almost universally held doctorates in divinity.[98] Without such credentials, the most Herbert could reasonably aspire to would be a richer benefice and a richer prebend's place. The overall conclusion seems inevitable: Herbert knowingly sold himself short. No one concerned with his career in a legitimate material sense would have advised such a choice.

Though we cannot answer as many questions concerning Herbert's "years in the wilderness" as we might like, then, we *can* perhaps put parameters on certain speculations. Herbert's long pilgrimage to Bemerton began with his retreat to his friend in Kent. From that point, there was either an acute crisis in patronage *or* Herbert did not truly decide to enter the priesthood until very late in this period. Even then, he received the barest nod of patronage, as his contemporaries were quick to perceive. The choice, however sound for his soul, undeniably involved serious self-effacement.

NOTES

1. Long before Amy Charles's biography, in response to the interpretation of Herbert by Joseph Summers David Novarr had stressed the difficulty of an overly religious interpretation of Herbert's early life: "[Summers's] treatment of Herbert as an Elizabethan idealist who would be both statesman and divine seems satisfactory until we ask why Herbert felt it essential to press so exclusively and so long for earthly preferment. It would seem that Herbert envisioned himself as a statesman with religious interests rather than as a divine who might wield civil influence." Novarr, *The Making of Walton's "Lives"* (Ithaca, NY: Cornell University Press, 1958), 354 n. 166.

2. Walton stressed that "very many" of Herbert's friends "have been mine." Izaak Walton, *The Lives of John Donne, Sir Henry Wotton, Richard Hooker, George Herbert, and Robert Sanderson,* ed. George Saintsbury (1927; reprint, London: Oxford University Press, 1966), 259.

3. "There was no single event which determined Herbert's retreat to the rural parish of Bemerton in 1630." Jeffery Powers-Beck, *Writing the Flesh: The Herbert Family Dialogue* (Pittsburgh, PA: Duquesne University Press, 1998), 220. Walton stressed Herbert's spiritual conflicts and a "sharp *Quotidian Ague*" afflicting Herbert in his thirty-fourth year (Walton, *Lives,* 277, 284). For the other matters see: Amy M. Charles, *A Life of George Herbert* (Ithaca, NY: Cornell University Press, 1977), 104, 111–12, 121, 131–34; Christopher Hodgkins, *Authority, Church, and Society in George Herbert: Return to the Middle Way* (Columbia: University of Missouri Press, 1993), esp. 127–48; and Cristina Malcolmson, *George Herbert: A Literary Life* (Basingstoke, England: Palgrave Macmillan, 2004), x–xi.

4. To emphasize Herbert's parliamentary career would have meant emphasizing Herbert's clientage to William Herbert, the third Earl of Pembroke, who led a parliamentary opposition to Buckingham and the king at this point (*Oxford Dictionary of National Biography,* hereafter cited as ODNB. s.v. "William Herbert."

5. Both Amy Charles and Cristina Malcolmson discuss Herbert's speech in praise of peace made in welcoming Prince Charles to Cambridge, with the prince still angry after the failure of the Spanish Match in 1624. Charles, *Life of George Herbert,* 100; yet see Malcolmson, *George Herbert,* 464–8.

6. Walton, *Lives,* 276–77.

7. For Walton's marriage to Rachel Cranmer, see Novarr, *Making,* 228–29; for his association with Sir Edward Dering, see especially, *Proceedings, Principally in the County of Kent, in Connection with the Parliaments Called in 1640,* ed. Lambert B. Larking, Camden Society, o.s., 80 (London: Camden Society 1862): xxii–xxix. Herbert's friendships with Kentish figures are not well known, but among them were with Sir Edwin Sandys, who served with Danvers, Ferrar, and Herbert in the 1624 Parliament (see note 10 below), and with Sir Robert Filmer, presumably Herbert's intimate from his childhood days in Westminster, who owned estates in Kent. Michael C. Schoenfeldt, *Prayer and Power: George Herbert and Renaissance Courtship* (Chicago: University of Chicago Press, 1991), 2, citing Bodleian Library, Tanner MS 233.

8. Charles, *Life of George Herbert,* 118–20, 130–32, 136–38, 143–45.

9. Cristina Malcolmson, *Heart-Work: George Herbert and the Protestant Ethic* (Stanford, CA: Stanford University Press, 1999), 6–7, 13, 15–25, 52–57. See, too, Powers-Beck, *Writing the Flesh,* esp. 13–18, 157.

10. Walton is almost certainly correct in naming Lodowick, the Duke of Rich-

mond, and James, the Marquess of Hamilton, as "two of [Herbert's] most obliging and most powerful friends" in this period (*Lives*, 276), although Charles casts some doubt upon the issue by calling them Herbert's "supposed patrons" (*Life of George Herbert*, 106). The marquess served with Herbert's stepfather, Sir John Danvers, on the Council of the Virginia Company, and was a close friend of Nicholas Ferrar, who likewise served on the council and served with Herbert in the Parliament of 1624. The marquess and the Earl of Pembroke staunchly defended the company in the Privy Council, and upon learning of Ferrar's becoming a deacon, the marquess immediately offered him preferment. P. Peckard, *Memoirs of the Life of Mr. Nicholas Ferrar* (Cambridge: J. Archdeacon, 1790), 115, 120–26, 130–32, 147–49, and 176, where he calls the marquess, Pembroke, and Sir Edwin Sandys Ferrar's "constant friends." The later contribution of the Duchess of Lennox toward Herbert's restoration of the church at Leighton Bromswold likewise argues for steady family associations (Charles, *Life of George Herbert*, 152). These associations were indeed powerful: in 1623 the marquess, in Chamberlain's opinion, belonged to the "junta for foreign affairs"; and the Duke of Lennox and the marquess both served with the Earl of Pembroke in the period on the Foreign Committee, associations suggesting the secular nature of Herbert's interests. Michael Van Cleave Alexander, *Charles I's Lord Treasurer: Sir Richard Weston, Earl of Portland (1577–1635)* (Chapel Hill: University of North Carolina Press, 1975), 49, 51.

11. Malcolmson, noting that previous scholars had stressed Herbert's ideas, quite properly stressed that Herbert's political alignments would have been equally significant (Malcolmson, *Heart-Work*, 6, 47, 230 n. 62).

12. Thomas Phillipps, *Institutiones Clericorum in Comitatu Wiltoniae, Ab Anno 1297, Ad Annum 1810* (Privately printed, 1825), pt. 2; 12, 14–16; Barrie Williams, ed., *The Subscription Book of Bishops Tounson and Davenant, 1620–40*, Wiltshire Record Society 32 (Devizes: Wiltshire Record Society, 1977), 41 (correcting Phillipps's dates). Chafin was probably William Herbert's chaplain, for he preached the earl's funeral sermon, "The Just Man's Memoriall," in April 1630. Nicholas Tyacke, *Anti-Calvinists: The Rise of English Arminianism, c. 1590–1640* (Oxford: Clarendon Press, 1987), 188.

13. Phillipps, *Institutiones*, pt. 2, 15; Williams, *Subscription Book*, 22 (correcting Phillipps's dates). Lee had received the living of East Wylie from William Herbert in 1619 (Phillipps, *Institutiones*, pt. 2, 10). In 1616, Lee had been collated to the prebend of Alton Australis by Bishop Robert Abbot; Archbishop George Abbot then advanced him to the dignity of treasurer of Salisbury "as his option" in 1624. John Le Neve, *Fasti Ecclesiae Anglicanae, 1541–1857*, vol. 6, *Salisbury Diocese*, ed. Joyce M. Horn (London: University of London Press, 1986), 2, 20, 12. He thus seems to have been a figure favored by the "Protestant alliance" between Abbot and the earl in this period.

14. Phillipps, *Institutiones*, pt. 2: 15. Nicholas was well established in Salisbury, having been advanced to the prebend of Gillingham Minor by the bishop in February 1628. Williams, *Subscription Book*, 16; Le Neve, *Fasti: Salisbury*, ed. Horn, 43–44.

15. Phillipps, *Institutiones*, pt. 2, 13; Le Neve, *Fasti: Salisbury*, ed. Horn, 98. Nicholas thus received three appointments in Salisbury within a two-year period.

16. *ODNB*, s.v. "Richard Steward"; Williams, *Subscription Book*, 32, 38. Amy Charles obscures various financial relationships. Curle first received the livings of Wilton St. Mary with Bulbridge from the Earl of Pembroke in 1611. It is difficult to calculate the value of the livings completely, but the living of Wilton alone was

worth £160 and with Bulbridge the appointments were likely to be near £200 in the early seventeenth century. John Lloyd, *Thesaurus Ecclesiasticus: An Improved Edition of the "Liber Valorum"* (London: T.N. Longman, 1796), 318. The following year the earl granted Curle the rectory of Ditchampton (worth at least £10), and in 1619 he favored Curle with the additional living of Mildenhall, worth £140, which he held with the earlier livings (315, 318). In 1620, Curle exchanged the livings of Wilton and Bulbridge for those of Fugglestone and Bemerton, worth £200 (318), retaining the living of Mildenhall. To these livings, Curle could add income from the prebend of Lyme and Halstock, in the gift of the earl, and from the deanery of Lichfield Cathedral (1622), the latter worth about £40 (155). At no point was Herbert offered like earnings. Compare Charles, *Life of George Herbert*, 143, 148. Curle lived at Mildenhall, moreover, where the rectory was in good repair. The rectory of Bemerton was in need of substantial repair at the time of Herbert's acceptance of the living (Walton, *Lives*, 291).

17. The bishop and the King thus worked together consistently in 1629 and 1630 on Steward's behalf (*ODNB*, s.v. "Steward"; Williams, *Subscription Book*, 47). Steward was collated to the prebend on March 18, 1630. William Henry Jones, *Fasti Ecclesiae Sarisberiensis, or a Calendar of the Bishops, Deans, Archdeacons, and Members of the Cathedral Body at Salisbury, from the Earliest Times to the Present* (Salisbury: Brown and Co., 1879), 353; Le Neve, *Fasti: Salisbury*, ed. Horn, 22, 98. In addition to Mildenhall, Aldbourne was worth £170 and the prebend of Alton Borealis at least £16 (Lloyd, *Thesaurus Ecclesiasticus*, 308, 314).

18. *ODNB*, s.v. "Steward."

19. Ibid.; Le Neve, *Fasti Ecclesiae Anglicani, 1541–1857*, vol. 2, *Chichester Diocese*, ed. Joyce M. Horn (London: University of London Press, 1971), 7.

20. Le Neve, *Fasti: Salisbury*, ed. Horn, 6, 55. Mason was a royal chaplain (Williams, *Subscription Book*, 47), as was Bates, who was also rector of the fashionable London parish of St. Clement Danes, and may well have been a client of Wentworth, receiving assistance from Laud. Jones, *Fasti Ecclesiae Sarisberiensis*, 399; Kenneth Fincham, "William Laud and the Exercise of Caroline Ecclesiastical Patronage," *Journal of Ecclesiastical History* 51 (2000): 78 n. 37. The following year the King presented him to a prebend in Westminster Abbey, and Bates retained both prebends until his death. John Le Neve, *Fasti Ecclesiae Anglicanae, 1541–1857*, vol. 7; *Ely, Norwich, Westminster, and Worcester Dioceses*, ed. Joyce M. Horn (London: University of London Press, 1992), 17–18.

21. Le Neve, *Fasti: Salisbury*, ed. Horn, 27–28.

22. See Malcolmson, *George Herbert*, 101.

23. Williams, *Subscription Book*, 31, 33, 36.

24. Ibid., 47.

25. Ibid., 18.

26. On Herbert and Bishop Davenant, see especially Ronald W. Cooley, *Full of All Knowledg: George Herbert's "Country Parson" and Early Modern Social Discourse* (Toronto: University of Toronto Press, 2004), 29–34.

27. Le Neve, *Fasti: Salisbury*, ed. Horn, 15, 21–22, 34, 41–2, 43, 45, 49, 51, 53, 55, 60–61, 62–63, 87–88. As bishop, Davenant had the right of collation to all but one of the prebends not attached to one of the cathedral dignities (Jones, *Fasti Ecclesiae Sarisberiensis*, 210; Le Neve, Fasti: Salisbury, ed. Horn [ix]). Five of these appointments were made in 1628 and 1629.

28. Walton, *Lives*, 50.

29. See these comments by Charles: "[T]he ordination itself would . . . close off most routes of secular preferment"; "If Herbert did not realize that his ordination

would close the way to virtually all advancement except that within the church"; "he had permanently removed himself from the way of secular preferment." Amy M. Charles, "George Herbert, Deacon," *Modern Philology* 72 (1974/5): 273–74, 276.

30. A. L. Maycock, cited by Schoenfeldt, *Prayer and Power,* 36–37. See, too, Nick Page's firm dismissal of Amy Charles's thesis: "[Herbert's] acceptance of this sinecure [Llandinam] signals no serious intent to enter the ministry." Page, *George Herbert: A Portrait* (Tunbridge, England: Monarch, 1993), 104.

31. Garrard noted, in his early petitioning for the mastership of Charterhouse in 1635, "Perhaps my Lord's Grace loving the Church, and a Divine being first placed in it [Charterhouse], he will persuade the King to bestow it again upon a Divine: That Strictness in *Eaton* College hath been long dispensed with, though there the Provost hath *curam animarum.*" George Gerrad, *The Earl of Strafforde's Letters and Dispatches,* 2 vols. (Dublin: Robert Owen, 1740), 1:361.

32. Chamberlain reported in April 1623 that Bacon was one of a number of distinguished suitors for the provostship. Sir Henry Wotton did not obtain the grant until July 1624, so negotiations for the provostship continued throughout the period of Herbert's service in Parliament. *The Letters of John Chamberlain,* ed. Norman Egbert McClure, 2 vols. (1939; reprint, Westport, CT: Greenwood Press, 1979), 2:487, 532, 538, 543, 552, 571; Novarr, *Making,* 132.

33. Charles, *Life of George Herbert,* 104.

34. Page, *George Herbert,* 104.

35. Robert Creighton was officially elected public orator on January 28, 1627/8 (Charles, *Life of George Herbert,* 135–36; Malcolmson, *George Herbert,* 81). For a sampling of various livings in the gift of Trinity College, Cambridge, see Lloyd, *Thesaurus Ecclesiasticus,* 102–6, 163, 210, 226, 243.

36. Herbert's strenuous effort to rid himself of his recently acquired prebend in Lincoln Cathedral, an incident reported by Nicholas Ferrar and identified by Barnabas Oley, is a good case in point. Ferrar's testimony is that he "did earnestly endeavour the resignation of an Ecclesiasticall dignitie, which he was possessour of" (Novarr, *Making,* 328–30). His sudden decision to deliver an oration to Buckingham after years of neglecting the office is another. See Nick Page's tart assessment of the performance (*George Herbert,* 109–10). As Page suggests (111), Herbert "remained in a peculiar limbo of indecision."

37. Compare, by way of contrast, Donne's actions in the summer of 1621, when instead of leaving London as usual, he remained there "to keep himself in the eyes of those who might help him" in his pursuit of a deanery. David Novarr, *The Disinterred Muse: Donne's Texts and Contexts* (Ithaca, NY: Cornell University Press, 1980), 156–57.

38. See, especially, Charles, *Life of George Herbert,* 145–46; Malcomson, *George Herbert,* 101.

39. Walton, *Lives,* 287.

40. John Aubrey, *"Brief Lives," chiefly of Contemporaries, set down by John Aubrey, between the Years 1669 & 1696,* ed. Andrew Clark, 2 vols. (Oxford: Clarendon Press, 1898), 1:309.

41. Walton, *Lives,* 3–4. Walton's presentation copy of the volume to Morley survives and can be seen in the Sterling Library at the University of London.

42. In her will, the Countess of Pembroke termed Morley "my true frind and godsonne" and "my first godson" and bequeathed him £40 to buy a piece of plate in her memory. George C. Williamson, *Lady Anne Clifford, Countess of Dorset, Pembroke & Montgomery, 1590–1676: Her Life, Letters and Work,* 2nd ed. (1922;

reprint, Wakefield, England: S. R. Publishers, 1967), 306, 467–69. Philip Herbert succeeded his brother as Earl of Pembroke on April 10, 1630 (*ODNB*). Since they were married the following June 3, Philip was undoubtedly wooing Anne at the time of the presentation.

43. For Herbert's letter to the countess, see Izaak Walton, *The Lives of Dr. John Donne, Sir Henry Wotton, Mr. Richard Hooker, Mr. George Herbert and Robert Sanderson,* 4th ed. (London: Richard Marriot, 1675), 347. I will deal with Morley and Lady Anne at a later date in my article, "The Early Life of George Morley, Bishop of Winchester," now in preparation.

44. Morley regarded Earle as his "dearest friend," and they "kept a constant friendship for above forty years." Anthony Wood, *Athenae Oxonienses,* 3rd ed. (1813–20; reprint, Hildesheim: Georg Olms, 1969), 4:151–52. The two were contemporaries at Christ Church College (Earle subsequently migrated to Merton College); both were great intimates with Lord Falkland at Great Tew; and, while in exile during the Interregnum, the two had lived together for a considerable period (Wood, *Athenae Oxonienses; ODNB,* s.v.v. "Earle," "Morley"). For Earle as Philip Herbert's chaplain and the presentation to the living of Bishopston, worth over £300 per year, see *ODNB,* s.v. "Earle"; Phillipps, *Institutiones,* pt. 2, 19; Lloyd, *Thesaurus Ecclesiasticus,* 311. Earle's relationships with the earls of Pembroke are not entirely clear, but he wrote a poem lamenting the death of the third earl, and he became his brother's chaplain sometime between 1630 and 1631. From that time on, he is seen as living with Pembroke at Wilton and Westminster, since as Pembroke's "chaplain in the house," Earle "was therefore entitled to a lodging at court." Wood, *Athenae Oxonienses,* 3:716; *ODNB,* s.v. "Earle"; J. S. Darwin, "The Life of John Earle" (BL thesis, Oxford University, 1963), 72–82.

45. "Dr. *Humphrey Hinchman,* now Lord Bishop of *London* (who does not mention him, but with some veneration for his life and excellent learning) tells me" (Walton, *Lives,* 293). As precentor, Henchman probably led the "singing men of Sarum," who Aubrey noted, led the burial service for Herbert (Aubrey, *"Brief Lives",* ed. Clark, 1:309–10). His house in the Close may have been one of the sites for the music making about which Walton is so informative. On Woodnoth, see Novarr, who finds it "quite likely" that Walton talked to Woodnoth before the outbreak of the English Civil War (Noverr, *Making,* 307–8, 331–33), and Charles, *Life of George Herbert,* 125, 129, 147, 153, 167–68, 202–3.

46. Charles (*Life of George Herbert,* 203) incorrectly stated that there was "no evidence that [Walton] was in touch" with Fuller. However, Fuller proclaimed Walton as his "worthy friend" as early as 1655, when he also praised Walton's lives of Donne and Wotton. Thomas Fuller, *The Church History of Britain,* ed. J. S. Brewer, 6 vols. (1845; reprint, Farnborough, England: Gregg International Publishers, 1970), 2:455, 5:566. Musical himself, Fuller may well have met Herbert. He was collated to the prebend of Netherbury in Ecclesia in June 1631 (Le Neve, *Fasti: Salisbury,* ed. Horn, 63).

47. This is even more the case when one recognizes that the easiest thing for Walton to do would have been to omit Herbert's name, since naming Philip Herbert meant associating Herbert with a major rebel against the King during the civil wars.

48. Walton, *Lives,* 273, also 271. William became lord chamberlain in 1615 (*ODNB,* s.v. "William Herbert").

49. Walton, *Lives,* 279.

50. Ibid., 287.

51. See, especially, Powers-Beck, *Writing the Flesh,* 15, 99, 177; Malcolmson, *Heart-Work,* 6–7, 15–25, 226–27.

52. Malcolmson, *Heart-Work,* 17–18, 21.

53. J. E. Neale, "Three Elizabethan Elections," *English Historical Review* 46 (1931): 228, who notes (230) that elections were often held in Montgomery Castle. Violet A. Rowe discusses a letter in 1625 from Philip as Earl of Montgomery to a borough, "angry at the neglect of the corporation to elect *his* nominee." Rowe, "The Influence of the Earls of Pembroke on Parliamentary Elections, 1625–41," *English Historical Journal* 50 (1935): esp. 245, 250; italics mine.

54. Although Jeffrey Powers-Beck stresses the role of William Herbert in promoting the career of George's brother, Henry, it is significant that Richard Dutton also finds strong evidence of the patronage of Philip Herbert. *ODNB,* s.v. "Henry Herbert"; Richard Dutton, *Mastering the Revels: The Regulation and Censorship of English Renaissance Drama* (Iowa City: University of Iowa Press, 1991), 227, 247–48.

55. See, for example, Joseph Summers, *George Herbert: His Religion & Art* (Cambridge, MA: Harvard University Press, 1968), 42–44. There is a provocative coincidence of dates. The dispensation from the archbishop of Canterbury allowing Herbert to be ordained immediately as a deacon is dated the day following the original date (November 2) set by King James for the second session of the 1624 Parliament. See Alexander, *Charles I's Lord Treasurer,* 53–63, 235 n. 69, for a brief history of the session and the reasons for the repeated postponement of the second session. Herbert does seem to be acting symbolically and precipitously to cut off further parliamentary engagement. He does not want to wait a full year to become deacon, as legally required.

56. Malcolmson, *Heart-Work,* 229 n. 43. I am in substantial agreement here with the perspective of Diana Benet, "Herbert's Experience of Politics and Patronage in 1624," *George Herbert Journal* 10 (1986–87): 36–37, 43.

57. Documentary evidence shows Donne and Herbert meeting at Chelsea during these years: see R. C. Bald, *John Donne: A Life* (Oxford: Clarendon Press, 1970), 474–76; Charles, *Life of George Herbert,* 118–19; Page, *George Herbert,* 108–9. It is tempting to imagine Donne encouraging Herbert to work out his reservations and doubts in verse, much as he did himself. On Herbert's friendship and literary interaction with Donne, see also *John Donne: The Divine Poems,* ed. Helen Gardner, 2nd ed. (Oxford: Clarendon Press, 1978), app. G; and Malcolmson, *George Herbert,* esp. 25–30.

58. Bald, *John Donne,* 424. Bald notes, in fact, that Donne's presence at the meeting of the governors on February 26, 1630/1 "was probably the last engagement away from home that he was able to keep" (528).

59. Bald discovered Donne's service as governor but was unable to examine the records directly. For a full account of Donne's service, see Robert C. Evans, "John Donne, Governor of Charterhouse," *John Donne Journal* 8 (1989): 133–50; Evans finds Donne "one of the most active and conscientious of all the Governors."

60. Evans records the members present at each meeting during Donne's tenure as governor ("John Donne, Governor," 135 and passim).

61. *ODNB,* s.v. "William Herbert." For Donne and William Herbert, also see Novarr, *Disinterred Muse,* 154–55.

62. Fincham, "Laud and Caroline Ecclesiastical Patronage," 74–75.

63. Donne, we recall, preached before the King in February 1630 and was a member of the royal household in his capacity as one of the royal chaplains-in-ordinary throughout April (Bald, *John Donne,* 312, 546). It may not be irrelevant in this light, in terms of the total context at court, that Donne wrote his last poem, "An Hymne to the Saints, and to Marquesse Hamylton," upon the death of the

Marquess of Hamilton early in 1625 (Bald, *John Donne*, 466). Equally intriguing are the books chosen by the countess to appear in her "Great Picture." Two of the thirteen works by English writers in the upper shelf are by Donne, where we also find "Georg Herbertt his Devine Poems" (Williamson, *Lady Anne Clifford*, 498–500).

64. Aubrey, *"Brief Lives,"* ed. Clark, 1:309. Fincham notes that the lord chamberlain had the right of presentation to livings falling in the gift of the Crown worth over £20 a year ("Laud and Caroline Ecclesiastical Patronage," 70 n. 3).

65. Barnabas Oley, "A Prefatory View of the Life and Vertues of the Authour, and Excellencies of This Book," in *Herbert's Remains* (London: Timothy Garthwait, 1652), sig. [b8].

66. Ibid., sigs. [a11v–a12r].

67. Amy Charles, for example, attempts to overturn Walton's description of the "decayd" condition of the church and rectory (*Life of George Herbert*, 153–54). Joseph Summers's description of Herbert's repairs at Bemerton makes them seem ordinary and minimal (*George Herbert*, 35). Even Cristina Malcolmson's description of the living of Bemerton as simply "a less prestigious position" and as "a logical alternative" to Herbert significantly mitigates the ruinous condition of the church and rectory there (*Heart-Work*, 24). Oley's concern is revealed in the fact that he confided such information in a prefatory life he dedicated "to the *Clergy-Reader* of the same Time, and Rank, and Mind, and in like Condition with the Epistler" ("A Prefatory View," sig. a).

68. John Gauden, "The Life & Death of Mr. Richard Hooker," in *The Works of Mr. Richard Hooker* (London: Andrew Crook, 1662), 11.

69. Walton, *Lives*, 287.

70. Aubrey, *"Brief Lives,"* ed. Clark, 1:309. "Bemerton is certainly humble," writes Schoenfeldt, noting that the church would normally accommodate only thirty-six parishioners (*Prayer and Power*, 36, citing Amy Charles). Those viewing Bemerton today are likely to overlook the circumstances in 1630. Herbert wrote to his brother Henry in the autumn of 1630 that he was "beggarly," for he had expended £200 in building and had as yet not received anything from the living (Charles, *Life of George Herbert*, 154, accepting Hutchinson's date for the letter). We should recognize that this was an extraordinary sum for the times, that the great majority of clerics in Herbert's time could never have afforded such expenditures, and that only his wife's dowry and his inheritance from the gift of the manor of Ribbesford made such an outlay of funds possible. Major repairs were clearly pressing both for the church and for the rectory, and although Charles chastises Walton for never having seen the quarters that he declares to have been "fall'n down, or decayed" (Walton, *Lives*, 291), that charge cannot be directed at Aubrey, who fully supports Walton, affirming that "[t]he old house was *very* ruinous" (Aubrey, *"Brief Lives,"* ed. Clark, italics mine). Here, too, Charles ignores the shared testimony of Aubrey and Walton.

71. *ODNB,* s.v.v. "Barnabas Oley," "John Gauden."

72. Charles (*Life of George Herbert*, 138) based her comparison on the assessment of tenths, reporting the "real value" of Fugglestone and Bemerton, but not of Wilton St. Mary (Lloyd, *Thesaurus Ecclesiasticus*, iv, 318).

73. *ODNB,* s.v. "John Hacket." The prebend of Aylesbury was valued at £36 in 1535, compared to the value of £13. 14s. for Leighton Ecclesia. John Le Neve, *Fasti Ecclesiae Anglicanae, 1541–1857*, vol. 9; *Lincoln Diocese*, ed. Joyce M. Horn and David M. Smith (London: University of London Press, 1999), 34, 85–86. The "real value" of the cure of St. Andrew's Holborne was £600 (Lloyd, *Thesaurus Ecclesiasticus*, 220).

74. Page, *George Herbert,* 137.

75. Fincham, "Laud and Caroline Ecclesiastical Patronage," 72, 82.

76. The fifteen clerics are: Ralph Hethcote, Nicholas Shaxton, William Bettes, Thomas Cator, Richard Sowthe, Robert Hooper, William Lewys, Walter Curle, George Herbert, Thomas Lawrence, Robert Jutt, Stephen Jay, Uriam Banks, Joseph Kelsey, and John Norris.

77. Jones, *Fasti Ecclesiae Sarisberiensis,* 354–56.

78. Joseph Foster, *Alumni Oxonienses: The Members of the University of Oxford, 1500–1714,* 4 vols. (1891–92; reprint, Nendeln, Liechtenstein: Kraus Reprint, 1968), 2:742; John Jones, *Balliol College: A History,* 2nd ed. (Oxford: Oxford University Press, 1997), 60, app. C.

79. He was collated to the prebend's place in 1674: Phillipps, *Institutiones,* pt. 2, 37; Le Neve, *Fasti: Salisbury,* ed. Horn, 64.

80. Le Neve, *Fasti: Salisbury,* ed. Horn, 45, 17, 100, 49–50.

81. *ODNB,* s.v. "Shaxton."

82. Jones, *Fasti Ecclesiae Sarisberiensis,* 105, 346; John Venn and J. A. Venn, *Alumni Cantabrigienses,* Pt. 1, 4 vols. (Cambridge: Cambridge University Press, 1922), 4:54. Mattishall had a "clear yearly value" of £120 (Lloyd, *Thesaurus Ecclesiasticus,* 256).

83. *ODNB,* s.v. "Shaxton"; Jones, *Fasti Ecclesiae Sarisberiensis,* 105.

84. Phillipps, *Institutiones,* pt. 2, 6 (Wilton St. Mary with Bulbridge); Foster, *Alumni Oxonienses,* 1:363; *ODNB,* s.v. "Walter Curle"; Jones, *Fasti Ecclesiae Sarisberiensis,* 398–99; Le Neve, *Fasti: Salisbury,* ed. Horn, 55.

85. Phillipps, *Institutiones,* pt. 2, 6, 10–11; Malcolmson, *Heart-Work,* 17.

86. Phillipps, *Institutiones,* pt. 2, 10–11; *ODNB,* s.v. "Curle."

87. Curle continued to appear in the Lenten lists until 1631 (*ODNB*).

88. *ODNB,* s.v. "Curle"; John Le Neve, *Fasti Ecclesiae Anglicanae, 1541–1857,* vol. 10, *Coventry and Lichfield Diocese,* ed. Joyce M. Horn (London: University of London Press, 2003), 6.

89. *ODNB,* s.v. "Curle."

90. Foster, *Alumni Oxonienses,* 3:888. For Duppa and Laud's election, see especially Nicholas Tyacke, ed., *Seventeenth-Century Oxford,* Vol. 4 of *The History of the University of Oxford* (Oxford: Clarendon Press, 1997), 199. Laud was probably responsible for Duppa's elevation to the see of Chichester (Fincham, "Laud and Caroline Ecclesiastical Patronage," 79–80).

91. Le Neve, *Fasti: Coventry and Lichfield Diocese,* ed. Horn, 18; Foster, *Alumni Oxonienses,* 3:888.

92. That achievement was far from typical. According to Kenneth Fincham, Philip Herbert was able to promote only one other of his chaplains to a royal chaplaincy—William Brough ("Laud and Caroline Ecclesiastical Patronage," 82).

93. Williams, *Subscription Book,* 58; Foster, *Alumni Oxonienses,* 3:888.

94. Jones, *Balliol College,* 99, app. C.

95. On the importance of preaching at court, see especially Julian Davies, *The Caroline Captivity of the Church: Charles I and the Remoulding of Anglicanism, 1625–1641* (Oxford: Clarendon Press, 1992), 41–42, especially Davies' comments on Richard Steward's frequent preaching at court from 1627 to 1631 (42 and note).

96. Issues of Herbert's patronage have recently focused entirely upon the Herbert family, but the matter is more complex. Fincham notes that the only domestic chaplains of Philip Herbert to advance were "fervent Laudians" ("Laud and Caroline Ecclesiastical Patronage," 82). Laud likewise procured the bishopric of Roch-

ester for Curle in 1628, as well as his future appointments (Davies, *Caroline Captivity*, 41 n. 190; *ODNB*, s.v. "Curle"; Fincham, "Lord and Caroline Ecclesiastical Patronage," 80). Fincham similarly sees Curle and Lawrence as Laud's "close allies" in another context (in Tyacke, *Seventeenth-Century Oxford*, 205, 208–10).

97. Joseph Summers, for one, suggests that Herbert "abandoned his hope for great place in civil affairs" after 1626 (*George Herbert*, 37), and Herbert's confession in "Submission" that "Perhaps great places and thy praise / Do not so well agree" registers significant doubt about the combination of devotion and high place. See, too, the careful observations of Christopher Hodgkins on this issue (*Authority*, 192–98, 202–5). Julian Davies writes that "Charles chose to prefer none but his chaplains in ordinary to higher ecclesiastical preferment" (*Caroline Captivity*, 39). See Fincham's very slight revision of this claim and his stress upon the considerably different situation under King James ("Laud and Caroline Ecclesiastical Patronage," 71–72).

98. Thomas Lawrence was "STB." at the time of his presentation to Bemerton and obtained his DD shortly thereafter (Williams, *Subscription Book*, 58); Kelsey was a bachelor of divinity (Le Neve, *Fasti: Salisbury*, ed. Horn, 64); Shaxton and Curle, the future bishops, had both earned a DD long before their appointments to Bemerton). All but one of those appointed canons residentiary at Salisbury from 1619 to the time of the civil wars held divinity degrees (Le Neve, *Fasti: Salisbury*, ed. Horn, 97–98). The sole exception was the son of a bishop of Worcester (Jones, *Fasti Ecclesiae Sarisberiensis*, 411).

The Country Parson's Flock:
George Herbert's Wiltshire Parish
John Chandler

FEW HERBERT SCHOLARS WOULD DENY THAT THE POET'S MINISTRY TO his parishioners at Bemerton during the last three years of his life was for him the culmination of his spiritual and pastoral journey; nor that his practical experience as rector of this Wiltshire parish to a great extent forms the backdrop to his prose manual, *The Country Parson*. It is somewhat surprising, therefore, that more interest has not been shown in the historical and topographical context in which Herbert was working and writing, and in the surviving local historical sources relevant to Bemerton around the period of his ministry.[1] This paper attempts to draw together some information, from a local historian's standpoint, about Herbert's parish—and the people who lived there.

The Wiltshire parish to which Herbert was instituted rector on April 26, 1630, and where he died on March 1, 1633, was known as Fugglestone with Bemerton. In fact, it included three communities (the third was Quidhampton), each with its own agricultural territory, and each with its linear village strung out along the ancient valley route between Salisbury and Wilton. (see figure 1).[2] In theory at least (though some may have managed to evade the list) a roll call survives of all adult males who were living in the parish in 1641/2, less than a decade after Herbert's death—forty-three in Fugglestone and Quidhampton together, and twenty-six in Bemerton. This is because all men were required to profess their support for the principles of the Church of England, and this "Protestation Return" survives and was published—many years ago—for the parish.[3] Multiplying this total, sixty-nine, by about three, to include women and children, gives a total population of about two hundred, perhaps split fairly evenly between the three villages. That round number, two hundred, was given again in the Compton Census, a return of religious allegiance about a generation later, in 1676, and it has been suggested that it referred to the total population of the parish.[4]

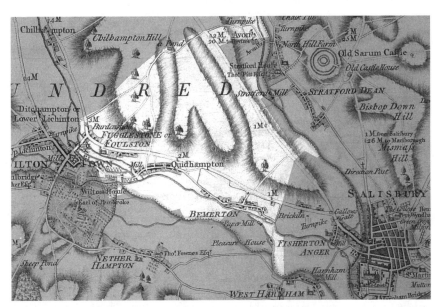

A facsimile section of a printed map of Wiltshire surveyed by John Andrews and Andrew Dury, first published in 1773, highlighted to show the approximate extent of George Herbert's parish, Fugglestone with Bemerton. The highlighted portion is adapted from John Chandler's photograph of the original (out of copyright) and was first published in *Sarum Chronicle* 6, 2006 (p. 31), copyright John Chandler.

Almost the whole parish belonged to, and was controlled through manorial courts, by one of two large landowners, and so most of these inhabitants were tenants of one or the other. In broad terms, the western half, Fugglestone and part of Quidhampton, belonged to the earls of Pembroke, of Wilton House, as successors to Wilton Abbey, the medieval owner. The eastern half, Bemerton and the rest of Quidhampton, had had many owners, but by about 1615 it had come entirely into the ownership of a family called Grobham, whose principal estate was at Great Wishford, farther up the Wylye valley in south Wiltshire. This manor was to stay with the Grob-hams (later Grobham Howe) for about two centuries, until about 1800 or a little later. When Herbert arrived in April 1630 both man-ors had new lords. Sir Richard Grobham had died in the previous July, and his whole estate, which included a portfolio of land all over Wiltshire, was inherited by his brother John Grobham.[5] Her-bert's kinsman, William Herbert, third Earl of Pembroke, had died even more recently, April 10, two weeks before the poet's institu-tion—he too was succeeded by a brother, Philip Herbert, who became the fourth earl. At about forty years of age, he was only a little older than the poet.[6]

So it was all change in 1630—two new landlords and a new rector. For any parish at around this time one might hope to find at least some documentary evidence. And for Herbert's there is the parish register, which would have been his responsibility.[7] During his incumbency it records fourteen baptisms, six marriages, and thirteen burials, though some parishioners who died in this period seem to have been omitted, or were buried elsewhere. There are also some twenty wills, between 1631 and 1647, nearly all of them, one assumes, of people the poet would have known personally.[8] Then there are court records, the minutes of business meetings held to run affairs in each manor, and, most importantly, a survey—a detailed written description—of all the tenancies held under the Wilton House manor (the western half of the parish), made in February 1632.[9] Another, briefer, survey (or extent), undated but a little earlier than Herbert's time, gives valuable information about farming in the Bemerton portion of the parish.[10] In addition, it is quite reasonable to extrapolate from records of rather earlier and later periods to draw conclusions about such things as topography, population, agriculture, and industry. An exhaustive study of a neighboring parish, Netherhampton, using Wilton estate records, has shown that there was a very considerable level of continuity there from one generation to the next.[11]

A few lines above the record of George Herbert's own burial, the parish register records that two tenant farmers, John Young and Richard Thring, were buried within little more than a week of each other, on April 8 and 17, 1631, respectively. Both left wills,[12] with inventories of their possessions taken soon after their deaths for probate purposes. Both described themselves as yeomen (small farmers) of Quidhampton.

Richard Thring, the later to die, was a widower, with two surviving sons, Richard and John (who took over the farm), and a daughter, Susan. Richard may have had a somewhat inflated view of his wealth, since in his will he left Susan £100, though as it turned out the total inheritance was assessed at £240. Susan, armed with this dowry, one assumes, went off and was married shortly afterward, and perhaps left the parish (since there do not seem to be any baptisms in the register attributable to her union). The sons, Richard and John, appear to have inherited an amalgamation of three virgates (or farming units of about twenty acres), since their father when he died was growing twenty acres of wheat, eighteen of barley, and three of oats and vetch (presumably another twenty acres or so was lying fallow, making about sixty acres in all). Some of their inheritance was out in the fields, shooting up now that spring had arrived, but there were also still stocks of barley and wheat in the barns and in a granary on staddle stones. There were eighty-six sheep, with sixteen lambs, four carthorses, four cows with two calves and two yearling bullocks, and four pigs. The younger Richard surrendered at least part of his interest in the farm a few years later, in 1638, but his brother John persevered, and began a new copyhold, in 1651.[13]

The farmhouse, a modest affair, was on two floors, with three rooms—the hall, the kitchen, and a bedroom—downstairs, and two more bedrooms and a wool loft upstairs. Altogether there were four beds—so one assumes that both sons and the daughter lived at home with their father. There were only two chairs, so at mealtimes the sons perhaps sat on the form, which is also listed. Other furnishings included two tables and a cupboard with two shelves.

John Young, the other casualty that April, was a married man, whose wife, and now widow, had the unusual name of Elflet, and there were two servants (by which they presumably meant farmworkers) living with them—these two had their own bedroom, but only one bed between them! After John died, Elflet lived on for another nine years, and she too left a will with probate inventory.[14] She had run the farm down a bit, it seems, as her estate was worth £127, down from £231 when her husband, John, had died. But then there were no surviving children, and her bequests were to various individuals. There is a whiff of George Herbert's caring country parson in her will. She asks that one of her appraisers (the valuers of her estate) be "[her] friend Hugh Chibnall, curate of Fugglestone." When John had died, he too had called on friends— "beloved friends," he called them—to witness his will and to act as appraisers. They were John Bacon and John Hillman, who both had interesting stories of their own.

John Hillman was the miller at Quidhampton, but it was not a corn mill.[15] His was a fulling mill, for the cleansing, felting, and finishing of cloth. The Salisbury area was still an important clothmaking center, though by now in decline, and the fulling mills dotted up and down the south Wiltshire rivers had been crucial to its prosperity. At Quidhampton the fulling mill was operating from about 1577 or earlier until it was finally destroyed during the agricultural laborers' revolt in 1830.[16] It stood on the river close to the present turning into the village from the Harnham main road. Hillman presumably employed staff, as in 1632 the will of John West, a fuller of Quidhampton, was proved.[17] In 1616 Hillman had been one of the "questmen," as they were known (churchwarden's assistants or sidemen), who had helped to draw up an account of the land and tithes that belonged to what would become Herbert's living.[18]

John Bacon, the other "beloved friend" who was to be an appraiser, was another small farmer in the parish, and by now something of a village patriarch. In his late seventies by 1631, his copyhold tenure dated back to 1575, fifty-six years before, when he was quite young.[19] Another named "life" on this copyhold was Margaret Elliott, a year older than John, and still alive in 1632, though widowed and known by her married surname of Forman. The parish registers are lost for the relevant years, but she surely must have married into the yeoman family of Forman, which in 1552 had produced Quidhampton's most famous son: the notorious astrologer, magician, and medical quack Dr. Simon Forman.[20] He had moved to Salisbury, then to London, fell in with Shakespeare and his circle, and become embroiled in scandals and lawsuits of various kinds. Margaret, seventy-nine in 1632, would have been Simon's exact contemporary, and it is likely, therefore, that her late husband had been one of his five brothers, and so she had been the colorful doctor's sister-in-law. Herbert would have heard of Forman's exploits and adventures (who hadn't?) and would doubtless have encountered many older parishioners, like Margaret, who remembered him from forty or more years before.

In "The Parson in Circuit" Herbert advises clergy to visit his parishioners on weekday afternoons, when they are "wallowing in the midst of their affairs." He goes on, "[W]herefore neither disdaineth he to enter into the poorest cottage, though he even creep into it, and though it smell never so loathsomely; for both God is there also, and those for whom God died." The probate inventories of people like John and Elflet Young, by no means the poorest cottagers, somehow enable us to creep in with Herbert's parson, find the sickly old man in his chamber within the hall, sitting up in his joined bedstead, wrapped in his feather bed, propped on a bolster, with coverlet green rug and mattress, his linen shirts over in a corner, a coffer, table, and two stools against the wall, and a fire burning. And when Elflet died, nine years after her husband, it was in the same room, now called the parlor, with much the same furniture around her. One recalls, in Walton's account, that Jane Herbert, George's wife, bought a pair of blankets to give to a poor widow in the parish—it would be pleasant to find the very blankets turning up in a probate inventory after the woman had died.

Just a month before Herbert took up his living, on March 12, 1630, a meeting was held of the manorial court in Bemerton.[21] This is interesting, because it relates, not to the Wilton estate part of the parish, but to the Grobham manor embracing Bemerton and part of Quidhampton. The Latin minutes of this meeting begin by listing all the farmers on the manor, eight freeholders (who would have sublet to tenants), four leaseholders, and ten copyholders (all of whom were probably hands-on farmers or, if not themselves, supervisors of employees or subtenants who were). There is a second list of the eight people who actually attended (the homage). The business dealt with several changes in tenancy, and then consideration was given to two requests from tenants. Robert Strugnell and the widow Katherine Scamell both needed wood to repair their barns. And both were given permission to cut down trees—three and two, respectively—on the land they tenanted, provided that they planted others in their place. Herbert was not the only person in Bemerton contemplating necessary repairs that spring, after the winter's ravages.

This 1630 meeting was recorded in a book that had seen service since 1595, and during the 1620s the minutes of one or two similar occasions were recorded each year. Little village tensions and gripes are played out in its pages, in curt Latin and eloquent English: Henry Bower the miller was presented in 1626, "for suffering his hoggs to go about the high ways and into the corn fields." Robert Smytten in 1623 took the law into his own hands by breaking down the pound to release his horses. He was made to pay one shilling to repair the damage but was pardoned the offense because the animals had been wrongfully impounded. James Jacobb, one of the principal farmers in Bemerton (occupying eight yardlands),[22] seems to have ridden roughshod over the proceedings more than once. In 1626 he kept sheep in the marsh when he should not, put mares on the common among the tenants' horses, dug a boundary ditch extending two feet onto his neighbor's land, and made an encroachment by extending his ploughland to the sheep down. It was time for the homage to beat the bounds, and settle such matters—which they did. But at the next court, in March 1627, we discover that they ran out of time and had not completed the job. So three days—Monday, Wednesday, and Friday—were set aside in Rogation Week "to view and bound out all the residue."

After 1630 there were no more meetings of the court for a few years (or if there were, the minutes were kept in a different book, which has been lost). Perhaps the new Grobham landlord decided that they were unnecessary. But the meetings resume in 1635, and standards seem to be slipping. The minutes begin in Latin, but soon the clerk lapses gratefully into English, "*in his verbis Anglorum se-*

quentur, videlicet." There are more changes in tenancies, fines for nonattendance, and more trees cut down for repairs; and clearly one tenant is planning to build a new house altogether, which will require the timber and planking from four trees. Everyone has to make sure that the fence in the marsh (part of the common meadow) is put into repair; arrangements are made too for managing the common sheep flock, including fines set if sheep or cattle stray onto the highway (except at sheertyme). The next year there are other problems—the tracks to Kingsmead and Oats Close need repairing; tenants have taken to keeping pigs on the common illegally and are fined. Judging by the names, the offenders are respectable members of society, so the fines are probably not punitive, but simply a way of collecting an unofficial rent for an activity not covered by commoners' rights. William Scammell is in trouble for not keeping his gate at the town's end in repair, and for neglecting a fence. These things mattered, of course, because everyone in the village would suffer if the stock got into their gardens through one person's negligence. The hayward, who is to be responsible for supervising taking the grass crop from the meadows, is appointed, and two other local worthies—Philip Stevens and John Best—are charged with organizing another beating of the bounds, for which they will be paid.

With a jolt we are back to George Herbert's concerns, though he was dead by the time that this particular perambulation was arranged. In his chapter, "The Parson's Condescending," he lists the four manifest advantages of processions: blessing of the fruits of the field; justice in preserving the bounds; the neighborliness of accompanying one another on the walk, and reconciling differences; and the opportunity to dole out poor relief. And who were Philip Stevens and John Best, the organizers of this event? As far back as 1616, twenty years before, they were the Bemerton churchwardens.[23] So these are the very men that Herbert was referring to when he wrote: "[T]he country parson doth often, both publicly and privately, instruct his churchwardens what a great charge lies upon them, and that indeed the whole order and discipline of the parish is put into their hands." And he was quite right. When trees were to be cut down for repairing houses, it was Philip Stevens who was to decide where their replacements were to be planted.

Such an office, Herbert decrees, was not to be vilified or debased by being cast on the lower rank of people—no indeed, both Stevens and Best were leaseholders, along with another man who attended the meetings, Edward Ward. He was a "questman" or sidesman, the churchwarden's deputy, but 1635 was his last meeting. He died in 1636 and left a will, in which he professed in simple piety the beliefs that Herbert had instilled or reinforced in him. His body was to be interred in Bemerton Church, and he left £1 to buy a pulpit cloth for the better adorning of the same church. St. Andrew's Church today is quite a plain building, but it has a spectacular and glorious modern altar cloth. Clearly this faithful worshipper wanted to do something to make his church special, just as its modern congregation has done, and as Herbert's manual itself advocated, in "The Parson's Church" (chap. 13): "that there be a fitting and sightly communion cloth of fine linen. . . ." Edward's considerable wealth enabled him to leave £100 each to his two daughters, to be paid them on their marriage (a dowry, in other words) but with the stipulation that they were "not to match or bestow themselves in marriage without the consent or good liking of their mother."[24]

All this came a little after Herbert had died, though during his lifetime Stevens, Best, and Ward, along with the curates, must have been Herbert's right-hand men, his trusted neighbors in Bemerton. But another record of a court meeting has survived from the Fugglestone and Quidhampton end of the poet's parish.[25] It took place in August 1633, a few months after he died, but one of the problems it addressed must have been dragging on for some time. In among the changes in tenancy, broken fences, and trees for mending (all in Latin) is a complaint—leveled against some of the leading small farmers, including John Bacon, whom we met earlier—that they had extremely dangerous hearths, and the fires were built up against the walls. This was causing great fear and concern on the part of their neighbors, and they were ordered to put matters right. Again we are back to Herbert's country parson, whose consideration of providence used the motif of fire—fire which unexpectedly overturns things, just when the farmer has safely gathered in his harvest. It was one of the stories—clearly a great worry in the minds of some of his parishioners—that he used to explain spiritual truths.

It may seem strange at first sight that it was the more affluent inhabitants who seemed to be taking risks, since they had the most to lose, but it was probably not their own homes that had the dangerous chimneys. It was probably those of the humble cottagers, their employees in what we would call tied cottages, about whose welfare Herbert is so concerned, but who at this date are largely absent from the records. Apart from their names—in the protestation rolls and the registers—we know almost nothing about them.

I want to introduce one more individual, like the churchwardens and the miller John Hillman a leaseholder (or tenant by indenture), in this case of the Wilton estate. His name was John Puxton, and he leased Fugglestone Farm. In fact, there were two John Puxtons, father and son, and they probably never resided in the parish, but installed tenants. John Puxton, Sr., lived in Salisbury and was an alderman, listed in a document of 1626 next to John Ivie, and alongside other city notables of the time, such as Henry Sherfield and Bartholomew Tookey.[26] A few months after this document (a list of ordinances) was signed, John Ivie became mayor of Salisbury, and during his mayoralty disaster struck, in the form of plague.

This was in spring 1627, just three years before Herbert came to Bemerton. Ivie, in recalling the terrible year, noted, "And as many persons of the city that had any friends in the country that would receive them into part of their houses or barns did fly as if it were out of an house on fire; insomuch they did load forth of goods and wares above three score carts a day until all of any ability were gone, and this in four days."[27] Puxton was doubtless part of this exodus (perhaps one of many who had sought refuge here and had risked exposing Herbert's parishioners to the plague). Although he had connections with various places around Salisbury, Fugglestone and Wilton were where much of Puxton's property lay. Any attempt at flight from the epidemic did him no good, however, as he died on April 10, 1627, and was succeeded by his son, John Puxton, Jr.[28] If we are to give credence to one of Walton's anecdotes, about the gentleman who used to walk into Salisbury with the poet, John Puxton, Jr., would fit the bill very well. Herbert is reported to have said to this man: "I do this (that is, ask about your faith) the rather because though you are not of my parish, yet I receive tithe from you by the hand of your tenant. . . ."

In the Wiltshire and Swindon Archives is a small, undated survey of Mr. Puxton's farm, as it was still described some years later.[29] Puxton had sold his lease of the farm to a Mr. Coker, and then it had been purchased by a Salisbury clothier, Thomas Cutler, probably in 1650, and he was responsible for making the survey. Cutler gave up the farm in 1677, passing the lease to his son, and died in 1684.[30] Cutler claims that, after letting the farm for an unspecified time, he "laid out £100 at least in setting up of hatches & in trenching [?] and drowninge the meadowes which are very much improved by it yeat not halfe soe much as they may bee." So it seems fairly clear that the water meadows in at least part of Herbert's parish (that belonging to the Earl of Pembroke's innovative Wilton estate) were not begun until sometime after 1650 and before 1677, long after his death. The court book for the other manor, described above, continues until 1639 without any mention of water meadows.

The history and operation of floated water meadows in south Wiltshire have received considerable scholarly attention in recent years,[31] and there can be little doubt that Herbert was aware of, and intrigued by, this technological innovation. His kinsman Rowland Vaughan had written a manual on the subject, dedicated to the Earl of Pembroke and published in 1610; water meadows had begun to be constructed along the south Wiltshire rivers Nadder and Wylye during the 1620s; and the poet himself seems to allude to the technique in poems such as "The Water-course."[32] For this reason, and because of a romantic notion like Sir Arthur Bryant's that associates Herbert with Bemerton's meadows,[33] it is perhaps worthwhile to emphasize that in Herbert's parish itself no evidence has so far come to light for the construction of water meadows during his lifetime.

Another common misapprehension concerns the nature of Bemerton as a "country" parish. Ronald Cooley has provided a valuable service in relating Herbert's experience of the countryside to the enclosure movement and the various agricultural regimes practiced in Wiltshire during the poet's sojourn.[34] The contrast between clayland north Wiltshire, an enclosed landscape where dairying predominated, and chalkland south Wiltshire, a country of open arable fields and sheep downland, has often been discussed, since its significance extended into the realms of social, religious, and cultural history.[35] Herbert, as Cooley notes, had experience of both south and north, "chalk and cheese," through his acquaintance with Dauntsey, Edington, and Bemerton. Dauntsey, in north Wiltshire, was certainly in the cheese country, but Edington (which Cooley brackets with Dauntsey) had far more of the character of the chalklands, with its extensive sheep runs on Salisbury Plain, and hillslope arable fields remaining open until 1842.[36] In many respects it was a more typical south Wiltshire parish than Bemerton.

Herbert's portrayal of the country parson, who preaches to country people, "thick, and heavy, and hard to raise to a point of zeal"—so that he must tell them stories, and for whom he must adopt "a slighter form of catechizing"—inclines the reader to assume that he is describing some isolated, backward community lost in the Wiltshire countryside. The impression is reinforced by Izaak Walton's anecdotes of what appear to be poor, ignorant rustics, stopping their plowing when they hear the church bell. This may be true of Dauntsey and Edington, but it does not fit seventeenth-century Bemerton.

Bemerton, or rather Fugglestone with Bemerton (the distinction is important), was a predominantly agricultural parish in Herbert's time, but it was not typical of south Wiltshire, for two reasons. First, because of its position close to the confluence of major rivers, with only a narrow spur of high ground between them, it possessed relatively little chalk downland; and the chalk spur that its territory straddled is here mantled by a loamy soil suitable for arable cultivation. The acreages devoted to arable and to rough sheep pasture were therefore quite disproportionate to those of the prevailing sheep-and-corn husbandry practiced throughout the chalkland parishes. These (including Edington) relied on intensively cultivated open arable fields, generally running up the valley sides, and extensive rough pasture for sheep on the downs beyond, the sheep being kept principally for folding on the fields in order to manure and so enrich them. But on the Wilton estate's Fugglestone Manor there were only 140 acres of downland, and at Quidhampton only 100 acres, far less than most of its neighbors farther upstream.[37]

The second atypical feature of Herbert's parish also relates to its position. Anyone who has made the pilgrimage will be aware that Bemerton today is suburban, rather than rural; its historic settlements and much of its farmland are engulfed by modern Salisbury. So familiar to us is suburban expansion that we make allowance for it, and imagine that in Herbert's day it was out in the country, separated from Salisbury by Fisherton, which was itself semirural. But Herbert's parish was not Bemerton, it was Fugglestone with Bemerton, and Fugglestone was very much a suburb—not of Salisbury, but of another town: its neighbor and historical rival, Wilton. Fugglestone extended right up to and embraced part of urban Wilton, several of its smaller suburbs, the site of its famous sheep fair, and the approach to Wilton House and some of what is now its park.[38] Looking the other way, the development of the parish was influenced by its proximity to Salisbury, still at this period one of the largest and most influential cities in southern England. The fulling mill has already been noted. A little farther toward Salisbury there were old and important paper mills (just over the parish boundary, but right next to Bemerton), and there are references to tentering racks (used for drying cloth in the woollen industry) and gravel pits. Salisbury gentry such as Puxton, businessmen such as Cutler, and intellectuals such as Forman had interests in or connections with the parish. Traffic was undoubtedly heavy (relatively speaking, in seventeenth-century terms) along the westward roads out of Salisbury through the parish, especially on market days. What is now, or should be, a country lane linking the three village streets was then a thoroughfare between major nearby towns. This was no sequestered downland parish.

And Salisbury itself, in Herbert's day, was not some genteel, Trollopean ideal of civilized living, to which the poet repaired for music and culture. It was a city in turmoil, ravaged by plague, in a kind of civil war with itself, between the reactionary, wealthy, St. Thomas's parish, and the radical Puritan, deprived poor of St. Edmund's. It was struggling to cope with an influx of vagrants, rough sleepers who tramped through places like Bemerton; they found that Salisbury's streets were not paved with gold, and were sent back again the way they had come.[39] Herbert would have seen the anarchic, infested Salisbury of John Ivie, not that of the Restoration culture that a generation later began to adorn the Close with its grand houses.

The social history of the Salisbury area in the early seventeenth century is beyond the scope of this paper, as are the many literary, cultural, and theological issues raised by a critical reading of Herbert's *The Country Parson*. But alongside all the diverse approaches to this great work, surely some consideration may be given to the pastoral context in which it was written and to the ordinary folk among whom Herbert chose to spend his final years, and who filled his little church each Sunday?

A recurring theme throughout *The Country Parson* is the number of apparently nonspiritual activities that his ministry involved. Much of the work may be read as a manual of common sense, to be used when dealing with the everyday problems thrown up by parish life. To be able to sit in, as this paper has tried to do, on the concerns and complaints aired at Bemerton manorial court meetings—the trespasses, broken fences, and cheating farmers—gives context to Herbert's advice in "Concerning Detraction" (chap. 37), or "The Parson in Sentinell" (chap. 18), or "The Parson's Completenesse" (chap. 23). Here is a man, we feel, who had to decide whether it was in the public good to expose a misdemeanor in open court. "For if he absolutely shuts up mens mouths, and forbid all disclosing of faults, many an evill may not only be, but also spread in his Parish, without any remedy. . . ." Herbert recommends, also, tact and humor to deal with the multitude of petty grievances that, only when all else failed, would come before the courts. "Besides, if he perceive in company any discourse tending to ill, either by the wickedness or quarrelsomnesse thereof, he either prevents it judiciously, or breaks it off seasonably by some diversion." The local records even enable us, when Herbert describes resolving a controversy by sending for "three of or four of the ablest of the Parish to hear the cause with him," to know the names and circumstances of these fellow adjudicators.[40]

In a similar vein the local records concerned with death—the registers, wills, and inventories—give depth to Herbert's remarks, in "The Parson's Completenesse," about treating the sick (another of the parson's manifold duties) through knowing and using the simples and remedies available in garden and hedgerow. When remedies failed and Herbert strove to comfort the bereaved, by going to them rather than calling the afflicted to him ("The Parson Comforting," chap. 15), the local records tell us the names and circumstances of the grieving widow, Elflet Young, and liberated daughter, Susan Thring, who would have received his ministrations.[41]

Finally, Herbert's country parson, "condescends even to the knowledge of tillage, and pastorage, and makes great use of them in teaching, because people by what they understand, are best led to what they understand not."[42] Only by exploring the local records can we condescend to a similar knowledge and a greater understanding.

NOTES

This paper is based on a lecture originally given to the Bemerton Local History Society and the Summer Evenings with the George Herbert Group, October 19, 2005, a version of which was published, as "The Country Parson's Flock: George Herbert's Bemerton in 1632," *Sarum Chronicle* 6 (2006): 29–40. I am grateful to Anne Trevett and Judy Rees of Bemerton for encouraging me to undertake this research, and to the staff of the Wiltshire & Swindon History Centre, Chippenham, for making source material available.

1. Modern exceptions are A. M. Charles, *A Life of George Herbert* (Ithaca, NY: Cornell University Press, 1977); and R. W. Cooley, *Full of All Knowledg: George Herbert's Country Parson and Early Modern Social Discourse* (Toronto: University of Toronto Press, 2004), esp. chap. 4. Charles's appendix E (228–33) includes a transcript of 1646 sequestration records relating to Herbert's successor, which are of considerable interest but, since they are readily available in print, are not discussed here.

2. The standard history of the parish, "A History of Wiltshire 6," by Margaret Morris, is in *Victoria History of Wiltshire* 6 (1962): 37–50.

3. Fry, E. A., "The Wiltshire Protestation Returns of 1641–2," *Wiltshire Notes & Queries* 7 (1911): 163–64.

4. A. Whiteman, ed., *The Compton Census of 1676: A Critical Edition* (London: British Academy, 1986), 126.

5. G. S. Fry, and E. A. Fry, eds., *Abstracts of Wiltshire Inquisitiones Post Mortem: Charles I,* (Devizes: Wiltshire Archaeological and Natural History Society, 1901), 103–7. W(iltshire &) S(windon) A(rchives) 753/1 is a detailed cartulary of

the Grobham estate, including copies of deeds relating to Bemerton and Quid-hampton.

6. *Oxford Dictionary of National Biography,* s.v.v. "William Herbert," "Philip Herbert."

7. WSA 930/1.

8. In WSA P1/ and P2/: searchable online at http://history.wiltshire.gov.uk/heritage/index.php.

9. E. Kerridge, ed., *Survey of the Manors of Philip, 1st Earl of Pembroke and Montgomery, 1631–2,* Wiltshire Record Society 9, (Devizes: Wiltshire Archaeological and Natural History Society, 1953), 49–55.

10. B(ritish) L(ibrary) Add Ch. 15156. Although undated some details are similar to a rental made in September 1620, which is recorded at the back of WSA 2057/M3.

11. H. Shute, *My Lord Pembroke's Manor of Netherhampton* (Netherhampton: H. R. Shute, 1986).

12. Thring: WSA P1/T/77; Young: WSA P1/Y/12.

13. WSA 2057/S12, Fugglestone court roll, September 18, 1651.

14. WSA P2/Y/29.

15. Kerridge, *Survey,* 49, 53.

16. K. H. Rogers, *Wiltshire and Somerset Woollen Mills* (Edington: Pasold Research Fund, 1976), 252–53.

17. WSA P2/W/354.

18. S. Hobbs, ed., *Wiltshire Glebe Terriers, 1588–1827,* Wiltshire Record Society 56, (Trowbridge: Wiltshire Record Society 56, 2003), 185 (no. 363).

19. Kerridge, *Survey,* 51, 53.

20. A. H. Rowse, *Simon Forman: Sex and Society in Shakespeare's Age* (London: Weidenfeld, 1974); J. Cook, *Dr. Simon Forman: A Most Notorious Physician* (London: Chatto, 2001).

21. WSA 2057/M3, covering 1595–1630, 1635–39.

22. His holding is given in the 1620 rental at the end of WSA 2057/M3.

23. Hobbs, *Wiltshire Glebe Terriers,* 185 (no 363).

24. WSA P2/W/373; quotation from George Herbert, *The Complete English Works,* ed. A. Pasternak Slater, (London: David Campbell, 1995), 216.

25. WSA 2057/M5.

26. P. Slack, *Poverty in Early Stuart Salisbury,* Wiltshire Record Society 31 (Devizes: Wiltshire Record Society 31, 1975), 93.

27. Ibid., 117.

28. Fry and Fry, *Abstracts,* 407–9.

29. WSA 413/74.

30. WSA 2057/S5 (the survey published by Kerridge—see note 10) includes marginal notes that Kerridge ignored. There is a reference to Cutler taking on the lease in 1646 (perhaps a confusion with Mr. Coker), but the date of the indenture is given as May 20, 1650. It was surrendered on June 13, 1677, in favor of his son, also Thomas, who finally surrendered the farm in 1696. Thomas Cutler, Jr., had acquired other property in Fugglestone in 1673. Thomas Cutler Sr.'s will was made in 1681 and proved in 1685 (WSA P4/1685/14).

31. J. H. Bettey, *Wiltshire Farming in the 17th Century* (Trowbridge: Wiltshire Record Society 57), xxx–xxxiv, 236–75; M. Cowan, *Wiltshire Water Meadows* (Salisbury: Hobnob Press, 2005); H. Cook, and T. Williamson, eds., *Water Meadows: History, Ecology and Conservation* (Macclesfield: Windgather Press, 2007).

32. Cooley, 2004, 104–7, 139–46.

33. E.g., in P. Magee, *George Herbert, Rector of Bemerton* (Bemerton: Friends of Bemerton 27, 1976), "the meadows of Bemerton where he once lived and worked are hallowed ground"; R. Blythe, ed., *A Priest to the Temple or The Country Parson,* by George Herbert ([Place?]: SCM Press, 2003), ix: "On Thursdays he walked via the water meadows to Salisbury Cathedral."

34. Cooley, *Full of All Knowledg,* 93–107.

35. Explored by D. Underdown, *Revel, Riot and Rebellion* (Oxford: Oxford University Press, 1985), 73–105.

36. K. H. Rogers, "Edington," *Victoria History of Wiltshire* 8 (1965): 239–50, esp. 243–45.

37. Morris, "A History of Wiltshire 6," 38, 44.

38. See maps in ibid., 196–97; and in more detail WSA T/A Fugglestone.

39. P. Clark and P. Slack, *Crisis and Order in English Towns, 1500–1700* (London: Routledge, 1972), 164–203; J. Chandler, *Endless Street* (Salisbury, Hobnob Press, 1983), 168–70. Herbert addresses the priest's attitudes to beggars, and to misfortunes in neighboring parishes, in *The Country Parson,* "The Parson's Charity" (chap. 12) and "The Parson in Reference" (chap. 19).

40. Quotations are from *The Works of George Herbert,* ed. F. E. Hutchinson (Oxford: Clarendon, 1941), 286–87, 252, 260.

41. Ibid., 260–62, 249.

42. Ibid., 228.

George Herbert and the Widow Bagges: Poverty, Charity, and the Law

Chauncey Wood

IN *THE COUNTRY PARSON* GEORGE HERBERT PRAISES ENGLAND'S POOR
Law Act of 1601 as "that excellent statute," but goes on to qualify
that praise and to show his preference for a completely different
way to deal with poverty.[1] To reconcile these divergent views we
need an appropriate critical framework, and, happily, Herbert himself supplies us with one in *Memoriae Matris Sacrum*. The phrase
he uses there, from which we can derive our critical frame, is *"Bel-
lum putamen, nucleus bellissimus"* (Hutchinson, 423)—"a beautiful shell, and a most beautiful nucleus." Herbert uses the phrase to
describe his late mother's writing, and it gives us the framework of
shell and nucleus for managing his own contradictory statements
in *The Country Parson*. As readers, we must sort out Herbert's divergent views so that we can put one statement into the compartment marked "beautiful shell," another into the compartment
marked "most beautiful nucleus." To make the proper selection we
need do only what we always do: read carefully and pay attention.
However, the process of extricating the nucleus from beneath the
shell will be complicated for us by the social and political winds that
buffeted England in the 1630s; winds whose crosscurrents did not
spare even country parsons.

In *The Country Parson* Herbert faced the problem of writing both
for would-be rural parsons and for other, far different, audiences.
Professor Ronald Cooley has observed that the work has "complex
and contradictory agendas," and that it is "hesitant, ambivalent,
and inconstant."[2] For example, Professor Cooley analyzes Herbert's treatment of the delicate question of kneeling for Communion by describing it as "neither a simple statement of his own
beliefs, nor a slavish formalism, but a complex negotiation among
a range of possible formulations: what he thinks he must say, what
he might like to say, and what different sorts of readers might need
or want to hear."[3] The "complex negotiation among a range of pos-

sible formulations" that Professor Cooley aptly describes is precisely what is likely to emerge when a writer sets out to present both a shell and a nucleus in his work. In the short passages that will be cited later, three sentences begin with an adversative "but" (not to mention two "thoughs"), which gives us some idea of the elusiveness of Herbert's meaning here. As readers of his poetry we are already familiar with his characteristically abrupt changes of direction, so we come to the prose well-prepared. Professor Cristina Malcolmson has argued that in *The Country Parson* Herbert presents a parson who is "calculating and alert in relation to social dynamics *but* committed to revealing his religious spirit in the midst of them."[4] Professors Malcolmson and Cooley have shown us precisely *what* Herbert does in *The Country Parson;* this essay attempts to show *how* he does it. For Herbert, laws and social dynamics are the *bellus putamen,* beneath which we can find the *nucleus bellissimus* of religious spirit. There is no oppositionality here; laws are not bad and religion good, but rather, as with Martha and Mary, one does well, the other does better. Indeed, as St. Augustine used the story of the two women in his essay "On the Good of Marriage," Martha's worldly engagement in ministering to the saints is good, but Mary's sitting at the feet of the Lord and hearing his words is better.[5] The key to understanding both the biblical story and Herbert's view of the correct approach to poverty is to recognize the invariable superiority of spiritual improvement over worldly engagement.

In the Middle Ages and in the years prior to 1601 poverty was generally viewed as an individual failing, not as a social issue, but several social, economic, political, and philosophical changes prompted Queen Elizabeth's government to avoid social disorder by setting up a means to assist the "deserving" poor—that is, those who were elderly, blind, or otherwise incompetent.[6] The "undeserving" poor were those who were both able-bodied and unemployed or unemployable. They were classified as "Sturdy Beggars," and the standard cure for this social problem was to whip the beggars and run them out of town. Edifying pictures of beggars being whipped out of town can be found in Holinshed's *Chronicles.* Professor Paul Slack has cited documents from Salisbury—noteworthy because of Herbert's proximity to Salisbury while serving as a priest—that give clear examples of both the deserving and undeserving poor.

Let us first consider some "Sturdy Beggars." In a forty-year period early in the seventeenth century some six hundred vagrants were whipped out of Salisbury, and the authorities were concerned about people like "John Sellevand an Ireshman . . . taken wandringe and begging, disordering hym[self]," or a man "taken dronke, not able to yeld any accompte of his ydle course of lyffe," or "Anne Harris, *wandring* . . . with William Gill who she sayth was her husband, he sayd she is his Sister."[7] Now look at some seventeenth-century case reports from Salisbury on the "deserving poor": "Widow Bagges, aged seventy-five, 'lame in her handes,' was allowed 1s a week relief; Melior Jones aged fifty was 'sometymes distracted,' while his daughter was 'crocke backed.' Three wives with children deserted by their husbands were other obvious cases for relief."[8] Two of the cases are of people with physical disabilities, one concerns a mental disability, and three treat cases of desertion where women and children have become effectively, if not legally, widows and orphans. It is all quite understandable to us today.

The local regulations for Salisbury are cited first because they contain illustrative details. Chronologically, however, they followed the Poor Law Act of 1601, which was national, not local. That remarkable law, which elicited Herbert's praise, and was to stand in England for almost two hundred years, is essentially a template for dealing nationally with the deserving poor. Administratively, the Poor Law Act called for parishes to name overseers of the poor, who, "by and with the consent of two or more Justices of Peace," should set to work children whose parents could not support them, set to work adults with no visible means of support, and raise, by taxation, "competent sums of money, for, and towards the necessary relief of the lame, impotent, old, blind, and such other among them being poor, and *not able to work*. . . ."[9] Thus, following the general societal distinction between the deserving and undeserving poor, a further distinction was made between the impotent deserving poor and the able-bodied but deserving poor; the former were to be given money, the latter were to be set to work. While the administrative structure of the act was based on parishes, and involved churchwardens as well as justices of the peace, *the act itself is devoid of any other sort of religious language or test*. This is important to note, since the local statute in Salisbury included a specific religious requirement. There, "the laws included the prohibition of relief to anyone who did not 'usually frequent his or her parishe Churche at Morning and Evening prayer and at Sermons,' and there sit on a bench with '*For the Poore* in great red letters' on it."[10]

This thoughtful branding of the correct place for the poor is to some degree evidence of concern for their ongoing religious instruction, but to a much larger degree it shows civil concern for social control. The poor may or may not be better for sitting in church, but social concerns about them, concerns both for their material welfare and for what might happen in society should they not receive it, could be assuaged by assigning them to marked benches. The poor were not examined on their church experience, because religious improvement was not the issue. Rather, the particular social contract in Salisbury demanded work from the poor who were able and church attendance from all who received relief. The bench was boldly marked to reassure the parishioners who were taxed for support of the poor that social control was indeed being exercised. It was the equivalent of the modern road construction signs that assure us of good government by saying "Your tax dollars at work."

To return to the national Poor Law Act, another passage of the act is important for us because it was to be important for Herbert: "And be it also enacted, that if the said Justices of peace do perceive that the Inhabitants of any Parish are not able to levy amongst themselves sufficient sums of money for the purposes aforesaid: that then the said two Justices shall and may tax, rate and assess, as aforesaid, any other of other Parishes, or out of any Parish within the Hundred where the said Parish is, to pay such sum and sums of money to the Churchwardens and Overseers of the said poor Parish. . . ."[11] The rich were to be taxed to support the poor, and it is this paragraph of the act that elicited Herbert's praise. Herbert's friend Nicholas Ferrar had noted that Herbert himself was willing to give up a church living or "ecclesiastical dignitie," (in Hutchinson 4) and Herbert was consistent in admiring the redistribution of wealth mandated by the Poor Law. As he put it in a letter to his mother, "[I]f we ha[ve] riches we are commanded to give them away" (Hutchinson, 373).

The most elaborate reference to poverty in *The Country Parson* is in Herbert's chapter "The Parson's Charity," in which he praises the major source of funds for the poor, tax money appropriated and distributed according to the Poor Law that we have been quoting. Beyond the poor box and the parson himself, the parson can make use

of that excellent statute, which bindes all Parishes to maintaine their own. If his Parish be rich, he exacts this of them; if poor, and he able, he easeth them therein. *But he gives no set pension to any; for this in time will lose the name and effect of Charity with the poor people, though not with God:* for then they will reckon upon it, as on a debt; and if it be taken away, though justly, they will murmur, and repine as much, as he that is disseized of his own inheritance. (Hutchinson, 244; emphasis added)

In characteristic fashion, Herbert praises the statute, refers to its third paragraph on assessing the rich to maintain the poor, and yet goes right on to ignore the act to protest against set pensions, about which the act is silent. Like so much in *The Country Parson,* Herbert's praise of the named, *national* statute is made equivocal by his rejection of a key part of the unnamed, uncited *local* statute. Praise and censure appear at first to be evenhanded, but, as we shall see, they are not. To unpack this complex little passage we must first recall the local scheme in Salisbury, which awarded, for example, one shilling per week to the lame-handed Widow Bagges. Herbert's praise of the national statute's *unevenness* in charitable support among parishes—the rich support the poor—leads to his condemnation of "set pensions," a kind of *evenness,* in local practice in Salisbury. Once a pension is set, it is no longer the right sort of charity in Herbert's eyes.

The passage on charity continues with a second adversative "But": "But the Parson having a double aime, and making a hook of his Charity, causeth them still to depend upon him; and so by continuall, and fresh bounties, unexpected to them, but resolved to himself, hee wins them to praise God more, to live more religiously, and to take more paines in their vocation, as not knowing when they shal be relieved; which otherwise they would reckon upon, and turn to idlenesse" (Hutchinson, 244–45).

Herbert's primary goal, as he says in the very first chapter of *The Country Parson,* is to "reduce" that is, to lead back—his parishioners to the "Obedience of God" (225). The civil authorities of Salisbury, it appears, were primarily concerned to maintain civil obedience, not to foster obedience to God. The first step in Salisbury was to banish the "impudent poor," those who were "Sturdy Beggars," which was seen as prima facie evidence of civil disobedience. The second was to provide for the deserving poor lest they start fomenting some similar sort of disobedience. In both cases the issue is social control. Herbert and his church also sought control, but the two interpreted it very differently. For Herbert control was not a matter of civil *pensions* but of charitable *rewards.* The parson "in all his Charity . . . *distinguisheth,* giving them most, who live best, and take most paines, and are most charged: So is his charity in effect a Sermon" (245; emphasis added).

George Herbert clearly took issue with the Salisbury pension scheme. Did he take issue with "that excellent statute" as well? Yes. Although he praises the statute and then condemns something in another law, he comes back to the underlying issue in the passage cited previously when he says that "the Parson having a double aime, and making a hook of his Charity, causeth them still to depend upon him. . . ." The double aim, he clarifies, is not only to relieve their poverty, but to win his parishioners "to live more religiously. . . ." Neither the Poor Law Act nor the laws of Salisbury propose to do anything more than to relieve poverty. Herbert's "double aim," is both to relieve poverty and to improve the spiritual lives of his flock. As he puts it a little earlier in his book: "So the Countrey Parson, who is a diligent observer, and tracker of Gods wayes, sets up as many encouragements to goodnesse as he can, both in honour, and profit, and fame; that he may, if not the best way, yet any way, make his Parish good" (244).

The total effect of all Herbert's "double aime" is very bold. In creating his model Parson Herbert takes issue with both local and national laws for the treatment of the poor, and tacitly censures both for ignoring the spiritual dimension of the poor. A shilling a week may make the lame-handed Widow Bagges comfortable, but it will not make her good, while her appearance on the Poor Bench serves others, not her. The great red letters "For the Poore" are not there to help the Widow Bagges to find her seat; rather, they are there to serve as an emphatic assertion of civil control of this particular social problem. By the same token, that "excellent statute" may take from the rich and give to the poor, but it will not make either group good. Both the local and national statutes, then, are to be placed in the compartment marked "shell," although we should not forget that it is a "beautiful shell." As Herbert concedes, a set pension may not appear to be charity to its recipients, but it is still charity in God's eyes. Only the "double aime" of the parish priest can address both the material and spiritual needs of his flock, and only that "double aime" can be placed in the compartment marked "most beautiful nucleus."

When Herbert expands on the parson's uneven charity he endorses the sort of religious test that is quite unfashionable today: "So doth hee also before giving make them say their Prayers first, or the Creed, and ten Commandments, and as he finds them perfect, rewards them the more. For other givings are lay, and secular, but this is to give like a Priest" (245).

The Poor Law Act of 1601 for all its detail does not specify religious quizzes; the documents from Salisbury are primarily concerned with physical or mental disability, not with religious knowledge. To "give like a Priest," then, is to give *un*evenly, to reward religious competence rather than only material need, and boldly to disagree with the secular thrust of both local and national laws. "Other givings are lay, and secular," Herbert wrote, so we can see that his praise of "that excellent statute" was very limited praise indeed. That praise is part of *The Country Parson*'s *putamen* or shell; the most beautiful nucleus lying beneath it is neither lay nor secular but endorses a form of charity that combines monetary support with spiritual development. It originates within the church and uses parish priests for its implementation, as opposed to the Poor Law Act of 1601, which originated in Parliament and used existing church structures for its civil implementation. The Poor Law was an excellent statute for a lay, secular statute, no doubt, but while it might contribute to the work of the parish priest, Herbert believed it could never replace it.

In "The Church Militant" Herbert envisioned a world in which commonwealths acknowledge God:

> And wrap their policies in [his] decree,
> Complying with [his] counsels, doing nought
> Which doth not meet with an eternall thought.

(lines 6–8)

However, in *The Country Parson* he outlines commonwealth policies regarding the poor that do not wrap themselves in God's decrees, do not comply with his counsels, and are enacted with only immediate, social thoughts, not eternal, religious ones. Those decrees can be socially good, and in that sense beautiful, but can only be praised superficially: as a shell.

George Herbert was consistent, although he had to be careful just how he phrased his concerns and so made use of both the beautiful shell and the most beautiful nucleus. He believed deeply in his own and his church's mission, and if his immediate "double aime" was to address both material and spiritual poverty, his ultimate aim was single and moral: to make Marys, not Marthas, to act so that he may—if not in the best way, yet in some way—make his parish good. And that is his *nucleus bellissimus*.

NOTES

1. F. E. Hutchinson, ed., *The Works of George Herbert* (Oxford: Clarendon Press, 1972), 244. Subsequent quotations of Herbert will be from this edition and will be cited in the text by page number for prose, line number for poetry.

2. Ronald W. Cooley, *Full of All Knowledg: George Herbert's "Country Parson" and Early Modern Social Discourse* (Toronto: University of Toronto Press, 2004), 20–21.

3. Ibid., 43.

4. Cristina Malcolmson, *Heart-Work: George Herbert and the Protestant Ethic* (Stanford, CA: Stanford University Press, 1999), 41; emphasis added.

5. St. Augustine, "On the Good of Marriage," trans. Rev. C. L. Cornish, http://www.newadvent.org/fathers/1309.

6. http://www.tiscali.co.uk/reference/encyclopaedia/hutchinson/m001254.html.

7. Paul Slack, "Poverty and Politics in Salisbury, 1597–1666," in *Crisis and Order in English Towns: 1500–1700,* ed. Peter Clark and Paul Slack (Toronto: University of Toronto Press, 1972), 166–67. Note here the importance given to idleness, which appears regularly in legal and social commentary of the times. Herbert shows his personal concern that his parishioners might turn to idleness in a passage cited later in this essay.

8. Ibid., 174.

9. http://www.sochealth.co.uk/history/poorlaw.htm. Emphasis added.

10. Slack, "Poverty and Politics," 185.

11. http://www.sohealth.co.uk/history/poorlaw.htm.

"To Do a Piece of Right": Edmund Duncon and the Publication of George Herbert

Anthony Martin

DESPITE HIS ROLE IN THE PUBLICATION OF A NUMBER OF WORKS BY AND associated with George Herbert, Edmund Duncon has been particularly neglected by biographers, critics, and scholars. Mentioned only in passing in major critical and biographical works, Duncon has received almost no attention, in comparison with Nicholas Ferrar and others associated with Herbert. However, Duncon played a vital part in the publication of Herbert's works, and without his efforts it is possible that not only *The Country Parson* but also much biographical detail on Herbert would have been lost. Any account of Herbert should thus recognize Duncon as a major agent in the reception history of Herbert and his works. Even where Duncon's role is acknowledged—in discussions of the provenance and reception history of *The Temple* by Daniel Doerksen and Frank L. Huntley, for example—Duncon is still relegated to ancillary status.[1] It is therefore necessary, first, to reconsider Duncon's activities in the publication not only of Herbert but also of his friend Nicholas Ferrar.

Moreover, as one of the few clerical associates of Herbert and Ferrar who lived long enough to witness both the Interregnum and the Restoration, Duncon is of particular interest, and a reassessment of his life is necessary and overdue. Not considered significant enough for a full entry either in the original or second edition of the *Dictionary of National Biography (DNB)*, Duncon has been slighted in both these works, and thus the scholarship and criticism reliant on them is unfortunately marred by misinterpretation and error. From a fuller and more accurate consideration of the traces of Duncon's professional and personal career, we may also learn a little more about Herbert's milieu as priest and poet, both in the 1630s, and also hypothetically how Herbert himself might have fared had he lived so long.

One particular piece of misleading biographical detail deserves

181

both elucidation and further consideration. Bearing as it does both on the publication history of Herbert's *The Temple* and on Duncon's clerical career, the story that money from the sale of Herbert's manuscript was used for rebuilding Duncon's rectory house connects the poet with the Norfolk country parson in yet another way, casting light on the activities of some of the active Christians associated with Herbert in the 1630s. Even if the story is not true—and though it appears in the new *DNB* it certainly should not be accepted without question—it does show how the material furnishings and structures of seventeenth-century Christian practice had a vital function, and how these material structures remain of significance for the modern reader of Herbert and student of the poet and his associates.

As is well known, Izaak Walton reports in his *Life of Herbert* that Duncon visited Herbert at Nicholas Ferrar's behest in 1633, when, Walton reports, the two prayed together the "prayers of my mother, the Church of England."[2] The description of this scene has been questioned by Herbert scholars: Amy Charles scorns the idea that Herbert would say "I see by your habit that you are priest" and then have Duncon ask "What prayers?"[3] However, we should note that Walton claims firsthand testimony for these details. "This Mr Duncon tells me . . ." Walton asserts, mentioning that Duncon is now rector of Friern Barnet, and also that the memory of Herbert is fresh in Duncon's mind.[4] While not disagreeing with the opinion held by Charles and other critics that Walton and/or Duncon may have embellished this scene at a distance of some forty years, and that the Restoration reading of Herbert, especially as constructed by Walton's *Life,* which was to be attached to subsequent editions of *The Temple,* tended to emphasize his Anglican tendencies, there is surely some degree of truth in the story. That is, Duncon met Herbert in 1633, prayed with him, and was thus one of the last of the Ferrar circle to see and speak with him. More importantly, Walton reveals Duncon's crucial role in transmitting the manuscript of *The Temple* to Ferrar, when on his return to Bemerton some days after his previous (possibly first) visit, he finds Herbert worse in health, and receives "this little book" to deliver to "my dear Brother Farrer" to publish if he considered it fit, or else to destroy it. Walton's repetition of mention of Duncon's role in transmitting the book to Ferrar later in the *Life of Herbert* seems to indicate that Duncon's personal input into this account must have been a major source for Walton's narrative of Herbert's final month at Bemerton, and the process of *The Temple* being published.[5] In this first edition of the *Life,* it is noticeable that Walton's account of Herbert's deathbed appointment of Woodnoth as executor is perhaps ambivalent in its positioning of Woodnoth as responsible for taking care of Herbert's wife and nieces and household goods, without mentioning the crucial question of the poet's manuscripts.

This matter of the rights to Herbert's writings was of some importance, as can be seen from the correspondence between Nicholas Ferrar and Arthur Woodnoth, an issue that is discussed by Amy Charles in her biography of Herbert, and also considered in depth by Daniel Doerksen. In his detailed analysis of the extant letters, Doerksen convincingly demonstrates that while Woodnoth clearly believed his rights and responsibilities extended to Herbert's literary works, Ferrar had his own plans for these texts, and had employed Duncon as a go-between in getting hold of the text of *The Temple* before Herbert died. While Woodnoth seems to have intended to have the book published by the London bookseller Philemon Stephens, who was to print later editions in the 1650s and 1660s, Ferrar had arranged for Thomas Buck and Roger Daniel at the University Press in Cambridge to publish *The Temple*. Moreover, Woodnoth appealed to Ferrar to keep in mind the claims of Herbert's family, reminding him that he, Woodnoth, had been appointed executor by the terms of Herbert's will. Indeed, it is apparent that Woodnoth betrays some irritation with "the delivering of the Booke to Mr Duncombe" and while Ferrar may have trusted Duncon, it seems that Woodnoth does not, though later in the correspondence he allows for Duncon's straight dealing. In the letters that have survived, which only show Woodnoth's side of the discussion, the eventual reconciliation between the men involved seems to have generated an accommodation with Stephens over future sales and editions of *The Temple,* an arrangement arbitrated by Duncon. Woodnoth also makes clear his personal devotion to Nicholas Ferrar, and his submission to Ferrar as his spiritual mentor.[6]

However, while Duncon may have been Walton's informant on the transmission of *The Temple* to Ferrar, and thus to its publication by Buck and Daniel at Cambridge in 1633, it is apparent from Walton's *Life* that Duncon's small role in the publication of the other major Herbert work, *The Country Parson* in 1652, was unknown to the biographer or to the public. Had it not been for Barnabas Oley's generous acknowledgment of Duncon in the 1671 edition of *A Priest to the Temple,* issued a short time after Walton's *Life,* this part of Duncon's role in the publication of Herbert's works would also have remained in oblivion. Walton had assumed that Arthur Woodnoth had had the manuscript, and that from him it passed to Barnabas Oley, who then had it published, along with a prefatory biography of Herbert, in the 1652 *Remains*. Perhaps partly as a consequence of the 1670 publication of Walton's *Life*, in 1671 Barnabas Oley brought out a second edition of the work, with a full declaration of the work's provenance in the preface: "My design in this Preface is to do a Piece of Right, an office of Justice to the Good man that was possessor of this Book, and transmitted it freely to the Stationers who first printed it, merely upon design to benefit the Clergy, and in them, the Church of England. He was Mr Edmund Duncon Rector of Fryarn-Barnet in Middlesex."[7]

There is some question, however, over how Duncon acquired the manuscript he gave to Oley. Elizabeth Clarke has examined an attempt at the publication of *The Country Parson* in early 1641, by Robert Cooke, who had married Herbert's widow, and who seems to have received a manuscript back from Woodnoth. However, Cooke had run into problems getting the work passed for publication, problems that may be ascribed to Laudian censorship. What is unclear is how the book, if it is the same manuscript, then ended up in Edmund Duncon's possession. Woodnoth died at some point between 1644 and 1651, and thus it might be reasonably assumed that the manuscript passed to Duncon. Alternatively, it may be that Duncon had come into possession of another manuscript copy of the work at some point between Herbert's death and Oley's first edition of *Herbert's Remains* in 1652.

Further attention should also be paid to Edmund Duncon's minor roles in the production and publication of other Herbert-associated works. He played an important part in persuading Nicholas Ferrar to undertake the translation of Carbone's *Instruction of Children in Christian Doctrine*, and was also engaged in the publication of that work along with Herbert's translation of Cornaro's *Treatise of Temperance*.[8] Moreover, the second edition of Valdesso's *Considerations*, translated by Ferrar, with notes by Herbert, was printed by Roger Daniel at Cambridge in 1646 "for E. D." according to the title page, an ascription almost certainly to Duncon. The variants in this edition, missing some sections printed in the first edition (1638), but also with some small additions, would seem to indicate that Daniel had recourse to some kind of fair copy, not just the first edition. Since Duncon clearly already had or gained possession of the manuscript of *The Country Parson* at this time, it seems likely that he provided further material or a revised manuscript of Valdesso to Daniel. It thus appears that in the 1630s and subsequent decades, Duncon was at the very least a provider of manuscript material from Herbert and Ferrar, either having these works published and republished himself, or providing others with the material to do so.

Elizabeth Clarke observes that by the time of the 1652 publication of *The Country Parson* Duncon was the only survivor of those connected to the publication process of *The Temple* in 1633. However, it is perhaps misleading to describe Duncon as a "non-Laudian minister from the 1630s," as she does, maintaining, "In 1652 he seems to have collaborated with the Laudian Barnabas Oley in an alliance which at that point made some kind of sense: the spectre of Laud as an enemy to Herbertian practice had long since faded, and they might have seen a common enemy in rampant Independency."[9] The idea that Duncon was anti-Laudian seems to have been developed by David Novarr in his revisionist work on the validity of Walton's *Lives,* but a closer look at what can be discovered about Duncon as a churchman would be corrective to this view. Indeed, the commonly held opinion, boldly declared by David Novarr, and followed by others, that Edmund Duncon was a Puritan, should be reassessed. Novarr cites the *Dictionary of National Biography* as his source for the assertion, while the *DNB* refers to Duncon's letter to John Ellis in February 1672 in support of the claim.[10] However, examination of the circumstances and the text of the letter hardly go to substantiate the *DNB*'s case. Although the addressee, John Ellis, had been an adherent of the Parliament side during the civil wars, and had written tracts and books in support of the Presbyterians, by 1659 he had recanted his views, and adopted a strongly Anglican position, much to the disgust of his former fellows and supporters. So, the close friendship between the two men that is evident in Duncon's letter, which mentions a number of familial and personal matters in common, would confirm that it was the Anglican, not the Puritan, version of Ellis with whom the rector of Friern Barnet was familiar. Moreover, the contents of the letter hardly bear out a Puritan Duncon; he writes principally about keeping a dietary and mental regimen in order to remain productive in old age, and refers to many of the concerns and people associated with Little Gidding and Herbert (though not to Herbert himself). At no point does Duncon mention any doctrinal or ecclesiastical point of order, but rather reiterates his continued reading of Valdesso and Thomas Jackson. In this letter, Duncon is an old man, writing to a contemporary, but still living with the practices and thoughts he had encountered some forty years previously.

While there seems no reason to believe that Duncon, or anyone else associated with Ferrar and Little Gidding, would have supported the kind of Laudian censorship noted by Elizabeth Clarke, it may be more accurate to suggest that even by the mid-1640s, at least, the sympathies of Duncon and his intimates would have been much more firmly with the former church establishment than with the Presbyterianism and Independency that had supplanted the bishops. Duncon himself was from a clerical Suffolk family, with two notable brothers, Eleazar and John, both of whom were also decidedly royalist and non-Calvinist in their views. All three brothers found difficulties and were removed from their livings in the 1640s; only Edmund, however, was to live to be restored.

Eleazar, older than Edmund by some three or four years, was a major figure in the Laudian group around Bishop Neile of Durham in the late 1620s and 1630s, having been ordained deacon by Laud in 1626, and priest by Neile in 1627. In the 1640s, after losing to sequestration the large number of benefices he had secured, he went into exile, active in the royalist cause; on at least one occasion he was involved in carrying money to Charles's court in Paris. Eleazar died in Italy in 1660, on his way home from exile. There is no evidence of any division or distance between Edmund and his elder brother; indeed, just before Eleazar's death, Edmund had been attempting to gain some recompense for his brother's loss of goods and property suffered during the Interregnum.[11]

Another brother, John Duncon, a year or two younger than Edmund, was also a clergyman, was patronized by Matthew Wren, the Laudian bishop of Norwich, and was appointed to a number of livings in the late 1630s. However, John also was ejected from his benefices in 1641, being accused of Laudian practices particularly in regard to the positioning of the altar, and he was ejected again in 1644 from the living at Rattendon in Essex, to which he had moved. John Duncon then became chaplain to Lettice Cary, Viscountess Falkland, whom he assisted in setting up a Little Gidding–style community at Great Tew. Though he was to die in 1652, John Duncon's spiritual biography of Lady Falkland, *The Returns of Spiritual Comfort,* had a considerable impact, being published in 1648 and subsequently in expanded editions in 1648 and 1652. (While the first edition of 1648 was published anonymously, the second and third editions name John Duncon and describe him on the title page as a sequestered minister.) If Edmund Duncon did not already know Laudians such as Oley, it might be supposed that his brothers' activities and publications in the late 1640s would have established some degree of contact.

Edmund Duncon seems to have led a humbler life than his brothers, apart from his contact with Ferrar and Herbert. He matriculated at Trinity Hall, Cambridge, in 1624, and was fellow of the college from 1628 to 1631. He was granted the vicarage of Wood Dalling in Norfolk, which lay in the gift of Trinity Hall, in 1629, and after being ordained at St. David's in 1630, was given the rectory of Swannington, about ten miles south of Wood Dalling, a living also within the gift of Trinity Hall. After his induction, which he noted took place on Christmas Day, 1630, Duncon remained at Swannington and Wood Dalling for the next fifteen years, marrying Elizabeth Eston in St. Margaret's Church, Swannington, on January 27, 1638. (The entry in the parish register is in Duncon's own hand.) They had at least four children: John, who succeeded his father as rector of Friern Barnet in 1673, but who died a few weeks later; Nicholas, who arranged his father's probate inventory; Ruth, named as executor of her brother John; and Elizabeth, who married John Hildeyerd in 1660. Other than his contacts with Nicholas Ferrar and George Herbert in this period, we know little of Edmund Duncon's activities until his sequestration in 1646.[12]

According to the records of the Committee for Plundered Ministers, the committee that oversaw the sequestrations of the 1640s, Duncon was deprived of his livings in August 1646, by order of the Earl of Manchester, the charge of delinquency being laid against him.[13] It is apparent from the parish records of Swannington in the 1630s and 1640s, however, that Duncon was a considerably more dutiful parson than his successor, the intruder at Swannington, Robert Cronshay by name, who remained in occupation until the Restoration and seems to have been a local man, as he was living in Wotton, Norfolk, when he was granted a preaching license in 1662. Although a fifth of the tithes and glebe was granted by the committee to Duncon's wife and children, it is unclear how he would have supported himself and his family at this time.[14] In the 1650s, however, he was acting as curate to Richard Ball, the chaplain to the Beaumont family, and rector of Tattingstone, Suffolk. Richard Ball, like Edmund Duncon's brother John, was closely associated with Bishop Matthew Wren, and had been similarly attacked by Puritan parishioners and others for his innovations with regard to the altar and other ceremonial matters.[15] Indeed, Edmund seems to have been connected to Wren at this point, since at least two children of the Beaumont family whom he baptized had members of the Wren family as godparents. Around this time—that is, 1654—Duncon also attempted to take up the benefice of Aveton Gifford (also spelled Aveton Giffard and Awton Giffard/Gifford) in south Devon, but because of his apparent inability to reside, the living lapsed. In 1660, however, Duncon was restored to both his Norfolk livings of Wood Dalling and Swannington, though he failed in his attempt to resume Aveton Gifford. He continued to hold the Norfolk livings until 1662, when he resigned both, and moved to the rectory of Friern Barnet, which was in the gift of the deanery of Saint Paul's.

In Duncon's travails during the Interregnum period, we may get a picture of how Herbert would have fared had he lived into the mid-seventeenth century. In view of the upheaval at the parish of Fugglestone with Bemerton in the 1640s and 1650s, a period that saw a succession of ministers installed and then excluded, we may imagine that Herbert's fate would have been very similar to Duncon's.[16] Moreover, it seems likely that Duncon's Cambridge connections, formerly with Ferrar and subsequently with Joseph Beaumont, not only helped him through the Interregnum years, but also may have contributed to his attempts at gaining livings in the 1650s and later.

The situation regarding Duncon's appointment at Aveton Gifford is unclear. The living was in the possession of one William Lane, who had been presented by Charles I in 1638; Lane had received half the advowson of the parish—that is, the legal right of presentation of a nominee to a church office or benefice—in 1627, and the other half sometime between 1627 and 1638. However, he seems to have fallen into debt and sold some property, including at least half the advowson, to his brother, John Lane, while William's son, also John Lane, received this half back in 1668. At some point, William Lane, who died in 1654, seems to have transferred the living of the parish itself to two men, Francis Barnard and John Morton (or Martin), though there is no record of either of these being officially instituted. John Lane, William Lane's son, attempted to appoint Edmund Duncon to the parish, but failed due to his (i.e., John Lane's) delinquency. Moreover, John Morton, appointed as rector, possibly unofficially in 1654 by William Lane, continued to his death in 1674 to officiate at the parish, from the evidence of the parish records, which he signed from 1661. However, the living remained in the gift of John Lane, as is apparent from later records, and Duncon himself seems to have continued in the belief that he had a claim to the parish, since it is as rector of Aveton Gifford, and not Swannington, that he subscribes in 1662.[17]

Although we cannot be sure of the exact circumstances of Duncon's relationship with John Lane, or indeed of his ever setting foot in the Devon parish, it is apparent that he was being assisted at the highest levels in his attempts to take up the living. Supported by John Lane, Duncon petitioned the king in 1660 for confirmation of his right, going back to 1654. Since John Lane had been delinquent, the living had relapsed with, we might assume, Morton as the man in place. In his petition, Duncon was supported not only by Lane as the holder of at least one half of the advowson, but also by Dr. Gilbert Sheldon, at this point bishop of London, prior to his appointment as archbishop of Canterbury.[18] Sheldon's intervention on Duncon's behalf, albeit ineffectual, not only provides more evidence of Duncon's position in a non-Puritan sector of the Church of England, but also situates the cleric well within the Restoration movement to reinstate and reward the suffering clergy of the previous decades.

The timing of the petition, and its evident failure, seems also to have closely preceded Duncon's leaving of the Norfolk parishes and induction into the much richer and better-connected Middlesex parish of Friern Barnet, in the gift of St. Paul's. From Friern Barnet, Duncon, who had left his Norfolk parishes to his son-in-law, could renew contacts with such as Oley and Sheldon, and enter into communication with Ellis, Walton, and others. Moreover, it would appear that after the difficulties of the Interregnum period, Duncon came into a position of some stability and relative affluence. At his death in October 1673, his possessions amounted to little—some twenty shillings each in value of clothes and books—but he had securities and other financial instruments of some four hundred pounds.[19]

A. G. Matthews, in his revision of Walker's *Sufferings of the Clergy,* asserts that Duncon lost his Norfolk livings, presumably because of nonsubscription, though this is doubtful for a number of reasons. Firstly, Duncon did not fail to subscribe: rather, he did so from Devon rather than from Norfolk. Presumably, Duncon was already in the process of moving from his Norfolk parishes, and when the Devon living failed to become his, gained Friern Barnet instead. Moreover, it is clear that rather than losing the livings, he managed to transfer them to his successor, John Hildeyerd, who had married Duncon's daughter, Elizabeth, at her father's church in Swannington two years previously, in 1660.

To the end of his life, as can be seen from his contact with Walton, and from his only extant letter, to John Ellis, he continued in the effort to publish and disseminate the Christian practices associated with Ferrar and Herbert. In the letter to Ellis, written in his seventy-first or seventy-second year, he is working on the publication of a discourse on "[b]ringing forth more fruit in our age," and asking Ellis to be a cowriter. Moreover, it is evident from his own church career up till his death in 1673, and from his family and other connections with Richard Ball, Matthew Wren, and his patronage by Trinity Hall and by the deanery of St. Paul's, that Duncon was never other than the man identified, in the words he himself may have ascribed to Herbert, a "priest of the Church of England."

As a country parson throughout the tumultous period of the seventeenth century's civil war and Interregnum, his ejection and eventual restoration may also give an example of how events might have transpired for Herbert, had he lived so long. Christopher Hodgkins's intriguing epilogue to his study of Herbert proposes as an example of how the poet would have fared the vicissitudes of Thomas Fuller, torn between conflicting principles of doctrine and discipline, surrounded by the violence and factionalism of war, and yearning nostalgically for the apparent unity of the Elizabethan Church.[20] In a minor and less public way, Edmund Duncon's experiences also provide something of a model for the troubled lives of a large number of the English clergy in the mid-seventeenth century. Unlike his friends Herbert and Ferrar, Duncon lived on through the English Civil War and the Commonwealth; unlike Fuller, who died in 1661, and many others of the ejected clergy, he lived long enough to enjoy the benefits of the Restoration and to see his contributions to Christian poetry and practice acknowledged by Walton and Oley. It is impossible to say, of course, how things might have turned out for Herbert, but it is surely the case that his friendship and reliance on the go-between, Edmund Duncon, would have survived.

One further aspect of Duncon's personal history should be mentioned. In a book of Trinity Hall memoranda and miscellanea compiled by Doctor William Warren, a fellow of the college in the early eighteenth century, Warren mentions a story about Duncon that has continued to be transmitted, even appearing in the recent *Oxford Dictionary of National Biography*. "I have been told," Warren says, "yt Mr Duncomb who built the Minister's House at Swannington got so much money by selling ye Manuscript of Mr Herbert's Poems as was sufficient to pay for the Building of it."[21]

The story as it stands seems unlikely, and was rejected out of hand by Frank L. Huntley and not even mentioned by Amy Charles.[22] Of course, there is a lack of evidence in the first place for how much a manuscript such as that of *The Temple* would have been worth. The few early modern references to theatrical texts being sold for forty shillings to publishers hardly count, considering that this "forty shillings" is itself proposed as a ludicrously meager amount for a manuscript, even a stage-play manuscript, which would, it might well be assumed, be far less than the value of Herbert's manuscript.[23] Later in the century, in 1667, Milton sold his manuscript of *Paradise Lost* for five pounds, with further sums depending on subsequent editions being produced.[24] It may thus seem unlikely that the value of the manuscript, and the price Buck and Daniel would have been willing to pay, was large enough to cover the major construction work involved in Swannington Rectory. And, even had this been the case, we might doubt Ferrar's willingness to devolve all the money to his go-between, Duncon. However, Swannington Rectory was in fact completely rebuilt in 1635, a major construction, since the house had been in considerable dilapidation until then. The restoration of the rectory still stands on the east (front) side of the house today.[25] It is doubtful that Edmund Duncon, the middle brother of a not particularly rich family, could have afforded the work himself, and since the rectory was not his own, whether he would have expanded the sums necessary for the renovation and new construction.[26] Furthermore, Herbert's poems may well have been a more valuable property to a seventeenth-century printer than a play script or *Paradise Lost*: the manuscript copy of *The Temple* was apparently the site of struggle between printers, and was destined to become a major piece of published property, with two editions in 1633, another in 1634, another in 1635, and as Walton accurately notes, ten editions by 1670.

In rebuilding the parsonage, Duncon's activity was similar to the reconstructions and renovations undertaken by the Ferrars, Herbert, and others in the 1620s and 1630s. Walton's *Life of Herbert* and John Ferrar's life of his brother Nicholas both describe at length how much the Little Gidding community and Herbert himself were greatly involved in the restoration and construction of church buildings in the country parsonages they occupied.[27] Moreover, while Amy Charles doubts Walton's description of Bemerton Rectory as a ruin, it is noticeable that Herbert spent considerable amounts—at least two hundred pounds—on renovation, which he evidently regarded as the duty of the incumbent, a duty that active and responsible ministers such as himself and Duncon seem to have found lacking in their predecessors.[28]

The evidence, such as it is, does not permit for any conclusive resolution to the Swannington story. Nevertheless, I feel that it should not be rejected out of hand. While the sums accruing from a sale of the manuscript itself, or from the sale of any rights to further editions, a matter in which Duncon seems to have been involved, would have hardly sufficed for the large scale of building work at Swannington Rectory, Ferrar and his circle were clearly interested in collecting and distributing funds for the restoration of church

buildings. In my opinion, it is therefore not impossible that some of
the proceeds from the printing of *The Temple* in Cambridge in 1633
found their way to Duncon's reconstruction of the parson's house
at Swannington.

The material remains—in churches, in the texts that were
painted and inscribed on walls, monuments, and mantlepieces, in
the pieces of church furniture and the church memorials—are now
the location in which we may find the church of Herbert, Ferrar,
Woodnoth, and Duncon. If Duncon is a fair example, many of the
active clerics of the seventeenth century were greatly concerned in
the preservation and renovation of the material, physical elements
of the church. In the traces that remain at St. Andrew's at Wood
Dalling, St. Margaret's at Swannington, St. James in Friern Barnet,
and at Little Gidding, and St. Andrew's Bemerton, we might still
discover some of the life of Herbert, the poet and parson, and his
friend and textual preserver, Edmund Duncon.

A visitor to St. James Church in Friern Barnet will search the
churchyard in vain for the resting place of Edmund Duncon, the
rector of the parish from 1663 to his death in 1673. Instead, one
will find Duncon's memorial on the interior north wall of the
church, where it was placed in 1974, taken inside the building because of the erosion it was suffering in the London rain and snow.
The memorial reads,

IN
M.S.
EDM DUNCON non ita pridem
Huius Parochiae Rector qui unimam
Suam inspitanti reddidit An Aetat
Suae septuagessimo secundo sal nostrae
MDCLXXIII quarto oct
Dormit in hoc tumulo fidelis Pastor Iesus
Cuius Mors docuit Vivere Vita Mori
Posuit I. D.

[In sacred memory of Edmund Duncon, not long ago rector of this parish, whose soul returned to its source of inspiration in his seventy-second year, and in the year of our salvation 1673, on the fourth of
October. He sleeps in this tomb a faithful shepherd of Jesus, whose
death taught him to live, whose life taught him to die. Placed by John
Duncon.][29]

It is indeed poignant that Duncon's memorial should now be
eroded almost to the point of illegibility, but has fortunately been

preserved, since his memory in scholarship has perhaps suffered a similar effacement. To do right to Duncon, as Barnabas Oley wrote, is to retain in memory his acts and his life, in Friern Barnet and Swannington and in our readings of texts written by Herbert but brought to us by the hands of his friend.

NOTES

1. Daniel W. Doerksen, "Nicholas Ferrar, Arthur Woodnoth, and the Publication of George Herbert's *The Temple,* 1633," *George Herbert Journal* 3 (1979/80): 22–44; Frank L. Huntley, "The Williams Manuscript, Edmund Duncon, and Herbert's Quotidian Fever," *George Herbert Journal* 10 (1986/87): 23–32.

2. Izaak Walton, *The Lives of John Donne, Sir Henry Wotton, Richard Hooker, George Herbert, and Robert Sanderson* (1927; reprint London: Oxford University Press, 1973), 308.

3. Amy M. Charles, *A Life of George Herbert* (Ithaca, NY: Cornell University Press, 1977), 161.

4. Walton, *Lives,* 308.

5. Ibid., 314.

6. The letters, from Woodnoth to Nicholas Ferrar, are among the Ferrar Papers, but for the most part are unpublished. In "Ferrar, Woodnoth, and *The Temple,*" Daniel Doerksen quotes extensively and provides the most detailed analysis of this episode. See also, Charles, *Life,* 188–92.

7. Barnabas Oley, "The Publisher to the Christian Reader," in *A Priest to the Temple, or The Country Parson,* 2nd ed. (London, 1671), sig. A5r–v.

8. Charles, *Life,* 187–89.

9. Elizabeth Clarke, "The Character of a Non-Laudian Country Parson," *Review of English Studies* 54 (2003): 495–96.

10. David Novarr, "Izaak Walton, Bishop Morley, and Love and Truth," *Review of English Studies* 2, no. 5 (1951): 33; Novarr, *The Making of Walton's "Lives"* (Ithaca, NY: Cornell University Press, 1958), 514. *Dictionary of National Biography,* ed. Leslie Stephen and Sidney Lee (London: Smith, Elder and Co., 1908), 6: 181–82. British Library Add MS 28930, fol. 24: letter from E. Duncon to J. Ellis, 1672.

11. For details of Eleazar Duncon's life, see Jason McElligott, "Duncon, Eleazar (1597/8–1660)," in *Oxford Dictionary of National Biography* (Oxford: Oxford University Press, 2004, http://www.oxforddnb.com/view/article/8242; A. G. Matthews, *Walker Revised: Being a Revision of John Walker's Sufferings of the Clergy during the Grand Rebellion, 1642–60* (Oxford: Clarendon Press, 1948), 141.

12. Basic details of Edmund Duncon's life are given, not altogether accurately, in the entry on Eleazar Duncon in the *Oxford DNB.* Also see Matthews, *Walker Revised,* 267; and John Dixon Wortley, *Swannington: Its Church, Rectors, and History* (Norwich, England: Goose and Son, n.d.)

13. British Library Additional MS 15670, fol. 196v.

14. Bodleian Library MS 324, fol. 45r.

15. Joseph Beaumont's son John was baptized by Duncon in 1654, and his daughter Anna Susanna was baptized in 1656 by Duncon, with Matthew Wren as one of the godparents: see John Gee, *Memoirs of Joseph Beaumont, Master of*

Peterhouse 1663–1699 . . . Annotated by Thomas Alfred Walker (Cambridge: Cambridge University Press, 1934), 4. For Richard Ball, see Matthews, *Walker Revised*, 326.

16. Herbert's successor at Fugglestone with Bemerton, Thomas Laurence, was ejected from the parish in 1645; see Charles, *Life,* 228–33; and *A History of the County of Wiltshire,* vol. 6, ed. Elizabeth Crittal, Victoria County History series, (London: University of London Press 1962), http://www.british-history.ac.uk/reort.aspx?compid=41774.

17. Details of the parish of Aveton Gifford during the 1650s and 1660s are taken from *A History of the Parish of Aveton Giffard,* compiled by the Reverend C. C. Shaw (Aveton Giffard: C. C. Shaw, 1966). This book has been scanned and made available on the Internet by Dr. Chris Burgoyne. Dr. Burgoyne points out that the book is still in copyright belonging to the estate of Rev. C. C. Shaw. http://wwwciv.eng.cam.ac.uk/cjb/ag/shaw/index.htm. I greatly appreciate Dr. Burgoyne's help on Aveton Gifford and John Lane.

18. Caldendar of State Papers Domestic, Charles II, August 7, 1660.

19. Duncon's probate inventory is in the Guildhall, London, MS 19504/18/34. I am extremely grateful to Dr. Christopher Whittick for his assistance with this matter.

20. Christopher Hodgkins, *Authority, Church and Society in George Herbert: Return to the Middle Way* (Columbia: University of Missouri Press, 1993), 210–14.

21. *Warren's Book,* ed. Alfred William Winterslow Dale (Cambridge: Cambridge University Press, 1911), 112.

22. Huntley, "Williams Manuscript," 30. Huntley argues that Duncon was an unreliable source for Walton, and that this story may be an example of Duncon's self-aggrandizement. Huntley, however, seems to find inconsistencies in all elements of Duncon's involvement with Herbert, a pervasive suspicion not shared by Herbert and his contemporaries, nor by most modern critics.

23. Peter W. M. Blayney, "The Publication of Playbooks," in *A New History of Early English Drama,* ed. John D. Cox and David Scott Kastan (New York: Columbia University Press, 1997), 395–96.

24. William Riley Parker, *Milton: A Biography,* 2nd ed. (Oxford: Clarendon Press, 1996), 1:601.

25. I would like to express my gratitude to Mr. Peter Day for his kindness and help in showing me St. Margaret's Church and the Old Rectory.

26. Rosemary O'Day observes that clergy were unlikely to invest their own money in land and buildings owned by the church, preferring to buy property that could be inherited by their children. O'Day, *The English Clergy: The Emergence and Consolidation of a Profession, 1558–1662* (Leicester: Leicester University Press, 1979), 181.

27. On the restoration of Leighton Ecclesia, see Charles Smyth, "Little Gidding and Leighton Bromswold," *Church Quarterly Review* 165 (1964): 290–305.

28. Charles, *Life,* 153–54.

29. Guides to the parish of Friern Barnet give the location of Duncon's memorial stone as outside the east wall of the church. The inscription is now almost illegible, though a transcription is provided in the church; see John Phillips, *Knights and (K)naves: A Short History of the Parish of Friern Barnet* (London: Parish of Friern Barnet, 1999); Frederick Teague Cansick, *A Collection of Curious and Interesting Epitaphs, Copied from the existing monuments of distinguished and noted characters in the churches and churchyards of Hornsey, Tottenham, Edmonton, Enfield, Friern Barnet and Hadley, Middlesex* (London: Wertheimer, Lea and Co., 1875).

III
Biblical and Liturgical Connections

George Herbert and the Liturgical Experience of Scripture
Paul Dyck

> Christ's gospel is not a ceremonial law . . . but it is a religion to serve God, not in bondage of the figure or shadow, but in the freedom of spirit, being content only with those ceremonies which do serve to a decent order and godly discipline, and such as be *apt to stir up the dull mind of man* to the remembrance of his duty to God *by some notable and special signification* whereby he might be edified. (Emphasis added)
>
> —Book of Common Prayer

To SPEAK OF GEORGE HERBERT AND THE BOOK OF COMMON PRAYER risks being an obvious business: Herbert used the book, and given his own book's section title "The Church," readers might imagine that the Prayer Book must have some relevance to Herbert's poetry. At the same time, Herbert's poetry has been so carefully marked out again and again as territory in the battle between high and low visions of church, that readers should be wary of making too-easy associations between Herbert, the Prayer Book, and given ecclesiological positions. This essay attempts to set aside for a moment the Prayer Book's status as a political and ecclesial disciplinary tool (which it certainly was) and consider it as a discipline of reading and more broadly experiencing scripture. Such a move is perhaps warranted by the fact that the Prayer Book has been through its entire history, culturally speaking, a protean object, a moving target for anyone trying to define it. At first a reforming book, then an illegal one under Mary, then, after the Elizabethan Settlement, a conservative book, it provided a negative rallying point for Presbyterians until the movement was quelled around 1590. Later, in the 1630s, the Prayer Book became increasingly a sign of autocratic monarchy, and even, in its form as Archbishop Laud's 1637 Scottish Prayer Book, a trigger of rebellion. Then again it was an illegal book under Cromwell, and then a conservative sign of Restoration. How the Prayer Book functioned at any given time was very much subject to its situation. And yet it remains a book with content, always received through interpretation and local practice, but nonetheless still a text remaining for us to read, a text that shaped Church of England worship perhaps most remarkably in the decades preceding the Civil War, when the nation could still be unified by religion.[1] The Prayer Book was, along with the English Bible and the homilies, a characterizing text of the English church for all of George Herbert's life. It bears asking, then, even given its contested status, how it functioned in worship, and how Herbert's verse might play upon and within this text of the church.[2] I will demonstrate here that Herbert's poetry operates within a biblical discursive space that has been significantly formed by Prayer Book worship, and that the most immediately important aspect of this worship for *The Temple* is that it positions the readers, and more particularly the reading church, as themselves being read by the living Word. Further, for Herbert, poetry can be an inspired act, but only when it works liturgically—that is, as a work to receive the Word.

In her *George Herbert: A Literary Life,* Cristina Malcolmson argues that for Herbert, "the church liturgy becomes spiritually significant when grace internalizes it within the worshipper." She goes on to say that "altars alone are idolatrous," since there is no holiness in the things themselves. However, "men without altars . . . replace the church's authority with their own, and follow their subjective responses rather than the authority of 'sacred ritual.'"[3] Malcolmson effectively summarizes the balance of Herbert's position, but we might ask whether her first statement, that "the church liturgy becomes spiritually significant when grace internalizes it within the worshipper," subtly gets things the wrong way around. Perhaps I can best get at my point through an anecdote: I am an Anglican who teaches at a Mennonite university, and one day a colleague noted to me that Anglicans, like Mormons, have two holy books. This struck me, and I think Herbert would have agreed, as precisely wrong. The functions of the Book of Common Prayer and the Book of Mormon are different, I pointed out; whereas the latter forms an addition to scripture, the former is largely an arrangement of scripture, one entirely without meaning apart from scripture. So, the liturgy of the Prayer Book is no more and no less important than any other liturgy: it is a way of worshipping. Its spiritual significance is not so much made possible by its internalization in the worshipper, but rather it, as an arrangement of scripture, makes possible prayer and communion. It does not do this exclusively, but it nonetheless does this regularly, disciplinarily, habitually. This is not to negate the contests around the Prayer Book, but to clarify that its liturgy is not an alternative to being Word-centered, but rather a way of being so.

How the liturgy is Word-centered is best established by a close reading of the text.[4] The opening sections of the Morning Prayer service follow the Psalms in blending subjective and objective texts, which together call for the involvement of the reader and locate that reader within the larger narrative of God's work in the world; *The Temple* goes on to take up this mode. Morning Prayer is a distinctly penitential rite: it begins with the minister reading "with a lowd voice" some sentences of scripture. Of the eleven given selections, three are from Psalm 51, that most well known psalm of penitence, traditionally identified as the composition of David after his adultery with Bathsheba and arranged killing of her husband, Uriah. A characteristic sentence of these is Psalm 51:17: "A sorrowful spirit is a sacrifice to God: despise not, O Lord, humble and contrite hearts." Immediately after reading these sentences, the minister leads the people in a prayer of general confession that itself is a catena or chain of biblical sentences, paraphrased for common reading. The congregation says together, "We have erred and strayed from thy wayes, like lost sheep we have followed too much the devices and desires of our owne hearts," an expansion of Psalm 119:176, "I have gone astray like a lost sheep." Likewise, they say, "We have left undone those things which we ought to have done, and we have done those things which wee ought not to have done," which reemploys the words of Christ in Matthew 23:23 and Luke 11:42 in which he, speaking of paying tithes and the "weightier matters" of "judgment, mercy, and faith," says "these ought ye to have done, and not to leave the other undone." And finally, they say, "Have mercy upon us miserable offenders," which echoes a familiar construction in the Psalms, such as in 123:3: "Have mercy upon us, O Lord, have mercy upon us." Next, the minister leads the people in the Lord's Prayer (from Matthew 6 and Luke 11) and then in versicles and responses, beginning with "O Lord, open thou our lips," to which the people respond, "And our mouth shall shew forth thy praise," a slight rewording of Psalm 51:15. Then, "O God make speed to save us" is followed by a close echo of Psalm 38:22, "O Lord make haste to help us."[5]

Whether Morning Prayer is constituted by scripture, then, is not the question, but rather how it is so constituted and to what end. The service treats scripture both as proclamation and as script, first asking the worshipper to listen to what it is saying, then asking the worshipper to enact it, speaking its words into action. As John Wall and Ramie Targoff have pointed out, Prayer Book worship differs from its medieval predecessor and the "free" Protestant worship that largely superseded it in not centering on individual and private experience but on the public experience of the church.[6] Notably, though, the Prayer Book's composition closely parallels the private psalms and poems of the time, characterized by Herbert's second "H. Scriptures" poem, in which verses make motions one to another, and combine to "make up some Christian's destinie."[7] The private modes of Bible reading and psalm composition and the public mode of common prayer are best seen as mutually informing (though of course not all early moderns would have agreed): the Prayer Book carefully draws the people of the church together into a scriptural understanding of God, the world, and the church, beginning with a moment of reckoning with sin, a moment both personal and universal, of the moment and of the psalmic past, and then going on to praise God, but only after taking the role of David in his deepest sin and recognizing that praise is itself a gift of God: "O Lord, open our lips, and our mouth shall shew forth thy praise." Through the Church of England liturgy, then, as Wall strikingly puts it, "the Bible becomes a living text in the world."[8]

Rosemary van Wengen-Shute, in her admirable 1981 study of Herbert and the Prayer Book, addresses the problem of sincerity and doubt in the variable worshipper, in particular whether a parishioner's voicing of prayers in the absence of corresponding feelings produces hypocrisy rather than true worship. Van Wengen-Shute argues that since liturgy is "the corporate voice of the Church, serving to unite the personal experience of the individual to that of all believers at all times," it helps individuals maintain their "spiritual equilibrium" by providing a "stable and unchanging background" to spiritual struggles.[9] While Herbert's poetry does work liturgically toward groundedness, the characterization of the Book of Common Prayer as a "stable and unchanging background" contributes to the false dichotomy between common prayers and personal poetry. While the Prayer Book, as with every other possible form of worship, can become an empty habit, it offers not only an experience of scripture but an encounter with God, and this encounter is precisely not stable and unchanging. The spiritual comfort of knowing that one belongs to a community comes only with the recognition that the whole church follows God or does not follow God as the Israelites did or did not in the wilderness. The church is a place that is exactly not a place, but a marker of a journey. As the theologian Catherine Pickstock puts it, the liturgy is an impossibility in that it is itself the condition of its own possibility, always happening in media res.[10] This impossibility is captured in the request, "Lord, open thou our lips." Only God can open our lips in holy acts, and since the request is itself a holy act, the request's desired outcome is also its condition. To be involved in liturgy is always to have been preceded by the actions of liturgy. Hence, as Herbert instructs in *The Country Parson,* the role of the priest exceeds the man who is priest and so his words are necessarily caught in paradox. He speaks "with a grave liveliness, between fear and zeal, pausing yet pressing" (Hutchinson, 231). The sincerity of the priest, or of any Christian in worship, is not the expression of the heart, a movement from internal to external, but rather the shaping of the heart by the external and alien Word. The priest, "when he is to read divine services, composeth himselfe to all possible reverence" since he is "truly touched and amazed with the Majesty of God" to whom the services are directed. So, what is unchanging about liturgy is that it is always interruptive. In this sense, the Reformation critics of set liturgy were exactly right: when they found themselves parroting empty words, they were not worshipping. Their mistake was in assuming that they had actually been doing liturgy, for, to take it by its own definition, liturgy always interrupts the self and even the church.

This interruption, if not clear enough in the opening sentences and prayers of Morning Prayer, becomes unmistakable in Psalm 95, which follows. With this psalm the church begins to praise, following the invitation "O come let us sing unto the Lord: let us heartily rejoice in the strength of our salvation." The church, through the psalm, goes on to declare that the world and everything in it is not neutral space but part of the created order: "[I]n his hand are all the corners of the earth," he is the "Lord our God" and we are the "sheep of his hands." Now (just when the reading is often curtailed in modern services) the psalm comes to its crux, the point that breaks the stability the liturgy may appear to have: "To day if ye will heare his voice, harden not your hearts: as in the provocation, and as in the day of temptation in the wildernesse. When you fathers tempted me: prooved me, and saw my works." Like no other, this verse makes it clear that saying the words of scripture does not secure or guarantee anything: the crucial time is always before us, "today." Now is when we must listen to a word that is not our own word, and not harden our hearts.

Herbert's poetry begins at exactly the point of instability that the liturgy makes possible: the realization that one must not harden one's heart, and yet, that one's heart is already hard. In fact, in *The Temple* the adjective "hard" almost always modifies "heart": within the opening series of poems, the word comes to signal a default internal state. "The Altar" and "The Sinner" both refer to "my hard heart" (lines 10 and 13, respectively) and, later, in "Grace," the speaker says that "Sinne is still hammering my heart / Unto a hardnesse, void of love" (lines 17–18). In opening "The Church" with frank admissions of inner hardness, Herbert takes up the penitential action of Morning Prayer. The remarkable sensitivity of these poems is not in somehow moving beyond the liturgy, but in recognizing the charged situation of prayer and in presenting that situation in its fully realized paradox. As I argue below, "The Altar" makes the hard heart—the very provocation of the scriptural past—into the very location of forgiveness. "The Sepulchre" emblematizes this action most memorably by finding the desolation of the grave with its "lodging" of "a cold hard stone" to be "pure" and hospitable compared to "our hard hearts," which are not fit to hold Christ (lines 2, 10, 13). However, it is in the hopelessly sepulchral state of the heart—and only that state—that Christ's love fully articulates: "Yet do we still persist as we began, / And so should perish, but that nothing can, / Though it be cold, hard, foul, from loving man / Withhold thee" (lines 21–24).

The interruptive quality of liturgy only intensifies in the service of Holy Communion, which was practiced infrequently in Herbert's time in parish churches.[12] This infrequency, however, does not necessarily reflect unimportance, especially for Herbert, whose poetry works eucharistically—that is, it often refers to the liturgical service of Communion, but more importantly, pervasively engages the ultimate ends of that service. Importantly, while Communion involves certainties, its uncertainties are more dramatically prominent, in that it destabilizes the regular categories of cultic practice. Communion operates within a specifically Jewish framework but also within a more generally recognizable structure of sacrifice-making. Those offering the sacrifice do so to a divine spirit in order to obtain divine goodwill, through atonement for sins, or blessing on future activities. While every cultic practice is much more complicated than this, and given that any encounter with a divine Other (however narrated) must be inherently unpredictable, Christian Communion nonetheless challenges given categories, particularly that of the sacrifice, in highly specific and destabilizing ways. As the biblical book of Hebrews thoroughly explores, the high priest in this case is himself also the sacrifice. This doctrine takes from worshippers their normal role as the bringers of sacrifice. Christians come to worship with nothing to offer, nothing that can purchase their atonement. Strangely though, they do end up offering themselves, their "praise and thanksgiving," but more, their "souls and bodies, to be a reasonable, holy, and lively sacrifice" to God (Booty, 164). This offering, though, comes not early in the ritual, to purchase something, but as one of the final acts of the service, only after the service's central sacrifice has been made. This central sacrifice, which does consist of the worshippers' presentation of gifts of bread and wine, turns out not to be a gift to God, but God's gift to humanity, a tangible sign of the spiritual body and blood of Christ, broken and shed for humanity's salvation. The basic instability to which I refer, then, is that the Communion service does not enact an exchange, but rather a counterintuitive overflow of the categories of sacrifice and forgiveness, a superabundance of blood and love.[13]

Herbert's poetry takes up the problem of Communion, even its impossibility, as Pickstock puts it, from the first poem of "The Church" to its last. Readers attempting to work out the liturgical shape of Herbert's work have often stumbled on the placement of the first poem, "The Altar." Obviously, an altar is not the first thing one encounters upon entering a church, particularly an English parish church, in which entry is typically from the rear side, so that one cannot immediately even see the far end of the church, where the altar is located. To this is added the problem that there was no altar in these churches during Herbert's lifetime, but rather a Communion table. However, this is to read Herbert as one would read his imitator, Christopher Harvey—that is, pedantically. Pickstock points out that in the Eucharist, the altar of God is an "infinitely receding place," a starting point never finally arrived at in earthly worship.[14] Even the high liturgy of the Catholic Reformation does not feature an altar that one can easily approach or name. Herbert's poem and its placement recognizes the altar's importance as the point of contact between humanity and God, an importance reflected in the persistence of symbolic altars in devotional works in reformed England.[15] Herbert's altar does not mark an accomplishment, but a starting point, a posture characterized by paradox. This altar is the work of the speaker—"A broken ALTAR, Lord, thy servant reares" (line 1)—and yet the work of God: "A HEART alone / Is such a stone, / As nothing but / Thy pow'r doth cut" (lines 5–8). It represents the gift of the speaker (line 16), and yet it is not the sacrifice itself, but rather the hopeful location of the sacrifice (line 15), who is identified in the following poem, "The Sacrifice," as the crucified Christ. The poem looks toward and celebrates the Communion of the speaker with Christ, but as the next poem makes agonizingly clear, that Communion is constituted by its own ex-

treme unlikeliness: the very inability of humanity to placate its
Lord, acted out in its extreme antagonism to Christ—the greatest
sin ever, according to Aquinas—becomes the moment of a super-
abundant love that overwhelms that antagonism.[16]

Communion, then, remembers not only the inability of humanity
to offer sacrifices, but its antipathy to its Lord, such that it offers
the Lord himself as a sacrifice. That the Lord turns this act of hatred into an effective overpayment for itself, thus physically and ag-
onistically turning hatred to love, is the immense problem that
Herbert's speaker strains to comprehend in the opening sequence
of "The Church." The very abundance of Christ's passion demands
from the speaker an attempt at revenge, "the remarkable vow of
"The Thanksgiving" to "revenge me on thy love" (line 17). However, the passion of Christ overwhelms any possibility of fair exchange: "Then for thy passion—I will do for that— / Alas, my God,
I know not what" (lines 49–50). What starts, then, as the apparent
presentation of the altar turns out to be the beginning of an ongoing
journey toward the point of Communion, the impossible point of
a redemption that has already happened, in which the sinner can
miraculously commune with an overwhelmingly offended and for-
giving God. This is the miracle to which "The Agony," two poems
later, points, in which Christ exceedingly strangely sounds the full
extent of both sin and love, which together produce the bittersweet
distance in which the rest of "The Church" operates. To commune
is to taste that passion: "Love is that liquor sweet and most divine, /
Which my God feels as bloud; but I, as wine" (lines 17–18). However, this reference to the rite of Communion not only celebrates
the connection, but serves to emphasize that it is a moment on the
journey to the altar, for it is not until the final lines of "The
Church" that Herbert gestures toward consummation. These lines,
in "Love" (III), notably, come as the culmination of an apocalyptic
sequence marking the four last things: death, judgment, heaven,
and hell. Notably, the expected title "Hell" does not appear, and
instead we find "Love." That Herbert's speaker is rescued from
hellish pride and self-isolation demonstrates the final overwhelming of hell by love, an ending gestured toward by the opening poems
of "The Church."

But, lest Pickstock's reading of the Roman rite seem too far afield
from Herbert and the reformed worship of the Prayer Book, let us
turn to a key Reformation account of the operations of liturgy, that
of Martin Luther. Richard Strier has argued for Herbert's commitment to Luther's doctrine of justification by faith and the impossibility of human merit, a doctrinal commitment that stands apart

from Herbert's disagreement with Luther on other matters, notably Luther's antiasceticism and doctrine of consubstantiation.[17] I wonder, though, whether we might reconsider the role of the liturgy in Luther's doctrine as important for Herbert's poetry, in particular Luther's description of the Gospel's as the "alieno verbo" or, as Heiko Oberman has translated it, "alien Word." Notably, for Luther, who was most strikingly shaped by his personal readings of scripture, the sacraments were a unique and irreplaceable location for encounter with God, for it was in them that one encountered not one's own knowledge of scripture, but rather the "alien Word," against which the devil—the master of subjectivity who lurks in the heart and is himself a master of the scriptures—has no defense.[18] Luther wrote in a letter on November 17, 1527, "The Prince of Demons himself has taken up combat against me; so powerfully and adeptly does he handle the Scriptures that *my scriptural knowledge does not suffice* if I do not rely on *the alien Word.*"[19] As Heiko Oberman puts it, the "'alien Word" is the Gospels, which is not "my own," but which I hear spoken "to me." The Christian can be justified in the sight of God only through trust in the extraneous righteousness of Christ and not through his own righteousness. Likewise, a Christian can only be promised absolution, the Word of forgiveness, "from outside." He cannot trust his own conscience, and the confusion will only increase in view of the fast-approaching end."[20] For Luther, baptism and Communion were the tangible pledges of God and the basis of Christian certainty, against the deceptions of the heart.[21]

One of Herbert's most Lutheran poems, "Conscience," dramatizes the contest between deceptive and isolating subjectivity and power of the Cross, experienced through Communion. While Luther has been popularly misunderstood as a champion of the "freedom of conscience," Herbert gets him right as freeing the self from papal authority in order to turn it over to biblical authority. The freed conscience is not a triumph but rather a tyranny of interiority. In this poem, Conscience is a "pratler," who works by naming: the fair foul, the sweet sour, music a "howl" (lines 2–4). Conscience's "chatting fears" rob the speaker of his "eyes and eares" (lines 5–6). However, the speaker has "physick to expell" this prattler: not words in response, but rather an unnamed physic, the "receit" of which is "My Saviours bloud." Notably, this blood is experienced not in the recesses of the heart, but in the objective life of the church: "when ever at his board / I do but taste it, straight it cleanseth me / And leaves thee not a word" (lines 14–16). Yet, if Conscience "talkest still," then the physic becomes a weapon:

"some wood and nails to make a staffe or bill / For those that trouble me" (lines 21–22). And so the speaker reveals that the public act of the church in Communion does not stand on its own, but refers to the central public act of Christian history, the crucifixion of Christ, and this is the only and sufficient answer to inner torment.[22] "Conscience" captures the way in which Herbert's poems work individually and yet necessarily refer to community. Herbert's enemy here is the self; his salvation is found in the church. As Wall argues, Herbert here imitates the work of the liturgy, opening the closed text to the present moment by inviting the reader into its individual and yet entirely common experience.[23] Luther's emphasis on the otherness of Christ's voice, though, has formal implications for our reading of Herbert, opening the possibility that one of Herbert's most remarkable poetic moves, inherited from Philip Sidney, has, within "The Church," a liturgical function.

A very different poem, "The Collar," takes place at the same location as "Conscience" and describes a like struggle with a seemingly untamable interiority. In this poem, though, the self speaks not as the inner legalist, but as the full-blooded rebel. Whereas the speaker of "Conscience" goes to the Lord's board, the Communion table, for solace, the action of "The Collar" begins there, as an intended point of departure: "I struck the board, and cry'd, No more. / I will abroad (lines 1–2). This well-known poem builds into an irreverent and even sacrilegious rant, framing the Christian life and more particularly the vocation of the priest as imprisonment, the sacrifice of freedom. The speaker would reject the "cage," the "rope of sands, / Which petty thoughts have made" (lines 21–23), and rather "Recover all [his] sigh-blown age / On double pleasures" (lines 19–20). The charge here is strikingly similar to that of "Conscience" in that, in both poems, the speaker identifies an inner disciplinary voice as the enemy. In fact, if freedom from conscience were the point of the first poem, then "The Collar" would start off as its apt expression. The difference between the conclusion of "Conscience" and the beginning of "The Collar," though, is found in both poems' treatment of the Eucharist. While the first poem's speaker comes to the board for relief, the second poem's speaker tries to escape it. His references to the eucharistic elements— "Have I no harvest but a thorn / To let me bloud" and "Sure there was wine / Before my sighs did drie it: there was corn / Before my tears did drown it" (lines 7–8, 10–12) are irreverent, but they are also desperate: rebellion itself must be articulated in the terms of the table. The poem is most remarkable, though, for the Sidneian speed and simplicity with which it resolves, sweeping away its storm of rage and wild meter with the final lines "Me thoughts I heard one calling, *Child!* / And I reply'd, *My Lord*" (lines 35–36).[24] The speaker, being at the table, hears the alien Word, that word that, unlike the many that have preceded it, is not the speaker's. In this one word, the fullness of the Word becomes present, for in chiding it also speaks the word of love, making manifest the speaker's identity not only as creature called to obey, but also as child, loved by a parent.[25] As has often been noted, the meter in these two lines is the eight and six syllables of the Psalter, showing that the verse, as well as the speaker, has been tuned, through a liturgical discipline, to the voice of God.

In *The Country Parson,* Herbert instructs ministers not to engage in controversial divinity in church, particularly around the question of kneeling at Communion, for "contentiousness in a feast of charity is more scandal than any posture" (Hutchinson, 259). This instruction seems not primarily a matter of propriety or of peacemaking, but rather firstly driven by the recognition that Communion is charged with its own tensions—and delights—of Host and guest, and that controversy displaces this proper difficulty with other self-driven and self-satisfying ones.

Why is it that Herbert in "Love" (III) belabors unworthiness even as "The Church" comes to its end? Some 160-odd poems after "The Altar," the speaker of "Love" characterizes himself as "guiltie of dust and sinne," the unworthy guest (line 2). It is as if we are back where we started, with a man on the ground with a broken heart. The beauty of the poem and its portrayal of a gently irresistible and perfectly graceful Love has kept it one of Herbert's most-read poems. Yet I think we will understand it better if we read it alongside the most jarringly antimodern prayer in the Prayer Book, the "prayer of humble access," which comes after confession and absolution, and even after the congregation has joined with the heavenly host in saying "holy, holy, holy," which logically should be the ultimate effect of having asked God for purification. Instead of immediately receiving Communion, however, the congregation now says,

> We do not presume to come to this thy table (O merciful Lord) trusting in our own righteousness, but in thy manifold and great mercies. We be not worthy so much as to gather up the crumbs under thy table, But thou art the same Lord, whose property is always to have mercy: grant us therefore (gracious Lord) so to eat the flesh of thy dear Son Jesus Christ, and to drink his blood, that our sinful bodies may be made clean by his body, and our souls washed through his most precious blood, and that we may evermore dwell in him, and he in us. Amen. (Booty, 263)

This prayer breaks the logical flow of the liturgy, which should move from confession to forgiveness to praise to Communion, instead returning us to abject unworthiness at the very moment of confidence. Pickstock calls this a "liturgical stammer" that does the work of liturgy precisely by denying the construction of a way to God. Instead, the stammer declares the impossible distance between the human and God, and that paradoxically "permits a genuine proximity with God."[26]

At the very moment when our place in the cosmos seems "meet and right" and we worship with the angels, all is cast down. Yet, at this very moment of acknowledgment that "we be not worthy so much as to gather up the crumbs under thy table" the church is not permitted a way to work up to those crumbs. Instead, the moment of acknowledgment becomes the moment of invitation to the table itself. This is why, as the poem "Sion" makes so astonishingly clear, Herbert is not building an edifice when he rears his altar. That "All Solomons sea of brasse and world of stone / Is not so deare to thee as one good grone" (lines 17–18) is the impossible realization of the liturgy itself, the work to receive the Word. The speaker of "Love" (III) is not being coy, but rather inhabits the common place of the church, the impossible position in which human unworthiness reveals the Lord "whose property is always to have mercy," and who invites us "to sit and eat."

· NOTES

1. See Judith Maltby, *Prayer Book and People in Elizabethan and Early Stuart England* (Cambridge: Cambridge University Press, 1998) on the relative popular success of the Prayer Book; and Anthony Milton, *Catholic and Reformed* (Cambridge: Cambridge University Press, 2002) on the broad but unstable unity of the Elizabethan and Jacobean church.

2. This essay leaves aside questions of the Prayer Book's exact doctrinal position on the Eucharist, which, within scholarship and the life of the Anglican Church has been treated as everything from Zwinglian memorialist to all-but-transubstantive. For an excellent recent reconsideration of the eucharistic doctrine of Herbert's church, see Robert Whalen's introduction in *The Poetry of Immanence: Sacrament in Donne and Herbert* (Toronto: University of Toronto Press, 2002).

3. Cristina Malcolmson, *George Herbert: A Literary Life* (Basingstoke, England: Palgrave Macmillan, 2004), 61.

4. "John Booty, ed., *The Book of Common Prayer, 1559: The Elizabethan Prayer Book* (Charlottesville: University of Virginia Press for the Folger Shakespeare Library, 1976), 19. All subsequent citations will be noted parenthetically in the text.

5. These prayers pluralize the scriptural tense. On the significance of this for

developing a communal identity in worship, see Ramie Targoff, *Common Prayer: The Language of Public Devotion in Early Modern England* (Chicago: University of Chicago Press, 2001), 22ff.

6. See John N. Wall, *Transformations of the Word: Spenser, Herbert, and Vaughan* (Athens: University of Georgia Press, 1988), chap. 1; and Targoff, *Common Prayer*, chap. 1. These two studies, along with Rosemary van Wengen-Shute's *George Herbert and the Liturgy of the Church of England* (Oegstgeest, [country?]: Drukkerij de Kempenaer, 1981) are significant studies to which this article is indebted.

7. F. E. Hutchinson, ed., *The Works of George Herbert* (Oxford: Clarendon Press, 1945), line 8. All subsequent references to *The Temple* and *The Country Parson* will be cited parenthetically in the text.

8. Wall, *Transformations of the Word*, 237.

9. van Wengen-Shute, *George Herbert ad the Liturgy*, 78, 85.

10. Catherine Pickstock, *After Writing: The Liturgical Consummation of Philosophy* (Oxford: Blackwell, 1998), chaps. 4 and 5. Pickstock's subject is the Tridentine Mass, which she reads, through Plato's *Phaedrus* and against Derrida, as a text consummated in its oral practice. I do not know how far, if at all, Pickstock would extend her celebration of the Catholic Reformation Mass, which she somewhat misleadingly describes as medieval, to the Book of Common Prayer, but I find her attempt to take liturgy seriously on its own terms generative to my reading of the Prayer Book and *The Temple*.

11. In *The Country Parson*, Herbert insists on "reasonable service," writing that in prayer "we speak not as parrats" (Hutchinson, *Works of George Herbert*, 232).

12. The Prayer Book required that "every parishioner shall communicate at least three times in the year" (Booty, *Book of Common Prayer, 1559*, 268), though it also requires that Communion take place at least every Sunday in cathedrals and collegiate churches (267). Herbert's residence in London, Cambridge, and then near Salisbury meant that he was never far from regular Communion services, should he have chosen to attend them. In his *Country Parson*, Herbert indicated that parsons should celebrate Communion "if not duly once a month, yet at least five or six times in the year" (*Hutchinson, Works of George Herbert*, 259). As Christopher Hodgkins points out, while Roman Catholics customarily received once a year, Calvin called for weekly Communion (*Authority, Church, and Society in George Herbert: Return to the Middle Way* (Columbia: University of Missouri Press, 1993, 31).

13. This eucharistic subversion of the usual propitiatory economy is not, of course, unique to the Book of Common Prayer, but characterizes the Christian tradition broadly, from Eastern Orthodoxy to Lutheranism.

14. Pickstock, *After Writing*, 183.

15. The 1604 Bishop's Bible title page, used subsequently in King James Bible folio editions, has a title page centered around a lamb on an altar. Some editions of the Prayer Book also featured a title page altar, as did the highly popular *Practice of Pietie*, by Lewis Bayly.

16. See Thomas Aquinas *Summa Theologiae* 3.48.2 on Christ's love as excess repayment for his murderer's sins.

17. Richard Strier, *Love Known: Theology and Experience in George Herbert's Poetry* (Chicago: University of Chicago Press, 1983), xiii–xiv.

18. Heiko Oberman, *Martin Luther: Man between God and the Devil* (New Haven, CT: Yale University Press, 2006), 227.

19. Ibid., 226. Emphasis added.

20. Ibid.

21. It seems unlikely that Herbert would ever specifically have encountered Luther's use of "alieno verbo," since the passages quoted here are from a letter. Yet, the idea, if not the term, is central to Luther's scriptural way of knowing and way of knowing scripture, and it resonates with Herbert's poetry, particularly in the frequent motions there of a "friend," the other who interrupts the speaker with a sudden and succinct voice. These interruptions, usually italicized, occur not only at the table, but also as the speaker struggles to properly hymn God, such as in "A True Hymn" or "Jordan" (II).

22. Notably, Herbert does not follow Luther in attributing the perversity of conscience to the devil, but here and in poems such as "Affliction" (IV) describes his own thoughts as disordered and thus an enemy without naming a further cause.

23. Wall, *Transformations of the Word*, 240, 248.

24. I refer to Sidney's dramatic endings in *Astrophil and Stella*, especially that of the first sonnet, which famously ends "Look in thy heart and write." As Anne-Marie Miller Blaise argues in "'Sweetnesse readie penn'd': Herbert's Theology of Beauty," *George Herbert Journal* 27, nos. 1–2 (Fall 2003/Spring 2004): 1–21, the apparent distinction between this line and Herbert's ending is not so great as commonly understood, for Sidney's turn is not to the self, but to the true image of Stella in his heart (9). Interiority is thus not necessarily isolating, as the self here, as in Herbert, becomes the site of the other.

25. The eucharistic confidence of this ending comes into relief when the poem is compared to those of Herbert's imitator Nathaniel Wanley, whose Puritan sensibilities seem not to allow the boldness of the ending of "The Collar." While Philip West argues that Wanley, in "Deceit," accomplishes a Herbertian turn, the poem's final stanza features not Christ speaking, but rather the speaker's self-reproach. See West, "Nathaniel Wanley and George Herbert: The Dis-Engaged and *The Temple*," *Review of English Studies* 57, no. 230, 1939: 353.

26. Pickstock, *After Writing*, 177.

Herbert and Early Stuart Psalm Culture: Beyond Translation and Meditation

Kate Narveson

A~NY~ INTRODUCTION TO HERBERT'S POETRY WILL LIKELY INCLUDE TWO standard assumptions: first, that Herbert's poetic craft was influenced by experiments in Psalms translation, and second, that his lyrics are rooted in devotional practice. Yet what has not been adequately recognized is the extent to which this combination of features makes "The Church" an anomaly in the early Stuart literary scene. In devotional works, even those rooted in the book of Psalms, ideas about the psalms as poetry do not influence composition. Instead, devotional writers focus on the individual Psalms verse as building material for shapeless prose meditations or repetitive "collage" prayers. Psalms translators were certainly concerned with literary matters—biblical genres, stanza form, and meter—but devotional writers ignored such issues in favor of the book of Psalms as a picture of godly affections and source of pious expression. The work of Phineas Fletcher, a pastor-poet contemporary with Herbert, is typical: when he turned to the Psalms in his devotional writing, he chose to write prolix prose meditations on Psalm 1 that show no concern for the psalm as poem.[1] Devotional writing was a distinct endeavor from literary Psalms translation.[2]

That in literary terms Herbert's verse was indebted to the work of Psalms translators has been well established.[3] But why, if no other devotional writers were imitating Psalms forms, did Herbert? I will argue that in focusing mainly on the discussions that surrounded Psalms translation to illuminate Herbert's poetic choices, we miss the ways in which Herbert's commitment to poetry was also connected to the aims of contemporary devotional writing. By examining points of similarity and difference between Herbert's lyrics and devotional writing rooted in the Psalms, we can gain a better sense of just how unprecedented was his choice to write poetry, and yet how his lyrics nonetheless exhibit the central concerns of early Stuart devotional literature, so that his choice can be seen not just as

211

a literary one but also as a new application of contemporary devotional concerns. Above all, the devotional context reveals how central a didactic aim was to Herbert's choice to write poetry and how closely his poems are in line with the impulse behind devotional prose: an evangelical sense of the pastor's duty.[4] It also calls in question how far we should accept Ramie Targoff's situating of the poems in the context of public worship. Although some of Herbert's lyrics could have been used by an individual or congregation to express devotion, as the Psalms were used, overall "The Church" is closer to the evangelical treatise than to a new Psalter.[5] As Herbert notoriously said, "A verse might find him who a sermon flies."

Early Stuart Psalms Devotions

To see the relation of Herbert's lyrics to evangelical Psalms devotion, we must look first at the kinds of devotional writing based on the book of Psalms, and then at the piety that shaped such works. There were three basic methods in use in early Stuart England, two methods of meditating on a psalm and one method of using the book of Psalms to create prayers. In meditations on a psalm, believers tended to contemplate one verse at a time, often drawing material from throughout scripture to develop the issues raised by each psalm verse. These meditations could be highly emotional—what the period called "affectionate"—or they could be primarily didactic. Alternatively, in what has been called "collation," verses were extracted from a wide range of psalms and reassembled to form devotional utterances, usually prayers.[6] In all three cases, the writers worked on the level of the individual Psalms verse.

The first type, affectionate meditations, were based on the view that the Psalms provided an exemplary picture of the expression of devotion. Proceeding verse by verse through a psalm, the meditator explored the emotions behind each verse, accounting for them in terms of doctrine, and applied the verse to the self, often concluding with a fervent prayer.[7] A translation of Guillaume du Vair's meditations offers a typical example. The speaker fervently responds to each verse: the meditation on Psalm 6:1, "O Lord, rebuke me not in thy anger, nor chasten me in thy wrath," opens thus: "Laie not upon me o Lord the arme of thy severe judgement: It wold throw me like a torrent into the depth of death and eternall damnation. It would devour mee like fier, and the remander of my body would fly away into ashes."[8] And so forth. The speaker starts with the situation or emotion suggested by a Psalms verse and elaborates on it in order to make vivid the experience assumed to be contained therein.

An example of the more didactic approach appears in John Norden's *Imitation of David*.[9] Pastors such as Norden, conscious of their lay readership, sought to connect the psalmist's affective expressions to doctrine. Such meditation was seen primarily as a preparation for prayer, since, as Norden tells his reader, "[P]rayer can never be so powerfull as upon holy premeditation."[10] "Premeditation" for Norden is doctrinal explication. For instance, he comments on Psalm 27:1, "the Lord is my light and my salvation," first by explaining the difference between "corporall" eyes and the light that allows them to see. He then tells his reader, "The ordinary meanes to apprehend Christ the light, is the word, which he taught and left unto us, yet [it is] not of it selfe that light, but onely sheweth it."[11] This discussion of spiritual sight fills several pages, and only subsequently does Norden make any connection to the psalmist, explaining, "[T]herefore, doth David joyne light and salvation together, because that without that light there is no salvation, for light goeth with or before salvation; for without the light of knowledge there can bee no faith, and without faith no salvation."[12] Norden also incorporates verses from, for instance, John, 1 Samuel, and other psalms as he elaborates on the theology behind the psalmist's words, operating according to the standard view that because all of scripture is coherent, like places from throughout the Bible may be brought together to illuminate a point. The emphasis in such meditations on logical clarity and specificity dictates the voice—first-person plural—and the syntax, with its "therefore . . . because . . . for" coordinating conjunctions.

The distinction between affectionate and didactic is not always clear-cut, and many meditations share both impulses. Meditators assumed that the Psalms are at once expressive and edifying because they are, in a frequently quoted phrase from Calvin, the "anatomy of the soul," and therefore (as one Psalms meditator put it) a psalm "displaieth, and laieth wide open before the world al mens motions, passions, and affections."[13] Believers find their own condition limned in the Psalms. Psalms meditations continue in that mode, displaying before others the motions of the godly soul even as they express the affections of the meditator. Sir John Bennet, for instance, explains first how he used the Psalms, and then how his own meditations may be useful to others. David's words were healing to his soul, for he cast the Psalms "into mine own mold, expressed the sense in mine owne plaine language, and paralelling [*sic*] mine with Davids perplexities, applied his plaisters to my sores." Bennett then chose to publish his meditations in the hope that "others may be mooved, as in Christian affection to condole with [him], so by a kinde of reflection, to mourne for themselves."[14] Like the Psalms themselves, Psalms meditations were felt both to express the believer's fervent affections and to anatomize the godly heart, so that others would see their experience laid out, feel that the speaker was voicing words that could be theirs, and be moved to devotion themselves.

Writers of meditation produced baggy, reiterative prose. The verse-by-verse approach exploded any tightness of structure a psalm may have had, and compounding the verbosity, instructions for meditation drew on early modern notions of rhetorical amplification. In one devotional guide, Elnathan Parr taught the use of "enlargement" through logical predicates and "ornaments," including apostrophes, "comely transitions," exclamations, interrogations, wishes, vows, and "ingeminations" or doublings.[15] Devotional works based on the Psalms shared this dependence on amplification, and it only contributed to their copiousness. A meditation or prayer on a single psalm verse was infinitely expandable. In the *Country Parson,* Herbert had written of country folk who "need a mountain of fire to kindle them."[16] For those who published meditations on the Psalms, apparently, the affections were to be heated rather by heaping on fuel than by the spark of a well-turned phrase.

The other main devotional use of the Psalms also gives evidence of the habit of reading them as a storehouse of individual verses rather than as literary forms to be imitated. In collation, believers compose what they variously called prayers, psalms, or hymns by taking individual verses from throughout the book of Psalms and recombining them, so that the whole prayer or hymn is composed simply of verses from the Psalms, culled and organized. Several factors seem to have informed this habit of reading. In describing the ways that Herbert brought similar habits of collation to his poetry, Chana Bloch notes that the marginal apparatus and concordances in Protestant Bibles encourage collation. Directions for reading scripture also teach collation. Nicholas Byfield recommends to his reader, "[M]ake thee a little paper booke . . . then write upon the toppe of every leafe the title for that that thou wouldest observe in reading." As the believer comes across striking and relevant verses, he is to record the book, chapter, and verse. The believer may then draw on this commonplace book to develop a prayer by "digesting" a number of verses on each topic to be covered.[17] Probably the most peculiar version of this use of the Psalms was that by John Clarke's

Some Choice places taken out of the singing Psalmes digested into a method of prayer and praises, in which Clarke extracts and re-arranges stanzas from Sternhold and Hopkins. Clarke's reference in the title to "some choice places" indicates the habit of extracting verses into a scripure commonplace book that lay behind his method. While this technique has roots in Christian liturgy, it was promoted in particular among English Protestants as a way to create devotion rooted in "scripture phrase."[18]

It might be thought that this technique would create something that looks like a psalm, but in fact the end result tended to have no structure or unity. Daniel Featley employed the method in *Ancilla Pietatis,* composing a "preparatory hymn" for each devotion "collected out of divers Psalms." For each, he is guided by a list of topics the hymn is to cover. For instance, in one case, the soul desires "Accesse. Audience. Assistance. Acceptance." Access is covered by means of three verses, taken from Psalms 27 and 51, while audience is covered by verses from Psalms 27, 5, and 45, and so forth. Subject matter controls the accumulation, with no concern for style or form. Within a collation, verse is heaped upon verse, the development merely additive. Further, the language is not crafted for that moment, but is drawn from scripture as a storehouse of conventional language.

To read Herbert's lyrics in the context of these types of Psalms devotion is to see at once a strong kinship and a striking divergence. Like Psalms meditations, Herbert's lyrics understand emotional experience in terms of doctrine—poems have as their nucleus a godly truth about Christian experience and, as Arnold Stein puts it, any particular poem "registers the felt significance and force of a personal apprehension of that truth."[19] Further, the lyrics share the rhetoric of affectionate Psalms meditations, giving voice to the believer's religious motions in apostrophes, expostulations, and exclamations. And, as has been often noted, Herbert shared the belief that verses from throughout scripture comment on one another so that, as Herbert put it, one verse "make[s] a motion" to another "that ten leaves off doth lie" ("The Holy Scriptures" [II], lines 5–6). Yet Herbert approached all these features as a poet. In his hands, for instance, the technique of collation was adapted toward poetic ends that someone like Featley seems never to have considered, enabling concision rather than rhetorical elaboration. Chana Bloch has beautifully demonstrated the way in which Herbert often uses collation to create resonant images: by taking scattered scriptural verses that share a common image and conflating them, Herbert creates an image in which multiple senses are simultaneously at play. Thus, as Bloch points out, in "The Sepulchre," Herbert brings together diverse ways in which stones figure in scripture, "from the sepulcher of Christ to the sinful impulses of man, to Christ's bounty, the true Church, and the Law inscribed in the heart." Bloch also identifies collations based on other modes of association, noting poems where Herbert brings together "like" or "unlike" places, sometimes conflating two verses sharing a common word (e.g., "least" in "The Posie" combines Gen. 32:10 and Eph. 3:8) or joining two phrases by rhyme (e.g., the refrain of "The Church Militant," "how deare to me, O God, thy counsels are! / who may with thee compare," joins Pss. 139:17 and 86:9).[21] Where other devotional writers used Psalms collation for amplification or proof-texting, Herbert employed it poetically, as a way to develop resonant, multivalent images.[22]

There is, then, a world of literary difference between Herbert's lyrics and the typical prolix Psalms meditation. Where Herbert was influenced by the metrical and stanzaic experiments of Psalms translators, devotional meditations on the Psalms published by others show no awareness of the Psalms' formal features. Remarkably, there is little to distinguish meditations on the Psalms from meditations on any other part of scripture. Further, the process of elaborating on each verse successively has the effect of obliterating any formal unity or internal development a psalm may have—the psalm as a poem disappears. Even though early Stuart devotional writers spoke of David as a poet and saw the Psalms as literary works with poetic integrity, they did not use them as formal models. Psalms verses are treated as discrete units rather than parts of a cohesive poem.[23] In writing meditations and prayers, believers show little concern for Psalms as literary wholes or as models for devotional lyrics.

What, then, do we make of Herbert's choice to write lyrics indebted to Psalms translation? Given that devotional writers and translators approached the book of Psalms with different sets of interests, and given that Herbert's lyrics reflect the metrical and stanzaic innovations of the translators and are as far, compositionally, from the congenitally diffuse prose meditation as they can be, it seems fair to ask whether, or in what sense, Herbert's choice to write poetry had any relation to his sense of what was involved in devotional writing. In what follows, I will argue that Herbert saw "The Church" as a work that served the function of a devotional guide and that he mined the resources of poetry for its effectiveness in instruction. His lyrics were to kindle the affections by aiding the understanding in a "holy premeditation," to use Norden's terms.

Broadly speaking, they are as close to sermons—or to didactic meditations—as to prayers. And this choice was deeply rooted in the culture of practical divinity in which Herbert participated. Despite the shapelessness of their own meditations on the Psalms, Herbert's fellow devotional writers did recognize in theory the instructional efficacy of the Psalms as poetry. Herbert put that recognition into practice.

"The Church" as Didactic Devotional Guide

The didactic quality of the lyrics of "The Church" has been stressed by Joseph Summers, who argues for the centrality of the instructional aim, insisting that "the expression of individual experience was valued not for the sake of self-expression but for its didactic effectiveness." Benet, holding that "Herbert's intent to instruct his readers is constant," acknowledges that Herbert's poetry "exploits its didactic possibilities with varying degrees of subtlety," but also demonstrates a remarkable range of techniques that make the poems effective as instruction. As Bloch points out, "[T]he didactic impulse is essential to *The Temple,* whether we like it or not."[24] The didacticism that these critics have identified marks the kinship of "The Church" with the early Stuart devotional guide.

It might seem odd to associate Herbert's lyrics with devotional guides rather than with collections of meditation and prayer. As scholars since Joseph Summers have reminded us, the poems of "The Church" are not simply Herbert's personal effusions but would have been taken to voice the Christian condition in general. But while a few of his lyrics may be open to use by others as their own devotional utterance, many (and arguably most) are not. Aside from those that are narratives, definitions, conversations, and speeches addressed to a personified abstraction such as Death or Justice, even those that involve prayer or meditation are usually representations of a speaker engaged in that act, and there is a difference between a meditation penned in the voice of a Christian everyman for general use and a representation of a particular speaker meditating, a representation that dramatizes developing awareness and emotion. Such lyrics display some aspect of Christian experience in a way that helps readers register its import and gain new insight that may directly speak to their own experience. But the particularity of the representation does not invite the reader to use the poem as his or her own meditation. In this, Herbert's lyrics are like Bennet's Psalms meditations, "the pious bequest of his soule" that is like a "tombe of black Marble" that others may look on and "be mooved, as in Christian affection to condole with him, so by a kinde of reflection, to mourne for themselves," although Herbert's lyrics bring the speaker's inward experiences to life in a way that Bennet and other prose meditators rarely manage.[25]

To align Herbert's lyrics with the private devotional treatise is also to argue against recent discussions of their primarily liturgical nature. *The Temple* is a book aimed not at public worship but at voluntary devotional reading. Ramie Targoff has shown that some of Herbert's lyrics fulfill the period's expectations for liturgical eloquence and provide texts that can serve as the congregation's voice, but while Targoff is right to blur the line between public worship and private devotional practice, she tends to go too far and collapse the distinction. Certainly, private devotion was not an arena for an individualistic quest for one's authentic inner experience, but it nonetheless played a distinctive role in constructing habits of self-understanding and patterns of emotion. Private devotion was voluntaristic and involved scripture reading, meditation, application of doctrine to the heart, and affective address to God. Most of Herbert's lyrics are in this mode rather than in the liturgical mode of official public worship. It is important to note that the distinction between public and private is not that one was communal and the other individual, since a major form of private devotion was household worship. The key difference is that public worship is the act of the community performing its duty to worship God—it is an act of the citizen in the public sphere. Household worship is voluntary. As a result, it tends to have a greater focus on the examination of the heart and applying the truths of scripture to the self. Daniel Featley summarizes the difference in his best-selling devotional work, *Ancilla Pietatis:* public devotion is more solemn and makes more noise, but private ought to be more frequent, and has "a deeper channel." Private devotion is a "preparative" that heats the individual's affections and "breedes this longing after the publike Ministerie."[26] The picture that Targoff gives of the creation of religious interiority through prayer, then, needs greater recognition of the major role of private devotion in the process. Herbert's lyrics are part of the voluntaristic, private, preparative process. Herbert's immediate reception also indicates that for his contemporaries, Herbert's lyrics are closest in aim to the didactic meditation.[27] Along with treatises and guides, such works were to be read and considered in the initial stages of devotion for the insight they give into godly experience and for the freshness with which they make the believer feel the import of a belief, thus preparing the believer to pray.

Thus, even poems that might seem most to belong to the "affectionate" category of meditation, Herbert's Psalms-like lyrics of complaint, ultimately take a didactic turn. It is true that "Longing," for instance, offers an open-ended expression of an emotional state. But it is a companion poem. "The Bag" follows and provides the lesson that drives away despair. "The Bag" at first seems to represent the same speaker's achievement of new clarity: "Away despair! my gracious Lord doth heare." Thus far Herbert could, like David in the book of Psalms, be offering the record of spiritual experience, first despair, then new hope. But the second stanza of "The Bag" makes the didactic turn: "Hast thou not heard, that my Lord Jesus di'd? / Then let me tell thee a strange storie" (lines 7–8). The addressee by this point is no longer "Despair" but the reader of the poem, who is to be instructed.

Similarly in other poems that voice strong emotion, Herbert shapes a narrative or an argument that points a lesson. For instance, an implicit didacticism informs a poem that at first seems to offer a meditator's expression of "inner weather," "The Storm." But it is in fact descriptive, aimed at edification. In it we seem to have a soul meditating on the need to seek mercy:

> *If* as the windes and waters here below
>   Do flie and flow,
> My sighs and tears as busy *were* above;
>   Sure they *would* move
> And much affect thee. . . .

(lines 1–5, emphasis mine)

Ideally his repentance should be so active that it would get a response, "knocking, to thy musicks wrong . . . Glorie and honour are set by, till it / An answer get" (lines 13, 15–16). Richard Strier points out that Herbert here develops a vision of how "God can be affected by human emotional need."[28] Yet in its overall structure the poem is hypothetical, teaching the sort of inner weather that *ought* to possess a believer. The poem is instructive, not expressive. "Repentance," likewise, seems at first to be a prayer of confession and to record the expression of an inner state. It opens with the cry "Lord, I confesse my sinne is great," and begs God, "Cut me not off for my most foul transgression." Following the conventions of a confession of sin, the speaker places his personal sin in the context of mankind's fall: "[W]e are all / To sorrows old, / If life be told/ from what life feeleth, Adams fall." The confrontation with his sin licenses the speaker's plea for forgiveness: "Sweeten at length this bitter bowl, / Which thou hast pour'd into my soul." To this point, the poem seems to be a prayer, a devotional utterance strictly understood. But the last two stanzas take a catechetical turn:

> When thou for sinne rebukest man,
> Forthwith he waxeth wo and wan:
> Bitternesse fills our bowels; all our hearts
>   Pine, and decay,
>   And drop away,
> And carrie with them th'other parts.
>
> But thou wilt sinne and grief destroy;
> That so the broken bones may joy,
> And tune together in a well-set song,
>   Full of his praises,
>   Who dead men raises.
> Fractures well cur'd make us more strong.

> (lines 25–36)

These two stanzas could be a poem on their own. The final stanza weds two images, the setting of bones and the setting of music, and two time frames, rebirth after the death of sin and eternal life after the resurrection, in a remarkable epitome of Christian soteriology and eschatology, driven home with one of Herbert's beloved proverbs. The expressive character of the poem's opening has completely given way to the catechetical, and the poem shifts from devotional utterance to a lesson on the theology of repentance.

This "didactic turn" appears even in "Deniall," one of Herbert's most Psalms-like poems. The first five stanzas resemble a penitential psalm. The soul cries to God unheard; it is like a "brittle bow" burst asunder and like dust; it is untuned, unstrung, hanging like a nipped blossom. Further, as the first stanza signals, the poem's form conveys the distress as well. The speaker cries, "Then was my heart broken, as was my verse" (line 3), and each stanza ends with an unrhymed line and feminine stress pattern. The didacticism of the conclusion in this case is muted: the speaker continues to address God rather than turning to the reader in a lecture:

> O cheer and tune my heartlesse breast,
>   Deferre no time;
> That so thy favours granting my request,

> They and my minde may chime,
> And mend my rhyme.
>
> (lines 26–30)

The petition not only appeals to God, but also instructs the reader, describing how distress may be resolved by a tuning of the speaker, the "chiming" of the speaker's mind with God symbolized by the restoration of masculine stress and rhyme. The poem represents not only distress but its answer.

"The Church" and Evangelical Piety

Even Herbert's most expressive poems, then, are calculated to drive a lesson home, and many of his lyrics, of course, are expressly didactic, either overtly teaching a lesson or telling a story that, as Herbert explains in the *Country Parson,* people "will well remember" (Hutchinson, 233). This didacticism is of a specific sort whose features and motive become clearer if we view them in the context of devotional guides produced by a particular strain of early Stuart piety, what Jerald Brauer called the "evangelical." Evangelical piety placed most weight on the experiential component of religion and therefore revolved around examination of and preaching to the heart, the center of the felt relationship to God.[29] Preaching was vital, because evangelicals emphasized that the heart must be kindled by a right understanding of its various affections. Phineas Fletcher, like Herbert a poet who was ordained relatively late in life, reminded his "deere Parishioners of Hilgay" that he has "laboured with all, nay above my strength, to bring you to that true knowledge of God, and our Lord Jesus Christ; and settle you in his grace. . . . [so that] you of this flocke whom God hath called, may be further builded in your most holy faith."[30] Parishioners needed guidance in interpreting the drama of the heart, which during the life of the believer was the site of a never-ending struggle between the fledgling efforts to serve God and the entrenched perversity of the "old man."

Herbert shared this piety. Critics have amply demonstrated his preoccupation with inward struggle, his many representations in "The Church" of the contrast between the hard heart and the heart suppled by grace, whether directly, as a dew or balm, or through affliction.[31] Herbert's evangelical tendencies appear in the *Country Parson* as well. His injunction that parsons are to preach by "dipping and seasoning all [their] words and sentences in [their] hearts . . . truly affecting and cordially expressing all that [they] say; so that the auditors may plainly perceive that every word is heart-deep," reflects the evangelical stress on felt experience (Hutchinson, 233). And as a teacher who must help his flock understand the ebbs and flows of godly affections, the parson must edify parishioners not only through preaching but also through prayer and sacraments, and, Herbert stresses, because attendance at worship meant nothing unless followed by the fruits of faith, the parson must spend weekday afternoons "in circuit." He is to discourse with his parishioners, to rebuke those who need it, to instruct them in matters such as medicine and law as well as faith, and to remind them of the proper attitude toward labor and worldly goods. Even the works of charity that Herbert prescribes fall generally under the rubric of edification; the parson is to distribute his charity so that the very weighing of worth and frequency of gifts serve as a lesson supplementing the advice or admonishment with which the parson addresses each person. The parson settles disputes in a fashion that teaches, and his very life is a lesson in temperance and charity.[32]

Evangelical piety cut across the spectrum from moderate Puritan to conformist.[33] John Favour, a conformist chaplain to Tobie Matthew, archbishop of York, for instance, held that the established church represented a return to the true doctrine and worship of the early church, and insisted on the need for ongoing instruction to fight what he saw as papal ignorance and superstition.[34] His concern to instruct even the meanest Christian appears in *Antiquitie Triumphing over Noveltie* (London, 1619), in which he uses colloquial phrases like "have the lucke on't" and "very good cheape."[35] Favour could be Herbert's country parson: he wrote his work despite impediments, "as preaching every Sabbath day, lecturing every day in the weeke, exercising justice in the Commonwealth, practising of Physicke and Chirurgerie, in the great penurie and necessitie thereof in the countrey where I live."[36] Another conformist evangelical, Thomas Tymme, wrote a tract celebrating Prayer Book worship and calling for a less exclusive emphasis on preaching, but also wrote *The Silver Watch-bell* (seventeen editions by 1634), whose epistle to the reader states that he framed his book as a watch-bell "to awake the most drowsie harted Sinners . . . [that] finding themselves, by their forepassed wicked life, not woorthy of the least of Gods mercies, they may reforme their lives, and seeke speedily to be reconciled unto our Lord and Saviour Jesus Christ. And I doe heartily wish that this labour of mine, may bee . . . so sweet a recreation in soule . . . and that it may yeeld a healing

plaster to everie wounded soule."[37] The main notes of Herbert's
piety are struck here—the sinner as worth less than the least of
God's mercies, grace as sweetness and healing to the wounded
soul, just as *The Temple* is to bring comfort to a "poor dejected
soul." This sort of piety, then, could exist comfortably within the
established church, and spurred a sort of publication that could illuminate the didactic impulse behind *The Temple*.

The challenge to the evangelical was to create devotional forms
that would foster godly and fervent affections while guiding the
reader in a right understanding and expression of that inner experience. Given the emphasis on understanding, evangelical works
tend to be warmly concerned to awaken and instruct the reader.
Phineas Fletcher's *Joy in Tribulation; or, Consolations for afflicted
Spirits* (1632) is typical. Addressing affliction and comfort, the
treatise offers expositions of the issues, considerations addressed to
the reader, meditations framed as the speaker's address to his soul,
and prayers seeking the sorts of comfort available to the afflicted, a
range of modes that resembles that of Herbert's poems. Fletcher's
meditations are typically verbose, preaching at length to the soul
to the point of noting and answering objections. The kinship with
Herbert's piety appears not in form but in Fletcher's treatment of
the heart, as when he states that comfort, "being nothing else but
a lenitive plaister for a wounded Spirit, is by our heavenly Physitian
prescribed onely to an heart sicke of sinne, and broken with godly
sorrow." Ministers are charged to apply that "Balme of Gilead" to
all who feel the smart of their sins.[38] Many of the lessons are also
Herbert's: what seems sinful despair at one's dullness is in fact an
indication that one is not dead to sin; what seems to be affliction is
in fact the gentle corrective of a loving father; God welcomes an
importunate beggar and heart-wracked groans.[39]

The kinship of "The Church" with evangelical treatises appears
also in a shared vocabulary of homely or scriptural figures focused
on the heart. Fletcher, for instance, writes, "[T]here is in us natu-
rally a deceitful heart, starting aside like a broken bow."[40] Afflic-
tions are a trial by fire, that "as in a furnace the most precious
mettal leaveth behind it some drosse, so I from this tryall might
come forth much more purified and clensed from my sinfull
steynes and pollution."[41] Christ conquers sin in our hearts: "[C]er-
tainly, the Lord Jesus hath set up his victorious Crosse in thee, and
he that now hangs out a flagge of defiance, will shortly set up his
banner of triumph."[42] Like Herbert, Fletcher celebrates the heart's
joy at the indwelling Spirit: "There let it abide, there let it reigne,
making thee to delight in the Lord, to turne and tune thy grones

and sighs, to hymnes and spiritual songs.''[43] And, in a passage that
shares Herbert's piety in several ways, Fletcher writes that God's
children are

> even swallowed with griefe, because they forget this comfortable truth,
> and doe not consider in the evill day, that the Lord hath . . . recorded
> and keepeth tale of their sighs, and bottles up their teares as a memori-
> all for them. . . . [T]hey make no question but God sees all their mis-
> deeds and sinnes, but that the Lord should behold their spirits sighing
> under the burthens, groaning under this oppression of Satan, that hee
> should in mercie, compassion, and love behold the wrastlings, stru-
> glings, and the bitter griefe of their hearts thus yoked with the body of
> death, they utterly forget. . . . This we must carefully amend, and fasten
> this truth in our memories, that the Lord cannot despise his owne
> worke in his creatures, but sees and perfectly knowes all the thoughts
> of our heart, so that our desires thirsting for his righteousnesse . . . are
> all heard and noted by him.''[44]

The Lord as a loving father, the tender, quickened heart oppressed
by sin and thirsting for righteousness, the sighs and groans—all
sound the characteristic notes of "The Church." The similarities
extend to imagery (tears bottled as a memorial [Ps. 56:8]) and tone
(the sweet compassion for the weak humans and the assured description of a tender God lovingly witnessing each soul's bitter
grief).

Such treatises illuminate the way evangelical piety wed together
both instruction and a sensitivity to the experience of the godly
heart, that peculiar marriage that also characterizes Herbert's lyrics. What distinguishes Herbert's work from that of other evangelicals is not its aim or conception of the godly condition but his
choice of poetic rather than rhetorical development of a topic. For
instance, when we compare the passage I have just quoted from
Fletcher's *Joy in Tribulation* with "Praise" (III), we can appreciate
how tightly Herbert could condense evangelical teaching by captur-
ing his subject in poetic form. Herbert's treatment of Fletcher's
subject is triumphant, that of a soul who has recognized that God
takes note of each believer.[45] Like Fletcher, Herbert draws on
Psalm 56:8: "I have not lost one single tear: / But when mine eyes /
Did weep to heav'n, they found a bottle there / . . . Readie to take
them in" (lines 25–29). But Herbert oddly and brilliantly extends
the tear imagery to encompass Christ's sacrifice and victory as well:

> But after thou hadst slipt a drop
> From thy right eye

> (Which there did hang like streamers neare the top
> Of some fair church, to show the sore
> And bloudie battell which thou once didst trie)
> The glasse was full and more.
>
> (lines 31–36)

Where Fletcher (among many) refers to Christ's banner planted in our hearts, Herbert conflates tears and banners, and thus offers in one image Christ's triumph over and satisfaction for sin.

Herbert also saw the possibility of using the expressive and dramatic qualities long recognized as characteristic of the Psalms, but turning them to the ends of evangelical didacticism. "Praise" (III) is typical here too: by speaking in his own person, Herbert can speak as one of the poor children that longs to feel grace, yet at the same time provide the authoritative pastoral perspective that Fletcher offers his reader.[46] This strategy was unprecedented; evangelical works do not develop the affective potential of this exemplary expressiveness. Fletcher's meditations, for instance, though addressed to his soul, make little pretence of verisimilitude; they do not even take advantage of the chance for dialogue and present the soul as the one objecting and needing instruction. The dependence on techniques of rhetorical amplification is in part to blame. In a prayer for a private person, Daniel Featley does convey something of the urgency of Herbert's poems of affliction:

> O Lord, despise not the sighing of a contrite heart: O cast him not from thy presence who valueth thy love above all things in Heaven and earth. . . . For all my hope is in thy promises, all my comfort in thy Word, all my riches in thy bounty, all my delight in the light of thy countenance, all my contentment in thy love. And now that my sins have cast a thicke cloud betweene me and thy face which sometime shined most brightly upon me: I am as unable to expresse, as long to endure my sorrow. . . . I returne to the closet of my heart; I shut the doore of my lips; I keepe silence even from good words though it be paine unto me; I vent my desires in sighes; I voice my prayers in groanes; I powre out my complaints in teares.[47]

Yet Featley simply states his condition. Even while he makes brief use of affective metaphor, his prayer tends to enumerate rather than develop, not only in the last sentence of the passage above, but in the sentence listing "all my hope . . . comfort . . . riches . . . delight."[47] The contrast with Herbert's "Longing" is instructive. The product of the same devotional stance, the poem opens with the speaker crying out:

With sick and famisht eyes,
With doubling knees and weary bones,
To thee my cries,
To thee my grones,
To thee my sighs, my tears ascend.

(lines 1–5)

But Herbert dramatizes the soul's desperate attempts to penetrate God's silence by the persistent clamor of arguments and inducements:

Lord Jesu, thou didst bow
Thy dying head upon the tree:
O be not now
More dead to me!
Lord, heare! Shall he that made the eare
Not heare?

(lines 25–30)

"Wilt thou deferre / To succour me. . . . Hast thou left all things to their course. . . . Is all lockt? hath a sinners plea / No key?" (lines 31–36, 39–40, 44, 47–48). Herbert's multiplication of reasons and his persistent questions replicate the desperation and incomprehension of the godly soul that feels deserted by God. Most evangelical works seek a generalized exemplarity, controlled and directed toward clear teaching, and the works do not attempt to represent or express the unfolding of the interior event. In Herbert's lyrics, though, spiritual experience is both dramatized and explicated; they offer psalmic expression and didactic meditation rolled into one.

The prissiness of evangelical devotional writing is especially surprising because of evangelical piety's fondness for the Psalms as records of a godly heart. That fondness can also help explain Herbert's sense of what his poems were to do.[49] Fletcher offers a picture of the Psalms that could apply to the lyrics of "The Church." He declares that all acknowledge the usefulness of the Psalms because they anatomize the godly man:

[W]e here behold lively drawne, by Gods owne finger, not onely the face, and hand (the outward profession, and actions) but the very heart of that man, who was according to Gods owne heart: and so may take there a full view of every limb, and be acquainted with every joynt, and feature of the new, and inward man: wee shall there see that heart ever in action, continualy drawing from that living fountain the word (to which it cleaves unseparable) the waters of life, and having throughly concocted them in the affection, returning them againe to every part for growth and practice.[50]

In speaking of poems in which are lively drawn each joint and feature of the inward man, Fletcher could be describing "The Church."[51] The effect of such poems is also telling. For Fletcher, David, "by expressing his holy affections, filled others, on all occasions, to lay open, and poure out their hearts to God in prayer." Fletcher even contrasts a doctrinal explication with the Psalms' dramatization: it is true that when we see "the combat between the spirit and the flesh doctrinally expressed," it gives no small light. "But," he continues, "when we behold it acted personally . . . it doth not only cleare our understanding but powerfully works on our affections."[53] This is why "the booke of Psalmes is by all acknowledged the most profitable, and usefull, because we here behold lively drawne . . . the very heart of that man, who was according to Gods owne heart."[54] We may see faith sometimes "soring so high that it is sing'd with presumption, sometime plunged in the deep, labouring for life," or the psalmist full of praise, "his heart well tuned and his tongue consorting with it," or mourning like a dove, his spirit "sticking fast in the mire, where no stay is."[55] Given Herbert's representation of these sorts of moments, and Ferrar's report that Herbert described his lyrics as "a picture of the many spiritual Conflicts that have passed betwixt God and my Soul," we can see Herbert aiming to create what Fletcher says the Psalms offer: a picture of the combat between flesh and spirit "personally acted" and therefore powerfully working on our affections.

This strategy was new. Despite the admiration voiced for David's psalms, and despite the centrality of inner experience, evangelical works described but did not dramatize the experience of the heart. What is surprising, ultimately, is that other contemporaries of Herbert were not quicker to use literary means to make their lessons effective, since in emphasizing the instructional impulse motivating Herbert's verse, I am only repeating what his contemporaries said about the Psalms: the choice of poetic form reflected a desire to teach more effectively. Fletcher's analysis may again be useful. He explains that God chose to provide holy songs because God perceived "our difficulty in learning, especially things spirituall" and saw "a certaine aptnesse in numbers to convey to our mindes, and settle in our memories these profitable lessons." God chose David because he had "the gift of Musicke."[56] In "Praise" (III), Herbert wishes, "O that I might some other hearts convert" (line 39). The aim is that of the evangelical pastor. The lyrics of "The Church" fit with the evangelical project in that they are intended to minister edification and comfort to poor, afflicted souls. The choice of poetry reflects the same desire to instruct in a way that will stick. Herbert combined the didacticism of evangelical manuals with the expressiveness of the Psalms and with the economy and focus of secular lyric, dedicating to God the effectiveness of poetry in ministering comfort to the "poor dejected soul."

A comparison between Herbert's lyrics and the various devotional uses of the Psalms highlights that of all the modes a writer might adopt, the didactic most consistently informs Herbert's verse, despite its vast distance from the shapeless Psalms meditation. Herbert shared the evangelical pastor's intent to inform the understanding and arouse the affections. Yet that commitment, while a point of identity with other devotional writers, can also help explain his remarkable departure from them, his turn from diffuse prose meditation to tightly crafted verse. There was a sense already potential in attitudes toward David as poet that the evangelical's goal was best realized by lyric verse, dramatizing figures "personally acting." Herbert acted on that sense.

NOTES

1. Phineas Fletcher, *The Way to Blessednes, a Treatise or Commentary, on the first Psalme* (London, 1632).

2. This is as true of devotional verse as prose. Fletcher is again representative; *The Purple Island,* his religious poem, is formally unadventurous. And aside from some experiments with hymns such as those by George Withers (intended for public worship) and some sonnets, the devotional verse of Nicholas Breton, the Fletchers, Martha Moulsworth, William Austin, Alice Sutcliffe, and scores of others likewise took the form of shapeless meditations in couplets.

3. Most of the scholarship on Herbert's use of the Psalms has focused on ways in which he shared the literary concerns of Psalms translators. See especially Coburn Freer, *Music for a King: George Herbert's Style and the Metrical Psalms* (Baltimore: Johns Hopkins University Press, 1972); Noel Kinnamon, "Notes on the Psalms in Herbert's *The Temple,*" *George Herbert Journal* 4, no. 2 (1981): 10–29; Rivka Zim, *English Metrical Psalms: Poetry as Praise and Prayer* (Cambridge: Cambridge University Press, 1987); Barbara Lewalski, *Protestant Poetics and the Seventeenth-Century Religious Lyric* (Princeton, NJ: Princeton University Press, 1979), 300–304; and Hannibal Hamlin, *Psalm Culture and Early Modern Literature* (Cambridge: Cambridge University Press, 2004).

4. The didactic character of Herbert's verse has been discussed by Joseph Summers, *George Herbert: His Religion and Art* (Cambridge: Harvard University Press, 1954), 102–3; and Diana Benet, *Secretary of Praise: The Poetic Vocation of George Herbert* (Columbia: University of Missouri Press, 1984), passim. Neither, however, situates Herbert's didacticism in the specific context of contemporary devotional discourse.

5. For Herbert's lyrics in relation to liturgy, see Ramie Targoff, *Common Prayer: The Language of Public Devotion in Early Modern England* (Chicago: University of Chicago Press, 2001), chap. 4. While Targoff is right to argue that Herbert saw Prayer Book worship as vital to the shaping of inward piety, it does not follow that he saw his lyrics as "comparable to the texts of public liturgy." The poems may "represent common devotional experiences," but those are usually the individual's experiences met with in private devotion, not public worship (99–100). In response to John Wall, Christopher Hodgkins has argued that the externalist, behavioral approach to public worship "slights a crucial question: was not the reformed English liturgy itself designed to teach?" Hodgkins argues that Herbert, like Cranmer and the other Tudor Protestant reformers, saw the externals of worship as means to pointedly evangelistic ends. See Hodgkins, *Authority, Church, and Society in George Herbert: Return to the Middle Way* (Columbia: University of Missouri Press, 1993), 4–5.

6. Susan Felch discusses collation in her forthcoming edition of Elizabeth Tyrwhit's prayers. I am grateful to Prof. Felch for sharing her work with me.

7. See, for instance, Theodore Beza, J. Bennett, *A Psalme of mercy* (London, 1625). William Hunnis's versified *Seven Sobs of a Sorrowfull Soule* could be called metaphrase in Louise Schleiner's sense, but he expands on each verse to the point that the original psalm almost disappears.

8. Guillaume du Vair, *Holy Meditations upon seaven Penitential and Seaven Consolatory Psalmes,* trans. W. Shute (London, 1612), 1–2.

9. John Norden, *The Imitation of David His godly and constant resolution . . . collected by way of Meditations and Prayers out of the 27 Psalme* (London, 1624). See also William Watkinson, *Moste Excellent Meditations upon the xxxii Psalme* (London, 1579); Sir John Hayward, *Davids Teares* (London, 1623); Samuel Page, *The Broken Heart: or Davids Penance* (London, 1637); and Sir Richard Baker, *Meditations and Disquisitions upon the Seven Psalmes of David* (London, 1639).

10. Norden, *Imitation of David,* sig. A8v.

11. Ibid., 14.

12. Ibid., 15.

13. John Calvin, *Commentary on the Book of Psalms,* trans. Arthur Golding (London, 1571), preface; Watkinson, *Most Excellent Meditations,* sig. *3v.

14. Bennet, *Psalm of Mercy,* sigs. A6r-A7r.

15. Elnathan Parr, *Abba Father* (London, 16xx), 37.

16. All of Herbert's works are cited from *The Works of George Herbert,* ed. F. E. Hutchinson (Oxford: Clarendon, 1941). Here the quotation is from p. 233.

17. Nicholas Byfield, *Directions for the private reading of the Scriptures* (London, 1618), sig. A10r. Examples of scripture commonplace books include Devon Record Office Z19/55/2, and Northampton Record Office FH 260.

18. One of the earliest printed examples was by the Catholic John Fisher, but was published without attribution and embraced by Protestants; see Fisher, *Psalmes or Prayers taken out of holye Scripture* (London, 1645). For other examples, see Thomas Becon, *The Pomander of Prayer* (London, 1558), sigs. 29v-31v; Henry Bull, *Christian Prayers and Meditations* (London, 1568); Thomas Rogers, *A Golden Chaine, taken out of the Psalmes of King David* (London 1579); and Christopher Stile, *Psalmes of Invocation upon God* (London, 1588).

19. Arnold Stein, *George Herbert's Lyrics* (Baltimore: Johns Hopkins University Press, 1968), 2. For the doctrinally rooted nature of Herbert's representation of emotion, see especially Richard Strier, *Love Known: Theology and Experience in George Herbert's Poetry* (Chicago: University of Chicago Press, 1983).

20. Chana Bloch, *Spelling the Word: George Herbert and the Bible* (Berkeley and Los Angeles: University of California Press, 1985), 59.

21. See ibid., 62.

22. Ibid., chap. 5.

23. John Donne may have been a partial exception; Barbara Lewalski has found that he responded to the Psalms as "organic, intricately contrived lyrics," but she also acknowledges that he made little overt use of the Psalms in his poetry (*Protestant Poetics*, 52).

24. Summers, *George Herbert*, 102–3; Benet, *Secretary of Praise*, 33–35; Bloch, *Spelling the Word*, 170.

25. Bennet, *Psalme of mercy*, sig. A7r.

26. Daniel Featley, *Ancilla Pietatis* (London, 1626), 2–6; Targoff, *Common Prayer*, chap. 4, and, on the shaping efficacy of worship, 6–13.

27. See Philip West, "Nathaniel Wanley and George Herbert: The Dis-Engaged and *The Temple*," *Review of English Studies* 57, no. 230 (2006): 337–58; Robert H. Ray, *The Herbert Allusion Book: Allusions to George Herbert in the Seventeenth Century* (Chapel Hill: University of North Carolina Press, 1986).

28. Strier, *Love Known*, 185.

29. Puritan and conformist come closest in piety when their basic outlook is evangelical. Evangelicals did not dismiss problems of outward order, but they tended to take a functional rather than a doctrinaire position, judging the outward according to the effect on the heart's expression. Similarly, evangelicals did not dismiss problems of theology, but their focus on inner weather and on aiding distressed souls inclined them to adapt the spiritual physic to the individual case rather than to attempt abstract or systematic formulations. They would, for instance, in one context carefully demolish any claim to merit on the part of the elect, and yet in another context stress that the believer must strive to increase God's graces in the heart. For a fuller discussion of evangelical piety, see Jerald Brauer, "Types of Puritan Piety," *Church History* 65 (1987): 47–50.

30. Fletcher, *Way to Blessednes*, sig. A5r.

31. In chapters 1 and 6 of *Love Known*, Strier deals with sin as a psychological and spiritual condition and with the inwardness of Herbert's sense of religious experience; Lewalski, *Protestant Poetics*, 309–11, discusses the heart.

32. Clearly, Herbert does not ignore questions of the conduct of life and morals, but he looks first to the heart for grace as the root from which service to God grows. The question of piety is which concern dominates. See also Hodgkins, *Authority, Church, and Society in George Herbert*, chap. 7.

33. Hodgkins has proposed that Herbert's piety was one of "regenerative nostalgia" for the Elizabethan church, but Daniel Doerksen has anticipated my argument that Herbert was not alone in his piety. See Hodgkins, *Authority, Church, and Society in George Herbert*, 1; and Doerksen, *Conforming to the Word* (Lewisburg: Bucknell University Press, 1997), 13–14 and passim.

34. For Matthew, see Kenneth Fincham, *Prelate as Pastor: The Episcopate of James I* (Oxford: Clarendon Press, 1990), 253–67.

35. John Favour, *Antiquitie Triumphing over Noveltie* (London, 1619), 71, 13.

36. Ibid., sig. A5r. That life also characterized Phineas Fletcher, who like Herbert came from a moderately distinguished family, gave up hope of court appointment, and took a rural call, publishing his religious poetry in 1633. Many of the ideas in his two prose tracts are usually classified as Puritan, yet Fletcher was content with the established church.

37. Thomas Tymme, *Silver Watch-bell*, 5th ed. (London, 1608), sig. A6r.

38. Phineas Fletcher, *Joy in Tribulation; or, Consolations for Afflicted Spirits* (London, 1632), 4–5.

39. Ibid., 4, 46–48, 120, 136; Herbert, "Gratefulness," "Sion," "Love Unknown," the affliction poems.

40. Fletcher, *Joy of Tribulation,* 45; compare "Denial," lines 6–7, and Psalm 78:57.

41. Fletcher, *Joy of Tribulation,* 52; compare "Love Unknown."

42. Fletcher, *Joy of Tribulation,* 329.

43. Ibid., 332. Fletcher's similes are typical of those that evangelical writers use to bring abstract doctrine to down to earth. In his own treatise on affliction, appended to *A Pathway to Pietie* (London, 1613), the moderate Puritan Robert Hill assembles several of Herbert's images when he asserts, "[W]ee are Gods trees, we shall grow better by pruning: Gods smell better by rubbing: Gods spice, bee more profitable by bruising: and Gods conduits, we are the better by running" (639).

44. Fletcher, *Joy of Tribulation,* 258–59.

45. See Strier, *Love Known,* 168.

46. Benet notes that in such cases, affective utterance is effective didactically because we as readers overhear rather than are directly addressed with a lesson to learn (*Secretary of Praise,* 39). She also demonstrates the way sequences as well as individual poems operate didactically, as we are called to exercise our "inferential and critical powers," which gives "the pleasure of detecting the speakers of the poems in an error, of applying an insight from an earlier to a subsequent, poem, of realizing that two apparently contradictory poems complement each other, or of formulating the conclusions implicit in the order of the poems" so that "the reader participates in his own edification" (96).

47. Featley, *Ancilla Pietatis,* 702–5.

48. Another prayer that adumbrates Herbert's more immediately personal representation of the Christian's inner life appears in Hill's *Pathway to Pietie.* In a "Prayer to be used by a mans selfe, or with others, changing the number," the speaker voices the sort of existential sinfulness common in Herbert's lyrics: "I feele, O Lord, (but it is thy Spirit that giveth me this feeling) that mine understanding is darkened, conscience feared, memory decayed, will bewitched, heart hardened, affections disordered, conversation corrupted" (*Pathway to Pietie,* 709). Hill, though, does not expand on any of these conditions.

49. See Lewalski, *Protestant Poetics,* 39–53, and Elizabeth Clarke, chap. 3, for views of the Psalms as divine poetry. Clarke offers a fuller account of Herbert's poetics as a development of Protestant uses of the Psalms for meditation than I am able to offer here. While I would argue that she overemphasizes the problems Herbert felt in writing poetry, her work should be central to any consideration of this topic.

50. Fletcher, *Way to Blessedness,* sig. A7v.

51. I am thinking of such lyrics as "The Temper" (I), "Frailty," "Ephesians 4:30. Grieve not the Holy Spirit," "Submission," "The Flower," "The Odour. 2 Corinthians 2," and "A Parody."

52. Fletcher, *Way to Blessedness,* 5.

53. Ibid., sig. A7r.

54. Ibid., A7v.

55. Ibid., A8r.

56. Ibid., 5.

IV
Pastor, Garden, and Pasture

Herbert's Pastor as Herbalist

Curtis Whitaker

In the chapter titled "the parson's completeness," approximately halfway through *The Country Parson,* George Herbert argues that his ideal pastor should possess expertise in herbal medicine in order to play the part of a physician.[1] This blurring of professional boundaries in Herbert's handbook for clergymen tells us much about the relationship of religion and science in the sixteenth and seventeenth centuries, demonstrating how these two areas of study were not separate and distinct in the way we usually think of them today. It was perfectly acceptable for a botanist to include biblical information in a scientific work such as an herbal and not unusual for a clergyman to dabble in the scientific study of plants. This essay will first put Herbert's apparently odd herbal recommendation in the context of early modern medicine—and science more generally—and then examine discussions of roses as a kind of medicinal test case, since they appear consistently in the herbals of the period as well as in Herbert's poetry.

Two main questions come up consistently in the sixteenth and early seventeenth centuries about prescribing medicines: first, what is being prescribed? and second, who is prescribing it? Both of these questions require some consideration of the many sixteenth-century additions to the materia medica, or herbal compilations, of the Middle Ages. First, many imports of spices and plants from Asia and the Americas appeared in the Renaissance as Europeans began colonizing and trading in these areas. Some of the best known of these included cinchona bark, from which quinine is derived, and guaiac, used in the treatment of syphilis. Then there were also many newly catalogued plants that were homegrown in England. Beginning with Continental herbalists such as Leonhard Fuchs in Germany, sixteenth-century naturalists catalogued many plants in northern Europe that did not appear in the ancient botanical texts of Dioscorides and Theophrastus. Finally, there were the new chemical substances associated with Paracelsus and his followers. Substances such as mercury and antimony were used both by

themselves as well as in mixtures combined with herbs of the materia medica.[2] Late medieval herbals contain a core of seventy plants;
that number grew to about seven hundred with the first edition of
the London *Pharmacopeia* in 1618, a tenfold increase within 150
years.[3] As a point of comparison, the herbal medicines currently
sold in Britain derive from about 550 plants,[4] so the Renaissance
saw a huge growth in the number of available pharmaceuticals.

Among these different substances that were available, Herbert is
clear about his preferences. He writes in *The Country Parson,* "In
the knowledge of simples [that is, an herb used individually rather
than in a compound], wherein the manifold wisedome of God is
wonderfully to be seen, one thing would be carefully observed;
which is, to know what herbs may be used in stead of drugs of the
same nature, and to make the garden the shop: For home-bred
medicines are both more easie for the Parsons purse, and more familiar for all mens bodyes" (Hutchinson, 261). The opposition
Herbert makes between herbs, or simples, and drugs has to do with
Renaissance pharmacy practices. Many apothecaries liked selling
complex combinations of herbs, called "Galenicals," which con-
sisted of expensive plants from other parts of the world. A substance such as theriac, which was thought to fight off poisons,
could require as many as eighty different simples to create. The
economic motive lying behind these elaborate concoctions was
often clear: hence Herbert's remark on the "Parsons purse." Herbert dismisses these foreign plants and spices as "vanities," much
preferring the "home-bred" ones, since they are more "familiar,"
or natural, to an English person's body than the expensive, unusual
ones apothecaries liked to sell.

Thus, rhubarb—an exotic plant at the time, imported from
China through Turkey or Russia—was popular with the druggist,
even though "damask or white roses," Herbert says, work just as
well as a purgative, or substance that evacuates the bowels. Herbert
continues with a discussion of bolearmena, or "Armenian bolus,"
an astringent earth from Armenia that was supposed to bind a loose
bowel: "So where the apothecary useth . . . bolearmena, the parson
useth plantain, shepherd's purse, and knot-grass." These last three
herbs are all common plants; indeed, the *OED* calls knot-grass "a
common weed in waste ground."[5] So Herbert is skeptical about
both the new plants from foreign parts and the new chemicals that
were being added to the Renaissance pharmacopeia. Such an attitude appears often in the poems as well, where Herbert considers
the attractiveness of, say, cloves, nutmeg, and cinnamon—all exotic spices in the Renaissance—in order to dismiss them in favor of

his own humble portion, or "size," as in the poem of that title. Thus, Herbert's preference for herbs over drugs corresponds to our general perception of him as a man with a distaste for flashiness, at least in his later years, when he wrote *The Country Parson* at Bemerton.[6]

But it would be unfair to see Herbert's preference for native herbs as solely economic in origin; his recommendation corresponds to current seventeenth-century thought on the physiological effects of local remedies. Nicholas Culpepper's herbal of 1652, for instance, states boldly on its title page that his herbal remedies are for an "English Physitian" looking after "English Bodies."[7] Alix Cooper has shown that this emphasis on local herbs for local populations was a widespread phenomenon in Europe in the sixteenth and seventeenth centuries, appearing in German and Dutch herbals as well as English ones.[8] Beginning with Paracelsus in the early 1500s, many compilers of herbals argued that natural sympathies existed between humans and their native environments, and that local medicinals were more effective than exotic ones. The original impetus behind such scientific nationalism may have been religious in nature, as countries sought to establish their own identities in the wake of the Protestant Reformation, but over time herbalists' preference for the indigenous over the exotic was rooted in the physiological thought of the time.[9]

We can see this line of thinking developed in further detail elsewhere in *The Country Parson,* as in Herbert's discussion of the parson's house, where red meat should be frequently served to suit "an English body" (Hutchinson, 243). Herbert presents the view that the cold, northern climate of England requires a diet heavy in red meat, unlike the more temperate countries of southern Europe. He (incorrectly) believes that a meat diet relieves rather than adds to constipation, and that the English in general, and scholars in particular, "are two great obstructed vessels" most helped by eating of "flesh." Local conditions are presented as bearing heavily on an individual's physiology, and religious customs such as fasting or eating fish on Fridays consequently require adjustment to suit the health of local populations.

This medical advice regarding the intake of herbs and meat is typical of the knowledge Herbert's parson can acquire with the reading of just three books: an herbal, an anatomy, and a "physic," or comprehensive book of physiology, such as that of Jean Fernel, whom Herbert mentions by name (261). Although Fernel's studies of physiology were to be eclipsed in the history of medicine by the accomplishments of other Renaissance medical writers such as

Vesalius and Harvey, in his time he was regarded much more highly, since he compiled existing Galenic thought in a systematic way and wrote the first comprehensive discussion of physiology.[10] His works were frequently reprinted in the seventeenth century,[11] and for Herbert, writing some seventy years after Fernel's death, he would still have enjoyed authority on many medical questions, especially those concerning humoral understanding of diet. When Herbert writes of Fernel, "Let his Method of Phisick be diligently perused, as being the practicall part, and of most use" (261), he shows the commonsense attitude toward medicine illustrated in his remarks on specific herbs as well as a general awareness of what was viewed as the current medical thinking of his time.

The second question mentioned above about medical prescriptions has to do with who is permitted to do the prescribing. Renaissance medicine was practiced in England by groups with competing interests: there were the physicians, who enjoyed the strongest claim to institutional support with the creation of the College of Physicians in 1518; the surgeons, who originally formed their guild in the time of Chaucer and merged with the barbers in 1540 to form the Barber-Surgeons Company; the apothecaries, who organized with James I's approval as a special body within the Grocers' Company in 1607; and finally, the "uneducated empirics," to use a term commonly applied to people without formal education who administered herbal remedies based on experiential or empirical knowledge.[12]

The obvious problem with these groups is that they were often encroaching on one another's territory. Some ailments required internal as well as external treatments, thus confusing the distinction between physician and surgeon; this situation was further complicated by the growing number of herbs and chemicals that fell into the apothecary's area of expertise. In the case of what had become one of the most common serious diseases of the Renaissance, syphilis, the physicians initially attempted classic Galenic treatments in the attempt to balance the humors. They had patients spend time in the sunshine or a dry climate, they gave many recommendations about diet and exercise, and they performed venesection, or bloodletting.[13] Of course, none of this worked. But because syphilis manifested itself with skin problems, the surgeons were also frequently involved. The surgeons were supposed to deal with problems concerning the body's surface—burns, knife wounds, skin diseases— and with mercury ointments they had some success in treating syphilis where the physicians had failed.[14] These two groups tended to lord it over the apothecaries; in the time of Henry VIII, for instance, the physicians gained the right to search apothecaries' shops whenever they wanted to.[15] All three of these groups of course disliked and felt threatened by the empirics and tried to make it illegal for them to practice at all. This fourth group did enjoy some parliamentary protection, though, with the so-called Quacks Charter of 1542, which chastised the surgeons who had "sued, troubled, and vexed divers honest persons, as well men as women, whom God hath endued with the knowledge of nature, kind and operation of certain Herbs, Roots and Waters."[16] The Quacks Charter did not protect empirics from physicians as much as it did from surgeons, but still it did give some legal rights to them.[17]

So when Herbert claims it is "easie for any Scholer to attaine to such a measure of Phisick" (Hutchinson, 261) to care for himself and his community, he was introducing his parson to a conflict that had been going on for some time. Herbert carefully comments that the parson is not to encroach on the livelihood of a physician, showing a professional's respect for other professionals. At the same time, Herbert clearly feels that a parson can do much that a lawyer or doctor can. Some of this ability comes from similar training: divinity, law, and medicine were the three learned professions that survived from the Middle Ages, and as such, some aspects of their educational programs overlapped. In the early sixteenth century the English physician's education emphasized classical languages, methods of reasoning, and moral and natural philosophy, not the clinical experience we associate with doctors today.[18] Much of this material was the same that a minister or a lawyer would have studied. As time went on, this humanistic education was combined with more practical knowledge in the study of anatomy, botany, and chemistry, but in Herbert's time physicians still "linked their professional authority to two key concepts, judgment and advice, just like their colleagues in church and law."[19] So if you were going to be a doctor, some clinical knowledge entered into it, but equally important was the classical training in language and reasoning, much the same as that of a minister or lawyer, as well as the general formation of character that was supposed to grow out of this disciplined course of study.

Herbert, then, has a few words to say about the parson acting as lawyer,[20] but it is medicine on which he really focuses, since knowledge of it affords spiritual benefits that any good parson would seize upon. Part of his motivation seems to have derived from larger professional concerns of the 1620s, as Ronald Cooley has argued: harder economic times prompted the secular authorities to assist the church in poor relief, and Herbert may have resisted this displacement of one of the church's central roles.[21] But one might argue that equally strong were Herbert's figurative, or metaphorical, concerns, as medicine and theology had a long history of overlapping and illustrating each other through powerful examples. Philipp Melanchthon, for instance, the architect of Lutheranism in Germany, wrote over twenty orations on medical topics. Medical commonplaces appeared frequently in humanist thought in general, as in the writings of Erasmus.[22] Herbert notes in several instances the importance of employing familiar images of rural life to illustrate spiritual truths,[23] and experiences related to medicine and health serve especially well this pedagogic function.

Herbert's most compelling example of the overlap between herbal medicinals and theology is of course the teaching of Jesus, who made use of "plants and seeds to teach the people" (Hutchinson, 261). Jesus referred to herbs in his parables, Herbert explains, for a number of reasons. First, they are easy to understand: the humblest listener—at least in an agrarian society—will comprehend the illustrations. Second, they provide therapeutic value: plants such as mustard seeds and lilies serve "labouring people" in that those who study them are now not "drowned altogether in the works of their vocation, but sometimes lift up their minds to better things, even in the midst of their pains." This therapeutic value extends to the parson himself, as "an help, and a recreation to more divine studies," offering the "comfort of diversion." Herbert's comments provide an early example of nature seen as therapy, a respite from both manual and intellectual labor. Herbal knowledge thus affords practical, pedagogic, and therapeutic advantages to the pastor, an example of medical information serving spiritual purposes.

Jesus's mustard seed appears in another work of Herbert's, further illuminating the relationship between scientific learning and theology in his thought. In 1620 Herbert wrote three poems honoring Sir Francis Bacon's publication of the *Instauratio Magna*. The longest of these, "In Honorem Illustr. D.D. Verulamij" (In Honor of the Illustrious Baron Verulam) lists what Herbert considered the senior statesman and scientist's greatest accomplishments. Bacon is considered "an archpriest of truth" (*veritatis Pontifex*), "Nature's own diviner" (*Naturae Aruspex intimus*), "Noah's dove" (*Columba Noae*), and "the world's and spirit's only priest" (*Mundique & Animarum sacerdos vnicus*).[24] The recurrent religious language demonstrates how capable Herbert was of mixing theology with science, even if one admits he does not do it often in his English poems.[25] As Christopher Hodgkins has noted, Herbert, as translator of Bacon's *Great Instauration* into Latin, would have been thoroughly familiar with both the particulars of Bacon's thought as well as with the scientist's larger goals of advancing human understanding through the empirical method.[26] Indeed, Herbert mentions Bacon's inductive method in the poem's opening lines and may even imitate it in providing such a long list of equivalences for Bacon's intellectual achievement.[27] The final comparison to Jesus's mustard seed clinches the idea that Bacon's work must be described in religious terms to comprehend its full significance:

> ínque Naturalibus
> Granum Sinapis, acre Alijs, crescens sibi:
> O me probè lassum! Iuuate, Posteri!

> (Mustard seed within the science of natural things,
> Sour to others flourishing unto itself.
> Oh, I'm all worn out. Posterity take over!)

William Sessions has noted the truly prescient quality of these lines, as they are apparently the first articulation of what Baconian science would mean to the future.[28] The sense of excitement here resembles the intellectual energy of "The Parson's Completeness" discussed above, where so many disciplines of knowledge lie within the capable, hardworking clergyman's grasp. Clearly, in Herbert's thought in general, especially the later poems that make up *The Temple,* spiritual knowledge supersedes all other forms of learning.[29] But in this early poem from Herbert's Cambridge days, science and theology freely mix, revealing the young writer's high level of familiarity with both areas of thinking and his comfort in combining them. Just as Jesus used mustard seeds to teach the people, drawing on herbal or scientific information to make a spiritual point, Herbert's Bacon becomes a mustard seed himself, showing how a religious parable can make a statement about secular knowledge.

The herbals of Herbert's time also freely mix various forms of discourse—the scientific, the religious, and the metaphorical—so Herbert's thinking was not at all unusual for his period. There has been some effort recently to show how sixteenth- and seventeenth-century botanicals were able to transcend the emblematic frame of mind that predominated in the Renaissance—that is, the episteme known as "resemblance," to use Foucault's word.[30] Brian Ogilvie, for instance, makes this argument in *The Science of Describing,* his account of the rise of natural history as an academic discipline. He cites naturalists such as Konrad Gessner and Joachim Camerarius who differentiated between what they knew about plants from direct observation and what they knew of them from literary sources.[31] This separation reveals, in Ogilvie's view, a scientific sensibility in which empirical information is filtered out from the surrounding cultural or literary material.

But many of the most accomplished herbals of the Renaissance still have a good deal of prescientific thinking mixed in with what are supposed to be empirical descriptions of plants. Rembert Dodoens's *Cruydeboek* (1554) and *Stirpium historiae pemptades sex sive libri XXX* (1583), for instance, were two of the most widely read herbals of the sixteenth century, the *Pemptades* providing much of the information for John Gerard's *Herball* of 1597.[32] Dodoens's work first appeared in English in 1578 in Henry Lyte's translation of the *Cruydeboek,* which broke the various plants down into discussions of "the description," "the place," "the time," "the names," and "the virtues."[33] In commenting on the rose, Dodoens begins in empirical fashion, according to Ogilvie's model, and goes on for three pages to give various factual information about the flower, such as the names of its various parts in nine different languages. Then something very odd happens, under the heading "The cause of the Name and historie thereof":

> We shall also find this written of Roses, that at the first they were all white, and that they became redde afterward with the bloud of the goddesse Venus, which was done in this sort.
>
> Venus loved the pounker Adonis better than the Warrier Mars (who loved Venus with all his force and might) but when Mars perceived that Venus loved Adonis better than him, he slew Adonis, thinking by this meanes to cause Venus not onely to forgoe, but also to forget her friend Adonis, and so to love Mars onely: of the which thing when Venus had warning how and where it should be accomplished, she was suddenly moved, and ranne hastily to have rescued Adonis, but taking no care of the way, at a sudden (ere she was a ware) she threw her selfe upon a bed of thicket of White-Roses, whereas (with sharpe and cruell thornes) her tender feet were so prickt and wounded, that the bloud sprang out abundantly, wherewhithall when the Roses were bedewed and sprinckled, they became all redde, the which colour they doe yet keepe (more or lesse, according to the quantitie of bloud that fell upon them) in remembrance of the cleare and pleasant Venus.[34]

This minidrama involving Venus and her "punker" Adonis is not set off from the surrounding scientific, factual information; the

short section in which it occurs, "The cause of the Name and historie thereof," is preceded by a comprehensive list of varieties of
roses to be found around Europe ("The Names") and followed by
extensive medical information ("The Nature" and "The Vertues"),
especially the "binding qualitie" of roses—that is, their possible use
as an astringent—as with the substance bolearmena referred to
earlier. Thus Dodoens allows empirical and mythic information to
mix freely, seeing no reason to understand them as separate do-
mains of knowledge.

William Ashworth has argued that an "emblematic world view"
pervades Renaissance natural history, as early scientists such as
Gessner and Aldrovandi sought to pull in as many associations as
they could in their accounts of plants and animals.[35] Much empirical information is included, but also much that is not empirical,
since for them the natural world was "a complex matrix of seemingly obscure symbols and hidden meanings" that must be viewed
from a variety of vantage points.[36] Although Dodoens's prose does
not contain the elements of wonder Ashworth identifies in that of
Gessner and Aldrovandi, something similar is going on in his willingness to combine empirical and allegorical, or at least mythic, information. Dodoens does not see any discontinuity in describing
where roses grow, what they are called, why Venus trampled on
them, and how they bind a loose bowel.

In juxtaposing his various materials, Dodoens does not necessarily make explicit connections between them; as with the symbolic
images of high modernist poetry, readers are left to make these
connections for themselves. In the spirit of Renaissance copiousness, the various forms of information are laid out for display, but
with the exact relationships still waiting to be articulated. As Ashworth has argued, the emblematic frame of mind predominated in
the second half of the sixteenth century, from the time of Alciati's
Emblems (1531) and Valeriano's *Hieroglyphics* (1556), at midcen-
tury, to the final years of the 1500s, with the publication of Ripa's
Iconologia (1593), Camerarius's *Collection of Symbols and Emblems* (1593–1604), and Aldrovandi's thirteen volumes of natural
history, beginning with the *Ornithology* of 1599.[37] One can see this
change in sensibility by comparing Dodoens's herbal to those of the
"German fathers of botany" in the generation before him: Otto
Brunfels's *Herbarium* (1530–36), Hieronymus Bock's *New Kreütter Buch* (1539), and Leonhart Fuchs's *De historia stirpium com-
menarii insignes* (1542). In all three of these writers, who
published their main works in the 1530s and 1540s, mythological,
emblematic material is largely missing.[38] Fuchs's entry for the rose,

for instance, includes scientific and medical writers from antiquity such as Theophrastus, Dioscorides, and Galen but not literary purveyors of myth such as Ovid and Bion, from whom the story of Venus and the rose originates.[39] Early herbals in English—such as the so-called Banckes herbal (1525) and William Turner's *New Herball* (1551, 1562)—reveal the same focus on empirical or medical information about plants, without emblematic myths added in.[40]

So in examining Dodoens's entry for the rose, we can see that he has followed Fuchs's example in part, as his drawing of the rose is an identical reversed image of that found in *De historia stirpium,* and his headings "The Kyndes," "The Description," "The Place," "The Time," "The Names," and so forth, follow Fuchs's model.[41] But the textual information in Dodoens has been expanded a great deal, with mythic or emblematic material interpolated with the scientific.

There are many other herbals following Dodoens's that reveal this emblematic worldview. Levinus Lemnius's *Herball to the Bible,* published in English about the same time as Lyte's translation of Dodoens, does so from an explicitly theological perspective: "Now, for that nothing sooner fadeth away and withereth than doth the Rose, therfore is the fraile, brittle, transitorie, and momentanie life of man, with all the gay glorie, pompe, pride & magnificence therof, which quickly passeth away, very aptly thereunto resembled."[42] The rose clearly serves an emblematic purpose here, as the brief life of man is "resembled" to it. This passage immediately follows an account of the purging qualities of roses and a comparison of the scents of different varieties of the flower, so we see again how comfortable these early writers of natural history are in merging empirical data with emblematic material. As with Dodoens, the connections between these forms of knowledge often are not explained; the various bits of knowledge, from diverse areas of experience, are laid out for readers, leaving them to find the correspondences for themselves.

One might argue that it is not surprising to find these mixtures of scientific and emblematic discourse in the early herbals, since the field of natural history was so new, but the same frame of mind appears in later ones as well. Take, for instance, John Parkinson's discussion of roses in his *Theatrum Botanicum* of 1640, a late date in the history of herbals. In the subsection entitled "The Names" under the entry for roses, Parkinson quotes for the most part the established scientific authorities on plants, writers such as Dioscor-

ides, Dodoens, Clusius, and Bauhin. But he then remarks, "A Lecture of much moralitie might be read upon the Rose, the parts
delivered by many authors both Greekes and Latines all which to
insert in this place is not my minde, onely I will recite a few of many
to give you a taste of the plenty and excellencie."[43] Parkinson then
goes on to quote several literary authors such as Philostratus and
Anacreon in order to present his "Lecture of much moralitie." The
rose thus takes on moral as well as scientific importance for him,
providing an emblematic message, just as with the herbalists cited
earlier. What does the rose represent? It is as "fresh young and delicate as Cupid, it is crowned with gold yellow haires, it beareth th-
ornes as darts and leaves as wings, the Crimson beauty of the
flowers as his glory and dignitie." Besides noting the "glory and dignitie" of the rose, Parkinson does not comment at great length on
what its moral is exactly. But he includes a good deal of speculative
material, also saying of the rose that "the miserably infatuated
Turkes will not suffer a Rose leafe to lye upon the ground, or any to
tread on them in honour of their Mahomet, from whose sweat they
are perswaded the Rose sprang up; somewhat like unto the old Pa-
gans, who held the Rose which formerly was white to become red
from the blood of Venus, falling thereon from her foote hurt by a
thorne, as shee ran among the bushes to helpe her Adonis." Parkinson may not believe that these stories are literally true—that roses
come from the sweat of Muhammad, or the blood of Venus—but he
clearly finds emblematic significance in them, "a Lecture of much
moralitie" that extends well beyond the scientific scope of his book.
The stories involving Venus, Muhammad, and the rose connect
him to the earlier herbalists such as Dodoens, Gerard, and Bauhin,
all of whom cite this material unquestioningly.[44] Parkinson does
not alter the details of the stories or the tone in which they are presented.

Parkinson did seek to distinguish himself from earlier herbalists
such as Gerard by including only botanical specimens he had seen
himself, a personal rule that enabled him to eliminate empirically
many of the errors he found in earlier herbals.[45] One of the most
successful apothecaries in London,[46] Parkinson brought high standards of professionalism to the simples he cultivated at his garden
at Long Acre and wrote to disseminate accurate information rather
than to entertain his reader, as Gerard was sometimes wont to do.[47]
Yet the emblematic frame of mind of the earlier writers persists at
select moments in the *Theatrum Botanicum,* as in Parkinson's discussion of roses. Most of the entries discuss only the scientific char-

acteristics of plants, but a number of key herbs—hyssop, bay leaves, and roses, for instance—are presented within their religious or mythic emblematic context. So Renaissance allegory—sometimes religious, sometimes secular—is alive and well, it seems, in early modern botanical texts through the mid-seventeenth century, even though these texts also contain passages that fall under the category of representation, Foucault's term for scientific discourse.[48] We have then in these examples residual and emergent ways of talking about the natural world, as is also the case in Herbert's poems.

Roses appear several times in *The Temple,* both as a sweet delight and as a purgative. In "Providence" Herbert informs us that "A rose, besides his beautie, is a cure" (line 78), or substance that purges; this duality also shows up in "Virtue," where Herbert writes, "Sweet rose, whose hue angrie and brave / Bids the rash gazer wipe his eye" (lines 5–6). These two senses of the rose as a sweet and as an irritant receive their greatest development in the poem "The Rose," which begins with the speaker rejecting the pleasures of the world in reply to someone who has tempted him. He tells his interlocutor that he does not want to argue, though; he will just give him a rose, which apparently says it all:

> But I will not much oppose
>   Unto what you now advise:
> Onely take this gentle rose,
>   And therein my answer lies.

(lines 13–16)

The speaker goes on in the following stanzas to identify the qualities of the rose we are familiar with, and not so familiar with:

> What is fairer then a rose?
>   What is sweeter? yet it purgeth.
> Purgings enmitie disclose,
>   Enmitie forbearance urgeth.

(lines 17–20)

The rose, then, which Herbert has identified in *The Country Parson* for its medical qualities—he observes that damask or white roses purge just as well as rhubarb does—becomes richly emblematic in the poem; that is, it is able to teach a moral lesson. For all its sweetness, the rose "bites" your palm if you close your hand around it, and so we need to exercise "forbearance" or restraint in pursuing pleasure. Herbert continues,

> So this flower doth judge and sentence
>   Worldly joyes to be a scourge:
> For they all produce repentance,
>   And repentance is a purge.
>
> But I health, not physick choose:
>   Onely though I you oppose,
> Say that fairly I refuse,
>   For my answer is a rose.

(lines 25–32)

The rose thus provides the lesson that worldly joys will scourge us, whipping us into repentance, but, as Helen Vendler has observed, it does so in the politest sort of way:[49] most "fairly" are the world's temptations refused. So really we find two kinds of restraint in the poem: restraint from pleasure, and restraint from arguing your opponent into submission. "The Rose" becomes all the more powerful in making its case through the gentleness in which its message is conveyed.

Michael Schoenfeldt has remarked upon Herbert's attention to the appetites in his poetry, with the recurrent emphasis on self-restraint.[50] Schoenfeldt connects this self-discipline to Galenic medical theory, where it was thought that good health depended upon a balance of humors. Thus, for Schoenfeldt, the instances where Herbert talks about consumption of food or purgatives are indicative of a struggle to find a humoral balance.

Herbert's herb poem "The Rose" therefore teaches a lesson in self-restraint, much as Jesus's herb parables teach their lessons. In both of these cases, medical properties of the herb are integrated with figurative ones, a mixing of discourses one also finds in the herbals by Dodoens, Gerard, Bauhin, and Parkinson. In his poems and in his handbook for clergymen, Herbert's account of herbal medicine is thus remarkably similar to the kinds of examples used by the professional scientists of his time. Since the seventeenth century is often thought of as the full flowering of the scientific revolution, it is tempting to hear exclusively what we think of as the language of science in the writings of early naturalists. But as historians of science such as Steven Shapin and Simon Schaffer have remarked, empirical scientific language that includes certain kinds of information and excludes others only became widespread at a later date through the self-conscious efforts of Robert Boyle and the members of the Royal Society.[51] In Herbert's time poet and scientist still spoke a common emblematic language, one in which Muhammad might appear as easily as a rose bush or Jesus as a mustard seed.

NOTES

1. George Herbert, *A Priest to the Temple; or, The Country Parson,* in *The Works of George Herbert,* ed. F. E. Hutchinson (1941; corr. reprint, Oxford: Clarendon Press, 1970), 259–62. All further quotations from or references to Herbert's prose and English poetry are taken from this edition and will be cited by page or line number in the text of my essay.

2. For a general history of these three medicinal groups, see Barbara Griggs, *Green Pharmacy: A History of Herbal Medicine* (New York: Viking Press, 1981). For more detailed consideration of plants from the Americas, see Sabine Anagnostou, "Jesuit Missionaries in Spanish America and the Transfer of Medical Pharmaceutical Knowledge," *Archives internationales d'histoire des sciences* 52 (2002): 176–97; for a comprehensive history of European cataloguing of herbals, first in Italy and later in northern countries, see Brian Ogilvie, *The Science of Describing* (Chicago: University of Chicago Press, 2006); for a history of Paracelsus, see Allen G. Debus, "The Pharmaceutical Revolution of the Renaissance," *Clio Medica* 11 (1976): 307–17.

3. John K. Crellin and Jane Philpott, *Herbal Medicine Past and Present,* vol. 1 (Durham, NC: Duke University Press, 1990), 11.

4. Ibid.

5. *OED,* s.v. "knot-grass."

6. Cristina Malcolmson discusses at length the contrast between Herbert's reduced circumstances at Bemerton and the courtly life he had led at Cambridge and London, arguing that the value of employment takes precedence over family or class in Herbert's later years. See Malcolmson, "George Herbert's *Country Parson* and the Character of Social Identity," *Studies in Philology* 85 (1988): 245–66.

7. Nicholas Culpepper, *The English Physitian; or, An Astrologo-Physical Discourse of the Vulgar Herbs of this Nation* (London: Printed by Peter Cole, 1652). Quoted in Alix Cooper, *Inventing the Indigenous: Local Knowledge and Natural History in Early Modern Europe* (Cambridge: Cambridge University Press, 2007), 21.

8. Cooper, *Inventing the Indigenous,* 21–50.

9. For a discussion of the close links between Protestantism and English national identity, see Claire McEachern, "Literature and National Identity," in *The Cambridge History of Early Modern English Literature,* ed. David Loewenstein and Janel Mueller (Cambridge: Cambridge University Press, 2002): 313–42. Although nationalism certainly existed before the Reformation, religious events of the sixteenth century and the accompanying emphasis on vernacular languages made national identities much more pronounced. See Andrew Hadfield, *Literature, Politics, and National Identity* (Cambridge: Cambridge University Press, 1994), 9.

10. John Henry and John M. Forrester, introduction to *The "Physiologia" of Jean Fernel (1567),* trans. John M. Forrester (Philadelphia: American Philosophical Society, 2003), 4–8.

11. Hutchinson, *Works of George Herbert,* 561. Hutchinson notes as well that Herbert's brother Edward left three volumes by Fernel to Jesus College, Oxford.

12. For a history of the professionalization of physicians, surgeons, and apothecaries, see Roy Porter, *The Greatest Benefit to Mankind: A Medical History of Humanity* (New York: W. W. Norton, 1997). For the dates given here, see 185, 186, and 194. For a history of unlicensed practitioners, or empirics, see Griggs, *Green Pharmacy*, 60–65.

13. Griggs, *Green Pharmacy*, 33.

14. Porter, *Greatest Benefit to Mankind*, 166–68, 174–75, 186.

15. Harold J. Cook, "Good Advice and Little Medicine: The Professional Authority of Early Modern English Physicians," *Journal of British Studies* 33 (1994): 8.

16. Griggs, *Green Pharmacy*, 61.

17. Cook, "Good Advice and Little Medicine," 8.

18. Harold J. Cook, "Physicians and Natural History," in *Cultures of Natural History*, ed. N. Jardine, J. A. Secord, and E. C. Spary (Cambridge: Cambridge University Press, 1996), 91. Nancy Siraisi uses the term "physician-polymaths" to emphasize the unspecialized world of sixteenth-century medicine. See Siraisi, "Medicine and the Renaissance World of Learning," *Bulletin of the History of Medicine* 78 (2004): 1–36.

19. Cook, "Good Advice and Little Medicine," 4.

20. Herbert specifically mentions Michael Dalton's *The Countrey Justice*, first published in 1618, and the *Abridgements of the Statutes*, a reference to the work of John Rastell and his son William. Dalton's book provided legal advice in a format similar to the organization of medical information in the herbals. A manual for lay magistrates, *The Countrey Justice* provided the justice of the peace with concise, alphabetized explanations of sessional duties. Since the justice of the peace did not have formal training but was usually a leading landowner or citizen of the town, the format of *The Countrey Justice* would have served just as well Herbert's parson. For a discussion of Dalton, see L. R. McInnis, "Michael Dalton: The Training of the Early Modern Justice of the Peace and the Cromwellian Reforms," *in Learning the Law: Teaching and the Transmission of Law in England, 1150–1900,* ed. Jonathan A. Bush and Alain Wijffels (London: Hambledon Press, 1999), 255–72. For a discussion of justices of the peace in general, see Daniel R. Coquillette, *The Anglo-American Legal Heritage: Introductory Materials,* 2nd ed. (Durham, NC: Carolina Academic Press, 2004), 441–42. John Rastell's *Magnum abbreviamentum statutorum Anglie* appeared in 1528; William's *Collection of All the Statutes,* in 1557. The latter was reprinted through the 1620s and was a common reference tool. See *Dictionary of National Biography,* s. v. "Rastell, William."

21. Ronald W. Cooley, "George Herbert's Country Parson and the Enclosure of Professional Fields," *George Herbert Journal* 19 (1995–96): 17.

22. Nancy G. Siraisi, "Oratory and Rhetoric in Renaissance Medicine," *Journal of the History of Ideas* 65 (2004): 191–211.

23. In chapter 4 Herbert writes that examples from "tillage, and pastorage" (Hutchinson, *Works of George Herbert,* 228) should be employed frequently; in chapter 21, he argues similarly that "a plough, a hatchet, a bushell, leaven, boyes piping and dancing" can all "serve for lights even of Heavenly Truths" (257).

24. George Herbert, "In Honorem Illustr. D.D. Verulamij, Sᵗⁱ Albani, Mag. Sigilli Custodis post editam ab eo Instaurationem Magnam" (In Honor of the Illustrious Baron Verulam, Viscount St. Alban, Keeper of the Great Seal, after the publication of his *Instauratio Magna*), in *The Latin Poetry of George Herbert: A Bilingual Edition,* trans. Mark McCloskey and Paul R. Murphy (Athens: Ohio

University Press, 1965), 168–71. I have translated *Auruspex* as "diviner" rather than reproduced McCloskey and Murphy's "cosmographer" in order to highlight the priestly connotation of the word. The haruspices of ancient Rome were a class of priests "who performed divination by inspection of the entrails of victims." *OED*, s.v. "haruspex."

25. Charles Whitney has noted that *The Temple* reveals, in fact, very little knowledge of Bacon's science. See Whitney, "Bacon and Herbert as Moderns," in *Like Season'd Timber: New Essays on George Herbert,* ed. Edmund Miller and Robert DiYanni (New York: Peter Lang, 1987), 235. Kenneth Hovey, "'Diuinitie and Poesie, Met': The Baconian Context of George Herbert's Divinity," *English Language Notes* 22 (1985): 30–39, argues that Herbert was following Bacon's recommendation in separating theology from science.

26. Christopher Hodgkins, "'Yet I love thee': The 'Wayes of Learning' and 'Groveling Wit' in Herbert's 'The Pearl,'" *George Herbert Journal* 27 (2003/2004): 24.

27. William A. Sessions, "Bacon and Herbert and an Image of Chalk," in *Too Rich to Clothe the Sunne: Essays on George Herbert,* ed. Claude J. Summers and Ted-Larry Pebworth (Pittsburgh, PA: University of Pittsburgh Press, 1980), 170.

28. Ibid., 169.

29. Christopher Hodgkins identifies Herbert's phrase "Nature serving Grace" as the poet's ideal approach to knowledge: science and philosophy should serve divinity without claiming any kind of sufficiency of their own. See Hodgkins "'Yet I love thee,'" 25.

30. Michel Foucault, *The Order of Things: An Archaeology of the Human Sciences* (New York: Pantheon Books, 1970), 17.

31. Ogilvie, *Science of Describing,* 15–16. Ian Maclean, "Foucault's Renaissance Episteme Reassessed: An Aristotelian Counterblast," *Journal of the History of Ideas* 59 (1998): 149–66, questions whether one can speak of any episteme at all in the Renaissance. Maclean sees Foucault's examples of the resemblance episteme as decidedly Platonic and unreflective of the Renaissance in general.

32. Gerard's debt to Dodoens has been interpreted in different ways. Frank Anderson, *An Illustrated History of the Herbals* (New York: Columbia University Press, 1977), 225, sees Gerard as Dodoens in "English dress"; Mats Rydén, "The English Plant Names in Gerard's Herball," in *Studies in English Philology, Linguistics, and Literature: Presented to Alarik Rynell 7 March 1978,* ed. Mats Rydén and Lennart A. Björk (Stockholm: Almqvist and Wiksell International, 1978), 142–50, finds more independence in Gerard's work.

33. Rembert Dodoens, *A Nevv Herball, or Historie of Plantes,* trans. Henry Lyte (London: Gerard Dewes, 1578).

34. Ibid., 656.

35. See William B. Ashworth, Jr., "Natural History and the Emblematic World View," in *Reappraisals of the Scientific Revolution,* ed. David C. Lindberg and Robert S. Westman (Cambridge: Cambridge University Press, 1990), 303–32; and Ashworth, "Emblematic Natural History of the Renaissance," in *Cultures of Natural History,* ed. N. Jardine, J. A. Secord, and E. C. Spary (Cambridge: Cambridge University Press, 1996), 17–37.

36. Ashworth, "Emblematic Natural History of the Renaissance," 23.

37. See ibid. for historical placement of all of these authors. Ashworth does note the fifteenth-century *Hieroglyphics* of Horapollo and the 1500 edition of Erasmus's *Adages* but argues that it was only with Alciati and Valeriano that emblematic thinking became widespread.

38. Hieronymus Bock, *Kreütterbuch darin underscheidt Nammen und Würck-ung der Kreütter* (1577; reprint, Munichi: Konrad Kölbl, 1964), 347–50, does mention Adonis briefly in his entry on roses, but almost all of the material is scientific. I have quoted from a later edition of the *Kreütterbuch,* but the absence of emblematic material is the same. Otto Brunfels, *Herbarum vivae eicones* (Argent-orati [Strasbourg]: apud Ioannem Schottu[m], 1530) does not have an entry on roses, but the authors writing throughout the herbal are almost exclusively scientific. On a prefatory page he lists his sources; with the exception of Apuleius, they are all scientific writers, such as Theophrastus, Dioscorides, Galen, and Pliny. Leonhart Fuchs, *De historia stirpium commentarii insignes* (Basileae: [Basel] In officina Isingriniana, 1542), 656–58, makes no mention of Adonis or any other mythological material in his entry on roses.

39. The earliest version of the myth appears in Bion's "Lament for Adonis," where the blood of Adonis and the tears of Venus create the rose and the anem-one, respectively. See A. S. F. Gow, *The Greek Bucolic Poets* (Cambridge: Cambridge University Press, 1953), 146. Ovid also tells this version of the story at the end of *Metamorphoses,* book 10, with some elaboration. The details of Dodoens's account correspond most closely, however, to the version of Natalis Comes, who describes how Venus wounds her foot with the thorn of a white rose, thereafter dying it the color of blood. See Comes, *Mythologiae sive explicationum fabularum libri X* (Venice, 1581), 349. The earliest extant version of Comes's text is from 1567, although the first edition is usually thought to have been printed in 1551, allowing ample time for Dodoens to have made use of its stories.

40. The Banckes herbal, named after its printer, was published anonymously under the title *Here begynnyth a newe mater* ([London]: Rycharde Banckes, 1525); it has no page numbers. William Turner's *A New Herball* (London: Steven Mierdman, 1551) appeared in two separate parts; for Turner's discussion of roses specifically, see *The seconde part of Vuilliam Turners herbal* (Collen [Country?]: Arnold Birckman, 1562), 117–18.

41. The reproduction of Fuchs's illustrations would not in itself suggest a deep familiarity with the earlier herbal; since woodcuts were expensive, it was usually printers rather than authors who made the decision to borrow illustrations from previous herbals. Still, Dodoens has borrowed many details from Fuchs, which he has then expanded upon and rearranged according to medical criteria rather than alphabetical order, as Fuchs had done. See Robert Visser, "Dodonaeus and the Herbal Tradition," in *Dodonaeus in Japan,* ed. W. F. Vande Walle and Kazuhiko Kasaya (Leuven: Leuven University Press, 2001), 49–50; and W. F. Vande Walle, "Dodonaeus: A Bio-Bibliographical Summary," in Vande Walle and Kasaya, *Dodonaeus in Japan,* 35.

42. Levinus Lemnius, *An Herbal for the Bible,* trans. Thomas Newton (London: Edmund Bollifant, 1587), 221.

43. John Parkinson, *Theatrum Botanicum: The Theater of Plants* (London: Printed by Tho. Cotes, 1640), 1021.

44. Caspar Bauhin, *Pinax Theatri Botanici* (Basil: Sumptibus & typis Ludovici Regis, 1623), 480. John Gerard, *The Herball or Generall Historie of Plantes* (London: By John Norton, 1597), 1077.

45. Parkinson was able to adhere to this personal rule until the final years of his research on the *Theatrum,* when he did accept some of his contacts' reports of plants he had not seen. See Anna Parkinson, *Nature's Alchemist: John Parkinson, Herbalist to Charles I* (London: Frances Lincoln, 2007), 257.

46. Parkinson played a key role in establishing the Society of Apothecaries, sep-

arating the group from the Company of Grocers during the years 1614–17 and enabling them to maintain stricter quality control over their products. See A. Parkinson, *Nature's Alchemist,* 144–57. Parkinson was also one of only five apothecaries who played a part in the creation of the first *Pharmacopoeia Londinensis* of 1618. See *Oxford Dictionary of National Biography,* s.v. "Parkinson, John."

47. In the publication of the *Herball,* Gerard consulted the Flemish botanist Matthias de l'Obel, or Lobelius, who was living in London at the time. Lobelius corrected many of the *Herball'*s errors, but Gerard insisted that many be left unchanged, arguing that the manuscript was "sufficiently correct and that de l'Obel had forgotten the English language." Quoted in A. Parkinson, *nature's Alchemist,* 119. For a description of Parkinson's garden, see John N. D. Riddell, "John Parkinson's Long Acre Garden, 1600–1650," *Journal of Garden History* 6 (1986): 112–24. Riddell notes that Parkinson's garden was created on a scale similar to those of John Gerard and the elder John Tradescant; one should add, however, that Parkinson funded his research out of his own business rather than relying on patronage, as the other herbalists did.

48. Foucault, *Archaeology of Knowledge,* 71ff. Foucault refers to the period from the mid-seventeenth century until the French Revolution as "the Classical age," in which Renaissance resemblance gave way to scientific thinking.

49. For Vendler, "The Rose" is the most elegant poem in *The Temple* and Herbert's most accomplished employment of the emblematic form. See Helen Vendler, *The Poetry of George Herbert* (Cambridge, MA: Harvard University Press, 1975), 83–87.

50. Michael Schoenfeldt, "George Herbert's Consuming Subject," in *George Herbert in the Nineties: Reflections and Reassessments* (Fairfield, CT: George Herbert Journal Special Studies & Monographs, 1995), 105–32.

51. Steven Shapin and Simon Schaffer, *Leviathan and the Air-Pump: Hobbes, Boyle, and the Experimental Life* (Princeton, NJ: Princeton University Press, 1985). See esp. 46, Shapin and Schaffer's analysis of Boyle's comments on the existence or nonexistence of a perfect vacuum.

V
Beyond Bemerton

Under Salisbury Spire with the Fictional George Herbert

Sidney Gottlieb

THE TRADITION OF FICTIONALIZING GEORGE HERBERT IS LONG-standing, going back at least to Barnabas Oley and especially, of course, Izaak Walton. (In some ways this fictionalizing process—the creation of a persona with a life story and experiences that are invented and dramatically reconfigured and carefully shaped as well as literally recalled—begins with Herbert himself, but that is a subject for another time.) My focus in the present essay is on one largely unnoticed but fascinating contributor to this process, the late-Victorian novelist Emma Marshall. Two of her novels, *Under Salisbury Spire* (1889) and *A Haunt of Ancient Peace* (1896), include George Herbert as a central character, and the way he figures in them gives us an interesting view of the image of Herbert in late nineteenth-century England, and perhaps reminds us of the extent to which a poet's reputation and persona, normally assumed (by academics, at least) to be understood as part of the realms of biography and critical commentary, are also mediated by the discourse of fiction. Far more people today know the Shakespeare of, say, *Shakespeare in Love* than of Samuel Schoenbaum. *Under Salisbury Spire* is in some ways an analogous case: as unlikely as it may seem, it is a kind of late nineteenth-century *Herbert in Love*.

Mrs. Marshall's "historical story" of George Herbert is, not surprisingly, largely based on Walton and Walton-influenced biographical legends. Historical fiction that is based on history based on fiction threatens to release a vortex that only a postmodernist could love, but I will try to proceed in a way that minimizes—or at least postpones—a dizziness that we must ultimately confront. I will concentrate on *Under Salisbury Spire,* although *A Haunt of Ancient Peace,* which presents Herbert in a tale more centrally about Nicholas Ferrar and Little Gidding, is also fascinating, as I attempt to illustrate in a companion essay to the present one. I will first give a little background on Mrs. Marshall's life and what led her to Herbert and then give an overview of the plot of *Under Salisbury Spire* with particular attention to the sections that focus on Herbert, noting not only how Herbert is represented but how he is integrated into the rest of the story. At the very least, I hope that we will gain a useful view of Mrs. Marshall's conception of Herbert, her adaptation and transformation of her sources, and her contribution to the public perception of Herbert at a time when his reputation was very much on the rise.

Emma Martin, later Marshall, was born on September 29, 1828, near Cromer, Norfolk, and raised if not as a Quaker (like her mother), then at least in a Quaker environment, the influence of which may be seen in her most characteristic personal qualities and activities: her sense of individuality and independence; her calm but determined outspokenness on a variety of controversial topics; her model of spirituality as personal, not highly formalized or institutionalized; her commitment to communal living, beginning with the extended family; and her dedication to a life of energetic activity, public service and charity, personal responsibility and morality, education, and peace. Somewhat less Quaker-like was "her keen and lifelong love of Nature," responsiveness to beauty—especially, as we shall see later, the "beauty of holiness"—and attraction to the arts, particularly music and literature.[1] She led what was in many respects an "unhistoric" life, characterized by domesticity. In a biographical sketch, her daughter foregrounds her "almost passionate maternity" (B. Marshall, 65–66): "[W]hatever else she may have been, she was pre-eminently a mother—a mother blindly devoted, heroically self-sacrificing, absolutely loyal to her children" (66), not only her own nine children but also "the succession of high-school girls" (264) she took on as boarders.

Other than her daughter's biography, she has garnered little attention: a brief *DNB* entry and, inevitably, one PhD dissertation. But some of the specifics of the "whatever else she may have been" and done are noteworthy. For example, she corresponded for many years with Longfellow, met regularly with leading scholars and literary critics of the time like T. H. Green and J. Addington Symonds, was active in the movement for women's right to vote, and helped establish a variety of lecture series and courses of study aimed particularly at expanding the educational opportunities for women. And along with this and so much more documented in her daughter's biographical sketch, between 1861 and 1899, the year of her death, she wrote nearly two hundred novels and shorter tales. No doubt Mrs. Marshall wrote out of a love of writing and storytelling, but she also wrote to make money to support her family, particularly after the failure of the bank her husband worked for, which left him with huge debts. "To clear him from this was now the object of my mother's unwearying literary endeavors," her daughter noted (149). Unwearying indeed: for example, in the year that she wrote the 344-page novel on which I will focus, she wrote six others as well.

This tremendous output commands respect, even as I offer the opinion that, alas, judged as literature, her writings are evidently weak, lacking such qualities as stylistic distinction or innovation, psychological depth, subtlety, and unusual insight. But her books are far from inconsequential. They were widely read, positively reviewed, and long in print. In her dissertation, Vera Rosemond Hughes notes that "during her lifetime she had more fiction titles on the shelves of Mudie's subscription library than any of her contemporaries, including popular writers for boys and Charlotte Yonge herself."[2] Her books were mainstays of her publisher Seeley's line, continuing into the 1920s, and advertisements in the books indicate that various titles of hers went into numerous editions and sold from four thousand to thirteen thousand copies (B. Marshall, 392)—not in the league of runaway best-sellers, like the novels of Hall Caine, for example, which sold upward of fifty thousand copies, but certainly respectable figures indicating solid interest in her works, which were also printed in America and translated into several foreign languages. Hughes argues convincingly that Mrs. Marshall's works should be taken into account in discussions of the history of popular Victorian fiction, particularly women's fiction, and accorded serious consideration as a vital part of the tradition of Charlotte Yonge and other writers of Victorian instructional literature aimed at children and young adults, particularly young women.

This is the genre to which Mrs. Marshall devoted most of her energy, but she also found the time to write numerous historical works that embedded fictional domestic instructional tales in scrupulously researched and often accurately described noncontemporary settings filled with romance, melodrama, and nonfictional characters and events. She wrote novels set in many periods, from the time of Queen Elizabeth to Victoria, but seemed to have a particular interest in Elizabethan and seventeenth-century England. Her "tales of modern life" (B. Marshall, 183) were often more popular and quicker to write: in a letter, she complained, "I am afraid I could not write two long historical books in one year. The effort of getting all the facts into order, and escaping blunders in dates, makes the writing of these stories far more laborious than one supposes" (273). Still, she turned repeatedly to historical subjects, alternating them with her contemporary tales. Early England fascinated her—and presumably her readers—and she diligently researched and wrote books on such subjects as William Tyndale; Sir Thomas Browne, a favorite work of hers, much praised also by Walter Pater; *Biographical Sketch,* 201, the seventeenth-century Bristol cleric Edmund Colston; an Elizabethan gentlewoman, a book based on material sent to her by one of her readers (237); and the disruptions of the English Civil War period. The title of this last book, *Memories of Troublous Times* (1880), reflects a recurrent concern of hers. "Troublous times" are not, of course restricted to the old days, and she turned her attention to a book about a poet closer to her time, William Cowper, who may have been of special interest to her not only because of his intense spirituality and his poetry, which she loved (219), but also perhaps because she, like him, was "given to introspective melancholy reflection on the mystery of death." (The comparison to Cowper is mine, but the description of her frequent state of mind is her daughter's; see B. Marshall, 242).

"Almost directly afterwards," her daughter notes, "she began to pass many hours in communion with George Herbert in preparation for another historical tale" (221–22). In a letter, Mrs. Marshall speaks generally of "the charm of George Herbert" (B. Marshall, 247), a quality that is much in evidence and described in particular detail in both *Under Salisbury Spire* and *A Haunt of Ancient Peace.* But we are fortunate also to have her specific comments about how and why she became attracted to Herbert, what he stands for, and how he can and should be used ideologically as well as dramatically:

> I am delighted with Shorthouse's preface to George Herbert's poems. To my mind it is the perfection of English, with the old-world fragrance of lavender and potpourri [sic] hanging over it. We want George Herberts nowadays. Rank unbelief and quasi-Romanism are rampant. I think the arrogance of Huxley reaches a pitch that almost approaches absurdity; Mrs.——'s egregious conceit, too, when she says "Having got the ear of the world, I am preparing a fuller exposition of my doctrines," or words to that effect. (B. Marshall, 239; quoted from a letter to her publisher in 1889)

We have here a good preview of why Mrs. Marshall would be hailed at the time by the dean of Salisbury as "a true daughter of the Anglican Church" (B. Marshall, 277), an institution envisioned as a refuge from and bulwark against Catholicism and modernism. But the

above description does not adequately prepare us for the significantly more complex character of Herbert that appears in *Under
Salisbury Spire:* his faith is by no means as "florid" as that of Shorthouse in the preface to his facsimile edition of *The Temple* (1882);[3]
his "belief" is solid but constantly tested and by no means always
victorious; he lives in a world of dung and clay as well as "lavender
and pot-pourri"; his humility is irreproachably admirable but maintained at some cost; and his struggle is not only with Rome but even
more so with particularly intemperate enemies of Rome. Still, these
words are a very good introduction to the novel, especially because
Mrs. Marshall acknowledges, first and foremost, that her Herbert is
enmeshed in a world of strife, in his day and hers.

The full title of the novel is *Under Salisbury Spire in the Days of
George Herbert: The Recollections of Magdalene Wydville,* and all
but the last chapter is told by Magdalene herself.[4] The story, set
primarily in various places close to Salisbury, begins in 1613 with
her marriage to Anthony Wydville. She is twenty; he is thirty-eight,
a "grave and austere man" (E. Marshall, 8) haunted, as he tells
her, by what he feels is a curse on his family and future because his
land was appropriated from the church years ago, resulting in
much harm to the original dwellers—an intimation to the reader
that the English Civil War stretches far beyond (in fact, both before
and after) the seventeenth century. Wydville is kin to the Danvers
family, and Magdalene soon becomes a close friend of Jane Danvers, future wife of George Herbert. Herbert is talked about repeatedly from the very beginning of the novel, setting the stage for his
entrance somewhat later, and he is never far from our attention,
because quotations from his poems are used as the epigraph to the
novel and each chapter.[5] The mood of the story is one of troubled
nostalgia: even the days of peace are far from calm, and we know
that they will not last long.

The household grows quickly. The Wydvilles' first child, Dorothea, is born, and soon shows signs of the "exceeding wilfulness
and proud spirit" (E. Marshall, 39) that sets in motion one of the
somewhat predictable central cautionary tales in the novel.[6] Soon
after, Anthony's half sister arrives, and before going off to marry
"the master of a band of performers" (E. Marshall, 36) arranges to
leave behind her son from a previous marriage to a "foreign creature" from Spain, part of the Earl of Pembroke's retinue (29).
Young Carlo Valdesarro adds an exotic element to the household,
and passes quickly from being Dorothea's relation to being her
friend and companion and then to being her beloved. The final
member of the family is born a few years later, Magdalene's son

Christopher, a sickly and physically deformed "winter's child" (58) who nevertheless blossoms under the beneficent influence of Herbert, in some ways becoming the son that Herbert never had.

The novel is punctuated by visits to nearby Wilton, where George Herbert makes his first appearance in person. Even at a quick glance, he is remarkable particularly for his kindness and sadness—"On his lips was writ the law of kindness" (45), and "there was in [his] eyes a sadness as he looked forth" (46)—and as a man of deep thought, fine speech, and quick action. It is perhaps no surprise that the well-known Cambridge orator would talk so impressively, and about matters of politics as well as faith—on this occasion, interestingly enough, about the sad fate of Raleigh and the ongoing Spanish threat—and that he is a calming presence, restraining Master Danvers from continuing his harsh critique of the "dotard king" and Buckingham (49). It is in fact this image of Herbert as a meliorating influence, a determined but gentle oppositional force and counterexample, that Mrs. Marshall emphasizes throughout the novel. That is the more reason why it is a bit of a shock to see Herbert leap into action, "quick as lightning" (51), to help Carlo save Dorothea when she falls into the lake (50–51), an incident most assuredly nowhere to be found in Walton.

The public world figures increasingly in the plot, and the "dark days in Salisbury" are a microcosm of impending troubles across the land. News of the "pushing and jostling at court to see who can get favour with Buckingham" (69) is brought to Wydville Grange by Magdalene's old friend Elizabeth, now Lady Beauchamp, and while this reinforces Magdalene's love of quiet retreat, Dorothea is drawn to the world of vanity fair. The nearby parish of Bemerton is in disarray, and Anthony Wydville grows increasingly puritanical and dour, lamenting the "coming ills of this nation," the "languishing" of "[t]rue religion in the church" (76), and the need for drastic measures to address the threats to the "liberty of the people" (100). Anthony's reminiscences of an earlier plague time and a "clumsy and graceless" king (81) soon prove to be not merely recollections but accurate prophecies of days to come.

There is a great need for (but, alas, lack of) heroic, exemplary figures. Shakespeare surfaces briefly as one such figure. Anthony tells of watching a performance of *Twelfth Night* at Wilton some years ago at which Shakespeare (and Massinger) were in attendance. The fact that Anthony's favorite character in the play is—*quel surprise!*—Malvolio ironizes but does not completely undermine his high praise for Shakespeare as a cultural icon of inestimable value. (Puritan though he is, Anthony owns a copy of the

First Folio—not entirely surprising when we recall that this book was dedicated to the earls of Pembroke, leaders of the Puritan party at court[7]—along with a scorched copy of a Tyndale Bible, an apt symbol of a culture at risk.) Magdalene tells of another person who emerges during the dark days: a Dr. Evans who, unlike most of the custodians of public health and safety during the resurgence of the plague in the mid-1620s, particularly the clergy (E. Marshall, 88), refused to abandon the needy and administered vital medicine and charity. The key exemplary figure, though, proves to be George Herbert, who from this point on becomes more prominent in the story, and embodies formidable literary, therapeutic, and spiritual qualities.

Perhaps for reasons of economy, but perhaps also as part of an artistic strategy of mixing modes of representation, Mrs. Marshall often alternates descriptions of Herbert and conversations about him with his direct appearances, and these indirect and direct appearances are themselves part of a larger pattern of alternation as Herbert weaves in and out of the story. But while he is by no means the constant focus, he is never far from our attention. We hear briefly that Herbert has been "made a deacon in the church, and has given up all Court life and interest" (98–99) and has begun an adventurous project of "the rebuilding of the decayed church of Layton Ecclesia" (99), initially against the advice of his revered mother but ultimately with the aid of her, Pembroke, Nicholas Ferrar, and Arthur Woodnot [Woodnoth], the latter two of whom become especially prominent at the close of the story. These actions clearly counterpoint and implicitly comment on moves in the opposite direction by some of the other key characters. Carlo, just back from serving in the low countries and gaining the favorable notice of King Charles, is about to join Buckingham's expedition to "retrieve lost honour at Rochelle" (96), but anything connected to the court seems to be suspect and dangerous. Not everybody goes as far as Anthony in his increasingly vigorous diatribes against the "tyranny and oppression" (102) of the times, but Magdalene, the narrative voice of careful and wise judgment, acknowledges the widespread sense of discontent and asks rhetorically "[W]ho shall say that such discontent was without reason?" (111). Mrs. Marshall's strong sense of the ravages and excesses of the English Civil War never erases her conviction that some forceful measures were necessary to alter the unjust and unfaithful ways of the world. As we shall see, she spends much of the remainder of the novel trying to envision that force as Herbertian rather than Cromwellian.

Back to our characters assembled at Carlo's leave-taking: Events come to a climax as Buckingham himself enters the scene, and, in the midst of a partly jeering, partly cheering crowd, is assassinated. It is a quasi-Dickensian moment, but functions in the novel mostly as a bit of a dramatic shock and as a bad omen, both for Carlo, about ready to continue in his path as a soldier-courtier, and for Dorothea, who is on her way to join the household of Lady Cheyney and move closer to the world of the court that, while we of course know better, seems so vibrant and attractive to her.

Herbert remains physically absent from the following scenes, but is much talked about. Woodnot and Jane Danvers arrive for a visit, and they have different stories to tell about their beloved friend. Woodnot describes Herbert's bout with a "quotidian ague" (118), a detail right out of Walton,[8] and both he and Jane present an extended defense of Herbert from the charges that he had "turned to the House of God because he had been grievously disappointed in not receiving a place about the Court, of distinction and honour" (E. Marshall, 119) and that "sacred orders are a mean and low employment for a man of gentle birth and parts" (119). But Jane stays longer in the household, deepens her friendship with Magdalene, and specifically shares with her the details of "the romance of her attachment to George Herbert" (120).

There is much that is familiar in Mrs. Marshall's picture of Herbert, and some that is new, but perhaps nothing is so unexpected as her attention to him as a lover, broadly defined, and the backstage view she presents of him, via Jane, as a suitor and then a husband. There is not much evidence on which to base such a picture, and what little there is is not always particularly promising. I have often thought of the great contrast there is between Donne and Herbert in this regard. We have plenty of information about Donne in love and marriage, capped by a memorable phrase in Walton's *Life of Donne* that I find endlessly telling and provocative. Said of Mrs. Donne, it reveals quite a bit about the mister as well: "She had yearly a child."[9] It is not difficult to imagine Donne—both Jack and Dean—leading a life of, shall we say, vigor (although to be sure this is associated with much pain as well as pleasure). Contrast this with what we know of Herbert: that he had no children; that he married his stepfather's cousin, virtually sight unseen, with a suddenness that Walton takes great pains to argue testified to "the strictest Rules of prudence" rather than any "Love-phrensie."[10] and that, in Aubrey's harrowing phrase, "[h]is marriage, I suppose, hastened his death."[11]

The phrase "let's not go there" comes to my mind when I consider contemplating such things. But Mrs. Marshall, more courageous, optimistic, and imaginative than I, did go there. It is especially important for her to incorporate the domestic and romantic as well as the spiritual, socially graceful, well-mannered, and artistic in her picture of an exemplary figure. And it is on all these counts that Herbert excels, and serves as an implicit and explicit foil to the major new character who enters the novel at this point, Sir Marmaduke Peel, a friend of Lady Cheyney. He is a caricatured Puritan: holier than thou, hypocritical, intemperately anticourt and anti-Catholic, and perhaps equally important, rude as a guest, friend, and suitor—overall the wrong engine for a much-needed change in church and state. His influence reinforces Anthony's growing rigidity and separation from the church, a regrettable action even though there is much evidence that the church has indeed fallen into disrepair. (Later on we will see that Anthony's growing friendship with Herbert has the exact opposite effect.)

Marmaduke is an unattractive figure, to say the least, not only because of his increasingly radical political and religious beliefs but also because of his relentless and in almost all ways improper pursuit of Dorothea. Carlo returns to Wydville Grange and it is now clear that he and Dorothea love each other, but they are blocked by her father's unwavering approval of Marmaduke as her future husband. In what turns out to be Herbert's most extended intervention into the purely fictional plot of the novel, he has several long talks with Magdalene, who is much in need of comfort. He helps her in three ways. First, he gives her predictably Herbertian advice: about the therapeutic force of keeping busy with one's daily round of activities, quite literally sweeping the rooms, as he described in "The Elixir," but making that action "fine" and recuperative by focusing on God's will, not our own, as the animating power of life (E. Marshall, 245). Magadalene notes that Herbert's recurrent and enormously helpful advice can be simply summarized: "Patience and faith, that God would overrule all for good" (251). The second way he helps is by reading some of his poems to her, specifically three of his "Affliction" poems (numbers 3, 4, and 5—interestingly, not number 1, the modern favorite, perhaps because it is more overtly autobiographical and self-directed). The effort here is not so much to prescribe practical advice as to offer compassion born of shared experiences. The last way he helps is much different than the first two: at a critical moment when Magdalene is especially distraught—Dorothea has disappeared—she goes to Herbert and he comforts her by simply walking quietly with her. She remarks that "Master Herbert knew, above all men that I ever met, to keep silence, even from good words, when it was better to do so"

(265). This is a fine insight, nicely conveying Herbert's personal delicacy and humility, and also resonating with our modern sense of him as someone deeply aware of both the power and the limits of words.

The romantic drama intensifies: Marmaduke nearly assaults Dorothea, attempting to kiss her as she sits quietly reading the *Faerie Queene* (217); schemes to discredit Carlo by claiming that a new arrival to the Grange, Juanita, is Carlo's wife (she turns out to be his sister); and ultimately insults Carlo, prompting a duel in which he is grievously injured, prompting Carlo to leave to seek his fortune elsewhere. One might expect all this to be foregrounded, but in fact it recedes somewhat, and for nearly 150 pages, until almost the end of the novel, Herbert becomes more the focus. Instead of primarily weaving him into the stories of others, from this point on Mrs. Marshall weaves the others in and around the story of the latter period of Herbert's life.

Prominent in this period is his marriage to Jane, the news of which is told to Magdalene by none other than Lord Herbert of Cherbury, Herbert's eldest brother, who repeats some of the few details we know from Walton's account, noting that "[i]t was love at first sight, fostered on the fair lady's side by her late father's constant reference to my brother and his perfections" (161). But he also adds an un-Walton-like glow by summing up their relationship as "like an old romance . . . and, indeed, my brother is a fit hero for it" (161). This is reinforced soon after by a letter from Jane to Magdalene that briefly tells of her "great bliss" being joined with Herbert in "mutual love," their "wedding feast" in the presence of one of her husband's other great loves, Christ, and her happiness in their new household.

Love is the driving force and key value and virtue for Mrs. Marshall, the many forms of which are embodied in her presentation of Herbert. Romantic love, as I have been suggesting, is a particularly important form, and the relationship between Herbert and Jane is a standard used to evaluate other relationships in the novel (Magdalene and Anthony's marriage does not measure up to it) and a model of the far reaches of human happiness on earth for others to emulate (Dorothea and Carlo will ultimately find a way to balance their passion with mutual support). "Hail wedded love" indeed. Beyond his exemplary romance, nearly everything Herbert does in the novel illustrates one or another kind of love, all harmoniously interrelated. As we might expect, there are recurrent references to his love of his mother (e.g., 163, 178), an extremely valuable relationship in itself as well as a synecdochic representation of the importance of the family. A mother's love and love of one's mother are the ground of one's being; not only for Herbert but for Dorothea. They both, of course, have a mother named Magdalene. Herbert is also the great example in the novel of a more broadly expansive love of humankind, manifested in his thoughtful and compassionate friendships—personal contact with him noticeably changes the lives of Magdalene, Anthony, Dorothea, Christopher, and even Marmaduke—and his many acts of charity. Charity serves not only individuals and the community at large, but is also perhaps the most significant expression of love of God, a kind of spirituality embedded in the physical. While Mrs. Marshall includes a few glimpses of Herbert at prayer and engaged in solitary spiritual struggles, he is emphatically not a recluse and by no means a contemplative.[12]

Finally, Mrs. Marshall's Herbert is also a lover of poetry and music, and the two frequently merge as he sings his poems, highlighting that these are primarily arts of celebration, social (or at least interpersonal) engagement, and communication, not self-expression and analysis. His attachment to poetry and music is related to his love of "beautiful things" (E. Marshall, 165), particularly when it comes to religious ceremonies. All these kinds of love that Herbert exemplifies are outer- and other-directed—specifically excluded from this ensemble is self-love, which characterizes the least attractive people in the book, such as Marmaduke and the ridiculous Lady Beauchamp—and exert such a radiating positive force that we might yet believe that, to coin a phrase, love is all we need.

There is much drama in this section of the novel, focusing not only on Dorothea's continuing difficulties repulsing Marmaduke's advances but also on broader public events that are increasingly disruptive and discouraging. Anthony is outspokenly critical of the state of the church and the clergy in his immediate neighborhood, and gives a description of the neglect of the parishioners, the disrepair of the church buildings, and the deservedly low esteem in which the church officials are held (169). Even Herbert does not disagree, but Anthony's proposed response—separating completely from this establishment—is not Herbert's. Herbert first counsels him privately, and though Mrs. Marshall does not include the details of what he says, she notes that the effect is to make Anthony "more gentle and lenient . . . towards the faults and deficiencies of the Church and the State" (180). Herbert soon gets a chance to do more than talk. The nonresident incumbent, Dr. Curle, has been made bishop of Bath and Wells, and Herbert is put forth by Pembroke as his replacement. This is a key turning point in the novel, which now concentrates primarily on building up Herbert as the ideal model of "the New Parson."

Mrs. Marshall relies very heavily on Walton in this section, and it is interesting to trace how she not only retells his stories but integrates them into her fictions (and vice versa). But she begins this section with a strategic transformation and expansion of Walton. She spends quite a lot of time stressing Dr. Curle's thoroughgoing unsuitability as a pastor to the local flock. He is, first and foremost, a "very grand gentleman" (195), vain, ostentatious, distant from the common people, and far more concerned with whether his clerical position is worthy of him rather than with whether he is worthy of it. All this is captured in his final sermon in Bemerton, "too full of scholarly references to be understood by the few poor folk who were present" (195), and the text of the day is his own well-deserved promotion and his suspicion that his rumored successor will probably be too ambitious to "hide his light under a bushel, and reside amongst you" (190). Walton alludes only briefly to Curle,[13] and in fact relates that it was Herbert himself whose first sermon was delivered "after a most florid manner; both with great learning and eloquence."[14] To be sure, Walton uses this incident as the exception that proves the rule, confirming that Herbert well knew that this "should not be his constant way of Preaching"[15] and that his ministry should be one of closeness to, not distance from, his beloved flock. Walton, here and elsewhere, is very much concerned with describing Herbert's inner debates and struggles with himself. Perhaps Mrs. Marshall altered the details here because her primary interest is not so much his complex and conflicted self as his determination and dedication, highlighting his unquestionable contrast with some of the contemporary custodians of the church, pictured as the unworthiest of the unworthy.

In what follows, though, she sticks close to details supplied by Walton, which I will summarize briefly. One of the few incidents of Herbert's inner conflict and self-debate retold by Mrs. Marshall comes as he questions his worthiness to take holy orders, and this process of self-examination and momentary hesitation, particularly as it contrasts with his predecessor's thoughtlessness and arrogance, testifies to how well-suited he is to this calling. As in Walton, Laud meets with Herbert at Wilton to talk him into accepting (a meeting that Amy M. Charles finds highly unlikely, noting that "Laud had no reason for being close at hand for consultation and persuasion"),[16] but the most dramatic moment comes when Woodnot and Magdalene glimpse Herbert "lying prostrate before the altar" in the little church at Bemerton, "holding communion with God" (E. Marshall, 202). According to Walton, Herbert himself identified this as a time when "he set some Rules to himself, for the future manage of his life" and there vowed to keep them,[17] but Mrs. Marshall—wisely, I think—refrains from embellishing this stunning moment with any prosaic commentary. (Walton, by contrast, gives an extremely detailed summary of those rules[18] that in effect specifically define Herbert's theology, a topic that Mrs. Marshall scrupulously avoids.) She similarly lets other incidents from Walton's *Life* speak for themselves: for example, she focuses extensively on Herbert's rebuilding of the church at Bemerton, and his restoration of proper attention to "the blessed meaning of the Church's holy days" (E. Marshall, 236). These activities come to make Herbert the embodiment of "the beauty of holiness" (288), but even more important, have an invigorating effect on the parishioners. The parishioners so affected include both fictional ones— for example, Anthony, who becomes noticeably softer, illustrating that Herbert is a powerful "antidote to the stern creed" (186) of Puritanism, and Christopher, who becomes increasingly his proté gé—and real, historical ones, that is to say, the particular, though unnamed, individuals "touched" by Herbert in Walton's *Life*. They include most memorably an old woman who comes to Herbert "in sore distress, body and mind" (212) and is speechless in front of the imposing new parson, but who is tenderly assisted by his patient listening as well as practical generosity; and the "man whose horse had fallen under a heavy load" (223), who Herbert assists while on his way with Christopher (Mrs. Marshall typically adds her fictional characters as witnesses to the events described by Walton) to a night of music in Salisbury, delaying and "lowering" himself in the process. It is such charity, however down and dirty it may be, that is Herbert's delight and the stuff of real holy music.

The end of Magdalene's recollections blends the personal conflicts of Dorothea, Marmaduke, and Carlo with the broader specter of civil war—she regularly calls attention to specific historical events that point to the heightening of the crisis, such as the imprisonment and death of Sir John Eliot in the Tower, part of the "perpetual kindling of fires, which, smouldering for a time, were to burst forth in a devouring flame in the coming years" (297)—but the focus of her last chapter is Herbert's final illness and death. Following Walton and the general pattern of spiritual biography, Mrs. Marshall ends the life of an exemplary figure with a description of his "good death," but her treatment of this is curious. It is a bit surprising that the story of Herbert's last days takes up only six pages here,[19] which tightly compress details from Walton about his declining strength, the final visits from Woodnot and Duncon, the preservation of his poems by Ferrar (without any mention of the licensing controversy), and how on his deathbed he sang several of his poems. And there are several striking contrasts with Walton's version. Walton has Herbert say *"I now look back upon the pleasures of my life past, and see the content I have taken in* beauty, *in* wit, in *musick, and* pleasant Conversation, *are now all past by me, like a dream, or as a shadow that returns not, and are now all become dead to me, or I to them"* (128). This is followed by an extended description of death as a portal to the *"new* Jerusalem," that *"happy place: And this is my content, that I am going daily towards it."* Walton notes that this "may be said to *be his* enjoyment of Heaven, before he enjoy'd it."[21] Mrs. Marshall, though, includes only the first sentence of this long paragraph (quoted above), eliminating the word "content," which Walton uses twice in his version. In the novel, Herbert's words are: "I now look back . . . upon the pleasures of my life past, and see the contrast . . ." (E. Marshall, 302),[22] and this is followed not by an extended description of the soon-to-come joys of heaven but a rather austere and brief commentary by Magdalene: "Ah, thus is it with us all. . . . And what, then, abideth? Sure we must say, but one thing, the love of God in Christ, the Word of the Lord, which endureth for ever." The result, I think, is a somewhat more dour and nervous scene than in Walton. She also omits Walton's subsequent reference to Herbert's "sudden Agony" on his deathbed, one last *"Conflict"* that he has to pass before he gives his *"last Will"* to Woodnot and is *"ready to dye."*

Perhaps she skips through and de-dramatizes Herbert's last days (as Walton does not) because the prospect was so grim for her. (Recall the comment by her daughter quoted earlier in my essay that her mother was somewhat morbidly preoccupied, "given to introspective melancholy reflection on the mystery of death," signs of which I believe we see in brief allusions here to the potentially overwhelming and incommunicable experience of the "loneliness of death" [E. Marshall, 304].) But it may also be that she wants to get more quickly to her more "positive" concluding point. She has another answer to the potentially disturbing question "And what, then, abideth?": not only Love of God and the Word of the Lord, but the memory of George Herbert. Magdalene ends her recollections by stressing Herbert's ongoing presence. The counterpart to the customary (and to my mind never particularly reassuring) invocation of the dead person's immortal life at Christ's side (307) is

Magdalene's reminder of how Herbert lives on: in the medlar tree that he and his wife planted (306), one of the great legends of Herbert's life, although not mentioned by Walton; and perhaps especially in the "fragrant memory" (305) of Herbert that is not only activated for her as she writes but conveyed to others through her writing. Not the least of Herbert's mercies, as it were, is the way he turns us to the "texts" of our lives: first and foremost, of course, is the Bible, his "exceeding love" of which "quickens" Magdalene's attention to it (305). But he also quickens her attention to her own book: "I think, when I first considered the task of writing the record of my life for those who came after me, over that life, the bright light of Master Herbert's teaching and example shone like a beacon to encourage me to do so, and to lead me on the way, so much did I feel his power" (304–5). It is not implausible, I think, to assume that this is not only Magdalene's credo, but Mrs. Marshall's as well.[24]

This is not the end of the novel. Magdalene's recollections are continued by her daughter, and one last chapter wraps up the fictional and historical stories. Dorothea quickly summarizes some events of the Civil War, including the deaths of Hampden and Falkland, the devastation of the countryside, and the restoration of both the King and courtly excesses, a grim narrative, Mrs. Marshall repeatedly notes, from which Herbert's death spared him. Dorothea also tells of her marriage to Carlo, and their children: a son, Marmaduke, named in memory of her erstwhile unwanted lover who eventually did reform, in large part under Herbert's influence, and became her protector and benefactor, and a daughter, Magdalene (every generation needs a Magdalene as well as a Herbert). Even Christopher ends happily married, to Juanita.

But particularly prominent at the end is Herbert, and also Jane, as in Walton's account, which similarly ends by telling of her life after his death and defending her remarriage.[25] Her love of Herbert was as "absorbing" as could be (E. Marshall, 329), but hers "was a clinging nature, that needed a prop, and when one failed sought another" (343). Far from a rebuke, it is a compassionate acknowledgment that we all need the help of another; it is part of Mrs. Marshall's recurrent celebration of the relationships that help us survive, flourish, and live in the world, envisioned with good reason as a social world. Not surprisingly, as Dorothea and Carlo return to Bemerton and serendipitously meet Jane's daughter by her second husband, Herbert has the last word. The novel ends in an evocative place where we see both the spire of the Salisbury Cathedral and Herbert's medlar tree, both symbols of faith and lives dedicated to

God's will. The dominant sight, predictably, is not the huge monument but the living tree, where "Master George Herbert's memory lingers . . . like the tender fragrance of faded flowers" (340), and where his voice still resounds, though others supply the breath to animate his words that animate us as we say, "Oh! let Thy sacred will / All Thy delight in me fulfil" (344).

I hope that I have managed to convey some sense of appreciation for Mrs. Marshall's achievement in mixing outright fiction and reported history, and making George Herbert a complex and dynamic figure rather than an unimaginative embodiment of a via media and a vehicle for knee-jerk nostalgia and dull hagiography. And I hope that in some small way I have generated interest in further work that remains to be done on Mrs. Marshall's representation of Herbert, including a close look at *A Haunt of Ancient Peace* to expand on my preliminary overview of her debt to and transformations of Walton and her strategic use of Herbert as a figure who embodies a model of spirituality, charity, love, and conflict resolution with historical as well as contemporary relevance. This kind of work would enhance our understanding of her role in the late nineteenth-century reevaluation of Herbert. Her books coincide with and contribute to the modern resurgence of interest in Herbert, and perhaps we can and should squeeze her name somewhere into the line running from Grosart to Palmer to Eliot to Hutchinson and onward, extending to this very day, of those who find a variety of ways to confirm that yes, "We want George Herberts nowadays."

NOTES

1. Beatrice Marshall, *Emma Marshall: A Biographical Sketch* (New York: E. P. Dutton and Co., 1901), 23. Further quotations from this book will be cited in the text.

2. Vera Rosemond Hughes, "The Works of Emma Marshall in Relationship to Her Life and the Educational Concepts of Her Time" (diss., University of Liverpool, 1986), 389.

3. C. A. Patrides does not include this preface in his Critical Heritage volume on Herbert, but he uses this word to describe it; see Patrides, *George Herbert: The Critical Heritage* (London: Routledge and Kegan Paul, 1983), 49.

4. Emma Marshall, *Under Salisbury Spire in the Days of George Herbert: The Recollections of Magdalene Wydville* (1890; reprint, New York: E. P. Dutton, n.d.). Quotations from this book are cited in the text.

5. It would be worth undertaking a more extensive analysis of the particular poems by Herbert quoted throughout the novel. Mrs. Marshall uses the following as epigraphs: "The Church-porch" (lines 457–62), "Mans medley" (lines 1–6), "Miserie" (lines 55–60), "Content" (lines 33–36, substituting "discerning" for

"discoursing"), "Content" (lines 13–16), "H. Baptisme" (II) (lines 1–5), "H. Baptisme" (II) (lines 6–10), "The Church-porch" (lines 307–12), "The Church-porch" (lines 349–52), "The Church-porch" (lines 397–98), "The Elixir" (lines 1–4), "Repentance" (lines 18–24), "Prayer" (I) (line 13), and "The Posie" (entire poem). The following poems are quoted in the text of the novel: "Antiphon" (II) (entire poem), "To my Successor" (entire poem), "Affliction" (V) (entire poem), "Affliction" (III) (entire poem), "Affliction" (IV) (entire poem), "The Thanksgiving" (lines 39–40), "Sunday" (lines 29–35), and "Obedience" (lines 16–20).

6. As Vera Hughes notes, "traumatic experiences as instrumental in bringing a girl to give up self-will" was a recurrent pattern in Mrs. Marshall's stories (Hughes, "Works of Emma Marshall," 85).

7. I am grateful to Christopher Hodgkins for reminding me of the relevance here of the Shakespeare-Pembroke connection.

8. Izaak Walton, *The Life of Mr. George Herbert* (1675); rpt. in Patrides, *George Herbert,* 107.

9. Izaak Walton, *Life of Donne,* in *The Lives of John Donne, Sir Henry Wotton, Richard Hooker, George Herbert, and Robert Sanderson* (New York: Oxford University Press, 1950), 31.

10. Walton, *Life of Herbert,* 108.

11. John Aubrey, *Brief Lives,* quoted in Patrides, *George Herbert,* 90. To be fair, I should note that Walton devotes two full paragraphs to the preparations for their marriage, emphasizes the importance for Herbert of this union of "mutual love and joy, and content" (*Life of Herbert,* 108), and, although in scattered references, treats Jane respectfully as person of interest and significance as he tells Herbert's life story: see esp. pp. 111–12 for a description of Herbert's instructions to his wife on her role as a "Ministers Wife" and her "unforc'd humility" and numerous acts of charity (for the latter, see also pp. 121–22). And see p. 122 for her careful attention to his condition as his health was failing; and the end of the *Life,* where Walton pays the "debt justly due to the memory of Mr. Herberts vertuous wife" by giving at least a "very short account of the remainder of her life" (130) after Herbert's death. This subtheme of Walton's *Life of Herbert,* the relationship of George and Jane, has not attracted much attention and has not caught on as a particularly important part of Herbert's biographical legend, and in some way this is perhaps just as well: Amy M. Charles suggests that "Walton's account of Herbert's marriage is so idealized as to be almost ludicrous"; see Charles, *A Life of George Herbert* (Ithaca, NY: Cornell University Press, 1977), 143. But Mrs. Marshall is very responsive to this dimension of Herbert's life.

12. For all that Mrs. Marshall wants to emphasize Herbert's spiritual kinship with Ferrar, she also contrasts Ferrar's withdrawal from society with Herbert's immersion in it. To complicate things further, in *A Haunt of Ancient Peace,* while still using Herbert and Ferrar as foils, she takes great pains to portray Little Gidding as a place of social beneficence and charity as well as spiritual retreat. Her point seems to be that Herbert is not a recluse like Ferrar—and neither is Ferrar!

13. Walton, *Life of Herbert,* 109, 112.

14. Ibid., 114.

15. Ibid.

16. Charles, *Life of George Herbert,* 47.

17. Walton, *Life of Herbert,* 110.

18. Ibid., 113–19.

19. By contrast, as David Novarr points out, "Walton spends 10 per cent of the *Life* on Herbert's holy dying." See Novarr, *The Making of Walton's "Lives"* (Ithaca, NY: Cornell University Press, 1958), 323.

20. Walton, *Life of Herbert,* 128.

21. Ibid., 129.

22. Mrs. Marshall also changes Walton's *"the content I have taken in beauty . . ."* (Walton, *Life of Herbert,* 128) to "I have joyed in beauty . . ." (E. Marshall, *Under Salisbury Spire,* 302). Novarr notes that Walton was evidently "dissatisfied with the looseness of the construction"—his reconstruction, that is—of this pivotal speech, and substantially revised the 1670 version in the 1674 edition of the *Life* (Novarr, *Making of Walton's "Lives,"* 359). Mrs. Marshall revises it even more extensively.

23. Walton, *Life of Herbert,* 129, 130.

24. The memorial words over Mrs. Marshall's tomb capture this nicely, and also remind us that Herbert was not the only exemplary figure who inspired her: "A lover of good men, and herself a follower of their faith and patience, she strove by her writings to make others love them" (B. Marshall, *Emma Marshall,* 342).

25. Novarr is perhaps a bit too blunt when he says that Walton "disposes of Mrs. Herbert in an appendix" (Novarr, *Making of Walton's "Lives,"* 325), but it is fair to say that while Walton ends by mentioning Jane, he by no means emphasizes her importance in the story of Herbert's life.

"Something Understood": From Poetry to Theology in the Writings of George Herbert
David Jasper

> Prayer the Churches banquet, Angels age,
>> Gods breath in man returning to his birth,
>> The soul in paraphrase, heart in pilgrimage,
> The Christian plummet sounding heav'n and earth. . . .

>> Church-bels beyond the starres heard, the souls bloud,
>> The land of spices; something understood.[1]

GEORGE HERBERT CONCLUDES HIS MEDITATION ON PRAYER WITH QUIET indefinition—with a series of syntactically incomplete images that employ the rhetorical trope of *scesis onomation* (lacking a main verb). The series of glorious and poetically musical images ends abruptly and perhaps necessarily in the silence of acceptance. Yet this indefinition paradoxically provides a definition of that silence which lies at the very heart of prayer's mystery.

It may be that all true poetry seeks for and finds its true end in silence, being not so much a matter of getting at some hidden meaning that is somehow resident within the verse, but rather, as the philosopher Martin Heidegger once put it, a "letting the unsayable be not said" in defiance of all propositional logic.[2] This is that "something understood" of George Herbert which constitutes the essential unspokenness of the language and images of true prayer, and in poetry an ending that, in the nice description of James Boyd White, "often (in a sense always) . . . concludes in silence, a silence given meaning by the words that have come before."[3] It is a silence at the very heart of language.

The very impossibility of adequate speech that is paradoxically admitted in the depths of Herbert's verse is also an eloquent recognition of the incapacity of all theological language finally to reflect the ineffable and the infinite.

Now I am here, what thou wilt do with me
        None of my books will show.
I reade, and sigh, and wish I were a tree;
        For sure then I should grow
To fruit or shade.[4]

But such an admission of linguistic limitation by no means confines
sacred poetry to the narrow uses ascribed to it by, for example, Dr.
Samuel Johnson in the eighteenth century, which are, he says, "to
help the memory, and delight the ear . . . but [they] suppl[y] nothing
to the mind. [For] the *ideas* of Christian Theology are too simple
for eloquence, too sacred for fiction, and too majestick for orna-
ment; to recommend them by tropes and figures, is to magnify for
a concave mirror the sidereal hemisphere."[5] Rather, indeed, for
Herbert, like St. Augustine before him, the mind is never more
theologically alive than in the energetic and vital language of the
poet as it seeks to bring to life the connection between what we say
and the most profound reality that we strive to express in our relationship with it. In Herbert's verse, the language provokes the
reader on competing, simultaneous levels, always profoundly aware
of its limitations while yet opening up a polyphony of meanings that
can be heard and felt not separately but only in the challenging
grandeur of their harmony and dissonance. Thus, our experience
of the literary moves beyond, and then returns to, the claims of
theological doctrine and dogma, at once exploring them and also,
at the same time, rendering them finally silent in our devout and
humble appropriation of them. Like the language of the Gospels
themselves, Herbert's poems are cryptic and often exploratory of
the impossible.[6] But if his verse is not so much precisely prayerful
as exploring and living within the impossibility of prayer (though is
there, in the end, a difference?), almost all of it is in the form of
spiritual autobiography,[7] its language crisp and almost clinically
exact, likened recently by David L. Edwards to the experimental
science advocated by Francis Bacon "(whether or not [Herbert
himself] was conscious of this)."[8]

    In thus recording in his poetry his own complex and profound
relationship with God and with Christ, Herbert takes his reader
through his words to the interior sanctuary of a life that, as Izaak
Walton admitted in his somewhat hagiographic manner in his *Life
of Mr. George Herbert* (1670), itself defeats description in words, a
life beyond common possibility demanding nothing short of the
golden tongue of a St. John Chrysostom himself: "I have now
brought him [says Walton] to the parsonage of Bemerton and to the

thirty-sixth year of his age, and must stop here, and bespeak the reader to prepare for an almost incredible story of the great sanctity of the short remainder of his holy life; a life so full of Charity, Humility and all Christian virtues that it deserves the eloquence of St. Chrysostom to commend and declare it."[9]

In short, in his very life we are brought within that space of literature and to the essential solitude that, in the words of the French literary and cultural critic Maurice Blanchot, writing not of Herbert himself, of course, "excludes the complacent isolation of individualism; it has nothing to do with the quest for singularity."[10] In this solitary literary space, the writer is lost in the greater work, the delimited site of an endless task, defined only by the restrictions of a particular poetic structure, or theological conclusion, the momentary vision that casts its passing light on a whole human life and its particularities. In Herbert's words in his poem "The Glimpse": "Thou cam'st but now; wilt thou so soon depart, / And give me up to night?"[11]

In Blanchot's thinking the solitude of the work has as its primary framework the very absence of any defining criteria or conclusion.

> "This absence," writes Blanchot, makes it impossible ever to declare the work finished or unfinished. The work is without any proof, just as it is without any use. It can't be verified. Truth can appropriate it, renown draws attention to it, but the existence it thus acquires doesn't concern it . . .The work is solitary: this does not mean it remains uncommunicable, that it has no reader. But whoever reads it enters into the affirmation of the work's solitude, just as he who reads it belongs to the risk of this solitude.[12]

It is necessary, perhaps, to expand further on this modern *literary* reflection in our reading of Herbert's poems. Within their complex linguistic structures the reader (who is always also the universal reader) enters a deeply solitary, interior place that is profoundly human, though one that entirely excludes any complacent individualism either of the Christian believer or of the nonbeliever. At the same time the reader cannot ignore Herbert's cultural, intellectual, and spiritual saturation in the language of the English Bible and the liturgy of the Church of England. Nor is this, for us, simply a hermeneutical issue between the horizons of the deeply religious language of the seventeenth century and the very different, more secular English of our own. For some of us, indeed, still familiar with the language of the Book of Common Prayer in our practice of worship, there may yet be heard a resonance in Herbert's words that is inaudible to those who are unfamiliar with this particular music: but it is not even a question of liturgical practice, of belief or unbelief. There is more to it than that. Thus, I want to move beyond the question posed by James Boyd White—that is, "[H]ow far is it possible to read Herbert's poetry, cast as it is in religious language, and with a theologically defined audience, without ourselves in some sense sharing in the beliefs that the language expresses?"[13] I move beyond that question inasmuch as the *authenticity* of the verse itself both embraces and expands the particularity of its immediate resonances and the references that are its landscape, but a landscape into which we are *all* graciously invited, its beauties and complexities open to us in manifold ways, whether they are familiar or strange, comfortable or alien in time, space, culture, or spirituality.

But before returning more specifically to George Herbert's poetry, it is necessary to ground the discussion in a somewhat broader context in both Renaissance and more recent literature. This is to seek to establish the close relationship between *religious experience* (which, as Dominic Baker-Smith has said, "results from a willingness to adopt a particular frame of reference [that] . . . in turn, structures the content of perception")[14] and *literary experience* that recognizes but does not necessarily adopt such a frame of reference. Or does it, although perhaps in a somewhat different way? Erasmus encouraged his reader to make a library of Christ in his own breast. But that library or book then has a linguistic energy of its own. It is, perhaps, that universal energy with which we as universal readers respond to the glorious description of scripture given us in 1611 by the translators of the Authorized Version of the Bible as "a tree, or rather a whole paradise of trees of life, which brings forth fruits every month, and the fruit thereof is for meat, and the leaves for medicine. . . . Finally a fountain of most pure water springing up into everlasting life."[15] Thus, we see that from the landscape of devotion emerges a space of literature that is a place of universal solitude, found also in John Donne's finest literary achievements, in which religion and its *particular* language are "treated as a repertory of roles to be enacted in a world demanding constant interpretation"[16] and constant expansion into the universal. So Donne writes in his *Devotions upon Emergent Occasions* (1624)—and we might here recall the Christ who is the library within our breasts: "The *stile* of thy *works,* the *phrase* of thine *Actions,* is *Metaphorical.* The *institution* of thy whole *worship* in the *old Law,* was a continuall *Allegory;* types & *figures* overspread all; and *figures* flowed unto *figures,* and powered themselves out into further figures. . . ."[17]

Such extraordinary literary energy is also characteristic of Sir Philip Sidney's 1595 *Apology for Poetry,* with its theologically intinctured and at the same time highly suggestive language (one might instance phrases such as "erected wit" or "infected will") that leads the reader into a world of art wherein the glories of the imagination and the poor stumblings of fallen humanity kiss and are found together: "[S]o no doubt the philosopher with his learned definition," says Sidney (and we might add the theologian to his picture)—"be it of virtue, vices, matters of public policy or private government—replenisheth the memory with many infallible grounds of wisdom, which, notwithstanding, lie dark before the imaginative and judging power, if they be not illuminated or figured by the speaking picture of Poesy."[18]

In the inspired imagination and in the continuances of literature, words, even those hallowed by the devotion that sanctifies language, are ever alert to the experience of the secular. As the poet Samuel Taylor Coleridge was to say to William Godwin in September 1800, "I would endeavour to destroy the old antithesis of *Words* & *Things,* elevating, as it were, Words into Things, & living Things too." And in 1822, objecting to the sole assumption to itself by the Roman Church of the word "Catholic," Coleridge calls words '*spirits* and *Living Agents* that are seldom misused without avenging themselves. . . ."[19] And, to sound one final note within the alchemy of language and its vicarious experience from a fellow poet in modern literature before returning to Herbert himself, here is a verse from D. J. Enright in his poem the "History of World Languages":

> They spoke the loveliest of languages.
> Their tongues entwined in Persian, ran
> And fused. Words kissed, a phrase embraced,
> Verbs conjugated sweetly. Verse began.
> So Eve and Adam lapped each other up
> The livelong day, the lyric night.[20]

And all this went on in paradisal innocence before the Fall, and Adam and Eve exercised their wits to conceive as love bade them welcome. Such is the space of literature.

In March 1615, Lancelot Andrewes, then bishop of Ely, was in attendance at the King's state visit to the University of Cambridge, where George Herbert, then only twenty-three, was a minor fellow of Trinity College, his ordination still more than ten years away. It is likely that on this occasion he was introduced to Bishop Andrewes, a meeting that led to a friendship and correspondence between the two men. Shortly afterward, Herbert sent Andrewes a letter (written in Greek) containing "some safe and useful aphorisms" on the subjects of predestination and sanctity of life, a letter, records Izaak Walton, "so remarkable for the language and reason of it, that, after reading it, the bishop put it into [his] bosom, and did often show it to many scholars, both of his and foreign nations; but did always return it back to the place where he first lodged it and continued it so near his heart till the last day of his life."[21] Such was the fate of this learned letter by a brilliant young man on the verge of worldly success, his courtly career seemingly assured. And it is precisely such success with words, though not at court, that would contribute to the textual confluence in his poetry of an utterly embodied spirituality. This poetry continues to address us directly today, in a union of body and soul such that no language of the body affronts the soul, but rather embellishes it in the space of literature as a truly aesthetic asceticism. In the most fragile, yet tenacious, of literary connections we can link the ancient brothers and sisters who were the first Christian saints of the desert with George Herbert, and then, in another unlikely leap of the imagination, to the twentieth century's Simone Weil, another ascetic who in fact read Herbert's poetry with remarkable insight and empathy.[22] In the chapter of his prose work *A Priest to the Temple* (1652, posthumous) entitled "The Parson's State of Life," Herbert writes of his subject:

> *He therefore thinks it not enough for him to observe the fasting days of the Church and the daily prayers enjoined him by authority, which he observeth out of humble conformity and obedience; but adds to them, out of choice and devotion, some other days for fasting and hours for prayers; and by these he keeps his body tame, serviceable and healthful; and his soul fervent, active, young and lusty as an eagle. He often readeth the Lives of the Primitive Monks, Hermits and Virgins, and wondereth not so much at their patient suffering and cheerful dying under persecuting emperors . . . as at their daily temperance, abstinence, watchings, and constant prayers and mortifications in times of peace and prosperity.*[23]

Thus, in prayer and devotion, the parson mirrors the ancients, while the "taming" of his body results in an extraordinarily "embodied" (and scriptural) description of the lusty soul rising upward like an eagle.

By far the best way to read Herbert's collection of poems *The Temple* is to take them as a whole in order to appreciate best their complex inner geography and the subtle interrelationships between texts and levels of reference. In the puns and riddles of language, words are continually slipping to different levels of meaning, even learnedly across different languages in the macaronic tradition of verse, yet without losing touch with the initial level, so that language becomes a medium that simultaneously embraces different worlds, at once interior and exterior, bodily and spiritual. The poetry both sacralizes the profane and profanes the sacred in an endless kenosis of certainty (a term to which I shall return later in this essay), and yet sustained by a profound and utterly real sense of presence in absence. Immersed as Herbert was in the Book of Common Prayer, it was article 28 of the Thirty-Nine Articles of Religion of 1562 that was central to his poetry: "The Supper of the Lord is not only a sign of the love that Christians ought to have among themselves one to another; but rather as a Sacrament of our Redemption by Christ's death: insomuch that to such as rightly, worthily, and with faith, receive the same, the Bread which we break is a partaking of the Body of Christ; and likewise the Cup of Blessing is a partaking of the Blood of Christ."[24] The language of the Articles of Religion is careful in what it avoids saying as much as in what it affirms: to "partake" (a word reaffirmed in the Archbishop Cranmer's eucharistic rite) skirts theological controversy while yet affirming a genuine sacramental presence. It allows Herbert to shift easily into a broad imagery that, in his most familiar poem, "Love" (III), permits the celebration of the Sacrament to entertain also the language of wayside hospitality and even overt eroticism. In the Sacrament all is transfigured—nothing is ever wasted.

The reader of Herbert's poems comes to know, in the very exercise of reading itself, a sense of transformed embodiment and real presence. To enter into the world of the poem is a transfiguring experience, words becoming real presences in sensual embraces, collating and colliding terms of reference in a merging of body, mind, and spirit and requiring an impossible dwelling in iconoclastic ways of thinking about what it means to be a human being. (We shall shortly return to the theme of "poetic dwelling" linking Herbert, in another unlikely conjunction, with the later thought of the twentieth-century German philosopher Martin Heidegger.) But Herbert's wit does more than pose puzzles or quibbles for the reader. Reversals of meaning, opaque endings, dialogues, and conversations, words opening out into ever new depths of reference, sometimes across different languages, lay a heavy burden of interpretation (or perhaps better call it "response") upon the reader. Herbert does not *tell* you, he *shows* you, and leaves you to accommodate yourself

as reader to violent intersections of being in words made flesh in
the body and soul. As in the biblical Song of Songs itself, moments
of sexual exchange become places of profound ascetic spirituality
(as the Cistercian monk Bernard of Clairvaux well knew), theology
is discovered in practice in dramatically conceived exchanges, and
familiar images from the Bible flood out in opposing voices and in
new complexities of relationship with the everyday. Words even
stand physically on the page in shapes that embody meaning and
narrative progress, as in Herbert's "Easter-Wings," or as biblical
quotations hidden within a larger body of language, so that scripture is found embedded in every verbal expression, giving new
meaning to the verse from Colossians 3:3: "Our life is hid with
Christ in God." Christ speaks directly from the verse through the
liturgical reproaches of Good Friday in "The Sacrifice." And behind
all is the enigmatic, priestly, courtly poet who engenders a world
that is at once familiar and yet utterly strange, a world that acknowledges the flesh, but a flesh transfigured and disciplined by the
spiritual.

Herbert's poetry both loses and finds itself in a language of opposites, a chiastic structure of verse that at once empties words and
fills them with their contraries, in weakness stout. Words in themselves are unreliable, like the impulse of the poet himself, sources
of delusion, until, emptied of meaning, they find themselves afresh
in a coincidence of opposites.[25] Only in such verbal kenosis, or
emptying,[26] can the word of the poet find its true being and poetic
dwelling become possible. Here I am deliberately employing the
language of Martin Heidegger, and for reasons that will gradually
unfold as we begin to draw this essay toward a close. Heidegger's is
a language that is born of his engagement with another, later, poet
who bears a deep, hidden, and mysterious relationship with Herbert—the German romantic Friedrich Hölderlin—though Herbert
is utterly removed from the world of Hölderlin's politics and, of
course, from German idealism. But in Heidegger's reading of Hölderlin we focus on the crucial feature of the artwork—that is, its singularity.[27] The poetic work (*Dichtung*), Heidegger says, is a "self-
sufficient presence,"[28] irreducible in our understanding. We rest in
its texture and images, our interpretations "disappearing before the
pure presence of the poem."[29] The poem then becomes a world
that embraces the reader, at once familiar and unfamiliar, but always finally unsusceptible to the grasping hand of "knowledge."
There is, at its heart, an essential unthought, a mode of being that
comes close, even in George Herbert, to a religion without an object. In Timothy Clark's words, this is a poetry that enacts "the pos-

sibility of other non-appropriative ways of knowing,"[30] and only thus, I would wish to say, can we even begin to draw closer to the sacred or what Heidegger calls the "mystery of the reserving nearness."[31] The task of the poet is to turn poetic language back upon its own foundations in the kenosis of language in which, in Herbert's words, "I am clean forgot."

It is this which Heidegger knows as "poetic dwelling," a being in the world in which words themselves dwell among us in their mystery and salvific potential. The philosopher James C. Edwards describes such poetic dwelling succinctly in this way: "To dwell poetically on the earth as a mortal is to live in awareness of the godhead, the clearing, the blank but lightening sky. It is to live so as to measure oneself against that Nothing—that No-thing—that grants the possibility of the presence of and the Being of the things that there are. Within that clearing, as Heidegger puts it, brightness wars with darkness. There we struggle against particular ignorances and incapacities to bring forth truth."[32] Within this very precise passage there are many resonances, and Herbert's poetry provides one of them. There is also, crucially, the first chapter of St. John's Gospel (which has never actually been far from our thoughts), negative theology, the theology of the death of God (from Hegel, through Nietzsche and the theologian Thomas J. J. Altizer), Heidegger, and Hölderlin. But let us not misunderstand this. I am not offering you a "positive" reading of Heidegger's interpretation of his poet, with the peculiar nationalisms and redemptive politics that such a reading would require. But neither am I offering a "positive" reading of Herbert, either in any traditional sense of him as a Christian poet, or as an Anglican of the early seventeenth century. The concern is more to move within and behind the poetry as the *embodiment,* not the reflection or statement, of theological *possibilities*—no more than that. It is to seek for a place within the disturbing semantic shifts of the verse.

Consider for a moment Herbert's poem "Christmas."[33] This is not a poem *about* Christmas, as such. To start with, its setting is temporally indeterminate, any time—"as I rid *one day.*" Rather, it is an exploration, a calling into question even, of the earthly hospitality granted to the heavenly child when the scene is transported from Bethlehem to the soul of the poet. Here is the first half of the poem:

> All after pleasures as I rid one day
>   My horse and I, both tir'd, bodie and minde,
>   With full crie of affections, quite astray;
> I took up in the next inne I could finde.

> There when I came, whom found I but my deare,
>   My dearest Lord, expecting till the grief
>   Of pleasures brought me to him, readie there
> To be all passengers most sweet relief?
>
> O thou, whose glorious, yet contracted light,
>   Wrapt in a nights mantle, stole into a manger;
>   Since my dark soul and brutish is thy right,
> To Man of all beasts be not thou a stranger:
>
>   Furnish & deck my soul, that thou mayst have
>   A better lodging, then a rack, or grave.

Here, indeed, is a poetic dwelling, and a dwelling of the word in the poet, a theology instantiated *within* language itself and our complex experience of words.[34] We begin after a journey, wearied from "pleasures," and setting down at the first inn at hand to rest, which becomes, in a sense, the humble inn of Christmas, but immediately moves to the interiority of the poet's "dark soul" burdened with "the grief of pleasures," its sinfulness awaited by the "contracted light" of its dear Lord. Moving between the different levels of reference (in a manner highly reminiscent of the Cranmerian Collects of the Book of Common Prayer), the reader is kept alert to shifts of place and inclusive slippages of language—theology, spiritual condition, and the inn itself intertwining at every level, even to complexities in single words. In the second stanza, which is almost a separate poem, a song to be sung in the conditions set up by the first stanza (a device Herbert also uses in his poems on Good Friday and Easter), an extended play on the word "sun" concludes with an harmonious exchange—"Till ev'n his beams sing, and my musick shine."

"Christmas" then concludes with a celebration, realized in defiance, almost, of all sophisticated hermeneutics. We know, as it were, 'something understood" even as the verse has simultaneously constructed and deconstructed the images and metaphors of the theological narrative in a new awareness of the possibility of presence of Being in the clearing of the poem. And here, as we move from poetry to theology, I make perhaps my most shocking move: from Herbert to the contemporary writings of the Italian philosopher Gianni Vattimo, who links the truth of Christianity with what he calls "postmodern nihilism" or "the end of metaphysics," "which is to say that Christianity's truth appears to be the dissolution of the (metaphysical) truth concept itself."[35] At the heart of Vattimo's post-Heideggerian deconstructed and (partly) reconstructed Christianity is a deeply poetic reading of kenosis, an understanding of the Incarnation as God's renunciation of his own sovereign transcendence, after Philippians 2:6–8. In what Vattimo calls a "reduced faith" he suggests that "the 'kenotic' interpretation of the articles of faith goes hand in hand with the life of every person, that is, with the commitment to transform them into concrete principles that are incarnate in one's own existence, and irreducible to a formula."[36] At the heart of this faith—its terms drawn from a century of existential thinking that includes Rudolf Bultmann, Martin Heidegger, and Paul Tillich—is "the recognition that the commandment of charity is the sole content of the myths of Scripture, of the history of spirituality and Christian theology."[37]

Now, we should not, of course, in any way attribute to George Herbert anything like the radical post-postmodern theology and "weak metaphysics" of Vattimo. That would be absurd and indefensible. But I do think that there are similarities between where each of them actually is, each in his own time, in the search for the truth of Christianity. (The phrase is Vattimo's, not mine.) The contemporary postmetaphysical philosopher finds such truth in those processes of secularization that allow him to move away from the, for him, impossible constraints of a church that still attempts to impose rules that cannot be accepted, but yet to acknowledge a culture that is still shaped by the biblical and specifically Christian message.[38] Reading the poetry of George Herbert, we find it in a space of literature that allows that truth to be "understood" without the imposition of doctrine, but acknowledges the authenticity of the Bible, the church, and its beloved liturgical discipline, but only through the appropriation of its impossible, living necessities. Herbert is a Renaissance Anglican clergyman: Vattimo is a radical Italian, Roman Catholic philosopher, rediscovering something like a Christian faith in terms that would have been utterly incomprehensible to the older poet. Strangely, however, we can read them both and find ourselves responding to the contemporary resonances of Herbert's call to his reader in all its interior earthiness, and in the defined freedom and continuances of the resulting intermediate space understand a little better Vattimo's claim to belief as still a crucial feature of our contemporary cultural and personal lives. And on a personal note, this odd transhistorical common ground between Herbert and Vattimo is important to me, because it is only through this literary space that I can continue to legitimate the continuing philosophical and cultural demands of theology—which is why Herbert remains such a major figure in my reading.

With this odd combination in mind, let us conclude with a brief reflection on a sonnet that links Herbert *back* through the Christian tradition to those early fathers and mothers of the desert whose lives became utterly one with scripture, such that reading finally becomes a totality of living. For to read Herbert is to become wholly one with the scriptures that inhabit not only almost every image and metaphor, but every word of his verse. The words of the Bible, "this book of starres" for our salvation, are realized in the flesh of the verse, and to read is to participate, shockingly, in the Word made Flesh.

> Oh Book! infinite sweetnesse! let my heart
> Suck ev'ry letter, and a hony gain,
> Precious for any grief in any part;
> To cleare the breast, to mollifie all pain.
>
> Thou art all health, health thriving till it make
> A full eternitie: thou art a masse
> Of strange delights, where we may wish & take.
> Ladies, look here; this is the thankfull glasse,
>
> That mends the lookers eyes: this is the well
> That washes what it shows. Who can endeare
> Thy praise too much? thou art heav'ns Lidger here,
> Working against the states of death and hell.
>
> Thou art joyes handsell: heav'n lies flat in thee,
> Subject to ev'ry mounters bended knee.[39]

The poem opens with a reference to Psalm 119:103, "O how sweet are thy words unto my throat: yea, sweeter than honey in my mouth." The heart of the reader of scripture is like a bee drawing sweetness from the flower, making for full health. The poet's address to the ladies daringly draws on a commonplace image from Jacobean theater of the vanity of women who admire themselves in the mirror.[40] Here, however, is the true mirror that does better than cosmetics, that does not merely reveal imperfection but washes it away. Throughout the sonnet, images and individual words expand in reference across the spiritual and the physical realms. The Bible is "heav'ns Lidger here"—a pun that refers at once to "resident ambassador" and "register" (book)[41] and is politically continued in the reference in the next line to the "states" of death and hell. Indeed, heaven itself lies flat between the pages of the Bible, its very words active in our salvation. In this brief sonnet, Herbert ranges across an extraordinary geography of different worlds and societies—in nature, the courtly lady, the politician—drawing them all together in the words of scripture.

Some readers will feel, no doubt, that I have taken considerable liberties with Herbert and his legacy, and have abandoned too cavalierly the haven of historical scholarship. In response I might suggest that such liberties in the realms of postmodern and post-structuralist literary criticism have often been taken with Herbert's fellow poet John Donne, to less evident consternation.[42] Further-more, Stanley Fish, in his influential book *Self-Consuming Arti-facts* (1972), writing of the "experience" of seventeenth-century literature, devotes an entire chapter to the dialectic of the self in Herbert's poetry from which, in many respects, what has been sug-gested here derives, though, after nearly forty years since Fish's book, with two major shifts. First, there is a more radical movement from the precise study of poetry to a consideration of theology in reading Herbert, and second, there is a claim that the Herbertian legacy does speak, most profoundly, to the state of religious experi-ence and expression that we now struggle with. Thus, close read-ings of the poems are linked with reflections on such major contemporary theological figures as Vattimo (after Heidegger) and their recovery of "poetic dwelling" in a secular sense of the liturgi-cal in current culture. Fish makes the point that "to read Herbert's poetry is to experience the dissolution of the lines of demarcation we are accustomed to think of as real . . . [and] in the course of this dissolution Christ is discovered to be not only the substance of all things, but the performer of all actions."[43] If this is indeed the case, then it is perfectly proper to link Herbert's poetry with issues in Christian theology after postmodernity, his legacy recognized in de-votional exercises within the radical culture of our own time.

In George Herbert we find another impossible saint—the court-ier turned country parson, whose poetry remains utterly immersed in the world even while sustaining an ascetic vision that is grounded entirely in the living word of scripture and in the sacra-ment of the Eucharist, which permeates every aspect of life lived to the full. The poet of *The Temple* is full of boundless energy, but it is an energy finally driven to an interiority within its language and its dramatic power, an interiority that suffers endless reversals and ne-gations. The frequent violence of the images and metaphors is fi-nally consumed in the still, insistent voice—the voice that calls silently from the wilderness without explanation and cannot be gainsaid. For, as something understood, it is the final negation of all language and its demands—and their complete fulfillment in si-lence of the total presence of God.[44]

NOTES

1. George Herbert, "Prayer" (I), in *The English Poems of George Herbert,* ed. Helen Wilcox (Cambridge: Cambridge University Press, 2007), 178.

2. See Timothy Clark, *Martin Heidegger* (London: Routledge, 2002), 118.

3. James Boyd White, *This Book of Starres: Learning to Read George Herbert* (Ann Arbor: University of Michigan Press, 1994), 29.

4. George Herbert, "Affliction (I)," lines 57–59, in *The English Poems of George Herbert,* ed. Helen Wilcox (Cambridge: Cambridge University Press, 2007), 162.

5. Samuel Johnson, *The Lives of the Poets* 1781; reprint, (Oxford: Oxford University Press, 1952), 1:204.

6. See White, *This Book of Starres,* 34. "For there is a strain running counter to such dogmatism, not only in writers like Herbert and Emerson and Augustine, but in the gospels themselves, which are full of the cryptic, the paradoxical, the impossible."

7. Joan Bennett, *Five Metaphysical Poets* (Cambridge: Cambridge University Press, 1966), 56.

8. David L. Edwards, *Poets and God* (London: Darton, Longman and Todd, 2005), 103.

9. Izaak Walton, *The Life of Mr. George Herbert,* in *George Herbert: The Complete English Poems,* ed. John Tobin (Harmondsworth, england: Penguin, 1991), 295.

10. Maurice Blanchot, *The Space of Literature,* trans, Ann Smock (Lincoln: University of Nebraska Press, 1982), 21.

11. Helen Wilcox, ed., *The English Poems of George Herbert* (Cambridge: Cambridge University Press, 2007), 530.

12. Blanchot, *Space of Literature,* 22.

13. White, *This Book of Sterres,* 43.

14. Dominic Baker-Smith, "Exegesis: Literary and Divine," in *Images of Belief in Literature,* ed. David Jasper (London: Macmillan, 1984), 175.

15. "The Translators to the Reader," in *The Bible: Authorized King James Version* (1611), ed. Robert Carroll and Stephen Prickett (Oxford: Oxford University Press, 1997), lvi.

16. Baker-Smith, "Exegesis," 175.

17. John Donne, *Devotions upon Emergent Occasions,* ed. A. Raspa (Montreal: McGill-Queen's University Press, 1975), 100.

18. Sir Philip Sidney, *An Apology for Poetry* (1595), in *English Critical Essays (XVI–XVIII Centuries),* ed. Edmund D. Jones (Oxford: Oxford University Press, 1947), 15.

19. Samuel Taylor Coleridge, *Collected Letters,* ed. Earl Leslie Griggs (1956; reprint, Oxford: Clarendon Press, 1971), 1:626; 5:228.

20. D. J. Enright, *Collected Poems* (Oxford: Oxford University Press, 1987), 206.

21. See Paul A. Welsby, *Lancelot Andrewes, 1555–1626* (London: SPCK, 1958), 107–9.

22. See Simone Weil, *Waiting on God,* trans. Emma Craufurd (London: Fount, 1959), 34–35, for Weil's reading of "Love" (III): "I learnt it by heart. Often at the culminating point of a violent headache, I make myself say it over, concentrating all my attention upon it and clinging with all my soul to the tenderness it enshrines. I used to think I was merely reciting it as a beautiful poem, but without

my knowing it the recitation had the virtue of a prayer. It was during one of these recitations that, as I told you, Christ himself came down and took possession of me."

23. John Tobin, ed. *George Herbert: The Complete English Poems of George Herbert,* (Harmondsworth, England: Penguin, 1991), 213.

24. See further, William J. McGill, *Poets' Meeting: George Herbert, R. S. Thomas and the Argument with God* (Jefferson, NC: McFarland and Co., 2004), 78–82.

25. The reference. of course, is to the *coincidentia oppositorum* that is at the heart of the theology of Nicholas of Cusa.

26. The biblical origins of the term are in the great poem in Philippians 2:6–11: "but emptied himself, taking the form of a slave" (2:7).

27. See, Clark, *Martin Heidegger,* 101.

28. Martin Heidegger, *Poetry, Language, Thought.* trans. Albert Hofstadter (New York: Harper and Row, 1971), 29.

29. Martin Heidegger, *Elucidations of Hölderlin's Poetry,* trans. Keith Hoeller (New York: Humanity Books, 2000), 22.

30. Clark, *Martin Heidegger,* 105.

31. Heidegger, *Elucidations,* 43, 47.

32. James C. Edwards, *The Plain Sense of Things: The Fate of Religion in an Age of Normal Nihilism* (University Park: Pennsylvania State University Press, 1997), 184.

33. Wilcox, *English Poems of George Herbert,* 292.

34. See, further, David Jasper, " 'The Wheels of the Chariot': Religious Language in English and German Romanticism," in *Transforming Holiness: Representations of Holiness in English and American Literary Texts,* ed. Irene Visser and Helen Wilcox (Leuven: Peeters, 2006), 95–97.

35. See Gianni Vattimo, "The Age of Interpretation," in *The Future of Religion,* ed. Santiago Zabala (New York: Columbia University Press, 2005), 43–54.

36. Gianni Vattimo, *Belief,* trans. Luca D'Isanto and David Webb (Cambridge: Polity Press, 1999), 77.

37. Ibid., 79.

38. Vattimo, "Age of Interpretation," 52.

39. George Herbert, "The H. Scriptures," (I) in Wilcox, *English Poems of George Herbert,* 208.

40. E.g., in Shakespeare's *Hamlet* and Webster's *The Duchess of Malfi.*

41. See Helen Wilcox, " 'Heaven's Lidger Here': Herbert's *Temple* and Seventeenth Century Devotion," in *Images of Belief in Literature,* ed. David Jasper (London: Macmillan, 1984), 153–68.

42. For example, Thomas Docherty, *John Donne Undone* (London: Methuen, 1986), which draws extensively on cultural and poststructuralist theory.

43. Stanley E. Fish, *Self-Consuming Artifacts: The Experience of Seventeenth Century Literature* (Berkeley and Los Angeles: University of California Press, 1974), 173.

44. This final image is drawn from Robert P. Scharlemann's book *The Reason of Following: Christology and the Ecstatic I* (Chicago: University of Chicago Press, 1991).

Contributors

JOHN CHANDLER, of East Knoyle, Salisbury, England, is proprietor of the Hobnob Press, which publishes books about Wiltshire and the surrounding area. He holds a PhD from the University of Bristol for research on the church in the later Roman Empire, but has spent his career in English local history, as a librarian, part-time lecturer, publisher, and researcher for archaeological investigations. He has written extensively about Salisbury and Wiltshire, has edited the Wiltshire Record Society series, and has produced editions of the travel writings of John Leland and John Taylor. An earlier version of his essay, "The Country Parson's Flock: George Herbert's Wiltshire Parish," appeared in *Sarum Chronicle*.

PAUL DYCK is associate professor of English, Canadian Mennonite University. He is currently doing research on the Gospel harmonies made by hand at Little Gidding (c. 1630–40) and the early editions of *The Temple*, and on the electronic publication of early texts. He has published articles on various aspects of Herbert's poetry, and on devotional practice and book production at Little Gidding.

DONALD FRIEDMAN is professor emeritus of English, University of California, Berkeley. His research interests include Milton, Shakespeare, and the sixteenth and seventeenth centuries. He is the author of numerous articles and of *Marvell's Pastoral Art* (1970), and editor of Eldred Revett's *Selected Poems, Humane and Divine* (1966) and Mildmay Fane, Earl of Westmoreland's *Otia Sacra* (1975).

SIDNEY GOTTLIEB is professor of media studies and digital culture, Sacred Heart University, and editor of the *George Herbert Journal*. His research interests include film history, literature and film, Alfred Hitchcock, Orson Welles, and seventeenth-century literature. His recent publications include *Roberto Rossellini's Rome Open City* (2004), *Alfred Hitchcock: Interviews* (2003), and *Framing Hitchcock: Selected Essays from the Hitchcock Annual* (2002).

Kᴇɴɴᴇᴛʜ Gʀᴀʜᴀᴍ is associate professor of English language and literature, University of Waterloo. His current research investigates the relationship between English poetry and post-Reformation church discipline. He has been published in *Renaissance and Reformation, Criticism, Journal of Medieval and Early Modern Studies,* and *Shakespeare Quarterly,* and he is the author of *The Performance of Conviction: Plainness and Rhetoric in the Early English Renaissance* (2004).

Cʜʀɪsᴛᴏᴘʜᴇʀ Hᴏᴅɢᴋɪɴs is professor of English at the University of North Carolina-Greensboro and founder of the ongoing George Herbert's Living Legacies project. He is author of *Authority, Church and Society in George Herbert: Return to the Middle Way* (1993), and co-editor, with Daniel W. Doerksen, of *Centered on the Word: Literature, Scripture, and the Tudor-Stuart Middle Way* (UDP, 2004). He also has published a wide-ranging study, *Reforming Empire: Protestant Colonialism and Conscience in British Literature* (2002). He is at work on *Anxious Beauty: George Herbert and the Protestant Aesthetic* for Stephen Prickett's series on the making of the Christian imagination, and on an edited collection of selected essays from UNCG's October 2008 international conference "George Herbert's Travels: International Print and Cultural Legacies."

Dᴀᴠɪᴅ Jᴀsᴘᴇʀ is professor in literature and theology, University of Glasgow. His research is an interdisciplinary attempt to examine the possibilities for theology (mainly but not exclusively Christian) in contemporary culture. His recent publications include *The Bible and Literature: A Reader,* with Stephen Prickett, (1999); *Religion and Literature: A Reader,* with Robert Detweiler, (2000); *The Sacred Desert* (2004); *A Short Introduction to Hermeneutics* (2004); and *The Oxford Handbook of English Literature and Theology,* with Andrew Hass and Elizabeth Jay (2007).

Cʟᴀʏᴛᴏɴ Lᴇɪɴ is professor of English, Purdue University. His research interests include British literature, seventeenth-century prose and poetry, choral music, and music in the Renaissance. He has been published in *English Literary Renaissance, University of Toronto Quarterly, Comparative Literature, Studies in English Literature,* and *Eighteenth-Century Studies.* He has edited the volume *British Prose Writers of the Early Seventeenth Century* (1995) and is editor of *English Renaissance Prose.*

CRISTINA MALCOLMSON is professor of English and department head, Bates College. She has taught on sixteenth- and seventeenth-century poetry, feminist literary criticism, and the news media. Her recent publications include *George Herbert: A Literary Life* (2004), *Debating Gender in Early Modern England, 1500–1700* (2002), *Heart-Work: George Herbert and the Protestant Ethic* (2000), and *Renaissance Poetry* (1998).

ANTHONY MARTIN is professor of English, Waseda University, Japan. His research interests include English poetry (especially Renaissance), African literature, literary theory (especially New Historicism), Renaissance drama, and Shakespeare. He has been published in *George Herbert Journal, Studies in Philology,* and *Shakespeare Studies.* He contributed to *Reader's Guide to British History,* ed. David Loades, (2003); *John Foxe and His World,* ed. Christopher Highley and John King, (2001); and *Anatomy of Tudor Literature: Proceedings of the First International Conference of the Tudor Symposium,* ed. Michael Pincombe, (2001).

KATE NARVESON is associate professor of English, Luther College. Her research interests include Elizabethan and early Stuart literature, medieval literature, Milton, and devotional writing. She has been published in *Studies in Philology, Seminary Ridge Review,* and *John Donne Journal.* Work in progress includes a book on the construction of emotion and identity in early Stuart literature, and a study of intersections between body and spirit in Grace Mildmay's medical and meditational writing.

GENE EDWARD VEITH is provost and professor of literature, Patrick Henry College. His research interests include Christianity and culture, classical education, literature, and the arts. His recent publications include *The Soul of the Lion, the Witch, and the Wardrobe* (2005), *A Place to Stand: The Word of God in the Life of Martin Luther* (2005), and *Loving God with All Your Mind: Thinking as a Christian in the Postmodern World* (2003). He is also author of *Reformation Spirituality: The Religion of George Herbert* (1985).

CURTIS WHITAKER is associate professor of English, Idaho State University. His research focuses on seventeenth-century literature and literary representations of nature. He has been published in *George Herbert Journal, Yale Milton Encyclopedia, Rendezvous,* and *Huntington Library Quarterly.*

HELEN WILCOX is professor of English, Bangor University, Wales. Her research interests include devotional writing (particularly lyric poetry), Shakespeare (particularly the tragicomedies), and women's writing (particularly poetry and autobiography). Her recent publications include *George Herbert: The English Poems* (2007); coeditor, *Transforming Holiness: Representations of Holiness in English and American Literary Texts,* (2006); and coeditor, *Betraying Our Selves: Forms of Self-Representation in Early Modern English* Texts (2000).

CHAUNCEY WOOD is professor emeritus of English, McMaster University. His research interests include medieval and Renaissance English literature. He is the author of *Chaucer and the Country of the Stars: Poetic Uses of Astrological Imagery* (1970) and *The Elements of Chaucer's "Troilus"* (1984). Other publications include *Herbert's Golden Harpe: A Transcription of Huntington Library Manuscript Hm 85* (1998).

General Index

Aaron, 94–95
Abel, 20
Abeles, Jennifer, 131 n. 14
Abbot, George, 143, 150 n. 13, 154 n. 55
Abbot, Robert, 150 n. 13
Acrasia, 18
Adam, 19, 45, 47, 57, 121, 277
Adonis, 242, 251 nn. 38 and 39
alchemy, 113
Alciati (Andrea Alciato), 243, 250 n. 37
Aldbourne, 137, 151 n. 17
Aldrovandi, Ulisse, 243
Alexander, Michael Van Cleave, 149–50 n. 10, 154 n. 55
All Souls College, 137, 147
Alpers, Paul, 37, 38, 49 nn. 9 and 10, 49–50 n.11
Althaus, Paul, 71 n. 11
Altizer, Thomas J. J., 281
Alton Australis, 150 n. 13
Alton Borealis, 137, 151 n. 17
America, United States of, 257
Americas, the, 128, 129, 235, 248 n. 2
Amos, William, 130 n. 1
Anacreon, 245
Anagnostou, Sabine, 248 n. 2
Anderson, Frank, 250 n. 32
Andrews, John, 159
Andrewes, Lancelot, 89 n. 32, 138, 277–78
Anglesey, Wales, 91; Marquess of, 91; Plas Newydd, 91
Anglicans/Anglicanism. See Church of England
Anti-Calvinists/Non-Calvinists. See Arminians/Arminianism
antimony, 235
Apuleius, 251 n. 38
Aquinas. See Thomas Aquinas
Armenia, 236
Arminians/Arminianism, 52, 53, 55, 82, 186

Asals, Heather, 50 n. 17, 76, 88 n. 24, 108 n. 60
Ashworth, William, Jr., 243, 250 nn. 35, 36, and 37
Asia, 235
Aubrey, John, 113–14, 116, 119, 122, 123, 130 n. 1, 131 n. 8, 132 nn. 35, 38, and 42, 140, 141, 143, 145, 262; *Brief Lives*, 114, 116, 130 n. 2, 131 nn. 7 and 22, 132 nn. 23 and 24, 152 n. 40, 153 n. 45, 155 nn. 64 and 70, 271 n. 11; "Memoires of Naturall Remarques in the County of Wilts.," 114, 130 n. 2
Augustine, 40, 50 nn. 17 and 18, 79, 81, 89 n. 33, 133 n. 60, 174, 180 n. 5, 274, 286 n. 6
Austin, William, 228 n. 2
Aveton Gifford (Aveton Giffard, Awton Giffard/Gifford), Devon, 187, 188, 194 n. 17
Aylesbury, 145, 155 n. 73

Bacon, Sir Francis, 134, 139, 240–41, 250 n. 25, 274; *Instauratio Magna (Great Instauration)*, 240–41, 249–50 n. 24
Bacon, John, 161, 162, 165
Bagges, the Widow, 25, 175, 177, 178
Baker, Sir Richard, 229 n. 9
Baker-Smith, Dominic, 276, 286 nn. 14 and 16
Bald, R. C., 154 nn. 57, 58, and 59, 154–55 n. 63
Baldwin, Robert, 119, 120, 131 nn. 14, 15, and 20, 132 nn. 26, 27, and 28
Ball, Richard, 187, 189, 193–94 n. 15
Balliol College, 147, 148
"Balme of Gilead," 223
Banckes, Rycharde, 251 n. 40
Banckes herbal, 244, 251 n. 40

292

Banks, Uriam, 156n. 76

Barnard, Francis, 188

Bates, Roger, 137, 151n. 20

Bath and Wells: bishopric of, 137, 147, 265

Bathsheba, 199

Battles, Ford Lewis, 89n. 36

Bauhin, Gaspard, 245, 247, 251n. 44

Baxter, John, 90n. 40

bay leaves, 246

Bayly, Lewis, 101, 209n. 15; *The Practice of Piety,* 101

Baynton House, 136

Beaumont, Anna Susanna, 193–94n. 15

Beaumont, John, 193–94n. 15

Beaumont, Joseph, 188, 193–94n. 15

Beaumont family, 187

Becon, Thomas, 229n. 18

Bedfordshire, 116

Bethlehem, 281

Bemerton, 15, 24, 38, 130n. 1, 134, 136–38, 140, 141, 143, 146, 150–51n. 16, 162, 163, 182, 188, 237, 248n. 6, 260, 269, 274–75; Church of St. Andrew, 16, 113, 155n. 67, 157n. 98, 165, 170–71n. 5, 192, 266; as "country" parish, 167–69; as Fugglestone with Bemerton, 158, 168, 188; Herbert's churchwardens at, 164; Herbert's congregation at, 24, 158–70; manorial court in, 162–64, 169; map of, 159; modern, 168, 170; obscurity of, as clerical preferment, 143–45, 150–51n. 16, 155nn. 67, 70, and 72; rectors of, sixteenth- and seventeenth-century, 156n. 76; rectory, 191, 275;   as urban suburb, 168–69

Bemerton Local History Society, 170

Beminster Secunda, 137

Benet, Diana, 53, 71n. 28, 107n. 30, 142, 154n. 56, 217, 228n. 4, 230n. 24, 231n. 46

Bennet, Sir John, 213–14, 218, 229nn. 7 and 14, 230n. 25

Bennett, Joan, 286n. 7

Berkshire, 138

Bermuda, 117

Bernard of Clairvaux, 280

Best, John, 164, 165

Bettes, William, 146, 156n. 76

Bettey, J. H., 171n. 31

Beza, Theodore, 229n. 7

Bible, 26, 106, 106nn. 9–12, 107nn. 18, 22, and 40, 108n. 67, 109n. 74, 200, 213, 214, 235, 244, 251n. 42, 269, 275, 280, 283, 284, 286n. 15, 287n. 26; Bishop's Bible (1604), 209n. 15; Gospels, 27, 86, 90n. 40, 107n. 27, 274, 281, 286n. 6; King James Bible (Authorized Version), 209n. 15, 276; and liturgical forms, 26, 102, 197–208; New Testament, 68, 199, 202, 213, 283, 287n. 26, doctrine and life in, 75, 79–80, and Herbert's poetic forms, 99; Tyndale Bible, 261

Biester, James, 90n. 45

Billing, Einar, 56, 71nn. 10 and 12

Bion, 244, 251n. 39

Birckman, Arnold, 251n. 40

Bishopton, 140, 153n. 44

Björk, Lennart, 250n. 32

Blaise, Anne Marie Miller, 210n. 24

Blanchot, Maurice, 275, 286nn. 10 and 12

Blau, Sheridan D., 88n. 20

Blayney, Peter W. M., 194n. 23

Bloch, Chana, 73, 87n. 5, 108n. 49, 214–17, 230nn. 20, 21, 22, and 24

Blythe, R., 172n. 33

Bock, Hieronymus, 243, 251n. 38

Bocking, Essex, 145

Bodleian Library, 149n. 7

bolearmena, 236, 243

Boleyn, Anne, 147

Book of Common Prayer. *See under* Church of England

Book of Mormon, 198

Booty, John E., 107n. 24, 108nn. 45 and 67, 203, 207, 208n. 4, 209n. 12

Boston (Salisbury alchemist), 119

Boyle, Robert, 247, 252n. 51

Bower, Henry, 163

Brauer, Jerald, 221, 230n. 29

Beton, Nicholas, 228n. 2

Brewer, J. S., 153n. 46

Bridges, Edward, 138

Bristol, 258

Britain, 236

Britton, John, 130n. 2, 132n. 24

Brooke, Dorothea, 29
Brough, William, 156 n. 92
Brown, Capability, 120
Browne, Sir Thomas, 258
Browne, William, 42
Brunfels, Otto, 243, 251 n. 38
Bryant, Sir Arthur, 167
Buck, Thomas, 26, 183, 191
Buckingham, Duke of (George Villiers), 135, 142, 149 n. 4, 152 n. 36, 260–62
Bull, Henry, 229 n. 18
Bulmer, Sir Bevis, 115, 130–31 n. 5
Bultman, Rudolf, 283
Bunyan, John, 82, 89 n. 40, 90 n. 41
Burgoyne, Chris, 194 n. 17
Burke, Kenneth, 49 n. 10
Bush, Jonathan A., 249 n. 20
Byfield, Nicholas, 214, 229 n. 17

Cain, 20
Caine, Hall, 257
Calendar of State Papers Domestic, 194 n. 18
Calvin, John, 52, 53, 63, 80, 89 n. 36, 90 n. 42, 213; and divine chastizement, 83; and divine vengeance, 83; doctrine of vocation, 54–55; *Institutes of the Christian Religion,* 80; on the Psalms, 229 n. 13
Calvinists/Calvinism, 60, 71 n. 16, 126, 133 n. 60
Cambridge University, 109 n. 71, 113, 125, 135, 138, 139, 145, 146, 149 n. 5, 183, 188, 209 n. 12, 241, 248 n. 6, 277
Cambridge University Press, 26, 183, 184, 192
Camerarius, Joachim, 242, 243
Canada, 118, 124
Cansick, Frederick Teague, 194 n. 29
Canterbury, 189
Carbone, Ludovico, 184
Cardwell, Edward, 88 n. 14
Carroll, Robert, 106 n. 9, 286 n. 15
Cartwright, Thomas, 79–80, 89 n. 34
Cary, Lucius, Lord Falkland, 153 n. 44, 269
Cary, Lettice, Viscountess Falkland, 186
Castiglione, Baldassare, 88 n. 22
Cator, Thomas, 156 n. 76

Caus, Isaac de, 122
Cefalu, Paul, 73, 85, 88 n. 9, 90 n. 47
Chafin, Thomas, 136, 150 n. 12
Chamberlain, John, 152 n. 32
Chandler, John, 16, 25, 159, 172 n. 39
Charles I, King, 117, 135–38, 141, 143–47, 149 n. 4, 151 n. 17, 153 n. 47, 154–55 n. 63, 188, 261; as Prince of Wales, and Spanish Match, 125, 149 n. 5
Charles II, King, 146, 186, 188, 269
Charles, Amy, 130 n. 1, 134, 139, 145, 149 nn. 1, 3, 5, and 8, 149–50 n. 10, 150–51 n. 16, 151–52 n. 29, 152 nn. 30, 33, 35, and 38, 153 n. 46, 154 n. 57, 155 nn. 67, 70, and 72, 170 n. 1, 182, 183, 190, 191, 193 nn. 3, 6, and 8, 194 nn. 28, 266, 271 nn. 11 and 16
Charterhouse, Clerkenwell, 139, 143, 152 n. 31, 154 nn. 58 and 59
Chastleton House, 121
Chaucer, Geoffrey, 238
Cheam, Surrey, 145
Chelsea, 136, 154 n. 57
chemistry, 113
Chibnall, Hugh, 161
Chichester Cathedral, 137, 156 n. 90
China, 236
Chippenham, 145, 170
Christ. *See* Jesus Christ
Christ Church College, 153 n. 44
Christmas, 282
Chrysostom, St. John, 81, 274–75
Church, The (section of *The Temple*). *See under* Index to Herbert's Writings, *The Temple*
Church of England, 26, 158, 182, 184, 185, 189, 190, 198, 200, 258, 281, 283; Anglo-Catholicism, nineteenth-century, 52; Arches, Dean of, 143; Articles of Religion, 279; attacked by Andrew Melville, 49 n. 6; Book of Common Prayer, 26–27, 53, 75, 97, 102, 103, 105, 107 n. 24, 108 n. 67, 197–208, 209 nn. 10 and 13, 222, 229 n. 5, 275, 282, Eucharist in, 208 n. 2, 209 n. 12, 279, Morning Prayer, 199, 201, 202, popular success of, 208 n. 1, prayer of humble access, 207, reception history of, 197–98; Book of Homilies, 198; Can-

ons of 1604, 75, 88n. 14; defended by George Herbert in *Musae Responsoriae,* 49n. 6; early Anglicanism, 52; interdependence of Bible and liturgy in, 26, 198–99; as middle way, 53; and poor relief, 25, 173–79, 239–40; priest's duties in seventeenth-century, 101–6; and salvation by grace through faith, 52, 53

Church Militant, The (section of *The Temple). See under* Index to Herbert's Writings

Churchwardens, 164, 176

Cistercians, 280

cinnamon, 236

city of gold. *See* El Dorado

Civil Wars, English, 28, 153nn. 45 and 47, 157n. 98, 185, 190, 198, 258, 259, 261, 267, 269

Clare College, 145

Clark, Peter, 172n. 39, 180n. 7

Clark, Timothy, 280–81, 286n. 2, 287nn. 27 and 30

Clarke, Elizabeth, 184, 185, 193n. 9, 231n. 49

Clarke, John, 214–15

Clerkenwell, 139

Clifford, Anne, Countess of Dorset, Countess of Montgomery and Pembroke, 140, 143, 152–53n. 42, 153n. 43, 154–55n. 63

cloves, 236

Clucas, Stephen, 131n. 14

Clusius, Carolus, 245

Coker, Farmer, 166, 171n. 30

Coleridge, Samuel Taylor, 277, 286n. 19

Colin Clout, 37

colonies/colonization. *See* empire

Colston, Edmund, 258

Comes, Natalis, 251n. 39

Committee for Plundered Ministers, 187

Commonwealth, 190

"Comus," 48. *See also* Milton, John

Compton Census of 1676, 158

Conformists/Conformity, 222, 230n. 29

Convocation, 147

Cook, Elizabeth, 41, 50n. 19

Cook, H., 171n. 31

Cook, Harold J., 249nn. 15, 17, 18, and 19

Cook, J., 171n. 20

Cooke, Robert, 184

Cooley, Ronald, 73, 87n. 7, 144, 151n. 26, 167, 170n. 1, 171n. 32, 172n. 34, 173–74, 180nn. 2 and 3, 239–40, 249n. 21

Coombe Martin, Devon, 120

Cooper, Alix, 237, 248nn. 7 and 8

Coquillette, Daniel R., 249n. 20

Cornaro, Luigi, 184

Cornish, C. L., 180n. 5

Countrey Parson, The, 17, 22, 25, 26, 31n. 7, 53, 56, 64, 69, 76, 77, 88n. 13, 95, 107n. 13, 169, 177, 179, 214, 237; and church discipline, 79; publication of, 26, 181–93; and social dynamics, 174; and *The Temple,* compared, 73–74; title of, 107n. 25; on "doctrine and life," 72–87; suspicious readings of, 88n. 22. *See also under* Index to Herbert's Writings

Cordelia, 106n. 7

Cormac, Bradin, 89n. 35

Cornelius Agrippa, 120

Coventry, Thomas, 143

Cowan, M., 171n. 31

Cowper, William, 258

Cox, John D., 194n. 23

Cranmer, Rachel, 149n. 7

Cranmer, Thomas, 147, 229n. 5, 279, 282

Crauford, Emma, 286–87n. 22

Creighton, Robert, 152n. 35

Crellin, John K., 248nn. 3, 4

Crittal, Elizabeth, 194n. 16

Cromer, Norfolk, 256

Cromwell, Oliver, 197, 261

Cronshay, Robert, 187

Culpepper, Nicholas, 237, 248n. 7

Cupid, 245

Curle, Walter, 137, 146–48, 150–51n. 16, 156nn. 76 and 87, 156–57n. 96, 157n. 98, 265, 266

Cutler, Thomas, Sr., 166, 168, 171n. 30

Cutler, Thomas, Jr., 171n. 30

Dale, Alfred William Winterslow, 194n. 21

Dalton, Michael, 249n. 20
Damon the Mower, 51n. 40
Daniel, Roger, 26, 183, 184, 191
Danvers, Henry, Earl of Danby, 138
Danvers, Jane (Herbert's wife), 28, 29,
    183, 184, 259, 262, 264, 269, 271n.
    11, 272n. 25
Danvers, Sir John, 138, 140, 143,
    149n. 7, 149–50n. 10
Danvers, Lady Magdelene. *See* Herbert,
    Magdelene
Darwin, J. S., 153n. 44
Dauntsey, 136, 138, 167
Davenant, Edward, 138
Davenant, John, 138, 151nn. 26 and
    27
David, 199, 200, 213, 216, 219, 227,
    228
Davies, Julian, 156n. 95, 157n. 97
Davis, John, 115, 118–20, 132n. 25
Day, Peter, 194n. 25
Dearing, Vinton A., 106n. 1
Debus, Allen G., 132n. 33, 248n. 2
Declaration of Independence, 41
Dee, John, 117–20, 121–27, 129, 130,
    131nn. 13, 14, and 15, 132nn. 26,
    27, and 28; *The Limits of the British
    Empire,* 124, 132nn. 47 and 48;
    *Mathematical Praeface to the Ele-
    ments of Geometry of Euclid,* 120,
    121, 124, 125; *Monas Hieroglyphica,*
    121–22
Dering, Sir Edward, 135, 149n. 7
Derrida, Jacques, 209n. 10
De Selincourt, Ernest, 106nn. 2 and 7
Devil, 205, 210n. 22
Devizes, 87n. 1
Devon, 115, 120, 189
Devon Record Office, 229n. 17
Dick, Oliver Lawson, 130n. 1
Dickens, Charles, 262
Dictionary of National Biography. See
    *Oxford Dictionary of National Biog-
    raphy*
Dioscorides, 235, 244–45, 251n. 38
D'Isanto, Luca, 287n. 36
Ditchampton, 150–51n. 16
DiYanni, Robert, 250n. 25
Docherty, Thomas, 287n. 42
Dodoens, Rembert, 242–45, 247,
    250nn. 32 and 33, 251nn. 39 and
    41; on redness of roses, 242–44

Doerksen, Daniel W., 70n. 3, 73, 87n.
    6, 88n. 14, 181, 183, 193nn. 1 and
    6, 230n. 33
Donne, Anne, 262
Donne, John, 35, 99, 107n. 31, 138,
    139, 142–43, 145, 152n. 37, 153n.
    46, 154nn. 58 and 61, 154–55n. 63,
    262, 285, 287n. 42; *Devotions upon
    Emergent Occasions,* 276, 286n. 17;
    and friendship with Herbert, 154n.
    57; and the Psalms, 230n. 23; "To
    Mr. Tilman . . . ," 99, 107n. 31
Donno, Elizabeth Story, 31n. 8
Downame, George, 89n. 38
Drayton, Michael, 42
Drummond, Christopher, 82, 90n. 40
Dryden, John, 92, 106n. 1
Dudley, Robert, Earl of Leicester, 118
Duncon, Edmund, 26, 181–93, 193n.
    12, 193–94n. 15, 194nn. 19 and 22,
    268; career of, 187–88; delivery of
    manuscript of *The Temple* to Ferrar,
    26, 182; family of, 187; and Herbert's
    dying wishes, 38; as literary agent for
    Herbert, 26, 181–93; memorial stone
    of, 192, 194n. 29
Duncon, Eleazar, 186, 193nn. 11 and
    12
Duncon, Elizabeth, 187, 189
Duncon, John, brother of Edmund,
    186
Duncon, John, son of Edmund, 187,
    192
Duncon, Nicholas, 187
Duncon, Ruth, 187
Duppa, Brian, 147, 156n. 90
Durham, 186
Dury, Andrew, 159
Dutch. *See* Netherlands
Dutton, Richard, 154n. 54
du Vair, Guillaume, 212–13, 229n. 8
Dyck, Paul, 26–27
Dyer, Robert, 23, 72–74, 79, 81, 86,
    87n. 1, 89n. 38

E. K., 37, 49n. 7
Earl of Manchester, 187
Earle, John, 140, 145, 153n. 44
East Wylie, 150n. 13
Eastern Orthodoxy, 209n. 13
Eaton College, 152n. 31

Eclogue, 37
Eden, Garden of, 57, 121–23
Edington, 167, 168
Edwards, David L., 274, 286n. 8
Edwards, Edward, 130–31n. 5
Edwards, James C., 281, 287n. 32
El Dorado, 115, 124
Eliot, George, 29
Eliot, Sir John, 267
Eliot, T. S., 270
Elizabeth I, Queen, 24, 115–18, 124, 130n. 4, 174, 257
Elizabethan miscellanies, 42
Elizabethan overseas exploration, 24, 113
Elizabethan Church, 208n. 1. *See also* Church of England
Elizabethan England: in fiction, 257, 258
Elizabethan Settlement, 197
Ellis, John, 185, 189
Ely, 277
Emerson, Ralph Waldo, 286n. 6
empire, 235; English / British, 115, 117–19, 123–24, 127, 128–30, 131n. 14, 133n. 62
Empson, William, 39, 42, 50n. 14
England, 235, 237–39, 248n. 9
Enright, D. J., 277, 286n. 20
Erasmus, 240, 250n. 37, 276
eschatology, 220
Essex, 145, 186
Eston, Elizabeth, 187
Eton College, 137, 139
Eucharist, 52, 71n. 20, 97, 104, 105, 202–4, 205–7, 279, 285; altar versus communion table at, 203; frequency of, 209n. 12; Jewish framework for, 202; kneeling at, 173, 207; and Protestant sacramentalism, 52; "real presence" in, 52, 53, 60; and Roman Catholic sacramentalism, 70n. 2; throughout *The Church,* 102, 103; transubstantiation, 208n. 2; Zwinglian memorialism, 208n. 2
Europe, 237, 243
evangelical piety: early Stuart, 221–28, 230n. 29, 231n. 43
Evans, G. Blakemore, 106n. 7
Evans, Robert C., 154nn. 59 and 60
Eve, 45, 57, 277

Faith: character in Bunyan's *Pilgrim's Progress,* 90n. 40
Fall, the, 57, 123, 277
Falstaff, 114, 130n. 1
Favour, John, 222, 230nn. 35 and 36
Fayes Mine, 120
Featley, Daniel, 215, 218, 225, 230n. 26, 231n. 47
Felch, Susan, 229n. 6
Fernel, Jean-François, 127, 133n. 59, 237, 238, 248n. 11; *Universa medicina,* 127
Ferrar, John, 191
Ferrar, Nicholas, 26, 38, 107n. 25, 149n. 7, 149–50n. 10, 152n. 36, 176, 181–84, 187–92, 193n. 6, 227, 255, 261, 268, 271n. 12
Ferrar Papers, 193n. 6
Filmer, Sir Robert, 149n. 7
Fincham, Kenneth, 151n. 20, 154n. 62, 155n. 64, 156nn. 75 and 92, 156–57n. 96, 157n. 97, 230n. 34
Fish, Stanley, 88n. 22, 102–3, 108n. 51, 285, 287n. 43
Fisher, John, 81, 82, 229n. 18
Fisherton, 168
Flannagan, Roy, 89n. 30
Flesch, William, 73, 79, 89n. 31
Fletcher, Giles, 42, 228n. 2
Fletcher, Phineas, 42, 211, 221, 223–27, 228nn. 1 and 2, 230nn. 30 and 36, 231nn. 38–44, 50, 52–56; *The Purple Island,* 228n. 2
Forest of Dean, 126
Forman, Margaret Elliott, 25, 162
Forman, Dr. Simon, 25, 162, 168
Formula of Concord, The, 60, 71n. 17
Forrester, John M., 248n. 10
Foster, Joseph, 156nn. 78, 84, 90, 91, and 93
Foucault, Michel, 241, 246, 250nn. 30 and 31, 252n. 48
Franck, Sebastian, 71n. 13
Freer, Coburn, 228n. 3
French, Peter, 119, 122, 131nn. 13, 15, 17, and 18, 132n. 34
French Revolution, 252n. 48
Friedman, Donald M., 15, 17, 22
Friern Barnet, 182, 184, 185, 187–89, 192, 193, 194n. 29
Frobisher, Martin, 115, 118, 131n. 14

Frost, William, 106n. 1
Fry, E. A., 170n. 3, 170–71n. 5, 171n. 28
Fry, G. S., 170–71n. 5, 171n. 28
Fuchs, Leonhard, 235, 243–44, 251n. 38 and 41
Fugglestone, 113, 145, 147, 150–51n. 16, 155n. 72, 158, 159, 161, 165, 166, 171n. 13, 188, 194n. 16
Fugglestone Manor, 168
Fuller, Joseph, 104, 108nn. 60 and 61
Fuller, Thomas, 140–41, 153n. 46, 190

Galen/Galenic thought, 238, 244, 247, 251n. 38
Galenicals, 236
Garden, the. *See* Eden, Garden of
gardening, 24, 113–30
Gardner, Helen, 154n. 57
Gardner, W. H., 106n. 6
Garrard, George, 139, 152n. 31
Garrod, H. W., 106n. 3
Gauden, John, 144, 145, 155n. 68
Gee, John, 193–94n. 15
Gentleman's Magazine, The, 130n. 1
George Herbert's Pastoral Conference, 15, 23, 24
Gerard, John, 242, 245, 247, 250n. 32, 251n. 44, 252n. 47
Germans, Germany, 235, 237, 240, 243, 280
Gessner, Konrad, 242, 243
Gibb, John, 89n. 33
Gilbert, Adrian, 24, 129, 130, 130nn. 1 and 2, 130–31n. 5; and alchemy, 119, 122, 123; and architecture, 119, 120, 123; and astrology, 121, 122; and chemistry, 116, 119, 123; compared to Falstaff, 114, 130n. 1; and John Dee, 117–22; and exploration overseas, 24, 113, 117; and garden design, 24, 113, 120–22, 126, 129, 130; and geometry, 119, 121; and magic, 24, 113, 117, 121, 122; and medicine, 116, 123; and mining, 119, 120, 126; and navigation, 119, 120; and Protestant empire, 24, 113, 117; and science, 24, 113
Gilbert, Sir Humphrey, 114–15, 118, 123, 124, 130nn. 2 and 3, 130–31n. 5

Gill, William, 175
Gillingham Manor, 150n. 14
Godwin, William, 277
Golding, Arthur, 229n. 13
Gonville Hall, Cambridge, 146–47
Good Friday, 280
Good Samaritan, 59
Gosse, Edmund, 15, 16
Gottlieb, Sidney, 28–29, 73, 87n. 6, 89n. 24
Gow, A. S. F., 251n. 39
Graham, Kenneth, 22–23, 88n. 16, 90n. 41
Grantham Australis, 146
Great Gransden, Huntingdonshire, 145
Great Tew, 153n. 44, 186
Great Wishford, 159
Greek/Greeks, 245, 278
Green, T. H., 256
Greenblatt, Stephen J., 130n. 4
Griggs, Barbara, 248n. 2, 249nn. 12 and 13
Griggs, Earl Leslie, 286n. 19
Grobham, John, 159, 163
Grobham, Sir Richard, 159
Grobham Howe, 159
Grobham manor, 163, 170–71n. 5
Grosart, Alexander, 30n. 2, 132n. 51, 270
Guiana, 115, 117, 124
Guildhall, London, 194n. 19
Guyon, 44

Hacket, John, 138, 142, 145
Hadfield, Andrew, 248n. 9
Hakluyt, Richard, 130n. 3
Halewood, William, 73, 87n. 4
Hall, Joseph, 89n. 24
Hamlin, Hannibal, 228n. 3
Hammond, Henry, 72
Hampden, John, 269
Hannay, Margaret, 131nn. 7, 10, and 22, 132n. 43
Harkness, Deborah, 123, 131n. 13, 132n. 41
Harnham, 161
Harrietsham, Kent, 137
Harris, Anne, 175
haruspices, 249–50n. 24
Harvey, Christopher, 203
Harvey, Gordon, 90n. 40

Harvey, William, 238
Hayward, John, 229n. 9
Heaney, Seamus, 92–93, 106nn. 4 and
  5; Nobel Prize for Literature, 92; *Redress of Poetry*, 93
Hegel, Georg Wilhelm Friedrich, 281
Heidegger, Martin, 273, 279–83, 285,
  287nn. 28, 29, and 31
Henchman, Humphrey, 140, 153n. 45
Henry VIII, King, 238
Henry, John, 248n. 10
herbals, 235–48. *See also* materia
  medica
Herbert, Sir Edward, Earl of Cherbury,
  141, 248n. 11, 264
Herbert, George:
  and alchemy, 123, 125, 126, 132n.
  54; and Anglo-Catholicism, 52; and
  antipastoralism, 15–21, 35–49; and
  asceticism, 61, 278, 285; and astrology, 127, 132n. 45; attacks Andrew
  Melville in *Musae Responsoriae*, 49n.
  6; as Augustinian, 40, 43, 50nn. 17
  and 18, 133n. 60; and Baconian science, 274 (See also under *Temple,
  The*); Bemerton congregation, 25,
  158–70, 266; and Bemerton priesthood, 38, 266, 274–75; and Bemerton Rectory, 191, 274–75; Bible,
  pervasive influence of, 26, 102, 275,
  284, 285; biographers of, 28; and the
  Book of Common Prayer, 197–208;
  burial of, 153n. 45, 160; calling and
  ordination of, 134–48; and Calvin-
  ism, 133n. 60; and catechizing, 103;
  and chemistry, 126–27; Church of
  England defended in *Musae Responsoriae*, 49n. 6; churchwardens of,
  164; and civil law, 124, 127, 239,
  249n. 20; and Lady Anne Clifford,
  153n. 43; commitment to "truth,"
  42; compared to Hopkins, 106n. 6;
  death of, 267, 271n. 19; and John
  Dee, 124; didacticism of, 221–28,
  228n. 4, 231n. 46; and divine chastisement, 83–86; on "doctrine and
  life," relation between, 72–87, 230n.
  32; and Edmund Duncon, as literary
  agent, 181–93; parallel career of,
  188; and early Stuart Psalm culture,
  27, 211–28; and early teachings of

Calvin, 52; and Elizabethan Church,
190; and empire, 123–24, 127, 128–
30, 133n. 62; and erotic desire, 18;
and Eucharist, 173, 279, 285, kneeling at, 207; and evangelical pastoral
duty, 27; uselessness, fear of, 46;
fictional portrayals of, 28–29,
255–70; and friendship with
Lancelot Andrewes, 277–78; and
friendship with John Donne, 154n.
57; and Thomas Fuller, 153n. 46;
and gambling language, 105; and
gunnery, 125; health of, 262, 267,
271n. 11; "Hell," absence of in "The
Church," 204; as herbalist, 27–28,
235–48 (*see also* herbs); hesitation of
in taking holy orders, 134–48, 266;
and *imitatio Christi* tradition, 43; institution at Bemerton, 159–60, 162,
266, 274–75; and justification by
faith, 82; and kenosis, 280, 287n. 26;
and limits of language, 273–85; and
liturgical experience of scripture,
26–27, 197–208; and liturgy, 229n.
5, 275; and Lutheranism, 22, 23, 52–
70, 205–6, 210nn. 21 and 22; and
Machiavellianism, 76; map of Herbert's parish, 159; and Marvell, 48;
and mathematics, 124–25; and marriage, 18–19, 262–64, 271n. 11; his
medlar pear tree, 269–70; and Milton, 48; and mining, 125–26, 128;
and monasticism, 61–62; and navigation, 124, 128, 129; ordination of,
as deacon, 154n. 55, 261; and parallel career of Richard Steward,
137–39; and parish register, 160;
Parliament, member of, 113, 135,
141, 142, 149nn. 4 and 7, 149–50n.
10, 152n. 32, 154n. 55, 179; and
pastoral romance, 18; and pastoral
tradition, 16–21, 35–49; and pastoral tranquility, 16; and patronage,
113–14, 130n. 1, 135, 136–42, 156–
57n. 96; and Pembroke (Earls of),
113–14, 130n. 1, 136, 140–42,
149n. 4, 153n. 44, 265; and perfectionism, 53; personification of *via
media*, 270; as physician, 235–48;
poetry and priesthood connected, 42,
48, 91–106; and Poor Law Act of

1601, 173–79; and the pope, 44; and postmodern theology, 282, 283, 285; and prebendary of Lincoln Cathedral, 152 n. 36; and Protestant politics, 44, 142, 150 n. 11, 173; and Psalms as poetry, 211–12, 228, 231 n. 49; Public Orator at Cambridge University, 109 n. 71, 113, 125, 141, 260; publication of *The Temple* by Ferrar, 26, 181–93, 268; and punishment, divine, 83–86; rector of St. Andrew's Church, Bemerton, and St. Peter's Church, Fuggleston, 113, 274–75; relation between theology and poetry, 273–85; repairs by, at Bemerton, 155 n. 67, 267; retreat from court, 134–35; and rhetoric, 88 n. 23, 90 n. 45, 109 n. 71; and Roman Catholic Church, 44, 49 n. 6, 52; and sacramentalism, 52, 108 n. 60; and sanctification, 90 n. 46; and scripture, 52; as "Secretary of praise," 68; and self-restraint, 247; and shepherds, 15–21, 35–49; and Sir Philip Sidney, 210 n. 24; and "sincerity," 38; tercentenary of death, 91; theology of presence, 52–70; in Victorian popular imagination, 28–29, 255–70; and virginity, 18–19; and vocation, 22, 56–70; and Nathaniel Wanley, 210 n. 25; on the Word and creation, 47

Herbert, Henry, Second Earl of Pembroke, 118

Herbert, Sir Henry (George's brother), 141, 154 n. 54, 155 n. 70

Herbert, Henry, Seventeenth Earl of Pembroke, 122, 132 n. 37

Herbert, Magdalen, 44, 134, 141, 143, 261, 264, 265

Herbert, Mary Sidney, Countess of Pembroke, 18, 31 n. 5, 114, 116–20, 129

Herbert, Philip, Fourth Earl of Pembroke, 119, 122, 129, 130 n. 1, 136, 140, 141, 144, 146–48, 152–53 n. 42, 153 nn. 44 and 47, 154 n. 54, 156 n. 92, 156–57 n. 96, 159–60; as Earl of Montgomery, 141, 143, 148, 154 n. 53; as Lord Chamberlain, 143

Herbert, Sidney, Sixteenth Earl of Pembroke, 132 n. 37

Herbert, William, First Earl of Pembroke, 118, 129, 130 n. 1

Herbert, William, Third Earl of Pembroke, 24, 116–18, 126, 129, 131 n. 12, 136, 139–43, 147, 149 n. 4, 149–50 n. 10, 150 nn. 12 and 13, 150–51 n. 16, 153 nn. 44 and 48, 154 nn. 54, and 61, 159, 167, 259, 261, 265–66; and Adrian Gilbert, 113–30

herbs, 27–28, 235–48

hermeticism: Renaissance, 121

Hethcote, Ralph, 156 n. 76

Hildeyerd, John, 187, 189

Hilgay: parish of, 221

Hill, Robert, 231 nn. 43 and 48

Hillman, John, 161, 165

Hirst, Derek, 88 n. 22

Hobbs, S., 171 nn. 18 and 23

Hodgkins, Christopher, 20, 31 n. 9, 70 n. 3, 73, 82, 87 n. 6, 89 n. 39, 107 n. 41, 130 n. 4, 131 n. 14, 132 n. 45, 133 nn. 60 and 62, 134, 142, 149 n. 3, 157 n. 97, 190, 194 n. 20, 209 n. 12, 229 n. 5, 230 nn. 32 and 33, 240–41, 250 nn. 26 and 29, 271 n. 7

Hoeller, Keith, 287 n. 29

Hofstadter, Albert, 287 n. 28

Hölderlin, Friedrich, 280, 281

Holinshed's *Chronicles*, 174

Holland. *See* Netherlands

Holy Communion. *See* Eucharist

Holy Spirit, 52

Homer, 38–39; *Iliad*, 38–39

Hooker, Richard, 79, 135, 144; *Of the Laws of Ecclesiastical Polity*, 89 n. 30

Hooper, Robert, 146, 156 n. 76

Hopkins, Gerard Manley, 93, 106 n. 6; compared to Herbert, 106 n. 6; "God's Grandeur," 93, 106 n. 6

Horace, 109 n. 72

Horapollo, 250 n. 37

Horn, Joyce M., 150 nn. 13 and 15, 151 nn. 17, 19, 20, and 27, 153 n. 46, 155 n. 73, 156 nn. 79, 80, 84, 88, and 91, 157 n. 98

Hospital of St. Nicholas, Salisbury, 136

Houghton House, 116

Hovey, Kenneth, 250 n. 25

Hughes, Vera Rosemond, 257, 270 n. 2, 271 n. 6

Hunnis, William, 229n. 7
Hunter, Lynette, 131n. 7
Huntingdonshire, 145
Huntley, Frank L., 181, 190, 193n. 1, 194n. 22
Hutchinson, F. E., 30n. 3, 49n. 2, 75, 87n. 2, 88n. 13, 90n. 43, 127, 132nn. 45, 46, and 54, 133nn. 57, 59, and 62, 155n. 70, 172n. 40, 176, 179n. 1, 207, 209nn. 7 and 11, 221, 222, 229n. 16, 236, 237, 239, 240, 248nn. 1 and 11, 249n. 23, 270
Hutchinson, Thomas, 106nn. 2 and 7
Hutton, Sarah, 131n. 7
Huxley, Thomas, 258
hyssop, 246
Hythloday, Raphael, 17, 78

imperialism. See empire
Incarnation, 96, 283
Independents/Independency, 185, 186
India, 117, 128–29
Innes, James, 89n. 33
Interregnum, 26, 153n. 44, 181, 186, 188–90
Ireland, 114
Italy, Italians, 186, 282
Ivie, John, 166, 169

Jackson, Thomas, 185
Jacobb, James, 163
Jacobean Church, 208n. 1. See also Church of England
Jacobean theater, 284
James I, King, 44, 49n. 6, 113, 115–17, 135, 141, 145, 147, 157n. 97, 238, 277
James, Marquess of Hamilton, 135, 149–50n. 10, 154–55n. 63
Jardine, N., 249n. 18, 250n. 35
Jasper, David, 29–30, 286n. 14, 287nn. 34 and 41
Jay, Stephen, 156n. 76
Jesus Christ, 174, 192, 197, 199, 202, 203, 205, 207, 209n. 16, 210n. 25, 213, 216, 221, 222–25, 240, 241, 247, 248, 264, 268, 274, 276, 279, 282, 285, 286–87n. 22; crucifixion of, 206; as high priest, 94–95, 202; as pastoral progenitor, 42
Jesus College, Oxford, 248n. 11
Johnson, Samuel, 274, 286n. 5

Jones, Inigo, 91
Jones, John, 156nn. 78, 82, 83, 84, and 94
Jones, Melior, 175
Jones, William Henry, 151nn. 17, 20, and 27, 156n. 77, 157n. 98
Jonson, Ben, 23, 31n. 11, 76, 87, 88n. 18, 90n. 48
Justices of the Peace, 57, 175, 176, 249n. 20
Jutt, Robert, 156n. 76

Kahn, Victoria, 88n. 21
Kasaya, Kazuhiko, 251n. 41
Kastan, David Scott, 194n. 23
Keats, John, 15, 92, 106n. 3; "Ode to Psyche," 92, 106n. 3
Keeble, N. H., 89n. 40
Kelsey, Joseph, 146, 156nn. 76 and 79, 157n. 98
Kent, 24, 135–37, 148, 149n. 7
Kermode, Frank, 49n. 1
Kerridge, E., 171nn. 9, 15, 19, and 30
Kingsmead, 164
Kinnamon, Noel, 89n. 25, 228n. 3
Kneidel, Gregory, 73, 76, 77, 88nn. 10 and 23, 89n. 27
knot-grass, 236
Kölbl, Konrad, 251n. 38
Krauth, Charles Porterfield, 52, 70n. 1
Kronenfeld, Judy, 79, 87n. 3, 88n. 17, 89n. 31
Kyne, Mary Theresa, 106n. 6

Lane, John, brother of William, 188, 194n. 17
Lane, John, son of William, 188
Lane, William, 188
Larking, Lambert B., 149n. 7
La Rochelle, 261
Latins. See Rome/Romans
Laud, William, 136, 146–48, 151n. 20, 156n. 90, 156–57n. 96, 185, 186, 197, 266
Laudians, 53, 156–57n. 96, 184–86
Lavington, 136
Lawes, Henry, 48
Lawrence, Thomas, 146–48, 156n. 76, 156–57n. 96, 157n. 98, 194n. 16
Lear, 106n. 7
Lee, F. N., 71n. 16
Lee, John, 136, 150n. 13

Leighton Bromswold, 141, 149–50n. 10, 155n. 73, 194n. 27, 261

Lein, Clayton D., 24, 130n. 1

Lemnius, Levinus, 244, 251n. 42; on redness of roses, 244

Le Neve, John, 150nn. 13 and 15, 151nn. 17, 19–21, and 27, 153n. 46, 155n. 73, 156nn. 79, 80, 84, 88, and 91, 157n. 98

Lennox, Duke and Duchess of, 149–50n. 10

Lent, 143

Lethe, 89n. 35

Lewalski, Barbara, 228n. 3, 230nn. 23 and 31, 231n. 49

Lewys, William, 156n. 76

Lichfield Cathedral, 147, 150–51n. 16

Lincoln Cathedral, 145, 152n. 36

Lincoln's Inn, 145

Lindberg, David C., 250n. 35

Lindheim, Nancy, 38, 49–50n. 11

Liturgical forms, 26; and biblical forms, 26

Little Gidding, 185, 186, 191, 192, 255, 271n. 12

Lloyd, John, 150–51n. 16, 151n. 17, 152n. 35, 153n. 44, 155nn. 72 and 73, 156n. 82

Lloyd, Rachel, 130–31n. 5

Lobelius (Matthias de l'Obel), 252n. 47

Lodowick, Duke of Richmond, 135, 149–50n. 10

Loewenstein, David, 248n. 9

London, 135, 143, 145, 151n. 20, 153n. 45, 162, 183, 189, 194n. 19, 209n. 12, 245, 252n. 47

London *Pharmacopeia,* 236

Long Acre Garden, 245, 252n. 47

Longfellow, Henry Wadsworth, 256

Lord's Supper. *See* Eucharist

Lucy, Countess of Bedford, 121

Lushington, Thomas, 137

Luther, Martin, 53, 59, 60, 63, 71n. 11; and the "alien Word," 205, 206, 210n. 21; and baptism, 205; and conscience, 210n. 22; doctrine of justification by faith, 204–5; doctrine of vocation, 54–70; and the Eucharist, 204–5; and *larva dei* (mask of God), 55, 66; and liturgy, 204–5; neighbor-centeredness of, 55–56;

theology of presence, 55, 60; and sacrifice, 67

Lutherans/Lutheranism, 52–70, 209n. 13, 240

Lyme and Halstock; churches of, 137, 138, 147

Lyte, Henry, 242, 244, 250nn. 33 and 34

Machiavelli, Niccolò/Machiavellianism, 76, 88n. 22

Maclean, Ian, 250n. 31

MacMillan, Ken, 131n. 14

Magdalen Hall, Oxford, 137

Magee, P., 172n. 33

magic, 118–19

Malcolmson, Cristina, 20, 24, 31nn. 10 and 12, 38, 50n. 12, 53, 56, 62, 67, 70nn. 4 and 7, 71nn. 13, 18, and 19, 73, 75–77, 87n. 6, 88n. 15, 89n. 24, 130 n.1, 132n. 53, 133n. 62, 136, 147, 149nn. 3, 5, and 9, 150n. 11, 151 n. 22, 152nn. 35 and 38, 153n. 51, 154nn. 52, 56, and 57, 155n. 67, 156n. 85, 174, 180n. 4, 198, 208n. 3, 248n. 6

Maltby, Judith, 208n. 1

Malvolio, 29, 260

Mars, 242

Marshall, Beatrice, 256–58, 270n. 1, 272n. 24

Marshall, Emma, 28–29, 255–70, 271nn. 6, 11, and 12, 272nn. 22 and 24; biography of, 256–57; *A Haunt of Ancient Peace,* 28, 255, 258, 270, 271n. 12; *Memories of Troublous Times,* 258; quality of work, 257; reception of work, 257; *Under Salisbury Spire,* 28–29, 255–70, 270n. 4, 272n. 22

Martha (sister of Mary and Lazarus), 174, 179

Martin, Anthony, 26

Martin, Sir Henry, 143

Marvell, Andrew, 19, 22, 31n. 8, 51nn. 38 and 40; "The Garden," 51n. 40; "Mower" poems, 51n. 40; "Upon Appleton House," 51n. 38

Mary, sister of Martha and Lazarus, 174, 179

Mary, mother of Jesus, 99

Mary I, Queen, 197
Mason, Edmund, 137, 151n. 20
Massinger, Philip, 260
materia medica, 235, 236
mathematics, 113
Matthew, Tobie, 222, 230n. 34
Matthews, A. G., 189, 193nn. 11 and 12, 193–94n. 15
Mattishall, Norfolk, 147, 156n. 82
Maxfield, John, 54, 70nn. 8 and 9
Maycock, A. L., 152n. 30
Mazzio, Carla, 89n. 35
McCloskey, M., 50n. 26, 249–50n. 24
McClure, Norman Egbert, 152n. 32
McEachern, Claire, 248n. 9
McElligot, Jason, 193n. 11
McGill, William J., 287n. 24
McInnis, L. R., 249n. 20
McKenzie, N. H., 106n. 6
McKenzie, Tim, 69, 70n. 5, 71nn. 27 and 28
McLehose, James, 133n. 60
McNeill, John T., 89n. 36
medicine: early modern, 116, 123, 235–48, 249n. 12; apothecaries, 236, 238, 245, 249n. 12; Barber-Surgeons Company, 238, 249n. 12; College of Physicians, 238, 249n. 12; Company of Grocers, 238, 251–52n. 46; empirics, 238, 239, 249n. 12; physician-polymaths, 249n. 18; Quacks Charter of 1542, 239; Society of Apothecaries, 251–52n. 46
Melanchthon, Philipp, 240
Melville, Andrew, 49n. 6
Mennonites, 198
mercury, 235, 238
Merton College, 153n. 44
Messiah, 94. See also Jesus Christ
Middle Ages, 174, 235, 236, 239
Middle Temple, 115, 130–31n. 5
Middlesex, 184, 189
Mildenhall, 137, 147, 150–51n. 16, 151n. 17
Miller, Clarence H., 132n. 54
Miller, Edmund, 250n. 25
Milton, Anthony, 208n. 1
Milton, John, 22, 40, 79; "Lycidas," 49–50n. 11; as Christian pastoral, 48; A Masque Presented at Ludlow Castle, 1634 ("Comus"), 48; Of Ref-ormation, 89n. 30; Paradise Lost, 40, 45, 47, 190–91
modernism: religious, 258
modernist poetry, 243
Moffett, Thomas, 118, 126–27, 133n. 56
Monro, Cecil, 130–31n. 5
Montgomery, 140–41, 154n. 53
More, Sir Thomas, 17, 30n. 4, 78; Utopia, 17, 79, 89n. 29
Morley, George, 140, 152n. 41, 152–53n. 42, 153nn. 43 and 44
Mormons, 198
Morris, Margaret, 170n. 2, 172n. 37
Morton, John, 188
Moses/Mosaic law, 86
Moulsworth, Martha, 228n. 2
Mountain, George, 143
Mudie's subscription library, 257
Mueller, Janel, 248n. 9
Muhammad, 245, 247–48
Murphy, P. R., 50n. 26, 249–50n. 24

Nadder River, 167
Narveson, Kate, 27
navigation, 113
Neale, J. E., 154n. 53
Neile, Richard, 186
Neoplatonism, 44
Nestrick, William, 73, 87 n.3
Netherbury in Ecclesia, 153n. 46
Netherhampton, 160
Netherlands, 237
Newfoundland, 114
Newmarket, 135
Newton, Thomas, 251n. 42
Nicholas of Cusa, 287n. 25
Nicholas, Matthew, 136, 150nn. 14 and 15
Nietzsche, Friedrich, 281
Noah, 240
Norden, John, 213, 216, 229nn. 9–12
Norfolk, 147, 182, 187, 188, 189, 256
Norris, John, 156n. 76
North Carolina, 114
Northhampton, 229n. 17
Northwest Passage, 114, 115, 117, 118, 120, 123, 129
Norwich, 186
Novarr, David, 130n. 1, 149nn. 1, 7, 152nn. 32, 36, 37, 153n. 45, 154n.

61, 185, 193n. 10, 271n. 19, 272n. 22, 272n. 25
nutmeg, 236

Oats Close, 164
Oberman, Heiko, 205, 209n. 18, 210nn. 19 and 20
O'Connor, Michael, 88n. 23
O'Day, Rosemary, 194n. 26
Ogilvie, Brian, 241–42, 248n. 2, 250n. 31
Oley, Barnabas, 26, 143–45, 152n. 36, 155nn. 65, 66, and 67, 183–86, 189, 190, 193, 193n. 7, 255
Ovid, 244, 251n. 39
Oxford University, 137, 145, 148
Oxford Dictionary of National Biography, 130nn. 2, 3, and 4, 130–31n. 5, 131n. 12, 132nn. 23 and 25, 149n. 4, 150–51n. 16, 151n. 17, 151nn. 18 and 19, 153n. 44, 154nn. 54 and 61, 155nn. 71 and 73, 156nn. 81, 83, 84, 86, 88, 89, 156–57n. 96, 171n. 6, 182, 185, 190, 193nn. 10, 11, and 12, 249n. 20, 251–52n. 46, 256
Oxford English Dictionary, 81, 82, 114, 122, 127, 130n. 1, 132n. 36, 133nn. 55 and 58, 248n. 5, 249–50n. 24

Page, Nick, 145–46, 152nn. 30, 34, and 36, 154n. 57, 156n. 74
Page, Samuel, 229n. 9
Palmer, George Herbert, 270
Papal Bull of 1493, 124
Papists. *See* Roman Catholicism/ Roman Catholic Church
Paradise. *See* Eden, Garden of
Paracelsus, 123, 127, 235, 237, 248n. 2
Paris, 186
Parker, William Riley, 194n. 24
Parkinson, Anna, 251n. 45, 251–52n. 46, 252n. 47
Parkinson, John, 244–47, 251nn. 43 and 45, 251–52n. 46, 252n. 47; on redness of roses, 245–46
Parliament, 113, 117, 130, 135, 141, 142, 149nn. 4 and 7, 149–50n. 10, 152n. 32, 154n. 55, 185
Parr, Elnathan, 214, 229n. 14
Pastoral. and golden age, 37; literary

conventions of, 42; as nostalgia, 37; and puns, 47; Renaissance traditions of, 36; as spiritual process, 42. *See also under* Herbert, George.
Pater, Walter, 258
Patrides, C. A., 132n. 54, 270n. 3, 271nn. 8 and 11
Paul, 19, 68, 76, 96, 97, 106
Pebworth, Ted-Larry, 73, 87n. 6, 250n. 27
Peckard, P., 149–50n. 10
Pembroke Circle, 113, 119, 123, 129, 131n. 15
Pembroke, Earls of, 16, 137, 138, 141, 146, 153n. 44, 159, 166. *See also* Herbert, George; Herbert, Henry; Herbert, Sir Philip; Herbert, Sidney; Herbert, Sir William
Persia/Persian, 277
Peterhouse, Cambridge, 147
Petrarch, 35
Phillips, John, 194n. 29
Phillipps, Thomas, 150nn. 12, 13, 14, and 15, 153n. 44, 156n. 79, 156nn. 84, 85, and 86
philosopher's stone, 119, 123, 126, 132n. 54
Philostratus, 245
Philpott, Jane, 248nn. 3 and 4
Pickstock, Catherine, 200, 203, 204, 208, 209nn. 10 and 14, 210n. 26
plantain, 236
Plato/Platonism, 36, 209n. 10, 250n. 31
Pless, John, 67, 71n. 25
Pliny the Elder, 251n. 38
Poor Bench, 175, 178
Poor Law Act of 1601, 25, 173–79
Pope. *See* Roman Catholic Church
Porter, Roy, 249nn. 12 and 14
Portugal, 124
Powers-Beck, Jeffrey, 70n. 7, 134, 149nn. 3 and 9, 153n. 51, 154n. 54
Prayer Book. *See under* Church of England, Book of Common Prayer
pre-Copernican universe. *See* Ptolemaic universe
Presbyterians/Presbyterianism, 185, 186, 197
Prickett, Stephen, 106n. 9, 286n. 15
Priest to the Temple; or, The Countrey Parson, A. See Countrey Parson, The

priesthood: of all believers, 107 n. 40; conveying God to humanity, 108 n. 62; and poetry: Celtic, 93, classical, 93, Jewish, 93, 94, Christian, 93; vulnerability of, 108 n. 62

Prince of Demons. See Devil

Privy Council, 149–50 n. 10

Protestants/Protestantism. See under Reformation

Protestation Return for 1641/2, 158

Psalms, 27, 35, 77, 89 n. 25, 199, 207, 211–28, 231 n. 40, 284; and ancient Hebrew liturgists, 27; collation of, 214–15; didactic use of, 217–21; meditations on, 212–16, 231 n. 49; as poetry, 211–212, 228, 231 n. 49; and private spiritual experience, 103, 201; and Psalm culture, early Stuart, 27, 211–28; and public worship, 103, 201. See also under Bible

Psalter. See Psalms

Ptolemaic universe, 121–23

Purchas, Samuel, 128–29; Purchas His Pilgrimes, 128–29, 133 n. 61

Puritanism, Puritans, 49 n. 6, 169, 185, 187, 222, 230 nn. 29, 36, 231 n. 43, 259–61, 263

Puttenham, George, 37, 49 n. 8

Puxton, John, Sr., 165–66, 168

Puxton, John, Jr., 166

Quakers/Quakerism, 256

Queens closet opened, The, 131 n. 9

Quidhampton, 158–62, 165, 168, 170–71 n. 5

quinine, 235

Quinn, David, 119, 130 n. 3, 130–31 n. 5, 131 nn. 16 and 21

Raleigh, Carew, 117

Raleigh, Sir Walter, 24, 113–17, 119, 120, 123, 124, 126, 129, 130, 130 nn. 3 and 4, 130–31 n. 5, 131 n. 12, 132 n. 23, 260; The Prerogative of Parliaments, 117

Raphael (Milton's angel), 45, 47

Rasmussen, Carl S., 71 n. 10

Raspa, Anthony, 286 n. 17

Rastell, John, 249 n. 20

Rastell, William, 249 n. 20

Rattendon, 186

Ray, Robert H., 230 n. 27

Rees, Judy, 170

Reformation:and Book of Common Prayer, 197–98, 201, 229 n. 5, 282; conservative, 52, 53, 55, 58, 62, 63, 65, 67–69, 70 n. 2; culture, 75, 123; and English national identity, 248 n. 9; and Eucharist, 203; and externals of worship, 229 n. 5; and free will, 81, 82; and justification by faith, 65, 79, 82, 204–5; and liturgy, 203–5; and medicine, 237; and preparation for grace/regeneration, 82; and priesthood of all believers, 65, 67; Protestant empire, 24, 113, 114, 123; and Protestant legalism, 55; and Protestant politics, 44, 142, 150 nn. 11 and 13; and Protestant work ethic, 56; and Psalms, 229 n. 18, 231 n. 49; radical, 52, 58, 62, 63, 67

Renaissance, 235–38, 241–43, 246, 250 n. 31, 252 n. 48, 276, 283; rhetoric and prudence in, 88 n. 21

Restoration, 26, 140, 169, 181, 182, 187, 189, 190, 197, 269

rhubarb, 236

Ribbesford, 155 n. 70

Rich, Sir Robert, Earl of Warwick, 145

Rickey, Mary Ellen, 51 n. 37

Riddell, John N. D., 252 n. 47

Ripa, Cesare, 243

Roanoke Island, 114, 124

Robynson, Ralph, 89 n. 29

Roche, Thomas P., Jr., 31 n. 6

Rochester, 147, 156–57 n. 96

Rogers, K. H., 171 n. 16, 172 n. 36

Rogers, Thomas, 229 n. 18

Roman Catholicism/Roman Catholic Church, 44, 49 n. 6, 52, 55, 67, 258, 259, 277, 283; anti-Catholicism, 89 n. 38, 259, 263; Catholic Reformation, 203, 209 n. 10; doctrine of vocation, 56–57; Eucharist in, 203–4, 209 n. 12, in Tridentine Mass, 209 n. 10; the pope, 44, 222; and preparation for grace/regeneration, 82; sacramentalism of, 70 n. 2

Rome/Romans, 245

Romantic poets: bardic responsibility of, 92

Rowe, Violet A., 154n. 53
Rowse, A. H., 171n. 20
Royal Society, 247
Russell, Sir Francis, 145
Russia, 236
Rydén, Mats, 250n. 32

Sacks, David Harris, 89n. 29
St. Andrew's Bemerton, church of. *See under* Bemerton
St. Andrew's Holborn: church of, 145, 155n. 73
St. Andrew's at Wood Dalling: church of, 192
St. Clement Danes: church of, 151n. 20
St. David's Cathedral, 187
St. Edmund's parish, Salisbury, 169
St. James's Church, Friern Barnet, 192
St. Margaret's Church, Swannington, 187, 192, 194n. 25
St. Paul's Cathedral, 188, 189
St. Stephen's Chapel, 147
St. Thomas's parish, Salisbury, 169
Salisbury, 15, 18, 23, 72, 119, 136, 145, 158, 161, 162, 169, 209n. 12, 259, 260, 267; Cathedral, 136–38, 140, 141, 146, 147, 150nn. 13, 14, and 15, 157n. 98, 269; Cathedral Close, 15, 16, 153n. 45, 169; dean of, 258; early Stuart era politics of, 25, 169; mayor of, 166; modern, 168; plague in, 166, 169; poverty in, 169, 174–78
Salisbury Plain, 167
Saltern, Thomas, 89n. 28
Sandridge, 115
Sandys, Sir Edwin, 149n. 7, 149–50n. 10
Sarum, 137, 153n. 45
Sarum Chronicle, 159, 170
Sarum College, 16
Sawley, 147
Scamell, Katherine, 163
Scamell, William, 164
scesis onomation, 273
Schaff, Philip, 89n. 33
Schaffer, Simon, 247, 252n. 51
Scharlemann, Robert P., 287n. 44
Schleinter, Louise, 229n. 7
Schoenbaum, Samuel, 255

Schoenfeldt, Michael, 73, 139, 149n. 7, 152n. 30, 155n. 70, 247, 252n. 50
science: early modern, 235–48; and emblematic thinking, 241, 243, 244, 247–48, 250nn. 31, 35 and 37; and Adrian Gilbert, 24; and religion, 27, 235, 237, 240, 241, 250 nn. 25 and 29
Sclater, William, 82
Scott, Thomas, 117
Scottish Prayer Book, 197
Secord, J. A., 249n. 18, 250n. 35
Seeley publishing house, 257
Sellevand, John, 175
Sessions, William, 241, 250nn. 27 and 28
Shakespeare, William, 25, 106n. 7, 114, 162, 255, 260–61, 287n. 40; First Folio, 260–61; *Hamlet,* 287n. 40; *King Lear,* 106n. 7; *Twelfth Night,* 260
Shakespeare in Love, 255
Shapin, Steven, 247, 252n. 51
Shaw, C. C., 194n. 17
Shaw, Robert B., 53, 70n. 5, 71n. 20, 88n. 14
Shaxton, Nicholas, 146–48, 156n. 76, 157n. 98
Sheldon, Gilbert, 147, 189
Shepherd, Geoffrey, 109n. 72
shepherd's purse, 236
Sherborne, 115, 116, 120
Sherfield, Henry, 166
Sherman, William, 119, 131nn. 14, 15, and 17
Shorthouse's preface to Herbert, 258, 259
Shuger, Debora, 73, 87n. 8
Shute, H., 171n. 11
Shute, W., 229n. 8
Sibthorpe, Christopher, 74, 88n. 11, 89n. 38
Sidney, Mary. *See* Herbert, Mary Sidney, Countess of Pembroke.
Sidney psalms, 134
Sidney, Sir Philip, 16, 18, 20, 30, 31n. 5, 41–42, 109n. 72, 118, 119, 126–27, 206–7; *An Apologie for Poetry,* 109n. 72, 277, 286n. 18; *Arcadia,* 17; *Astrophil and Stella,* 210n. 24; self-mockery of, 18

Sidney-Herbert circle. *See* Pembroke circle
Singleton, Marion, 77, 89 nn. 24 and 26
Siraisi, Nancy, 249 nn. 18 and 22
Slack, Paul, 171 nn. 26 and 27, 172 n. 39, 174, 180 nn. 7, 8, and 10
Slater, A. Pasternak, 171 n. 24
Sloane, Thomas O., 88 n. 21
Smith, David M., 155 n. 73
Smock, Ann, 286 n. 10
Smyth, Charles, 194 n. 27
Smytten, Robert, 163
soteriology, 220
Sowthe, Richard, 156 n. 76
Spain/Spanish, 115, 117, 124, 259; Infanta of, 125
Spary, E. C., 249 n. 18, 250 n. 35
Spenser, Edmund, 16–18, 20, 30, 31 n. 6; and anti-Spenserianism of Herbert, 17; as Colin Clout, 37; E. K. on Spenser as Colin Clout, 37; *The Faerie Queene*, 18, 44, 264; *The Shepheardes Calendar*, 17, 20, 49 n. 7
Spenserians: allegorical, 42. *See also* Browne, William; Drayton, Michael; Fletcher, Giles; Fletcher, Phineas; Wither, George
Stella (of Sidney's *Astrophil and Stella*), 210 n. 24
Stein, Arnold, 215, 229 n. 19
Stephens, Philemon, 26, 183
Sterling Library, University of London, 152 n. 41
Sternhold and Hopkins, 215
Stevens, Philip, 164, 165
Steward, Richard, 137, 139, 145, 148, 150–51 n. 16, 151 n. 17, 156 n. 95
Stile, Christopher, 229 n. 18
Stoics/Stoicism, 77, 89 n. 24
Strier, Richard, 65, 71 n. 23, 73, 87 n. 6, 88 n. 22, 90 nn. 43 and 44, 204–5, 209 n. 17, 219, 229 n. 19, 230 nn. 28 and 31, 231 n. 45
Strong, Sir Roy, 121, 132 nn. 31–32
Strugnell, Robert, 163
Stuart Psalm culture: early, 27, 211–28
Sturdy Beggars, 174–75, 177
Suffolk, 186
Summer Evenings with George Herbert, 170
Summers, Claude, 73, 87 n. 6, 250 n. 27

Summers, Joseph H., 149 n. 1, 154 n. 55, 155 n. 67, 157 n. 97, 217, 228 n. 4, 230 n. 24
Surrey, 145
Sutcliffe, Alice, 228 n. 2
Sutton's Hospital, 143
Symonds, J. Addington, 256
syphilis, 235, 238
Swannington, 187–90, 192, 193; rectory rebuilt by Edmund Duncon, 190–92, 194 n. 25
Swartz, Douglas, 88 n. 22

Talkative (character in Bunyan's *Pilgrim's Progress*), 90 n. 40
Targoff, Ramie, 108 n. 54, 199–200, 208–9 n. 5, 209 n. 6, 212, 218, 230 n. 26
Tattingstone, Suffolk, 187
Taylor, E. G. R., 124, 132 n. 50
Taylor, John, the Water Poet, 114, 116–17, 121–23, 130 n. 2; *A new discouery by sea*, 114, 130 n. 2, 131 n. 11, 132 nn. 30, 38, 39, and 40
Temple, The, 17, 22, 23, 25, 26, 40, 42, 43, 64, 65, 69, 95, 99, 101, 102, 143, 154–55 n. 63, 182, 198, 199, 201, 209 n. 10, 217, 223, 241, 259, 278–79, 285.aesthetic principles of, 100–101, 105; and Baconian science, 250 nn. 25, 26, 27, and 29, 274; and character of holiness, 75; compared to *The Countrey Parson*, 73–74; doubleness in, 37; editions of by 1670, 191; humility of, 104; and liturgical forms, 197–208; manuscript of delivered by Edmund Duncon to Nicholas Ferrar, 26, 182, 183; manuscript possibly sold by Edmund Duncon, 190–91; pervasive influence of Bible, on, 102, 275, 284, 285; and prayer, 103; priestly calling in, 93–106; and private versus public worship, 218; proceeds from printing of, 191–92; publication of, 25, 181–93; rose imagery in, 246–48; temple imagery in, 97; tercentenary of, 91; Williams manuscript of, 38. *See also under* Index to Herbert's Writings for individual poems
Ten Commandments, 178

Terry, Edward, 128–29; "A Relation of a Voyage to the Easterne India," 128
Thacker, Christopher, 116, 131 n. 6
Theocritus, 16, 30, 36; *Idylls,* 36
Theophrastus, 235, 244, 251 n. 38
theriac, 236
Thomas Aquinas, 204, 209 n. 16
Thomas, R. S., 104, 108 n. 64; "Silence," 104
Thring, John, 25, 160–61
Thring, Richard, Sr., 25, 160, 171 n. 12
Thring, Richard, Jr., 160–61
Thring, Susan, 25, 160, 161, 169
Throckmorton, Elizabeth, 130 n. 4
Tillich, Paul, 283
Tobin, John, 57, 71 n. 14, 286 n. 9, 287 n. 23
Tookey, Bartholomew, 166
Tower of London, 115, 116, 143, 267
Tradescant, John, 252 n. 47
Trevett, Anne, 170
Trinity (Godhead), 121
Trinity College, Cambridge, 145, 152 n. 35, 277
Trinity Hall, Cambridge, 186, 187, 189, 190
Turkey, Turks, 236, 245
Turner, William, 244, 251 n. 40
Twickenham Park, 121
Tyacke, Nicholas, 150 n. 12, 156 n. 90
Tymme, Thomas, 222–23, 230 n. 37
Tyndale, William, 258, 261
Tyrwhit, Elizabeth, 229 n. 6

Underdown, David, 172 n. 35
University of London, 152 n. 41
Uriah the Hittite, 199

Valdes, Juan (Valdesso), 83, 184, 185
Valdesso. *See* Valdes, Juan
Valeriano (Piero Valeriano Bolzani), 243, 250 n. 37
Vande Walle, W. F., 251 n. 41
van Wengen-Shute, Rosemary M., 108 n. 53, 200, 209 nn. 6 and 9
Vatja, Vilmos, 67, 71 n. 26
Vattimo, Gianni, 282–83, 285, 287 nn. 35, 36, 37, and 38
Vaughan, Rowland, 167
Veith, Gene Edward, Jr., 22, 70 n. 3, 71 nn. 10 and 21, 90 n. 46

Vendler, Helen, 132 n. 54, 247, 252 n. 49
venesection, 238
Venn, J. A., 156 n. 82
Venn, John, 156 n. 82
Venus, 242–44, 251 n. 39
Vesalius, 238
Victoria, Queen, 257
Virgil, 16, 30, 38, 92
Virginia, 117
Virginia Company, 130–31 n. 5, 135, 149–50 n. 10
Visser, Irene, 287 n. 34
Visser, Robert, 251 n. 41
Vitruvius, 120

Wales, 91, 104
Wall, John, 199–200, 206, 209 nn. 6 and 8, 210 n. 23, 229 n. 5
Walsingham, Sir Francis, 37, 118
Walton, Izaak, 24, 38, 50 n. 13, 54, 70 n. 6, 135, 149 nn. 3 and 7, 149–50 n. 10, 153 nn. 46 and 47, 155 nn. 67 and 70, 182, 183, 189–91, 193 n. 2, 194 n. 22, 255, 260, 262, 264, 266–70, 272 n. 25, 274, 278; Herbert's calling and ordination, his account of, 134–48, 150–51 n. 16; *Life of Donne,* 262, 271 n. 9; *Life of Herbert,* 140, 162, 182–84, 191, 262, 266, 267, 271 nn. 8, 10, 11, 13–15, 17–23, 274, 286 n. 9; *Lives,* 140, 149 nn. 2 and 6, 149–50 n. 10, 151 n. 28, 152 nn. 39 and 41, 153 nn. 43, 45, 46, 48, 49, and 50, 155 n. 69, 185, 193 nn. 2, 4, and 5, 271 n. 9
Wanley, Nathaniel, 210 n. 25
"Deceit," 210 n. 25; Ward, Edward, 164–65
Ward, Samuel, 76, 80, 88 n. 19, 89 n. 35
Warren, Dr. William, 190
Watkinson, William, 229 nn. 9 and 13
Webb, David, 287 n. 36
Weber, Max, 56, 71 n. 13
Webster, John, 287 n. 40; *The Duchess of Malfi,* 287 n. 40
Weil, Simone, 278, 286–87 n. 22
Welsby, Paul A., 286 n. 21
Wentworth, Thomas, Earl of Strafford, 151 n. 20

West, John, 161
West, Philip, 210n. 25, 230n. 27
Westman, Robert S., 250n. 35
western planting movement. *See* empire
Westminster, 24, 134, 153n. 44
Westminster Abbey, 137, 140, 151n. 20
Westminster School, 137, 145, 149n. 7
Whalen, Robert, 208n. 2
Whistler, Rex, 91, 105
Whitaker, Curtis, 27–28, 123
White, Francis, 81, 82, 88nn. 37 and 38
White, James Boyd, 273, 276, 286nn. 3, 6, and 13
Whitelaw, Wesley, 130–31n. 5
Whiteman, A., 170n. 4
Whitney, Charles, 250n. 25
Whitney, Geffrey, 89n. 35
Whittick, Christopher, 194n. 19
Wijffels, Alain, 249n. 20
Wilcox, Helen, 23, 29, 66, 71n. 24, 106n. 8, 109n. 71, 286nn. 1, 4, and 11, 287nn. 33, 34, 39, 41
William III, King, 146
Williams, Barrie, 150nn. 12, 13, and 15, 150–51n. 16, 151nn. 17, 20, 23, 24, and 25, 156n. 93, 157n. 98
Williams, John, 138, 142, 145
Williams manuscript of *The Temple,* 38
Williamson, T., 171n. 31
Wilton, 145, 158, 163, 166, 168, 260
Wilton Abbey, 159
Wilton St. Mary with Bulbridge, 150–51n. 16, 155n. 72, 156n. 84
Wilton, Richard, 132n. 51
Wilton House, 16, 18, 24, 91, 105, 113–17, 120, 122, 123, 130n. 1, 132n. 37, 153n. 44, 159, 160, 168; Palladian bridge at, 120
Wiltshire, 16, 23–25, 72, 87n. 1, 136–38, 140, 159, 161, 168; Herbert's congregation in (*see under* Bemerton); history of, 16; landscape of, 15, 25; map of, 159; south and north

("chalk and cheese") contrasted, 167; water meadows of, 166–67
Wiltshire and Swindon Archives, 166
Wiltshire and Swindon History Centre, Chippenham, 170
Wiltshire Record Society, 150n. 12, 171n. 9
Winchester, 153n. 43
Winchester College, 139
Wingren, Gustaf, 71nn. 10 and 22
Wither, George, 42, 228n. 2
Wittgenstein, Ludwig, 73
women's right to vote, 256
Wood, Anthony, 153n. 44
Wood, Chauncey, 25
Wood Dalling, 187, 192
Woodford, 136
Woodnoth, Arthur, 26, 28, 140, 153n. 45, 183, 192, 193n. 6, 261, 262, 266, 268
Worcester Cathedral, 137, 157n. 98
Wordsworth, William, 92, 106nn. 2 and 7; "Ode. Intimations of Immortality," 92, 106n. 2; "Tintern Abbey," 106n. 7
Wortley, John Dixon, 193n. 12
Wotton, Norfolk, 187
Wotton, Sir Henry, 135, 152n. 32, 153n. 46
Wren, Matthew, 186, 187, 189, 193–94n. 15
Wylye River, 167
Wylye Valley, 159

Yates, Frances, 118–20, 131nn. 15, 17, and 19, 132nn. 29 and 49
Yonge, Charlotte, 257
York, 222
Young, Elflet, 25, 161, 162, 169, 171n. 12
Young, John, 160–62, 171n. 12

Zabala, Santiago, 287n. 35
Zim, Rivka, 228n. 3
Zwingli, Huldrych, 55
Zwiinglians, Zwinglianism, 60

Index to Herbert's Writings

Alia Poema Latina: In Honorem D.D. Verulamij, Sti Albani., 240, 249–50 n. 24

Briefe Notes on Valdesso's Considerations, 83, 90 n. 43

Countrey Parson, The: chapter 1, "Of a Pastor," 60–61, 95, 177; chapter 3, "The Parson's Life," 78; chapter 4, "The Parson's Knowledg," 79, 249 n. 23; chapter 6, "The Parson praying," 201, 209 n. 11; chapter 7, "The Parson preaching," 75, 102, 221–22; chapter 9, "The Parson's state of Life," 18, 20, 96, 278; chapter 10, "The Parson in his house," 61; chapter 11, "The Parson's Courtesie," 59; chapter 12, "The Parson's Charity," 25, 59, 102, 172 n. 39, 176–78, 222; chapter 13, "The Parson's Church," 105–6, 165; chapter 14, "The Parson in Circuit," 59–60, 62, 162, 222; chapter 15, "The Parson Comforting," 59, 169; chapter 16, "The Parson a Father," 61; chapter 18, "The Parson in Sentinell," 169; chapter 19, "The Parson in reference," 77, 172 n. 39; chapter 21, "The Parson Catechizing," 59, 249 n. 23; chapter 22, "The Parson in Sacraments," 207, 209 n. 12; chapter 23, "The Parson's Completenesse," 19, 27, 61, 127, 169–70, 235–41, 246; chapter 24, "The Parson arguing," 75, 88 n. 12; chapter 26, "The Parson's eye," 20; chapter 27, "The Parson in mirth," 61; chapter 30, "The Parson's Consideration of Providence," 19; chapter 32, "The Parson's Sur-veys," 20, 57–59, 124, 125, 130; chapter 35, "The Parson's Condescending," 21, 164; chapter 37, "Concerning detraction," 169

Lucus: epigram 24, *In Angelos,* 44; epigram 31, *In Solarium,* 44; epigram 32, *Triumphus Mortis,* 125

Memoriae Matris Sacrum, 173; epigram 2, Corneliae sanctae, graues Semproniae, 173; epigram 14, Psyches asthenes erkos, amauron pneumatos aggos, 44
Musae Responsoriae: epigram 39, *Ad Seren. Regem,* 49 n. 6

Notes on Valdes. See *Briefe Notes on Valdesso's* Considerations

Outlandish Proverbs, 124, 132 n. 45

Remains, 26, 155 n. 65, 184

Temple, The: The Church-porch, 16, 17, 20, 50 n. 16, 69, 101, 103, 107 n. 30, 108 n. 56, 109 n. 72, 270–71 n. 5; *Superliminare,* 101; *The Church,* 27, 38, 43, 44, 46, 47, 76, 79, 80, 101–3, 197, 202–4, 206, 207, 211, 212, 216–28: "Aaron," 64–65, 93–95, 96, 98; "Affliction" (I), 51 n. 38, 231 n. 39, 274, 286 n. 4; "Affliction" (II), 231 n. 39; "Affliction" (III), 231 n. 39, 263, 270–71 n. 5; "Affliction" (IV), 210 n. 22, 231 n. 39, 263, 270–71 n. 5; "Affliction" (V), 231 n. 39, 263, 270–71 n. 5; "The Agonie," 108 n. 57, 204; "The Altar," 69, 101, 103, 108 n. 56, 202, 203, 207; "Antiphon" (I), 103, 108 n. 50; "Antiphon" (II), 35, 49 n. 2, 103, 270–71 n. 5; "Avarice," 125; "The Bag," 219; "The Banquet," 69, 108 n. 57; "H. Baptisme" (I), 108 n. 57; "H. Baptisme" (II), 108 n. 57, 270–71 n. 5; "Charms and Knots," 108 n. 47; "Christmas," 35, 49 n. 4, 95, 107 n. 15, 108 n. 53, 281–82; "The Church-floore," 103, 108 n. 56; "Church-monuments," 103, 108 n. 56; "Church-musick," 108 n. 50; "Clasping of hands," 83; "The Collar," 64, 69, 104–5, 107 n. 16, 108 n. 66, 206–7, 210 n. 25; "Coloss. iii.3. *Our life is hid with Christ in God*," 100, 108 n. 50, 280; "The H. Communion," 108 n. 57, 109 n. 70; "Conscience," 205–6; "Constancie," 74, 76–78, 89 nn. 24 and 26; "Content," 270–71 n. 5; "The Crosse," 46, 69; "Death," 217; "Deniall," 104–5, 107 n. 16, 108 n. 66, 220–21, 231 n. 40; "A Dialogue-Antheme," 103; "The Discharge," 108 n. 52; "Discipline," 23, 82–86, 90 n. 41; "Doomsday," 108 n. 60; "Easter," 107 n. 16, 108 nn. 50 and 53, 282; "Easterwings," 280, 282; "The Elixir," 40, 50 n. 16, 66–67, 97, 126, 132 n. 54, 263, 270–71 n. 5; "Employment" (I), 43, 63, 65; "Employment" (II), 62, 65; "Ephes. iv.30. *Grieve not the Holy Spirit, etc.*," 108 n. 50, 231 n. 51; "Even-song," 96, 97, 108 n. 53; "The Familie," 63; "The Flower," 46, 47, 50 n. 22, 100, 107 nn. 14 and 39, 231 n. 51; "The Forerunners," 103, 108 n. 58; "Frailtie," 231 n. 51; "The Glimpse," 275; "Good Friday," 282; "Grace," 202; "Gratefulnesse," 231 n. 39; "Grief," 46; "A true Hymne," 46, 69, 97, 98, 210 n. 21; "The Invitation," 108 nn. 44 and 57; "Jesu," 103–4, 108 n. 60; "Jordan" (I), 17, 19, 23, 29, 35, 41, 42, 46, 100, 105, 108 n. 50, 109 n. 72; "Jordan" (II), 36, 99, 210 nn. 21 and 24; "Justice" (I), 217; "Justice" (II), 50 n. 16, 107 n. 35, 217; "Lent," 80–

82, 88 n. 12; "Longing," 84, 219, 225–26; "Love" (I), 108 n. 60; "Love" (III), 21, 46, 102, 107 n. 14, 108 nn. 44 and 57, 204, 207, 208, 279, 286–87 n. 22; "Love unknown," 69, 102, 108 n. 52, 231 nn. 39 and 41; "Man," 45, 69; "Mans medley," 270–71 n. 5; "Mattens," 107 n. 14; "Miserie," 270–71 n. 5; "Obedience," 270–71 n. 5; "The Odour. 2 Cor. ii. 15," 107 n. 14, 108 n. 50, 231 n. 51; "A Parodie," 231 n. 51; "Peace," 102; "The Pearl. Matt. xiii.45," 19, 108 n. 50, 127, 133 n. 60, 250 n. 26; "The Posie," 216, 270–71 n. 5; "Praise" (III), 224–25, 227; "Prayer" (I), 29, 103, 108 n. 55, 270–71 n. 5, 273, 286 n. 1; "The Priesthood," 98–100, 106 n. 4, 108 nn. 50 and 62; "Providence," 44–45, 68, 99, 107 n. 34, 125, 127–29, 246; "The 23d Psalme," 35, 49 n. 3, 108 n. 50; "The Quidditie," 105; "Redemption," 95, 102, 107 nn. 15 and 16; "Repentance," 219–20, 270–71 n. 5; "The Rose," 28, 246–48, 252 n. 49; "The Sacrifice," 43, 50 n. 16, 102, 203, 280; "The H. Scriptures" (I), 50 n. 16, 284, 287 n. 39; "The H. Scriptures" (II), 200, 215; "Sepulchre," 202, 216; "The Sinner," 202; "Sion," 108 n. 63, 208, 231 n. 39; "The Size," 237; "The Sonne," 47; "The Starre," 98; "The Storm," 219; "Submission," 157 n. 97, 231 n. 51; "Sunday," 270–71 n. 5; "The Temper" (I), 231 n. 51; "The Thanksgiving," 43, 107 nn. 14 and 16, 204, 270–71 n. 5; "Trinitie Sunday," 86; "Unkindnesse," 107 n. 14; "Vanitie" (I), 126; "Vertue," 39, 50 n. 15, 246; "The Water-course," 167; "Whitsunday," 99, 108 n. 53; "The Windows," 23, 50 n. 16, 65–78, 95–98, 100, 108 n. 62; "A Wreath," 23, 72, 79, 86, 87 n. 3

Church Militant, The, 50 n. 16, 102, 179, 216

Temple, The, Williams Manuscript: "Perfection," 66–67, 126